I0120752

W. Little

Reports of the Royal Commission on Labour

W. Little

Reports of the Royal Commission on Labour

ISBN/EAN: 9783741199608

Manufactured in Europe, USA, Canada, Australia, Japa

Cover: Foto ©Suzi / pixelio.de

Manufactured and distributed by brebook publishing software
(www.brebook.com)

W. Little

Reports of the Royal Commission on Labour

ROYAL COMMISSION ON LABOUR.

THE AGRICULTURAL LABOURER.

VOL. V.

PART I.

GENERAL REPORT

BY

MR. WILLIAM C. LITTLE
(SENIOR ASSISTANT AGRICULTURAL COMMISSIONER).

Presented to both Houses of Parliament by Command of Her Majesty.
February 1893.

LONDON:
PRINTED FOR HER MAJESTY'S STATIONERY OFFICE,
BY EYRE AND SPOTTISWOODE,
PRINTERS TO THE QUEEN'S MOST EXCELLENT MAJESTY.

And to be purchased, either directly or through any Bookseller, from
EYRE AND SPOTTISWOODE, EAST HARDING STREET, FLEET STREET, E.C., and
32, ABINGDON STREET, WESTMINSTER, S.W.; or
JOHN MENZIES & Co., 12, HANOVER STREET, EDINBURGH, and
90, WEST NILE STREET, GLASGOW; or
HODGES, FIGGIS, & Co., LIMITED, 104, GRAFTON STREET, DUBLIN.

1894.

ROYAL COMMISSION ON LABOUR.

THE AGRICULTURAL LABOURER.

SUMMARY OF CONTENTS.

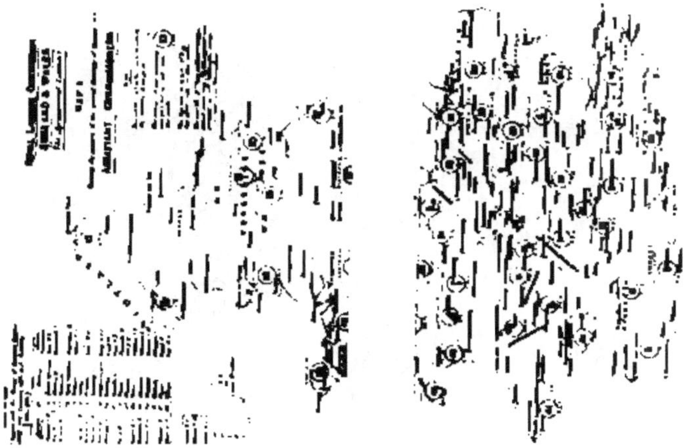

IRELAND

TABLE OF CONTENTS.

ROYAL COMMISSION ON LABOUR.

THE AGRICULTURAL LABOURER.

To Geoffrey Drage, Esq.,
Secretary to the Royal Commission on Labour.

Sir,

I have now the honour to present my Final Report on the subject of the Inquiry into the condition of the Agricultural Labourer in different parts of the United Kingdom which has been carried out under the direction of the Royal Commission on Labour. In this Report I have described the nature and scope of the Inquiry; the method which has been pursued; the area which has been surveyed; the characteristic features of the several districts of inquiry; and finally the conclusions which may be drawn from the information and evidence which has been obtained. Preface.

I have previously in my Review of the Inquiry summarised these conclusions. In the following pages I have stated them at greater length and supported them by extracts from the reports of my colleagues.

I regret to state that I have found it impossible, within the time at my disposal, to deal with the Reports upon Wales, Scotland, and Ireland in the same manner as I have done in the case of England. I cannot venture to hope that the inferences and conclusions which I have drawn from the evidence before me will be accepted by all persons as fair and reasonable. I trust, however, that I may be credited with having endeavoured to preserve an impartial attitude in discussing those subjects upon which differences of opinion are inevitable.

1. On the 12th of August 1891 I had the honour of receiving a letter from the Marquis of Hartington, the Chairman of the Commission, inviting me to undertake the work of analysing and condensing the evidence collected within the last few years on the subject of Agricultural Labour, by Commission or otherwise, with a view to its being placed before the Commission in a convenient form as a preliminary to further inquiry, either by the examination of witnesses before the Commission or the collection of information by the aid of Assistant Commissioners. Introduction.

It was with great pleasure that I accepted the work thus offered me, and I immediately placed myself, as I was directed to do, in communication with Lord Derby, who was the Chairman of the Committee of the Commission to whom this branch of the inquiry had been referred.

In correspondence with his Lordship I requested directions as to—

(i.) The area of inquiry;
(ii.) The period of time to be embraced;
(iii.) The particular sources of information to be examined.

On the first of these points I ascertained that my inquiry was not to be confined to England and Wales, but extended to Ireland and Scotland.

2. With regard to the period of time to which my attention was to be given, Lord Derby wrote thus:— Scope of inquiry.

> "The period of time over which information is wanted has been nowhere defined.
>
> "But as the inquiry is for practical and not historical purposes the rule to follow would seem to be not to go back to a date when the state of things was widely different from what it is now. Twenty or twenty-five years back, I think, should be the outside limit."

Upon the question as to the sources of information to be consulted, Lord Derby defined them as, "all papers laid before Parliament within the time named."

ROYAL COMMISSION ON LABOUR.

THE AGRICULTURAL LABOURER.

To Geoffrey Drage, Esq.,
Secretary to the Royal Commission on Labour.

Sir,

I have now the honour to present my Final Report on the subject of the Inquiry into the condition of the Agricultural Labourer in different parts of the United Kingdom which has been carried out under the direction of the Royal Commission on Labour. In this Report I have described the nature and scope of the Inquiry; the method which has been pursued; the area which has been surveyed; the characteristic features of the several districts of inquiry; and finally the conclusions which may be drawn from the information and evidence which has been obtained. Preface.

I have previously in my Review of the Inquiry summarised these conclusions. In the following pages I have stated them at greater length and supported them by extracts from the reports of my colleagues.

I regret to state that I have found it impossible, within the time at my disposal, to deal with the Reports upon Wales, Scotland, and Ireland in the same manner as I have done in the case of England. I cannot venture to hope that the inferences and conclusions which I have drawn from the evidence before me will be accepted by all persons as fair and reasonable. I trust, however, that I may be credited with having endeavoured to preserve an impartial attitude in discussing those subjects upon which differences of opinion are inevitable.

1. On the 12th of August 1891 I had the honour of receiving a letter from the Marquis of Hartington, the Chairman of the Commission, inviting me to undertake the work of analysing and condensing the evidence collected within the last few years on the subject of Agricultural Labour, by Commission or otherwise, with a view to its being placed before the Commission in a convenient form as a preliminary to further inquiry, either by the examination of witnesses before the Commission or the collection of information by the aid of Assistant Commissioners. Introduction.

It was with great pleasure that I accepted the work thus offered me, and I immediately placed myself, as I was directed to do, in communication with Lord Derby, who was the Chairman of the Committee of the Commission to whom this branch of the inquiry had been referred.

In correspondence with his Lordship I requested directions as to—

(i.) The area of inquiry;
(ii.) The period of time to be embraced;
(iii.) The particular sources of information to be examined.

On the first of these points I ascertained that my inquiry was not to be confined to England and Wales, but extended to Ireland and Scotland.

2. With regard to the period of time to which my attention was to be given, Lord Derby wrote thus:— Scope of inquiry.

> "The period of time over which information is wanted has been nowhere defined.
>
> "But as the inquiry is for practical and not historical purposes, the rule to follow would seem to be not to go back to a date when the state of things was widely different from what it is now. Twenty or twenty-five years back, I think, should be the outside limit."

Upon the question as to the sources of information to be consulted, Lord Derby defined them as, "all papers laid before Parliament within the time named."

Period of time embraced in retrospect.

3. Acting upon the instructions thus received, I selected for the starting point of my investigation the year 1867. The main reason for choosing that particular year was that a Royal Commission was then appointed to inquire into "The Employment of "Children, Young Persons, and Women in Agriculture." That Commission carried out a most comprehensive and searching investigation of the condition of the agricultural labourer in England, Wales, and Scotland. The Reports of the Commissioners and those of their Assistant Commissioners present a most complete picture of the circumstances and surroundings of the agricultural labourer throughout Great Britain at that period, and they form a basis for a comparison with the present times.

Royal Commission on employment of children, &c., 1867.

1867 convenient point of departure in the history of rural population.

4. But if the existence of the Reports recording the results of such an inquiry as has been described supplied one reason for the adoption of the year 1867 as a convenient point of departure, other reasons for the selection of that date were not wanting.

The period was a distinct epoch in the social and economical history of the rural population of this country. The inquiry followed very closely after the passing of the Union Chargeability Act of 1865, though too soon for that Act to have had much effect in remedying the evil results of "close" parishes. It was immediately succeeded by the Elementary Education Act of 1870, for which it undoubtedly paved the way.

That Act for a short time powerfully affected the agricultural labourer's position, by restricting juvenile labour and diminishing the aggregate amount of the family earnings.

Agriculture was flourishing, and was, indeed, approaching the zenith of her prosperity. Labourers' unions, strikes, and lock-outs * had not yet disturbed the relations of employers and employed. In almost every respect the conditions of the various classes engaged in and dependent on agriculture have since then experienced a remarkable change.

Transfer of landowners' and farmers' profits to labourers.

5. It is no exaggeration to say that in the quarter of a century which has elapsed since the inquiry of which I have been speaking was in progress, a quiet economic revolution, accomplished with little aid from legislation, has transferred to the labourers from one-fourth to one-third of that profit which the landowners and farmers then received from the cultivation of the land.

Memorandum prepared on Reports of Royal Commission, 1867.

6. Commencing then with the inquiry of 1867, I proceeded to prepare an abstract of the information contained in a series of volumes issued by the Commission † with particular reference to the following subjects:—

1. The employment of women and children in agriculture.
2. The system of hiring and engagement of labourers.
3. Hours of work.
4. Wages and earnings.
5. Housing of the labourer.
6. Allotments and gardens.
7. Benefit Societies, &c.

It must be remembered that this Commission dealt only with Great Britain and had no reference to Ireland.

I may at this point explain that in dealing with this and other Reports of a similar character I thought it desirable to present a pretty full *résumé* of the evidence in place of bare references to volumes which are not always accessible to inquirers.

Memorandum on Richmond Commission, 1879–1882.

7. I next proceeded to abstract from the Reports and proceedings of the Royal Commission on Agricultural Interests (the Richmond Commission) 1879–82 so much of the evidence as relates to the agricultural labourer in Great Britain and Ireland and I subsequently prepared, and laid before the Commission, papers epitomising the contents of various Blue Books which are relevant to the subject of inquiry, and to these reference will be made hereafter.‡

The progress of the work upon which I was engaged was interrupted by my being directed to consider a scheme for an inquiry into the present condition of the agricultural labourer.

Proposed inquiry by Assistant Commissioners.

8. In the month of November 1891 I was informed by you that it had been proposed, at a meeting of Committee B. of the Commission, to circulate throughout the country a series of questions bearing upon the condition of the agricultural labourer; and to

* The Assistant Commissioners, Royal Commission 1867–[illegible] [illegible] and [illegible].

† Reports, with Appendices, [illegible] (1867–8); [illegible] (1868–9); [illegible] (1870).

‡ These papers are included in the Appendix to this Report, Vol. V. Part II.

divide England and Wales into four districts, corresponding with those adopted by the Richmond Commission in 1879, within which districts an inquiry by Assistant Commissioners was to be carried out.

I was requested to consider the draft circular of inquiries and the proposed mode of circulating them.

In reply to your communication I pointed out that while it was desirable to obtain information upon the several subjects included in the draft circular it would be found extremely difficult, if not impracticable, to obtain generally such definite replies as would be sufficient to give a full and fair representation of the very varied conditions existing in different parts of the country.

I urged the fact that there were no parochial officials who could be called upon to collect the detailed information required, and I said that I saw no way of getting the circulars widely distributed amongst those who would be able and willing to answer the questions contained in them.

9. As an alternative scheme to that proposed, I submitted, in mere outline, a plan of inquiry, the main feature of which was the selection of sample or typical districts within which a more minute investigation might be made than would be possible within any reasonable space of time, if the inquiry were to be extended to every parish in the country.

10. I was subsequently instructed to prepare a plan of inquiry, and after several conferences with His Grace the Chairman of the Commission and yourself, I drew up and submitted a memorandum on the subject, the main features of the plan proposed being as follows:—

(1.) The inquiry to be conducted by Assistant Commissioners within certain selected districts.

(2.) The selected districts to be representative of various conditions as regards agriculture, population, competing industries, &c.

(3.) The area of each selected district to be that of a Poor Law Union.

(4.) A separate Report on each district to be presented by Assistant Commissioners.

(5.) Assistant Commissioners to be transferred to different parts of the country and not restricted to particular groups of counties.

11. As regards the area of inquiry, the Poor Law Union naturally suggested itself as an aggregation of parishes grouped together for administrative and registration purposes, and as generally containing within its limits parishes exhibiting different characteristics in respect of the ownership and tenure of lands and cottages—for it the various statistics relating to population, pauperism, &c., are readily obtainable—and it is usually of such a size as permits to many of those connected with the administration of local affairs an intimate acquaintance with the circumstances of the people throughout the whole district.

If it were decided to carry out the inquiry in districts and not by counties, there seemed to be no necessity to assign to the Assistant Commissioners certain groups of contiguous counties, and in this respect it was suggested that the precedent of the Richmond Commission should not be followed, but that of the Commission on "the Employment of Children, &c.," should be adopted.

In support of the proposal to transfer Assistant Commissioners from one part of the country to another, I pointed to the advantage it must be to anyone engaged upon an inquiry of this character to be able to contrast the practices, habits, and conditions of the labourer in widely different districts; and also to the use which some of the Assistant Commissioners had made of similar opportunities in the before-mentioned inquiry of 1867–70.

In the case of Wales, however, it was obviously desirable to appoint an Assistant Commissioner who should be able to speak the language of the people, and to place all the Districts of inquiry within the Principality under his charge.

12. The plan of inquiry thus proposed was adopted, and as regards England and Wales and Ireland, it has been substantially adhered to; but in Scotland, owing to the absence of any local area of administration similar to that of the Poor Law Union, it was found necessary to pursue a slightly different course.

13. The Scheme having been settled by the Committee, draft instructions to the Assistant Commissioners, and notes as to the specific subjects to be inquired into, were submitted to the Committee, and after discussion and some amendment they were approved and adopted. A copy of the notes for the inquiry are appended to this Report. [Page 165.]

Appointment of first Assistant Commissioners for England and Wales.

14. On the 14th of March Messrs. E. V. P. Bouverie, Cecil M. Chapman, Aubrey Spencer, and D. Lleufer Thomas, barristers-at-law, were appointed Assistant Commissioners for the purpose of conducting inquiries in England and Wales. I was definitely appointed the Senior Assistant Commissioner, and to me was assigned the duty of selecting the districts of inquiry and superintending the work of my colleagues.

On the 17th of the same month the Assistant Commissioners met the Chairman of the Commission for the purpose of receiving preliminary instructions. On the 28th the notes for inquiry were definitely arranged, and on the following day I met my colleagues, who immediately began their work.

It became necessary before attempting to estimate the time which would be required for carrying out the inquiry on the lines proposed to determine the number of districts to be selected for inquiry; and as the Board of Agriculture had very kindly promised to furnish certain detailed statistics with reference to those districts which might be chosen, it was desirable to settle at once the areas of inquiry, and I immediately proceeded to frame a Scheme, which was laid before the Committee B. and adopted.

This Scheme embraced 36 Poor Law Unions in England and eight in Wales. The distribution of these districts is shown by the accompanying map.*

I shall have to state hereafter the general principles which guided me in making the selection which I did.

Additional Assistant Commissioners appointed.

In the middle of April Mr. Bouverie was compelled to resign his appointment in consequence of serious illness, and his post was not immediately filled up; but as soon as the list of districts had been settled the sanction of the Treasury was obtained for the appointment of three additional Assistant Commissioners, and on the 4th June Messrs. A. Wilson Fox, R. C. Richards, and E. Wilkinson, barristers-at-law, and Mr. W. E. Bear, journalist, were appointed, and at once commenced their duties.

Ireland.

15. The subject of the inquiry in Ireland and Scotland next engaged my attention.

Assistant Commissioners appointed.

On the 20th of June I went to Dublin, where I met and conferred with Mr. W. P. O'Brien, C.B., late Vice-President of the Prisons Board (Ireland), and Mr. R. McCrea, late Sub-Commissioner under the Land Commission (Ireland), who had consented to act as Assistant Commissioners in Ireland.

Assistance rendered by Local Government Board (Ireland).

16. I had an interview with Mr. G. Morris, the Vice-President of the Local Government Board, and Mr. Henry A. Robinson, a Commissioner of the Board, and I beg to acknowledge gratefully the great assistance which I received from these gentlemen, who most cordially responded to my requests for information, and, with a view to aid me in the selection of districts of inquiry, procured from the several Poor Law inspectors particulars respecting the industrial conditions of all the Poor Law Unions of their districts.

And also by the Constabulary.

I also had an interview with Sir Andrew Reed, Inspector-General of Constabulary, who very kindly promised to issue instructions to members of the Constabulary Force to aid in every possible way the work of the Assistant Commissioners, and I may here remark that the Assistant Commissioners have frequently acknowledged their obligations to the members of that force for assistance in the prosecution of their inquiries.

Scheme of inquiry adopted.

17. Mr. O'Brien and Mr. McCrea commenced work immediately after my visit to Dublin, and shortly after my return I was able to submit a scheme of inquiry which was approved, and which included 30 Poor Law Unions, extending into every county of Ireland, and fairly distributed over the whole country.

Scotland: Assistant Commissioners appointed.

18. On the 11th of July I visited Edinburgh, where I met Mr. G. R. Gillespie and Mr. Andrew Mitchell, advocates, who had accepted nominations for the post of Assistant Commissioner, and discussed with them the best mode of procedure.

Assistance by Board of Supervision.

I also saw Mr. Skelton, the Secretary to the Board of Supervision, and Mr. Peterkin, one of the General Superintendents under that Board, who assisted me in various ways, and furnished me, for the use of the Assistant Commissioners, with a copious list of officials and others in different parts of the country who might be consulted in their respective localities. Very shortly after my return from Edinburgh, Mr. Gillespie presented a plan for the inquiry in Scotland, which was considered and approved.

Mr. Mitchell, after accepting the appointment, found himself unable to undertake the work, and in his place Mr. H. Rutherfurd, barrister, was appointed.

Death of Mr. G. R. Gillespie, Assistant Commissioner.

19. On the 13th of October Mr. Gillespie, who had just completed the survey of his third district of inquiry, died very suddenly.

* See map of England and Wales, Frontispiece.

I have taken an opportunity of expressing elsewhere my high opinion of the services of my late colleague, and of my deep regret at his untimely death.

Mr. R. Hunter Pringle was appointed in his place on the 29th of October. He met me in London on the 4th of November, and immediately afterwards commenced his inquiries in Scotland.

20. In the month of December all the English districts had been assigned to one or other of the Assistant Commissioners, and as the survey both in Ireland and Scotland was in a much more backward state I asked and obtained from the chairman permission to transfer two of my colleagues to Ireland, and one to Scotland, and in January Mr. Wilson Fox and Mr R. C. Richards proceeded to Ireland, and Mr. E. Wilkinson to Scotland. I have reason to believe that these gentlemen were put to some inconvenience by their acceding to my request that they would extend their work, and I desire to acknowledge the readiness with which they accepted the proposal which I was commissioned to make to them. During the winter of 1892–3 Mr. D. Lleufer Thomas was unable to continue his work owing to ill-health, and early in the month of March he was appointed to the secretaryship of the Welsh Land Commission; and Mr. Cecil M. Chapman, upon the conclusion of his work in England, obligingly consented to conduct an inquiry in the district of Builth, in Wales, thus completing the scheme which had been originally settled.

21. The Reports of each Assistant Commissioner have been issued as a separate section or part of a volume with three exceptions; Mr. Chapman's Report on the Builth district is attached to Mr. Thomas's Reports on the other districts in Wales; Mr. Gillespie's Reports are issued with those of Mr. Rutherford, and Mr. Wilkinson's two Reports on districts in Scotland are published in the same part as Mr. Hunter Pringle's Reports on that country.

The district Reports of the Assistant Commissioners are preceded by Summary Reports written after the completion of their survey, an opportunity being thus afforded them of recording their mature conclusions after comparing the conditions existing in different parts of the country and in districts varying widely in character.

The Reports are arranged in four volumes, which relate to England, Wales, Scotland, and Ireland respectively.*

The particular districts reported upon by each Assistant Commissioner are shown in Appendix, page 167, where also will be found an alphabetical list of counties with a reference to districts of inquiry within them.

22. It will be convenient at this point to state the principles upon which the selection of districts of inquiry was made, and as the sole responsibility for the choice of these districts rested with me, and as the list which I had prepared was accepted by the Committee, I may be permitted to describe at length what I had in view. For this purpose it will be desirable to deal separately with England, Wales, Scotland, and Ireland.

I. ENGLAND.

23. In the first place it was obviously desirable that these districts should be generally distributed over the whole country.

A reference to the map of England and Wales which has been prepared and is annexed, and to Table A, Appendix, page 167, will show how far this object has been obtained. In England only four counties are unrepresented, namely, Middlesex, Durham, Westmoreland, and Rutland. In the two counties first named the

* Reports of Assistant Commissioners.

Vol. I.—England.
Part I.—Mr. W. E. Bear.
II.—Mr. C. M. Chapman.
III.—Mr. A. Wilson Fox.
IV.—Mr. R. C. Richards.
V.—Mr. A. Spencer.
VI.—Mr. E. Wilkinson.
Vol. II.—Wales.—Mr. D. Lleufer Thomas, and Mr. C. M. Chapman.

Vol. III.—Scotland.
Part I.—Mr. H. Rutherfurd, and Mr. G. E. Gillespie.
II.—Mr. R. Hunter Pringle, Mr. E. Wilkinson.
Vol. IV.—Ireland.
Part I.—Mr. R. McCrea.
II.—Mr. W. P. O'Brien, C.B.
III.—Mr. R. C. Richards.
IV.—Mr. A. Wilson Fox.

agricultural labourers are not a well defined class, and they form a very small percentage of the population (in Durham they are less than 1 per cent., and in Middlesex, outside the Metropolitan area, they are less than 2 per cent.). In Westmoreland less than one-fifth of the cultivated area is arable (the average proportion for England being 48 per cent.), the growth of corn and root crops, which require a considerable amount of manual labour, is at a minimum. Rutland, though a purely agricultural county, is very small in extent, and the conditions do not differ materially from those of neighbouring counties. The three Ridings of Yorkshire have been treated as separate counties, and in the important agricultural county of Lincolnshire two districts were selected, one of which, Louth, includes a large tract of wold farming, and the other, Holbeach, is a type of the mixed agricultural and intensive culture which characterises the "low country."

Undoubtedly there are several other counties which contain within their limits very distinct types of soil and cultivation, and it would have been an easy task to extend the inquiry considerably, but I was of opinion that if nearly every county had one selected district within it all the possible conditions under which the agricultural labourer lives and works would find a representation.

24. The following table shows the distribution of the districts of inquiry over the four divisions into which England has been divided by the Board of Agriculture for statistical and produce returns.

Agricultural Divisions, England.	Number of Counties in each Division.	Cultivated Area in each Division, Acres.	Selected Districts of Inquiry in each Division.	Cultivated Area in Districts of Inquiry.	Ratio of Cultivated Area in Districts to that in Divisions.
					Per cent.
I. E. and N.E. Counties	9	6,173,000	10	694,337	11·25
II. S.E. and E.M.	13	5,830,000	10	575,694	9·94
III. S.W. and W.M.	10	6,300,000	10	655,940	10·11
IV. N. and N.W.	10	6,131,000	8	573,920	8·86

25. In the next place it was desired to observe the conditions affecting labour under the various systems of agriculture and on different descriptions of soil.

In any given area of land the amount of manual labour required and the character of the work to be done will be greatly influenced by the use to which the land is put; the proportionate extent of the arable land; the nature of the crops that are grown; and the method of disposing of those crops; the numbers and descriptions of live stock, and the objects for which they are kept.

As a rule on every considerable farm a variety of objects are pursued—the growth of corn and green crops and the rearing and fattening of stock—but in different parts of the country one branch of farming becomes the principal or most important object of the farmer, and any classification of systems of agriculture must be regarded as indicating only the more important of the various objects to which the farmers under that system direct their attention.

26. The simplest classification which can be made is that of (1) corn-growing, and (2) pastoral districts; but corn-growing districts will vary greatly in respect of the kind of corn which is grown, and also in respect of the live stock associated with the production of corn. In some such districts sheep are largely bred and reared; in others they are purchased and fattened; in others again few sheep are kept, and cattle are kept to produce the manure which is required for the corn crop.

In some such districts root crops which require labour at particular seasons are largely grown; in others bare fallows which employ the smallest modicum of labour are resorted to.

Similarly in pastoral districts the amount of labour required will be powerfully affected by the purposes for which the live stock are kept. Sheep-breeding will occupy on the hill farms only a few shepherds, while in another pastoral district dairying, milking, and cheese-making, with the production and securing of crops in connexion with these industries will demand a special class of labour.

27. Outside of the ordinary range of farming there are to be found special industries which employ a considerable amount of labour, such as hop and fruit growing, and

market gardening, and in many parts of the country employment on the farm is supplemented at certain seasons of the year by work in other industries.

28. The Agricultural Returns, which have been compiled for the use of the Labour Commission by the Board of Agriculture, enable us to ascertain the characteristics of the agriculture in each of the several selected districts of Inquiry, and to classify a considerable proportion of the whole number as representing distinct types of husbandry; but it must be pointed out that these returns were obtained after the selection of districts had been made, and though they will be used hereafter to illustrate the different conditions under which the agricultural labourer works, it cannot be pretended that the original selection was based upon such precise knowledge of the agriculture of those districts as is now possessed. *Agricultural Returns compiled by Board of Agriculture.*

29. The general distribution of the districts having been decided upon, it was considered desirable to select, as a rule, a union which was distinctly agricultural in character, and with this object in view, unions which contained a considerable town, or had a large proportion of the population engaged in other industries, were avoided. For the purpose of fixing on distinctively agricultural unions, the following returns were carefully examined. *Poor Law Unions chosen.*

30. (1.) A return of the rateable value of (1) Lands, (2) Buildings, (3) Railways, (4) Mines, and (5) all other kinds of property according to the valuation list . . . . in force in 1870 in each parish and union in England and Wales. [[illegible]. [illegible].] *Land value in proportion to other property.*

At the date of the return referred to in 32 of the selected districts, land represented more than two-thirds of the entire rateable value, and in 15 it was four-fifths of the whole rateable property. The districts are arranged in the following table from the highest to the lowest per-centage of the total value of property assessed to the Poor Rate which was represented by lands, including in that term farmhouses, farm buildings, and tithe rentcharge:—

RATEABLE VALUE.

RATIO of LAND to TOTAL VALUE 1870.—DISTRICTS of INQUIRY arranged in order from Highest to Lowest Per-centage.

Table 2

1. Land Value		2. Land Value		3. Land Value	
[illegible] of Total	Per-centage	[illegible] of Total	Per-centage	Less than [illegible] Total	Per-centage
1 [illegible]	[illegible]	16 [illegible]	[illegible]	33 Monmouth	[illegible]
2 [illegible]	[illegible]	17 Pershore	[illegible]	34 Atcham*	[illegible]
3 [illegible]	[illegible]	18 [illegible]	[illegible]	35 Truro	[illegible]
4 Pewsey	[illegible]	19 [illegible]	[illegible]	36 [illegible]	[illegible]
5 Wigton	[illegible]	20 North Witchford	[illegible]	37 Belper	[illegible]
6 Langport	[illegible]	21 Dorchester	[illegible]	38 Godstone	[illegible]
7 Swaffham	[illegible]	22 Wantage	[illegible]		
8 [illegible]	[illegible]	23 Maldon	[illegible]		
9 [illegible]	[illegible]	24 Driffield	[illegible]		
10 Thame	[illegible]	25 Thakeham	[illegible]		
11 Melton Mowbray	[illegible]	26 Thingoe	[illegible]		
12 Louth	[illegible]	27 [illegible]	[illegible]		
13 Southwell	[illegible]	28 St. Neots	[illegible]		
14 Uttoxeter	[illegible]	29 Cirencester	[illegible]		
15 [illegible]	[illegible]	30 Hollingbourn	[illegible]		
		31 Woburn	[illegible]		
		32 [illegible]	[illegible]		

The six unions which are ranged in the third column of the preceding table are, with the exception of Godstone, industrial districts, as will be shown hereafter by other statistics. Godstone is a residential district. There is little doubt that since this Return was compiled, land has receded in position in all parts of the country, but most in those districts where the assessment of buildings, railways, mines, and other kinds of property, formed a large part of the rateable value in 1870; but probably the relative position of the several districts to each other has not greatly changed.

31. (2.) The other statistical authority consulted for the purpose of selecting districts of Inquiry, was the Census Returns for 1871, which contain what the later Returns do not give, namely, particulars of the occupations of the people in registration divisions, which are as a rule identical with Poor Law Unions. *Agriculturists in ratio to population.*

An examination of these Returns showed the unions in each county containing the largest proportion of agriculturists.

* Atcham and Shrewsbury.

The following TABLE shows the PERCENTAGE of the MALE POPULATION aged 20 Years and upwards who were classed as Agriculturists in Fields and Pastures in the DISTRICTS selected for Inquiry:—

Agriculturists 50 per cent. and upwards			Agriculturists 33·3 per cent. and under 50 per cent.			Agriculturists Less than 33·3 per cent. of total		
Order	Districts	Per-centage.	Order	Districts	Per-centage.	Order	Districts	Per-centage.
1	Wantage	[illegible]	21	Crediton	[illegible]	34	[illegible]	[illegible]
2	Thingoe	[illegible]	22	Melton Mowbray	[illegible]	35	[illegible]	[illegible]
3	Garstang	[illegible]	23	[illegible]	[illegible]	36	Truro	[illegible]
4	[illegible]	[illegible]	24	Langport	[illegible]	37	Monmouth	[illegible]
5	Easingwold	[illegible]	25	Wigton	[illegible]	38	Belper	[illegible]
6	North Witchford	[illegible]	26	Southwell	[illegible]			
7	Pershore	[illegible]	27	Wetherby	[illegible]			
8	Thame	[illegible]	28	[illegible]	[illegible]			
9	Brixworth	[illegible]	29	[illegible]	[illegible]			
10	Pewsey	[illegible]	30	Dorchester	[illegible]			
11	Bromyard	[illegible]	31	Ulverston	[illegible]			
12	Thakeham	[illegible]	32	[illegible]	[illegible]			
13	Louth	[illegible]	33	Cirencester	[illegible]			
14	Holbeach	[illegible]						
15	[illegible]	[illegible]						
16	[illegible]	[illegible]						
17	[illegible]*	[illegible]						
18	[illegible]	[illegible]						
19	St. Neots	[illegible]						
20	[illegible]	[illegible]						

These figures will be better understood when it is stated that there was only one county in England in 1871 where 50 per cent. of the males aged 20 and upwards were classed as agriculturists, and that was Huntingdonshire, in which there is not a town of 5,000 population. Rutland, which is a purely agricultural county, had only 47 per cent. of adult males thus classed.

If to the numbers represented by the percentages given in the preceding table, there could be added those of the wives and children and others maintained by agriculturists it would be seen that a very large proportion of the population must be dependent upon agriculture in the 20 districts which are in the first column of the table referred to.

In the five districts which are placed in the third column of this table the industrial class outnumbered the agriculturists.

The following table will show the relative importance of the agriculturists and of the industrial class with that of certain branches of the latter class in these five districts:—

TABLE showing the PERCENTAGE of the TOTAL NUMBER of MALES aged 20 Years and upwards in certain Occupations in Five Districts of Inquiry in 1871.

Class and Order, Census Returns	Class IV.	Class IV., Order 9	Class V.	Class V., Order 10	Class V., Order 11	Class V., Order 15	Class VI.
Districts	Agricultural Class	Agriculturists in Fields and Pastures	Industrial Class	Persons engaged in Art and Mechanical Productions	Persons working and dealing in Textile Fabrics and Dress	Persons working and dealing in Minerals	Indefinite and Non-productive Class
Belper	[illegible]	[illegible]	[illegible]	[illegible]	[illegible]	[illegible]	[illegible]
Monmouth	[illegible]	[illegible]	[illegible]	[illegible]	[illegible]	[illegible]	[illegible]
Truro	[illegible]	[illegible]	[illegible]	[illegible]	[illegible]	[illegible]	[illegible]
[illegible]	[illegible]	[illegible]	[illegible]	[illegible]	[illegible]	[illegible]	[illegible]
[illegible]	[illegible]	[illegible]	[illegible]	[illegible]	[illegible]	[illegible]	[illegible]

It was thought desirable to include some districts where other industries than agriculture were predominant, and the five districts just noticed may be taken to represent industrial districts where the competition for unskilled labour is always present and often severe.

32. The preceding statement established the fact that a large proportion of the districts chosen for the purpose of inquiry were agricultural in character.

It must not, however, be inferred that in all cases the districts where the agricultural interest was most predominant was selected.

In the final choice many other circumstances than those alluded to were taken into consideration.

33. In some cases an exceptional decrease of population suggested an inquiry. The general decrease of the rural population of this country is a notorious fact. By many this depopulation is

* The County is merged in the [illegible] Registration Division; the figures given are for the whole [illegible].

attributed to the unfavourable conditions under which the agricultural labourer lives and works. The irregular distribution of the decrease is familiar to all investigators. It seemed possible that an inquiry in some of the districts where the decrease of population was most marked, and a comparison of the conditions obtaining in such districts with those existing in others where a similar decrease had not occurred, might throw some light on the subject.

Census Returns.

34. It will not be out of place to notice at this point the result of a comparison of the Census Returns for 1871, 1881, and 1891, as regards the 38 selected districts in England. It will be seen from the table which follows this paragraph that in 25 districts of the inquiry there has been a continuous decrease of population since 1871, and that the rate of decrease varies from 14·30 per cent. in 10 years to an insignificant quantity; that in five of these districts* an increase during the first period of 10 years was followed by a decrease in the next and most recent decade, and that in two districts† the reverse had happened, and a decrease was followed by an increase; while in only six districts was there a continuous increase, these six‡ districts including three out of the five industrial districts already noticed, and, in addition, Godstone, a residential district. On the other hand, Truro, which is one of the industrial districts of the former table, stands second in the list in respect of decrease of population, and Monmouth, another industrial district, has also decreased in each of the two decades.

In consequence of alterations of boundary, which have taken place since 1871, an exact statement of the results of 20 years is not very easily made, but the sum of, or the difference between, the percentages for the two decades gives an approximate result, which is sufficient for comparison between the several districts.

Comparative density of population.

35. But the importance of a decrease in population depends generally upon the density of the population, and a decrease of 17 per cent. in the population of a sparsely peopled district may have much greater effect than a decrease of 21 per cent. in a much more thickly populated region. A column representing the density of population in the districts of inquiry has been added to the table which shows the decrease of population.

It will be seen that the density of population varies from 6·9 to 93·5 per 100 acres of gross area.

As, however, some of the districts include a considerable urban population while others have no town of 5,000 inhabitants, the density of the rural parts of those which contain towns has been calculated by deducting the area and population of all places having 5,000 or more inhabitants.

For the purpose of comparison the following Table, representing the density of the population in some of the counties of England, has been prepared:—

Table 5.

Counties.	Population per 100 acres. Average for County.	Average for Rural Districts.
Westmorland	13·0	10·7
Rutland	21·0	13·0
Hereford	22·5	15·0
Huntingdon	25·0	20·0
Yorkshire N.R.	25·0	18·[illegible]
Lincoln	25·0	15·1

Increase or decrease of population.

TABLE showing the INCREASE (+) or DECREASE (−) of POPULATION in the DISTRICTS of INQUIRY between 1871 and 1881, and between 1881 and 1891. Also the DENSITY of the POPULATION in such DISTRICTS, and in the RURAL PARTS of such DISTRICTS in 1891.

Table 6.

Order from greatest Decrease to Increase.	Districts.	Increase or Decrease. 1871–1881.	1881–1891.	1871–1891.	Density of Population. No. of Persons per 100 Acres of Districts.	Order from least to greatest.	No. of Persons per 100 Acres Rural Portions of Districts.
1	Woburn	−14·10	−8·99	−22·12	27·5	33	29·5
2	Truro	−12·78	−6·88	−19·71	87·7	35	35·6
3	St. Neots	−8·10	−9·87	−17·44	33·1	31	35·1
4	Langport	−11·76	−5·43	−17·18	34·8	25	34·3
5	Glendale	−10·30	−7·11	−16·44	6·9	1	6·9
6	Crediton	−7·61	−6·62	−14·70	18·1	10	18·1
7	Pewsey	−7·86	−5·82	−13·80	18·0	5	15·0
8	Buntingford	−6·70	−8·17	−13·40	19·9	8	18·0
9	Southwell	−7·11	−5·41	−12·83	20·5	9	19·0
10	Brixworth	−1·02	−9·02	−12·11	20·4	18	19·4
11	Easingwold	−3·80	−7·69	−11·18	16·5	5	15·6
12	Bromyard	−1·57	−9·86	−11·40	20·4	7	18·0
13	Thame	−2·42	−8·51	−10·80	35·1	30	29·1
14	Thingoe	+0·97	−4·60	−10·40	13·7	11	18·7
15	Monmouth	−5·80	−4·70	−10·31	77·1	40	18·0
16	Louth	−2·13	−7·84	−9·79	19·7	13	12·0

* Stamford, Driffield, Garstang, Wetherby, Atcham.
† Uttoxeter and North Witchford.
‡ Wigton, Melton Mowbray, Basingstoke, Belper, [illegible] and Godstone.

17	Swaffham	[illegible]	[illegible]	[illegible]	[illegible]	[illegible]	[illegible]
18	Pershore	[illegible]	[illegible]	[illegible]	[illegible]	[illegible]	[illegible]
19	Holbeach	[illegible]	[illegible]	[illegible]	[illegible]	[illegible]	[illegible]
20	Maldon	[illegible]	[illegible]	[illegible]	[illegible]	[illegible]	[illegible]
21	Hollingbourn	[illegible]	[illegible]	[illegible]	[illegible]	[illegible]	[illegible]
22	Wantage	− 1·15	[illegible]	[illegible]	[illegible]	[illegible]	[illegible]
23	[illegible]	[illegible]	[illegible]	[illegible]	[illegible]	[illegible]	[illegible]
24	Thakeham	[illegible]	[illegible]	[illegible]	[illegible]	[illegible]	[illegible]
25	[illegible]	[illegible]	[illegible]	[illegible]	[illegible]	[illegible]	[illegible]
26	[illegible]	[illegible]	[illegible]	[illegible]	[illegible]	[illegible]	[illegible]
27	[illegible]	[illegible]	[illegible]	[illegible]	[illegible]	[illegible]	[illegible]
28	[illegible]	[illegible]	[illegible]	[illegible]	[illegible]	[illegible]	[illegible]
29	Wetherby	[illegible]	[illegible]	[illegible]	[illegible]	[illegible]	[illegible]
30	Uttoxeter	[illegible]	[illegible]	[illegible]	[illegible]	[illegible]	[illegible]
31	[illegible]	[illegible]	[illegible]	[illegible]	[illegible]	[illegible]	[illegible]
32	Wigton	[illegible]	[illegible]	[illegible]	[illegible]	[illegible]	[illegible]
33	Atcham	[illegible]	[illegible]	[illegible]	[illegible]	[illegible]	[illegible]
34	Melton Mowbray	[illegible]	[illegible]	[illegible]	[illegible]	[illegible]	[illegible]
35	Basingstoke	[illegible]	[illegible]	[illegible]	[illegible]	[illegible]	[illegible]
36	Belper	[illegible]	[illegible]	[illegible]	[illegible]	[illegible]	[illegible]
37	Nantwich	[illegible]	[illegible]	[illegible]	[illegible]	[illegible]	[illegible]
38	Godstone	[illegible]	[illegible]	[illegible]	[illegible]	[illegible]	[illegible]

36. It is difficult to find in the figures thus brought together any direct connexion between the comparative density of the population and its decrease or increase. It is true that the first four districts in the list which show the largest decrease of population are those of more than average density, but the next eight on the list are, in comparison with the first four, sparsely populated.

Of the 38 districts five, namely, Atcham, Belper, Louth, Nantwich, and Truro, contain towns of more than 10,000 inhabitants; 16 other districts comprise some urban sanitary areas, which are, however, for the most part agricultural towns. In these, with only two exceptions,* the population of the rural parts has either decreased to a greater extent or increased to less extent than that of the urban districts. Seventeen districts are entirely rural sanitary areas.

Woburn, which stands first on the list, has probably lost population in consequence of the decay of the straw plaiting and lace making, which used to employ a very large number of the wives and daughters of cottagers. Truro is a mining district, and there the urban as well as the rural population has decreased. St. Neots, Langport, and Glendale are almost entirely agricultural in character, and it will appear subsequently that one of these, Glendale, is a district where the condition of the agricultural labourer is equal, if not superior, to that in any other part of England, while another, namely, Langport, is a low wage district.

Some other considerations which led to the selection of particular districts may be mentioned.

37. The successful results which have attended the wise and consistent administration of the Poor Law in the Unions of Atcham and Brixworth pointed out these districts as exceptionally interesting for an inquiry.

The very able Reports made by the late Bishop Fraser and Mr. J. J. Henley to the Royal Commission on the Employment of Children and Women in Agriculture, about 20 years ago, suggested the desirability of comparing the present condition of the labourer in Swaffham (Norfolk) and Glendale (Northumberland) with what it was when these Reports were made.

Thingoe Union in Suffolk is believed to be the first district in which a county council has held a public inquiry under the Housing of the Working Classes Act, 1890, and in the neighbouring county of Essex the cottage accommodation of the labourers in the Union of Maldon has been the subject of a recent and very careful investigation by Dr. J. C. Thresh, the Medical Officer of Health to the Rural Sanitary Authorities of Chelmsford and Maldon, and it seemed desirable to take advantage of these circumstances and to include these unions in the list of districts.

* In Holbeach and Nantwich the urban population decreased at a greater rate than that of the rural districts.

In many other instances a particular reason for choosing a district existed. Stratford-on-Avon attracts interest as the birthplace of the National Agricultural Labourers' Union, and Thame had been the scene of a recent strike.

Again, while some districts were selected as representing distinct and special types of agriculture, others were chosen because they embraced within their limits a considerable variety. Districts exhibiting great variety.

Thus Cirencester includes farms on the Cotswold Hills, an arable tract of more fertile land on the East, and a dairying district in the centre. Basingstoke includes a district of large farms on the Chalk, and an entirely different district in what is known as the "Woodlands" of Hampshire.

It would be tedious, and it is, I think, unnecessary to state the reasons for the selection of each district. Enough has been said to show that an attempt was made to secure a representation of all the various systems of agriculture and the different conditions under which the agricultural labourer has to live, and to distribute the several districts fairly over the whole country. How far the object which was aimed at has been attained must be finally decided upon a consideration of the Reports of the Assistant Commissioners who visited the several districts, but the special Agricultural Returns prepared for the use of the Commission by the Board of Agriculture supply the means of ascertaining how far the selected districts illustrate and represent different types and classes of agriculture.

38. For the purpose of comparing the statistics relating to each district the per-centage of the whole cultivated area which is under each of the crops specified in the returns and numbers of cattle and sheep per 100 acres of cultivated area have been calculated, and the results are appended to the Returns. The per-centage of these crops and live stock in the different counties are also there given.* Statistics of agriculture in districts.

39. The first point to which attention may be directed is that of the proportionate extent of arable and grass land. The whole area which is returned as under crops, bare fallow, and grass is designated cultivated area. Inasmuch as, on the average, one acre of arable land requires as much manual labour as from three to five acres of grass, it will be obvious that the proportionate extent of arable land has a most important bearing upon the employment of the labourer. Arable and pasture.

In the following table the districts of inquiry are arranged in order from the highest to the lowest percentage of arable land. They are classed in three divisions:—

(A.) Arable Districts, those which have an excess of arable land, at least 25 per cent. greater than the average for England.

(B.) Mixed Arable and Grass Districts, which do not vary from the average of England by as much as 25 per cent.

(C.) Pastoral Districts, where the arable area is 25 per cent. or more below the average for England.

Table showing Districts of Inquiry arranged in respect of the Per-centage of the Cultivated Area which is Arable. Table I.

(A.) Arable Districts, having an Arable Area 25 per cent. in excess of the Average for England.			(B.) Mixed Arable and Pastoral Districts, having an Arable Area not more than 25 per cent. above or below Average.			(C.) Pastoral Districts, having an Arable Area 25 per cent. below Average.		
Order from Highest to Lowest.	Districts.	Per cent. of Cultivated Area which is arable.	Order.	Districts.	Per cent. of Cultivated Area which is arable.	Order.	Districts.	Per cent. of Cultivated Area which is arable.
1	[illegible]	[illegible]	15	Pewsey	[illegible]	32	Bromyard	[illegible]
2	Driffield	[illegible]	16	Easingwold	[illegible]	33	Monmouth	[illegible]
3	[illegible]	[illegible]	17	[illegible]	[illegible]	34	Garstang	[illegible]
4	Thingoe	[illegible]	18	[illegible]	[illegible]	35	Melton Mowbray	[illegible]
5	Swaffham	[illegible]	19	[illegible]	[illegible]	36	Nantwich	[illegible]
6	[illegible]	[illegible]	20	Hollingbourne	[illegible]	37	Belper	[illegible]
7	Wantage	[illegible]	21	Thakeham	[illegible]	38	Ulverston	[illegible]
8	Maldon	[illegible]	22	[illegible]	[illegible]			
9	Holbeach	[illegible]	23	Pershore	[illegible]			
10	Louth	[illegible]						
11	Glendale	[illegible]		[illegible]	[illegible]			
12	Cirencester	[illegible]						
13	[illegible]	[illegible]	24	Godstone	[illegible]			
14	St. Neots	[illegible]	25	Stratford-on-Avon	[illegible]			
			26	Thame	[illegible]			
			27	Wetherby	[illegible]			
			28	[illegible]	[illegible]			
			29	[illegible]	[illegible]			
			30	Langport	[illegible]			
			31	Bosworth	[illegible]			

* App. Vol. V. Pt. II. Sec. I. D.

It will be seen that 14 districts are included in Class (A) as most distinctively arable, two of these having upwards of 80 per cent., four between 70 and 80 per cent., and eight from 63 to 70 per cent. of land under the plough.

In Class (B.) nine districts have more than the average and eight less than the average of England.

In Class (C.) seven districts are classed as most distinctively pastoral, the arable area in no case exceeding 35 per cent. of the total, while in three of them it is less than 25 per cent., the grass area being correspondingly large, reaching in Uttoxeter to 88 per cent.

Appended to the Agricultural Returns for districts are tables showing the per-centages of arable &c., in the several counties, for the purpose of comparison with those of the districts.

It may be interesting to compare some of the districts at each extreme of high and low per-centage of arable land with the counties in which they lie thus.

CLASS A.—ARABLE DISTRICTS.

Order in respect of per-centage Arable Area.	Districts.	Per-centage of Arable.	Per-centage of Grass.	Counties.	Per-centage of Arable.	Per-centage of Grass.
1	North Witchford	81·77	18·23	Cambridgeshire	77·9	22·1
2	Driffield	81·50	18·50	Yorkshire E.R.	69·7	30·3
3	Buntingford	79·14	20·86	Hertfordshire	64·2	35·8
4	Thingoe	78·48	21·52	Suffolk	73·7	26·3
5	Swaffham	78·18	21·82	Norfolk	73·1	26·9
6	Basingstoke	73·60	26·4	Hampshire	61·6	38·4
7	Wantage	68·35	31·65	Berkshire	68·7	31·3
	CLASS C.—PASTORAL DISTRICTS.					
12	Bromyard	35·00	65·00	Hereford	31·0	69·0
13	Monmouth	30·85	69·15	Monmouth Gloucester Hereford	23·1 44·5 37·0	77·0 55·5 63·0
14	Garstang	20·00	71·00	Lancashire	28·6	71·4
15	Melton Mowbray	20·40	78·60	Leicester	26·6	73·4
16	Nantwich	20·06	79·94	Chester	33·8	66·2
17	Belper	21·77	78·23	Derby	19·5	80·5
18	Uttoxeter	17·00	83·00	Stafford Derby	30·2 19·5	69·8 80·5

This table shows that these districts present, in an intensified form, the characteristics of the counties to which they lie; the arable counties are represented by districts which are in a marked degree arable in character; the pastoral counties by districts which in four instances conform pretty closely to the county standard. In two instances, Uttoxeter and Nantwich, there is considerable excess of pasture. The Union of Monmouth, which lies in three counties, blends their different characteristics.

40. Turning next to the purposes to which the arable land is applied, it may be observed that of all the several classes of crops which are generally grown corn crops require the greatest amount of manual labour. Leaving out of sight for the present those districts where hops and fruit are grown, or market-gardening is carried on, those districts which have the largest extent of corn land will give the greatest amount of employment.

41. The Returns which are available show the area of white corn (wheat, barley and oats) only, but the other corn crops (rye, beans, and peas) being less than one-tenth of the whole, could not materially affect the result.

In the following table those districts which have more than the average acreage of white corn are arranged in two classes, (a) those which have 50 per cent above the average, and (b) those which have an excess not so great as the others. The proportionate area of the same crops in the several counties represented is also given.

CORN DISTRICTS.

(a.) No.	Districts having 50 per cent. excess of Average Area in White Corn.	Per-centage of Cultivated Area.	Counties in which the Districts lie.	Per-centage of Cultivated Area.	(b.) No.	Districts having an Area of White Corn in excess of Average of less than 50 per cent.	Per-centage of Cultivated Area.	Counties in which the Districts lie.	Per-centage of Cultivated Area.
1	North Witchford	51·81	Cambs	42·8	10	Basingstoke	36·10	Hants	27·6
2	Buntingford	45·42	Herts	31·8	11	St. Neots	32·45	Huntingdon Beds	33·1 31·4
3	Driffield	41·80	Yorks E.R.	36·8	12	Bromyard	30·10	Yorks N.R.	31·1
4	Thingoe	37·33	Suffolk	37·9	13	Pewsey	31·46	Wilts	29·0
5	Swaffham	38·28	Norfolk	37·1	14	Cirencester	35·33	Gloucester	18·0
6	Louth	35·56	Lincoln	35·9	15	Samford	36·29	Notts	25·6
7	Holbeach	35·9			16	Crediton	31·81	Devon	19·1
8	Wantage	33·8	Berks	30·8	17	Glendale	23·48	Northumberland	19·6
9	Maldon	30·73	Essex	33·8	18	Thakeham	30·64	Sussex	22·6
					19	Mallingbourne	32·01	Kent	21·6

AVERAGE FOR ENGLAND, 23·4

Thus exactly half the districts have an excess and half have less than the average extent of the crops in question.

It will be observed that in North Witchford more than one half of the cultivated area is devoted to the growth of wheat, barley, and oats. A reference to the Returns,* in which particulars as to the white corn area in all districts is given, will show that at the other extreme Uttoxeter has less than 6 per cent. occupied by these crops.

In 13 out of 19 districts the per-centage of white corn is greater than in the counties to which they belong, and in six it does not vary by as much as two per cent., and it may be counted as practically the same as in the counties.

It will be interesting to carry the investigation one step further to ascertain which of three kinds of grain is most cultivated in these 19 corn districts, and in others where one or more descriptions of white corn are extensively grown.

In the following table those districts which have an acreage of wheat, barley, and oats, 50 per cent. in excess of the average quantity are given. Wheat, barley, oats.

Table 10.

Order in respect of White Corn	Order in respect of Wheat	Wheat Districts	Per-centage of Cultivated Area	Order in respect of White Corn	Order in respect of Barley	Barley Districts	Per-centage of Cultivated Area	Order in respect of White Corn	Order in respect of Oats	Oats Districts	Per-centage of Cultivated Area
1	1	North Witchford	[illegible]	4	1	Thingoe	[illegible]	5	1	Driffield	17·31
9	2	[illegible]	19·[illegible]	3	2	[illegible]	[illegible]	[illegible]	2	†Wigton	16·17
3	3	Huntingdon	19·[illegible]	2	3	Huntingdon	[illegible]	1	3	North Witchford	13·19
7	4	Holbeach	[illegible]	6	4	Louth	14·70	18	4	†[illegible]	12·[illegible]
11	5	†St. Neots	17·[illegible]	19	5	†[illegible]	[illegible]	12	5	†Glendale	11·[illegible]
21	6	§Pershore	11·77	17	6	†[illegible]	[illegible]	[illegible]	6	†[illegible]	11·[illegible]
4	7	Thingoe	14·76	5	7	Driffield	11·[illegible]				
10	8	†[illegible]	14·47	8	8	Wantage	10·[illegible]				
8	9	Wantage	13·10								
15	10	†Cosford	13·27								
5	11	Driffield	13·19								
		Average for England	8·7			Average for England	7·10			Average for England	6·6

47. Next in importance to corn crops come root crops, as creating employment for labourers. The Agricultural Returns supply details of the acreage of turnips and swedes, mangold and potatoes. Root crops.

The districts in which the growth of these crops is most marked are shown in the following Table:—

Districts having 50 per cent. in excess of the average Proportion:—

Table 11.

No.	Turnips, Swedes, and Mangold Districts	Per-centage of Cultivated Area	No.	Potatoes Districts	Per-centage of Cultivated Area
1	Swaffham	17·76	1	North Witchford	9·[illegible]
2	Driffield	14·25	2	Holbeach	7·[illegible]
3	Thingoe	13·[illegible]	3	Ormskirk	[illegible]
4	Glendale	12·[illegible]	4	[illegible]	[illegible]
5	Louth	11·90	5	Wigton	5·70
6	Depwade	11·[illegible]	6	Nantwich	5·57
7	Cosford	10·[illegible]			
	Average for England	6·3		Average for England	1·5

The Returns give particulars of the acreage of hops and small fruit in the selected districts.

43. Hops are grown in the five undermentioned districts. The extent and proportionate part of the cultivated area occupied by the crop in those districts and the several counties in which they lie are as follows:— Hops and fruit.

Hops.

Table 12.

District.	Acreage.	Per-centage of Cultivated Area.	Counties	Per-centage of Cultivated Area.
1 Hollingbourn	[illegible]	4·50	Kent	4·5
2 Bromyard	[illegible]	3·67	Hereford	1·5
3 [illegible]	[illegible]	0·79	Surrey	0·7
4 Pershore	117	0·31	Worcester	0·3
5 Thakeham	6	0·02	Sussex	1·1

—	Average	
Basingstoke	4·11	1·24
Pershore	[illegible]	1·70

44. One other class of crops may be noticed as affecting the amount of labour required on farms, and it is that of clover and grasses in rotation. These crops may be regarded in the same light as pasture in respect of the labour employed.

Following the course pursued with regard to other crops, the districts which have an exceptional area of these crops amounting to 50 per cent. over average are given below.

District	Percentage of Cultivated Area
Truro	21·31
Glendale	25·91
Wigton	23·10
Glenwarton	[illegible]
Basingstoke	19·[illegible]
Crediton	17·[illegible]
Driffield	17·[illegible]

The position of these districts in respect of labour is materially changed, when the extent of the crops under notice is taken into consideration, as will be seen from the following statement, which shows the per-centage of arable land (nominal), and that actually under crops demanding a considerable amount of labour.

Districts having an Area of Clover, &c., 50 per cent. in excess of the Average for England	Percentage of Cultivated Area			
	Arable.	Pasture.	Arable not including Clover, &c.	Pasture and Clover, &c.
Truro	64·[illegible]	35·67	30·42	67·10
Glendale	[illegible]	[illegible]	[illegible]	[illegible]
Wigton	[illegible]	[illegible]	[illegible]	[illegible]
Glenwarton	85·07	19·91	[illegible]	17·[illegible]
Basingstoke	77·50	[illegible]	34·74	45·[illegible]
Crediton	[illegible]	11·16	[illegible]	39·[illegible]
Driffield	[illegible]	18·50	64·10	35·[illegible]

45. Examining next the statistics as to Cattle and Sheep in the selected districts, and taking Cattle as first in order, we find that in eight of these districts the numbers for every 100 acres of cultivated area are 25 per cent. in excess of the average for England, which was in 1891 19·4 per 100 acres. These districts are as follows, the proportionate numbers for the counties in which the districts lie being added for the purpose of comparison.

CATTLE.

No.	District	Number per 100 acres Cultivated Area	Counties	Number per 100 acres Cultivated Area
1	Nantwich	33·83	Cheshire	32·1
2	Uttoxeter	27·40	Stafford	21·8
			Derby	20·6
3	Garstang	27·[illegible]	Lancaster	20·5
4	Truro	26·13	Cornwall	22·6
5	Belper	25·[illegible]	Derby	20·6
6	Melton Mowbray	25·07	Leicester	20·[illegible]
7	Wigton	25·[illegible]	Cumberland	22·7
8	Brixworth	21·95	Northampton	18·[illegible]

AVERAGE FOR ENGLAND—19·4

Seven other districts have more than the average proportionate number of cattle of all ages. They are as follows:—

No.	District.	Number per 100 acres Cultivated Area.	Counties.	Number per 100 acres Cultivated Area.
9	Atcham	25·71	Salop	[illegible]
10	Langport	25·70	Somerset	[illegible]
11	Holbeach	[illegible]	Lincolnshire	16·0
12	Wetherby	[illegible]	Yorks W.R.	[illegible]
13	Southwell	[illegible]	Notts	[illegible]
14	Woburn	19·78	Beds	[illegible]
15	Thame	19·75	Oxon and Berks	[illegible] / [illegible]

If we take the different classes of Cattle into consideration we find that some of the districts in the second list, which are not very remarkable for the total number of Cattle, have a very large representation of one or more of these classes as will appear from the following table which shows those districts which have an excess in any one class amounting to 25 per cent. above the average for England.

CATTLE IN THREE CLASSES.

Districts having an excess of 25 per cent or more over average.

(1.) Cows and Heifers. Order	Districts	Number per 100 acres Cultivated Area	(2.) Cattle 2 years old and above. Order	Districts	Number per 100 acres Cultivated Area	(3.) Cattle under 2 years. Order	Districts	Number per 100 acres Cultivated Area
1	[illegible]	[illegible]	1	[illegible]	[illegible]	1	Garstang	[illegible]
2	Uttoxeter	[illegible]	2	Melton Mowbray	[illegible]	2	Thame	[illegible]
3	Belper	[illegible]	3	Wetherby	[illegible]	3	Uttoxeter	[illegible]
4	Garstang	[illegible]	4	Holbeach	[illegible]	4	[illegible]	[illegible]
5	Thame	[illegible]	5	Thame	[illegible]	5	Wigton	[illegible]
			6	Langport	[illegible]	6	Belper	[illegible]
			7	Easingwold	[illegible]	7	Melton Mowbray	[illegible]
			8	Wigton	[illegible]	8	Atcham	[illegible]
			9	[illegible]	[illegible]			
			10	Atcham	[illegible]			
			11	Louth	[illegible]			
	Average for England	[illegible]		Average for England	[illegible]		Average for England	[illegible]

The five districts in column 1 may be described as Dairy districts; those in the second column are Grazing and Fattening districts, and those in the third are districts in which a large number of Cattle are Reared.

46. Dealing next with Sheep we find that nine of the districts of inquiry have more than 25 per cent. above the average number for England, which is 71·10 per 100 acres of cultivated area.

These districts are shown in the following table which also gives particulars of the stock of Sheep in the counties containing the districts in question.

SHEEP per 100 ACRES of CULTIVATED AREA.

Order	Districts having upwards of 25 per cent. above the Average for England.	Number per 100 acres	Counties in which the Districts lie.	Number per 100 acres
1	Glendale	[illegible]	Northumberland	[illegible]
2	Dorchester	[illegible]	Dorset	[illegible]
3	Pewsey	[illegible]	Wilts	[illegible]
4	Hollingbourne	[illegible]	Kent	[illegible]
5	Louth	[illegible]	Lincolnshire	[illegible]
6	Driffield	[illegible]	Yorks E.R.	[illegible]
7	Holbeach	[illegible]	Lincolnshire	[illegible]
8	Wantage	[illegible]	Berks	[illegible]
9	Brixworth	[illegible]	Northamptonshire	[illegible]

It will be seen that with the exception of Hollingbourn all these districts are more distinctly Sheep districts than the counties to which they belong. Glendale is remarkable for having more than three times the average number for England and 50 per cent. more than that of the county of Northumberland.

It should, however, be pointed out that as Sheep are not entirely maintained on the cultivated area, and that in hilly districts they have a wide range over land which is not under crops, bare fallow, or grass, and therefore a comparison between a highly cultivated and enclosed district and a hill district on the basis of numbers in proportion to cultivated area is misleading.

In the case of Glendale, which includes in its area part of the Cheviot range of hills, the total area is far in excess of the cultivated area, and the number of Sheep per 100 acres of total area is in that district 114·83, while the proportionate number for Northumberland is 61·46 and for England 54·98.

If the number in proportion to total area were given for each of the nine districts in the preceding table they would all of them retain their position as notably Sheep districts whether they were compared with England generally or with the counties to which they belong.

With respect to the two classes into which Sheep are divided in the Returns, that is—(1) Sheep of one year old and above; (2) Sheep under one year old (lambs); the following Table shows those districts in which either of these classes is specially prominent:—

SHEEP and LAMBS.—NUMBER per 100 ACRES CULTIVATED AREA.

Sheep.			Lambs.		
Order.	Districts having 25 per cent. over average for England.	Number per 100 acres.	Order.	Districts having 25 per cent. over average for England.	Number per 100 acres.
1	Glendale	[illegible]	1	Glendale	[illegible]
2	Holbeach	76·49	2	Pewsey	[illegible]
3	[illegible]	[illegible]	3	Louth	[illegible]
4	Hollingbourn	63·95	4	Dorchester	[illegible]
5	Driffield	49·15	5	Hollingbourn	[illegible]
6	Pewsey	[illegible]	6	* Thingoe	[illegible]
7	Louth	39·66	7	Wantage	[illegible]
8	Brixworth	[illegible]	8	Driffield	[illegible]
9	Wantage	[illegible]	9	* Swaffham	[illegible]
			10	* Cirencester	[illegible]
	AVERAGE FOR ENGLAND	[illegible]		AVERAGE FOR ENGLAND	[illegible]

The only thing which need be noted in respect of this Table is that Holbeach and Brixworth are evidently Sheep Feeding districts, while the remainder, being all of them notable for their number of Lambs, are Breeding districts.

47. In the following Table an attempt is made to exhibit in a compendious form the characteristic features of the several districts of inquiry as shown by Agricultural and other Returns. The Reports of the Assistant Commissioners, of course, exhibit in much greater detail differences which are not apparent from the statistical Returns.

TABLE showing the CHARACTERISTIC FEATURES which distinguish the several DISTRICTS of INQUIRY in ENGLAND.

Index Number.	[illegible]	1. [illegible]	2. [illegible] (a)	2. [illegible] (b)	3. [illegible]	4. [illegible] (a)	4. [illegible] (b)	4. [illegible] (c)	5. [illegible] (a)	5. [illegible] (b)
1	[illegible]	Ind.	—	—	PA	—	—		C [illegible] Cn(a) Cs(a)	—
2	[illegible]	Agl.	—	—	A	C W O	B	—		
3	[illegible]	Ind.	—	—	P	—	—	—	C(a) [illegible](a) Cs(a)	
4	[illegible]	Agl.	Dec.	[illegible]	PA	—	—	—	C(a) Cn(a)	[illegible](a) [illegible](a) [illegible]
5	[illegible]	Agl.	Dec.	[illegible]	P	—	—	[illegible]	[illegible] Cs	—
6	[illegible]	Agl.	Dec.	[illegible]	A	C(a) W B	—			—
7	[illegible]	M.	—	—	A	C	B	—		[illegible] [illegible] L(a)
8	[illegible]	Agl.	Dec.	[illegible]	AP	C W	B(a)	—	Cn Cs	[illegible] [illegible] L(a)
9	[illegible]	M.	—	—	AP	—	B(a)		[illegible]	[illegible](a) [illegible](a) L(a)
10	[illegible]	Agl.	—	[illegible]	A	C(a) W B O	B(a)	—		[illegible](a) [illegible](a) L(a)
11	[illegible]	Agl.	Dec.	[illegible]	AP	C B O	B	P	Cn(a)	—
12	[illegible]	Agl.	—	[illegible]	P	—	—	P	C(a) [illegible](a) Cn Cs(a)	—
13	[illegible]	Agl.	Dec.	[illegible]	A	C B O	B(a)	—		[illegible](a) [illegible](a) L(a)
14	[illegible]	Dec.	—	—	PA	—	—	[illegible]		—
15	[illegible]	Agl.	—	—	A	C(a) W	—	P	C Cn(a) Cs	[illegible](a) [illegible](a)
16	[illegible]	Agl.	—	—	AP	C	—	[illegible] F		[illegible](a) [illegible](a) L(a)
17	[illegible]	Agl.	Dec.	—	PA		—		C [illegible] Cn(a) Cs	[illegible]
18	[illegible]	Agl.	—	[illegible]	A	C(a) B	B(a)	—	Cb(a)	[illegible](a) [illegible](a) L(a)
19	[illegible]	M.	—	—	A	C(a) W	—		Cn	—
20	[illegible]	Agl.	—	—	P	—	—	—	C(a) [illegible] Cn(a) Cs(a)	[illegible] [illegible]
21	[illegible]	Ind.	Dec.	—	P	—	—	—	Cs	[illegible] L
22	[illegible]	Ind.	—	—	P	—		P	C(a) [illegible](a) Cs(a)	—
23	North Witchford	Agl.	—	—	A	C(a) W O	—	P		
24	[illegible]	Agl.	—	—	AP	W	—	[illegible] F		—
25	[illegible]	Agl.	Dec.	[illegible]	AP	C	B	—		[illegible](a) [illegible](a) L(a)
26	St. [illegible]	Agl.	Dec.	—	A	C W	—	—		—
27	[illegible]	Agl.	Dec.	[illegible]	AP	C	—	—	C Cb(a) Cs	—
28	[illegible]	M.	—	—	PA	—	—	—		L
29	[illegible]	Agl.	—	[illegible]	A	C(a) B	B(a)	—		[illegible] L(a)
30	[illegible]	Agl.	—	[illegible]	AP	C	—	[illegible]		—
31	[illegible]	Agl.	Dec.	—	PA	—	—	—	C [illegible] Cn	—
32	[illegible]	Agl.	Dec.	[illegible]	A	C(a) W B	B(a)	—		[illegible] [illegible] L(a)
33	[illegible]	Ind.	Dec.(a)	—	A	—	—		C(a) [illegible](a) Cn(a) Cs(a)	[illegible] [illegible] L
34	[illegible]	Agl.	—	—	P	—	—		C(a) [illegible](a) Cs(a)	—
35	[illegible]	Agl.	—	—	A	C(a) W B	B	—		[illegible](a) [illegible](a) L(a)
36	[illegible]	M.	—	—	PA	—	—	—	C Cn(a)	—
37	[illegible]	Agl.	—	[illegible]	AP	O	—	P	C(a) [illegible] Cn(a) Cs(a)	[illegible]
38	[illegible]	Agl.	Dec.(a)	—	PA	—	—	—	C Cb Cs	—

Col. 1. Agl.—Agricultural. Ind.—[illegible]. M.—Mixed. Dec.—[illegible]. See Tables [illegible].

[illegible]

II.—WALES.

48. The agricultural conditions of Wales differ so widely from those of England that it would be impossible to find in it such diversity as is represented by the English districts. The wide extent of commons and hill pasture which helps to maintain Cattle and Sheep in Wales vitiates any comparison of districts in respect of the proportionate numbers of these animals, and the cultivation of arable land is nowhere very extensive as compared with England.

49. A comparison of the agricultural statistics relating to the two parts of the country will indicate the wide difference between their requirements in respect of agricultural labour. The ratio which the cultivated area bears to the total area is little more than three-fifths, while in England it exceeds three-fourths.

Thus the arable land in England occupies twice as large a part of the whole surface as it does in Wales.

PER-CENTAGE OF TOTAL AREA

—	Cultivated Area	Hill, Mountain, Woods, Waste, Water	Arable	Pasture
England -	77·25	22·75	37·00	40·25
Wales -	61·16	38·84	18·54	42·62

50. The proportionate part of the cultivated area devoted to different classes of crops is shown by the following table:

PER-CENTAGE OF CULTIVATED AREA

—	Arable	Pasture	Corn Crops	Green Crops	Clover and Rotation Grasses	Arable land, less Clover, &c.
England -	47·9	52·1	24·7	10·1	11·0	36·9
Wales -	30·3	69·7	14·1	4·2	11·3	19·0

It will be seen from these figures that while in England 35 acres out of 100 acres of cultivated area are under crops which require much labour, only 18 acres in Wales are so cultivated.

By way of comparison it may be stated that only six counties in England have so small a proportion of arable area as the average of Wales. They are as follows: Westmorland, 16·3; Derby, 18·5; Monmouth, 22·6; Somerset, 23·5; Middlesex, 27·9; Stafford, 30·2 per cent. of cultivated area.

51. In the selection of districts of inquiry in Wales the same principles of distribution and representation of different classes of farming were kept in view as in England. Eight districts were selected; of these three are in South Wales and five in North Wales.

These districts extend into 10 out of the twelve counties, and they include within their area nearly one-fifth of the whole cultivated area of Wales.*

In these districts, if judged by the same standard as was employed in the case of England, the agriculturists are nowhere so strong numerically as they were found to be there.

52. In the following Table the districts are arranged in order from the highest to the lowest percentage of agriculturists among males of 20 years and upwards in 1871 (the latest available returns

* Cultivated area of Wales [illegible] acres; that of the districts of inquiry is [illegible] = 19·[illegible] per cent. of total.

for the purpose); the per-centage of the industrial class, and that of the sub-order engaged in working or dealing in minerals are added:—

Order.	District.	Agricultural Class. IV.	Agriculturists in Fields and Pastures. IV. 1.	Industrial Class. V.	Persons Working and Dealing in Minerals. V. 18.
1	Builth	36·36	37·30	34·18	3·62
2	Llanfyllin	34·43	35·10	33·46	3·66
3	Ruthin	31·03	30·10	27·05	10·61
4	Pwllheli	30·50	40·04	35·51	8·15
5	Narberth	29·54	47·56	29·2[illegible]	10·45
6	Dolgelly	21·64	29·70	41·61	[illegible]
7	Anglesey	[illegible]	33·05	24·99	4·71
8	Bridgend	14·03	34·71	40·09	30·91

It will be seen that in Bridgend the industrial class had double the number of the agriculturists, and as the population of that Union has enormously increased since 1871, the disparity in the numbers of the two classes has no doubt become much greater.

In only one other district, Dolgelly, did the industrial class outnumber the agriculturists. Anglesey, which had a smaller per-centage of agriculturists than Dolgelly, had also a smaller number in the industrial class, but in that Union the commercial and the indefinite and non-productive classes formed nearly one-fourth of the male population of 20 years and upwards.

53. Classifying these districts in the same manner as was done in the case of England we have—

Agricultural districts.—Builth, Llanfyllin, and Ruthin.

Mixed districts.—Pwllheli, Narberth, Dolgelly, and Anglesey.

Industrial district.—Bridgend.

In respect of comparative density of population the districts follow in this order from the least to the greatest:—

Llanfyllin	4·64	Pwllheli	22·38
Builth	6·23	Anglesey	24·13
Dolgelly	9·39	*Bridgend	46·57
Ruthin	13·08	Rural district	38·69
Narberth	14·63		

In respect of increase or decrease of population the Welsh districts exhibit the same diversity as the English.

In five of these there has been a continued decrease in the last two decades. In two an increase during the first decade has been followed by a decrease in the second, and in one district only has there been a continuous increase.

Districts in order from greatest Decrease in Population.	Population as stated in Census Returns 1881: 1871.	Census Returns 1881: 1881.	Census Returns 1891: 1881.	Census Returns 1891: 1891.	Increase (+) or Decrease (−) Per cent. 1871–1881.	1881–1891.	1871–1891.
1. Builth	13,[illegible]	14,215	14,215	12,[illegible]	− [illegible]	− [illegible]	−15·0
2. Llanfyllin	21,671	19,[illegible]	19,[illegible]	18,[illegible]	− [illegible]	− 7·12	−15·6 approx.
3. Narberth	[illegible]	19,517	19,541	18,[illegible]	− 4·[illegible]	− 6·[illegible]	−10·[illegible]
4. Anglesey	16,[illegible]	15,114	15,102	11,[illegible]	− [illegible]	− [illegible]	−10·[illegible] approx.
5. Ruthin	[illegible]	8,1[illegible]	8,[illegible]	7,[illegible]	− 1·09	− [illegible]	− 4·3
6. Dolgelly	15,311	15,130	15,175	14,[illegible]	− 3·37	− 1·27	− 1·01 approx.
7. Pwllheli	[illegible]	[illegible]	23,911	[illegible]	+ 0·[illegible]	− 0·76	+ 6·3
8. Bridgend	31,371	[illegible]	42,[illegible]	51,[illegible]	+ [illegible]	+ [illegible]	+ [illegible] approx.

54. The Agricultural Returns furnished by the Board of Agriculture yield the following results:—

DISTRICTS of INQUIRY arranged in order from Highest to Lowest per-centages of CULTIVATED AREA under different kinds of CROPS.

Arable Area.		White Corn.		Wheat.		Barley.	
1. Ruthin	49·46	1. Ruthin	23·77	1. Llanfyllin	4·11	1. Ruthin	11·[illegible]
2. Anglesey	47·35	2. Anglesey	16·30	2. Ruthin	3·[illegible]	2. Bridgend	5·[illegible]
3. Pwllheli	40·11	3. Llanfyllin	16·[illegible]	3. Bridgend	3·[illegible]	3. Pwllheli	5·06
4. Llanfyllin	31·1	4. Pwllheli	14·[illegible]	4. Builth	2·55	4. Llanfyllin	4·[illegible]
5. Bridgend	31·[illegible]						
Average for Wales	[illegible]	Average for Wales	15·3	Average for Wales	[illegible]	Average for Wales	[illegible]
6. Builth	28·5[illegible]	5. Bridgend	13·16	5. Narberth	0·[illegible]	5. Narberth	3·74
7. Narberth	21·[illegible]	6. Builth	12·77	6. Dolgelly	0·[illegible]	6. Builth	2·[illegible]
8. Dolgelly	17·[illegible]	7. Narberth	11·[illegible]	7. Anglesey	0·35	7. Dolgelly	2·[illegible]
		8. Dolgelly	7·[illegible]	8. Pwllheli	0·0[illegible]	8. Anglesey	1·[illegible]

Oats.		Turnips.		Potatoes.		Clover and Grasses under Rotation.	
1. Anglesey	12·75	1. Ruthin	5·76	1. Pwllheli	4·67	1. Anglesey	26·[illegible]
2. Ruthin	9·[illegible]	2. Bridgend	4·[illegible]	2. Anglesey	2·[illegible]	2. Ruthin	19·[illegible]
3. Pwllheli	9·[illegible]	3. Anglesey	3·[illegible]	3. Dolgelly	1·[illegible]	3. Pwllheli	17·[illegible]
		4. Llanfyllin	2·73				
Average for Wales	6·3	Average for Wales	2·7	Average for Wales	1·8	Average for Wales	11·8
4. Builth	7·70	5. Pwllheli	2·34	4. Ruthin	1·[illegible]	4. Llanfyllin	10·[illegible]
5. Llanfyllin	7·18	6. Builth	2·[illegible]	5. Builth	0·73	5. Bridgend	10·[illegible]
6. Narberth	6·55	7. Narberth	1·16	6. Narberth	0·[illegible]	6. Narberth	7·[illegible]
7. Bridgend	5·37	8. Dolgelly	0·61	7. Llanfyllin	0·66	7. Dolgelly	7·37
8. Dolgelly	1·[illegible]			8. Bridgend	0·40	8. Builth	6·81

Cattle and Sheep.

Districts of Inquiry arranged in order from Highest to Lowest Numbers per 100 Acres of Cultivated Area.

Cattle.

Cattle of all Ages.		Cows and Heifers.		Two Years Old and upwards.		Under Two Years Old.	
1. Pwllheli	39·46	1. Pwllheli	12·44	1. Pwllheli	7·[illegible]	1. Pwllheli	19·[illegible]
2. Anglesey	34·56	2. Narberth	11·[illegible]	2. Anglesey	7·[illegible]	2. Anglesey	15·[illegible]
3. Narberth	31·69	3. Anglesey	11·45	3. Bridgend	4·[illegible]	3. Narberth	14·[illegible]
4. Llanfyllin	29·77			4. Llanfyllin	4·[illegible]	4. Llanfyllin	13·[illegible]
5. Ruthin	26·91			5. Narberth	4·[illegible]	5. Ruthin	13·[illegible]
				6. Dolgelly	4·[illegible]		
Average for Wales	26·3	Average for Wales	10·[illegible]	Average for Wales	4·[illegible]	Average for Wales	11·70
6. Dolgelly	25·[illegible]	4. Ruthin	9·[illegible]	7. Ruthin	3·[illegible]	6. Dolgelly	11·48
7. Bridgend	22·[illegible]	5. Llanfyllin	9·[illegible]	8. Builth	3·[illegible]	7. Bridgend	9·[illegible]
8. Builth	19·72	6. Dolgelly	9·[illegible]			8. Builth	6·[illegible]
		7. Bridgend	8·[illegible]				
		8. Builth	7·[illegible]				

Sheep.

Sheep of all Ages.		One Year Old and upwards.		Lambs under One Year Old.	
1. Dolgelly	[illegible]	1. Dolgelly	[illegible]	1. Dolgelly	[illegible]
2. Builth	[illegible]	2. Builth	157·[illegible]	2. Builth	61·[illegible]
3. Llanfyllin	[illegible]	3. Llanfyllin	[illegible]	3. Ruthin	47·[illegible]
4. Ruthin	[illegible]	4. Ruthin	[illegible]	4. Llanfyllin	44·[illegible]
				5. Bridgend	[illegible]
Average for Wales	[illegible]	Average for Wales	71·1	Average for Wales	[illegible]
5. Bridgend	[illegible]	5. Bridgend	[illegible]	6. Pwllheli	[illegible]
6. Pwllheli	[illegible]	6. Pwllheli	[illegible]	7. Anglesey	[illegible]
7. Anglesey	[illegible]	7. Anglesey	[illegible]	8. Narberth	[illegible]
8. Narberth	41·[illegible]	8. Narberth	[illegible]		

In none of the districts does the arable area amount to 50 per cent. of the cultivated area, and in only three of them is it as much as one-third of it. If we class these districts as those of England were classed, three will be mixed, pastoral and arable districts, with a preponderance of pasture [P.A.], and five distinctly pastoral in character [P].

TABLE showing the CHARACTERISTIC FEATURES of the several DISTRICTS of INQUIRY in Wales.

Districts.	Industrial Character.	Population (a) Density.	Population (b) Sparse under 25 per 100 acres.	Character of Cultivation.	Crops of more than average extent: Corn.	Roots.	Pasture.	Cattle.	Sheep.
Anglesey	Mixed	Den.	—	PA	C O	R	P	C Cows C B C 1	—
Bridgend	Ind.	—	—	P	W	—	—	C b	L
Builth	Agl.	Den.	S	P	W	—	—		SS S L
Dolgelly	Mixed	—	S	P	—	—	P	C b	SS S L
Llanfyllin	Agl	Den	S	P	C W B	R	—	C C B C 1	SS S L
Narberth	Mixed	Den.	S	P	—	—	—	C Cows C B C 1	—
Pwllheli	Mixed	—	—	PA	C B O	—	P	C Cows C b C 1	—
Ruthin	Agl.	Den	S	PA	C W B O	R	—	C C 1	SS S L

Under Column Crops.—C. White corn. W. Wheat. B. Barley. O. Oats. R. Turnips and mangolds. P. Pasture.
" Cattle.—C Cattle of all ages. C B Cattle two years old and above. C 1 One year and above.
" Sheep.—S S Sheep of all ages. S Sheep one year and above. L Lambs.
Agl. Agricultural. Ind. Industrial. Population [illegible] 21 per 100 acres, county of [illegible] taken for comparison.

III.—SCOTLAND.

56. The inquiry in Scotland has been carried out on rather different lines to those laid down for England, Wales, and Ireland. Finding, after inquiry, that there existed in that country no definite area of local government analogous to the Poor-law Union of the other countries, I proposed the grouping of counties, or portions of neighbouring counties of somewhat similar agriculture, to form districts of inquiry.

Upon the appointment of the late Mr. Gillespie and Mr. Andrew Mitchell as Assistant Commissioners, I discussed the whole subject with them, and they prepared and submitted a scheme which was accepted by Committee B. of the Commissioners, and this, with a slight addition to it, has been carried out by the late Mr. Gillespie, Mr. H. Rutherford, Mr. Hunter Pringle, and Mr. Wilkinson.

57. The scheme accepted divided the country first of all into two broad divisions, the pastoral or sheep country, and the agricultural districts. It was thought that the conditions of labour in the pastoral districts might be ascertained by the survey of two districts, one in the Highlands and the other south of the Highland line. The agricultural part of Scotland was divided into eleven districts or groups. The proposed arrangement as regards the agricultural districts has been observed. Mr. Gillespie, who worked out the plan, had not fixed upon the locality of the Highland pastoral district. Had he lived to assist in the work it is probable that it would not have been necessary to add another Highland district to the list, but when the whole scheme as prepared had been carried out it appeared that the extensive counties of Inverness and Ross had received little attention, and Mr. Pringle very kindly undertook, though his engagement under the Commission had terminated, to make a rapid survey of the district, which includes North Inverness and South Ross, and it is the subject of his Report B. IV.

58. The districts of inquiry and the counties, or portions of counties, included in them, may be stated in geographical order from north to south in a zig-zag line, an order which coincides pretty closely with that adopted for the Census Returns.

Districts of Inquiry:—

1. Orkney, Caithness, East Sutherland, and Easter Ross.
2. Inverness (North) and Ross (South).
3. Nairn, Elgin, Banff.
4. Aberdeen and Kincardine.
5. Forfar and East Perth.
6. Perth West (Breadalbane).
7. Fife, Kinross, Clackmannan.

8. Stirling and Dumbarton.
9. Argyll (South), Bute, Renfrew, Ayr.
10. Lanark and Linlithgow.
11. Edinburgh and Haddington.
12. Berwick and Roxburgh.
13. Peebles and Selkirk.
14. Dumfries, Kircudbright, and Wigtown.

Of these 14 districts Nos. 6 and 13 are pastoral. No. 2 includes an arable and pastoral district; the other 11 districts are largely arable.

As the inquiry in this country covered the whole ground where any considerable amount of agricultural labour is employed, it is not necessary at this stage of my Report to discriminate between the several districts as in the case of England and Wales, where it was desirable to prove that the districts were representative and typical.

I shall take an opportunity hereafter of noticing the characteristics of the agriculture in different parts of Scotland and their bearing upon the employment of labour.

IV.—IRELAND.

59. The Poor Law Union is in Ireland, as in England and Wales, an important unit of local government, and a convenient area for an inquiry such as the present one, which is much facilitated by the minutely detailed statistics collected and published by the Registrar General for Ireland. The Census Returns for that country contain statistics as to the different classes and sub-classes of occupations of persons of 20 years and upwards in each union, a similar return in the case of England having been discontinued since 1871. They also give the number of agricultural holdings in each union classified in respect of value and area, the population resident on different classes of holdings and the house accommodation thereon.

The Agricultural Returns which are issued annually are not only more full of information than those which are published in England, they are also given in detail for each Union.

60. I have already stated that through the kind offices of Mr. H. Robinson, one of the Commissioners of the Local Government Board (Ireland), I was put in possession of a series of short minutes by the Inspectors of the Board as to the general characteristics of the several unions in their respective districts. In these minutes the unions were classed in respect of population as (1) Agricultural, (2) Mixed, other industries being of sufficient importance to afford to the labouring population employment to an appreciable extent; (3) Migratory districts, where the scarcity of employment compels a number of people to go elsewhere in search of work.

I desire to acknowledge gratefully the information thus communicated by the officials of the Local Government Board.

On the occasion of my visit to Dublin, I conferred with my colleagues, Mr. O'Brien and Mr. McCrea, and with their assistance I prepared a list of unions to be chosen as districts of inquiry in Ireland, and the selection having been approved by the Committee, they have been surveyed.

These districts, which are 20 in number, extend into every county, and owing to the circumstance that many of the unions overlap the county boundaries, no fewer than nine counties are represented by more than one district.

61. The map of Ireland prefixed to this Report* shows the locality and the distribution of the districts, and gives the name of the Assistant Commissioner reporting on each district.

In the following Table the area and population of each district and the province in which it is situate are shown.

TABLE showing the AREA and POPULATION of each DISTRICT of INQUIRY classed under the PROVINCE or PROVINCES in which it is situated, with the Industrial characteristics of each District as described by Local Government Board Inspectors.

A.—Agricultural. I.—Mixed Industries. M.—Migratory.

No.	District of Inquiry.	Industrial Characteristics.	Connaught. Area Acres.	Connaught. Population 1891.	Leinster. Area Acres.	Leinster. Population 1891.	Munster. Area Acres.	Munster. Population 1891.	Ulster. Area Acres.	Ulster. Population 1891.
1	Ardee	A	—	—	66,219	14,777	—	—	—	—
2	Bailieborough	A	—	—	—	—	—	—	66,911	16,731
3	Ballymahon	A	—	—	109,246	14,600	—	—	—	—
4	Ballymena	I	—	—	—	—	—	—	102,148	36,897
5	Ballyshannon	A	33,416	5,879	—	—	—	—	63,894	17,[illegible]
6	Balrothery	A	—	—	74,800	17,119	—	—	—	—
7	Carlow	A	—	—	143,130	28,887	—	—	—	—
8	Cashel	A	—	—	—	—	180,137	30,[illegible]	—	—
9	Castleblayney	A	—	—	—	—	—	—	94,301	30,391
10	Castlerea	A	163,446	37,476	—	—	—	—	—	—
11	Clones	A	—	—	—	—	—	—	73,900	17,656
12	Cookstown	I	—	—	—	—	—	—	96,730	27,164
13	Dublin	A	—	—	74,880	9,365	—	—	—	—
14	Downpatrick	I	—	—	—	—	—	—	147,641	43,[illegible]
15	Dromore	I	97,053	16,919	—	—	—	—	—	—
16	Ennistymon	I	—	—	—	—	99,361	30,[illegible]	—	—
17	[illegible]	A	—	—	—	—	165,695	28,178	—	—
18	[illegible]	A	—	—	—	—	195,163	14,319	—	—
19	[illegible]	A	—	—	—	—	145,169	24,169	—	—
20	Letterkenny	I	—	—	—	—	—	—	209,267	18,910
21	Limavady	I	—	—	—	—	—	—	146,711	23,700
22	Listowel	A	—	—	—	—	91,[illegible]	18,181	—	—
23	Loughrea	A	196,[illegible]	23,244	—	—	—	—	—	—
24	Mountmellick	I	—	—	200,627	31,431	—	—	—	—
25	Naas	A	—	—	216,188	24,879	—	—	—	—
26	[illegible]	A	—	—	65,994	10,[illegible]	47,800	9,[illegible]	—	—
27	Skibbereen	A	—	—	—	—	111,836	20,950	—	—
28	Thomastown	I	—	—	107,207	11,876	—	—	—	—
29	Westport	M	345,791	37,391	—	—	—	—	—	—
30	Wexford	I	—	—	188,[illegible]	35,182	—	—	—	—
	TOTAL		887,[illegible]	114,696	1,267,735	222,760	1,034,617	169,[illegible]	993,[illegible]	268,079

The following Table is a summary of the preceding one, with the addition of the number of agriculturists of 20 years and upwards in the districts within each province, and also the number of districts classed by the Local Government Board Inspectors as —1. Agricultural; 2. Mixed; 3. Migratory.

—	No. of Districts. 1. Agricultural.	2. Mixed.	3. Migratory.	Area.	Population, 1891.	Agriculturists 20 Years of age and above.
Connaught	5	1	1	887,[illegible]	114,696	[illegible]
Leinster	7	1	—	1,267,735	222,760	41,791
Munster	7	[illegible]	—	1,034,617	169,[illegible]	[illegible]
Ulster	4	5	—	993,[illegible]	268,079	60,314
Ireland	[illegible]	10	1	4,[illegible]	754,[illegible]	[illegible]

The area, population, and number of agriculturists in the districts as compared with the provinces in which they lie, are as follows:—

Province.	Percentage of Total included in Districts of Inquiry. Area.	Population.	Agriculturists.
Connaught	19·15	16·89	15·85
Leinster	20·07	19·14	20·66
Munster	17·78	14·13	15·45
Ulster	23·06	15·81	14·97
Ireland	19·67	16·04	15·16

It will be seen that one-fifth of the area of the whole country, and nearly one-sixth of the population and of the agriculturists, are included in the districts of inquiry, and that the different provinces are not very unequally represented.

62. The distribution of the districts in the different counties is shown in the Appendix, where I have also shown the characteristics of each district in respect of population and agriculture. I shall here briefly notice only the subjects of comparison, pointing out the districts which exhibit the most striking differences.

As I have already stated, the Census Returns give the occupations of persons of 20 years and above in each district. The per-centage of the total number of persons, and also of the total number of males classed as agriculturists in each district is shown in the Appendix*.

63. The extreme range in respect of the proportionate part of the population engaged in agriculture is from 45·7 per cent. in Castlerea, and 45·1 in Dromore, both of which are in Connaught, to 24·9 in Naas, and 25·9 per cent. in Balrothery (both of which are in Leinster). If males only are considered, the range is from Dromore with 81·4 per cent, to Naas with 31·8 per cent. The average proportions for the whole of Ireland are 29·1 per cent. of all persons, and 53·0 per cent. of males.

64. In every district of inquiry the population decreased between 1881 and 1891, and the same may be said with regard to the period from 1871 to 1881, excepting the three districts of Westport, Kenmare, and Skibbereen.

In four districts the decrease amounted to 15 per cent. in 10 years, and in each of these the decrease was continuous, and exceeded 24 per cent in 20 years.

They were as follows:—

District.	Decrease, 1881 to 1891.	Decrease, 1871 to 1881.	Decrease, 1871 to 1891.
Castleblayney (Ulster)	17·55	7·65	25·20
Bailieborough (Ulster)	15·72	9·91	24·07
Cashel (Munster)	15·22	10·65	27·21
Ardee (Leinster)	15·71	11·50	24·73

In four districts the decrease between 1881 and 1891 was less than 10 per cent. They were as follows:—

District.	Decrease, 1881 to 1891.	Increase or Decrease, 1871 to 1881.	Decrease, 1871 to 1891.
Wexford (Leinster)	9·10	+1·06	13·10
Mountmellick (Leinster)	8·69	−6·03	14·21
Westport	4·77	+0·35	5·14
Naas (Leinster)	7·70	−9·60	16·84

It does not seem that in either period the decrease was very distinctly connected with the preponderance of the agricultural population. If Castleblayney and Bailieborough rank high in respect of agriculturists, this is not the case with either Cashel or Ardee; and again Westport, which has a population almost entirely agricultural, shows the least decrease during the 20 years of any district of inquiry.*

It may be, and probably is, the case that migration from Westport takes the place of emigration.

65. The Census Returns contain a most interesting table, showing the number of persons resident on agricultural holdings of different classes, the classification being made in respect of value, for which purpose rateable value is taken.

Table 60 of these Returns gives the per-centage of the population on holdings above and below 15*l.* annual value, and of those not resident on such holdings. From Table 50 I have compiled similar statistics as to each of the districts of inquiry, and the result is given in the Appendix.*

Taking the whole of Ireland, the proportions are as follows:—

Persons resident on agricultural holdings—	
Not exceeding 15*l.* in value	34·7
Exceeding 15*l.* in value	28·4
	63·1
Persons not resident on agricultural holdings	36·9
	100·0

* Vol. V., Part II., Section III., F.

The following COUNTIES represent the MAXIMUM and MINIMUM, (excluding COUNTY DUBLIN and ANTRIM,) in each of the three classes named above:—

	Maximum.		Minimum.	
		per cent.		per cent.
Persons resident on Agricultural Holdings:—				
Not exceeding 15l. annual value	Leitrim	75·2	Waterford	15·7
Exceeding 15l.	Meath	48·3	Leitrim	10·9
Not resident on Agricultural Holdings	Louth	60·4	Mayo / Roscommon	9·3 / 9·3

Among the districts of inquiry there are four which have upwards of two-thirds of their population resident on agricultural holdings not exceeding 15l. annual value, and six other districts have more than one-half of the people on holdings of the class. In nine districts less than 25 per cent. of the whole number are living on these small holdings, as will appear from the following Table:—

POPULATION RESIDENT on HOLDINGS not exceeding 15l. annual value.

Districts having two-thirds and above.		Districts having one-half and not exceeding two-thirds.		Districts having 25 per cent. and not exceeding 50 per cent.		Districts having under 25 per cent.	
Castlerea	81·19	Ballyshannon	63·77	Letterkenny	41·26	Wexford	23·47
Westport	70·07	[illegible]	59·[illegible]	[illegible]	43·14	Carlow	23·17
Kenmare	70·62	Castleblayney	58·[illegible]	Ballymahon	40·71	Naas	22·80
Dromore	67·76	Lisnaskea	55·57	Clones	44·6	Thomastown	21·95
		Cookstown	51·63	Cavan	40·31	Ardee	21·60
		[illegible]	50·53	Mountmellick	40·03	Cashel	20·85
				Kanturk	42·39	Downpatrick	19·43
				[illegible]	35·77	Kilmallock	15·15
				Limavady	32·53	Balrothery	11·64
				Lismore	29·10		
				[illegible]	29·44		

Of the last two named in the above Table, Balrothery has the least number of people resident on agricultural holdings of all descriptions, viz., 46·88 per cent., but Kilmallock has no less than 71·60 of population resident on agricultural holdings, a large per-centage being therefore resident on holdings of higher value.

Dromore with 93·19 per cent., and Castlerea with 93·10 per cent. have the largest proportion of the population on agricultural holdings.

64. The number of holdings classified according to value and area with the per-centages have been calculated for each district, and will be found in the Appendix.*

Taking the annual value of 15l. again as a dividing line, we find eight districts which are conspicuous for the high per-centage of holdings not exceeding that limit either in respect of number, the ratio to the total value of all holdings, or the ratio to the total area.

These districts are as follows:—

AGRICULTURAL HOLDINGS not exceeding 15l. in value.

(1) Percentage of Total Number			(2) Per-centage of Total Rateable Value			(3) Per-centage of Total Area		
1	Westport	93·14	1	Kenmare	60·19	1	Kenmare	60·45
2	Castlerea	91·40	2	Westport	54·05	2	[illegible]	56·77
3	Kenmare	87·09	3	Castleblayney	47·67	3	Castlerea	57·23
4	Ballyshannon	81·67	4	Ballyshannon	45·63	4	Ballyshannon	55·[illegible]
5	[illegible]	81·63	5	[illegible]	44·19	5	Cookstown	55·11
6	Castleblayney	73·44	6	[illegible]	41·25	6	Castleblayney	51·71
7	Cookstown	73·40	7	Castlerea	40·77	7	Westport	51·34
	Average for Ireland	69·2		Average for Ireland	20·35		Average for Ireland	27·0

Examining these statistics a little more in detail, as to the proportionate part of the whole rateable value which is in these small holdings, it appears that in the seven districts named in column 2 in the above list, the per-centage of rateable value in the separate classes of value not exceeding 15l., for which particulars are given, is as follows:—

AGRICULTURAL HOLDINGS.—Per-centage of Total Value

In Holdings

At the other end of the scale the seven districts where a large number of the holdings exceed 100l. rateable value are these:—

AGRICULTURAL HOLDINGS exceeding 100l. Rateable Value.

(1.) Per-centage of Total Number.		(2.) Per-centage of Total Value.		(3.) Per-centage of Total Area.	
1. Balrothery	16·30	1. Balrothery	61·01	1. Balrothery	46·74
2. Ardee	10·24	2. Ardee	60·55	2. Ardee	35·99
3. Kilmallock	10·37	3. Naas	57·60	3. Delvin	34·97
4. Naas	9·12	4. Delvin	57·35	4. Naas	40·71
5. Cashel	7·01	5. Carlow	49·86	5. Cashel	30·88
6. Carlow	8·74	6. Cashel	45·10	6. Carlow	29·64
7. Delvin	6·36	7. Lismore	45·33	7. Roscrea	29·66
Average—Ireland	3·10	Average—Ireland	34·35	Average—Ireland	21·1

These seven districts may be regarded as those of the larger occupations. The Returns do not discriminate between holdings exceeding 200l. value. The per-centages of holdings over that value in the seven districts included in column 2 of the above table are as follows:—

AGRICULTURAL HOLDINGS above 200l. Rateable Value.

—	Per-centage of Total Number.	Per-centage of Total Value.	Per-centage of Total Area.
Balrothery	7·36	37·79	34·98
Ardee	7·24	25·18	25·86
Naas	1·70	22·25	16·58
Delvin	1·77	31·92	30·66
Carlow	1·17	18·40	17·79
Cashel	1·98	11·63	14·85
Lismore	0·75	15·74	20·51
Average—Ireland	0·45	11·15	7·86

The average value of the holdings in the districts of inquiry ranges from 49·48l. in Balrothery, and 47·02l. in Ardee, both of which are on the extreme east of the country to 6·56l. in Westport and 8·72l. in Kenmare, both of which are on the western coast. Out of 15 districts* which are above the average value of the whole country, which is 20l. 4s. 6d., eight are wholly in Leinster, three in Munster, two in Ulster, and one partly in Leinster and partly in Munster; not one of them is in Connaught.†

67. Viewing the districts next in regard to the disposition and cultivation of the land, the official agricultural statistics give the most ample information, and a series of tables, in some cases extracted and in others compiled from those Returns, are given in Appendix.† It should be stated that the figures for 1891 have been taken because the Census Returns were for that year, and a comparison of the statistics where the two sets of Returns are contemporaneous is thus made more easy.

68. The proportionate part of the whole area which is under crops of all kinds, grass or fallow, that is, the cultivated area, excluding woods and plantations, turf bog, marsh, barren mountain land, water, roads, fences, &c., varies from 93·5 per cent. in Balrothery and 92·2 per cent. in Ardee, to 45·6 per cent. in Westport, and 50·1 per cent. in Kenmare, the average percentage for Ireland being 74·5.

69. In the Irish Agricultural Returns, the permanent grass which is mown for hay is reckoned with crops of various kinds, and grass includes only what is actually depastured. The area under crops and hay includes, therefore, the arable land, and so much of the grass as gives considerable employment. The per-centage of the whole area thus classed varies from 47·6 per cent. in Downpatrick to 6·1 per cent. in Westport, the average for Ireland being 23·8 per cent. Out of 16 districts‡ having more than the average extent, 7 are in Ulster, and 7 in Leinster, and 1 in Munster.*

70. The area and proportionate extent of different classes of crops in districts are given in the Appendix,† with particulars as to the more important corn and green crops. The two northernmost districts have the largest proportion of their crops in corn, Limavady having 50·36 per cent., and Letterkenny 49·61 per cent., but it must be noted that these districts have a comparatively small area under crops. In proportion to total area or cultivated area, Downpatrick with 21·94 per cent. of the former, and 24·70 per cent. of the latter, stands highest in respect of corn crops, and is really the only one in the list where the growth of wheat is at all considerable.‡

71. The very large extent of the potato crop in Ireland raises the class of green crops, in which potatoes are included, to great importance, particularly in the western and southern parts of the island, where the area of this crop exceeds that of the corn. In Skibbereen, Westport, and Kenmare potatoes are over 30 per cent. of all crops. In Ennistimon they are more than four times as extensive as corn crops. Green crops.

Mangolds, turnips, and carrots are most grown in Wexford, Mountmellick, Roscrea, Skibbereen, Limavady, Ardee, and Letterkenny. (*See Appendix.**)

72. In the North of Ireland flax is grown to an extent which forms an appreciable per-centage in 13 of the districts of inquiry. Of these nine are in Ulster; and outside of that province the crop is nowhere as much as 1 per cent. of all crops. Flax.

In Ballymena it forms 11·15 per cent.; in Cookstown 7·50 per cent., and in Castleblayney 6·59 per cent. of all crops. (*See Appendix.**)

73. Throughout Ireland the hay crop occupies a large share of the farmer's attention: it is in none of the districts now under consideration much below one-fifth of all the crops grown, and in Kilmallock it reaches to 75·84 per cent. The average extent of the crop in Ireland is 43·74 per cent. of all crops, which is, however, only 13·60 per cent. of the cultivated area. In 11 districts this crop exceeds the total of all other crops and in 8 others it exceeds the corn crops in extent. (*See Appendix.**) Hay.

74. In the Appendix I have inserted tables showing the numbers of different kinds of live stock and the relative number per 100 acres of cultivated area. Live stock.

The districts which are most conspicuous in respect of each kind of stock are shown below, with particulars as to the relative numbers of each kind of stock in them.

Table 49

Horses.	No. per 100 Acres.	Cattle.	No. per 100 Acres.	Sheep.	No. per 100 Acres.	Pigs.	No. per 100 Acres.
1. [illegible]	6·91	1. Kilmallock	[illegible]	1. [illegible]	[illegible]	1. Wexford	[illegible]
2. Wexford	6·71	2. Mitchelstown	[illegible]	2. Ross	[illegible]	2. [illegible]	[illegible]
3. [illegible]	7·11	3. [illegible]	[illegible]	3. Dromore	[illegible]	3. Castleblayney	[illegible]
4. [illegible]	5·11	4. [illegible]	[illegible]	4. Westport	[illegible]	4. [illegible]	[illegible]
5. Castleblayney	[illegible]	5. [illegible]	[illegible]	5. Dublin	[illegible]	5. Skibbereen	[illegible]
6. Ballymena	6·91	6. Cashel	[illegible]	6. [illegible]	[illegible]	6. Ballymena	[illegible]
				7. [illegible]	[illegible]		

75. The Returns relating to agricultural holdings in Ireland which have been already made use of to illustrate the characteristics of the districts of inquiry contain minute details as to the classes of dwellings which are to be found on each class of holdings in every Poor Law Union. Houses on agricultural holdings.

In the Returns houses are divided into four classes in respect of their extent, quality, and construction.

In the lowest class are comprised *houses built of mud or other perishable material, having only one room and window*. In the THIRD CLASS a better description of *houses varying from one to four rooms and windows*. In the SECOND what may be considered as *a good farm house, having from five to nine rooms and windows*; and in the FIRST CLASS *all houses of a better description than the preceding*.

To this classification has been added a further distinction in respect of accommodation. For this purpose also, four classes are distinguished. In the first of these are first class houses occupied by one family, in the second class houses of the second class occupied by one family, and houses of the first class occupied by two or three families, and so on, but the details as to house accommodation are not given for smaller areas than those of counties. I have not thought it necessary to tabulate particulars on this point as regards each district of inquiry. It will be sufficient to select those districts where the proportionate number of houses of the fourth classes is greatest. In this respect three districts in Munster are pre-eminent. Taking the whole of Ireland, the per-centage of fourth class houses upon agricultural holdings is 2·95. The particulars for the three districts alluded to are given in the following table:—

POPULATION, INHABITED HOUSES, and FOURTH CLASS HOUSES on AGRICULTURAL HOLDINGS in two classes in respect of ANNUAL VALUE.

Table 50.

—	Per-centage of Total Population resident on Agricultural Holdings.		Number of Inhabited Houses on such Holdings.		Number of Fourth Class Houses on such Holdings.		Per-centage of Inhabited Houses, on such Holdings, which are of the Fourth Class.	
	Not Exceeding 15*l.*	15*l.* and upwards.	Not Exceeding 15*l.*	15*l.* and upwards.	Not Exceeding 15*l.*	15*l.* and upwards.	Not Exceeding 15*l.*	15*l.* and upwards.

The percentage of fourth class houses on all agricultural holdings is in Kenturk 0·69, in Kilmallock 0.53, in Kenmare 8·11, and for the whole of Ireland 2·94.

In marked contrast with the districts which have been noticed are two of the districts in Ulster, namely, Ballymena, which has 0·51 per cent., and Downpatrick, with 0·66 per cent. of fourth class houses on agricultural holdings. Lismore, the most favourable instance in Munster, has 1·07 of that class. Roscrea, with 1·43 per cent. partly in Munster but mainly in Leinster, is the best example among the districts of inquiry in the province of Leinster.

Families on holdings of different classes.

76. The Census Tables give, as has been already stated, particulars not only as to the percentage of houses in each class, but also as to the number and percentage of the total number of families occupying each class of house accommodation. A diagram illustrates the former, and a map indicates by shading the prevalence of the lowest class of accommodation in the several counties.

In respect of houses Munster has the worst record, with 3·6 per cent., and Ulster the best with 1·1 per cent. in the fourth class. In the case of counties Kerry heads the list with 7·9 per cent., next comes Limerick, with 6·0 per cent., and Meath is third in the list, with 4·8 per cent. of fourth class houses.

On the other hand Antrim has only 4, Down 7, and Londonderry 8 per thousand of that class. In the other Table showing accommodation the same three counties in Ulster have the smallest proportionate (1·1 to 1·4 per cent.) number of families in the lowest class, while Meath, Galway, Limerick, and Kerry have 5·3, 6·0, 7·6, and 10 per cent. respectively.

Districts exhibit wide range of variety.

77. Enough has been said to prove that the districts of inquiry in Ireland exhibit a wide range of variety in respect of population and agriculture.

It is some indication that a fair representation of the conditions generally prevailing has been secured when it can be said that if compared with the average for the whole country the several districts in their agricultural characteristics are not very unequally divided into those above and those below the average, as will be seen from the following Table:

Table H.

—	Districts.	
	Above	Below.
Holdings not exceeding 15*l.* annual value	Average	Average
Proportionate part of total number	13	17
" " value	14	16
" " area	15	17
Holdings not exceeding 30 acres	15	15
Average value of all agricultural holdings	15	15
Agriculture—		
Extent under crops of all kinds	15	15
" corn crops	14	16
" green crops	14	16
" hay	15	15
Live stock—Horses	16	14
Cattle	13	17
Sheep	14	16
Pigs	18	19

Reference to reports of Assistant Commissioners.

78. Having indicated the more special features which distinguish the districts of inquiry in England and Ireland, I must refer to the Reports of my colleagues for detailed information as to the conditions under which the agricultural labourer lives and works. Those Reports deal with each separate district as a whole, and the conclusions which each individual Assistant Commissioner has formed are presented on a systematic plan.

Indexes.

79. The work of consulting those Reports is much facilitated by the full indexes which have been prepared under your directions.

It is not for me to estimate the value of those Reports, but I may be permitted to say that each one of my colleagues has endeavoured to carry out the inquiry committed to him thoroughly, completely, and in the most conscientious and impartial spirit. With regard to the survey as a whole I venture to say that it has never been surpassed as a minute and searching inquiry into all those circumstances which influence and concern the position of the agricultural labourer.

V.—THE AGRICULTURAL LABOURER.

80. Before proceeding with the inquiry as to the condition and circumstances of the agricultural labourer, it will be desirable to indicate broadly who are those included under this comprehensive term, and what are the grades and sub-classes into which the whole class is divided. The term agricultural labourer is used commonly as comprehending all those who are habitually engaged in work for wages upon the lands of others, supporting themselves and those dependent upon them chiefly by their earnings in such employment. [illegible]

A survey of the condition of the agricultural labourer, such as that which has been undertaken by the Royal Commission on Labour, would, however, be very incomplete if a rigid adherence to this definition were observed. No doubt a large proportion of those who work fulfil the conditions described, but a considerable amount of the work of the farm is done in many parts of Great Britain and Ireland by casual labourers, and by those who have other occupations and resources, not to speak of those who work on their own farms, or of the labour of the different members of farmer's families.

In the case of Ireland, as I have pointed out elsewhere,* the term agricultural labourer as descriptive of those entitled to benefit by the Labourers Acts, has been by successive enactments extended, so that whereas it at first included only—

> "a person who habitually works for hire upon the land of some other person, and
> "whose principal means of living is such hire," and includes a herdsman,

it now comprehends—

> "a man or woman who does agricultural work for hire at any season of the year
> "on the land of some other person or persons, and shall include handloom
> "weavers and fishermen doing agricultural work as aforesaid, and shall also
> "include herdsmen."

This extension of the term was doubtless the consequence of the peculiar conditions of the country and the fusion of farmers, labourers, and other classes which is so marked a feature in rural Ireland. No similar state of things prevails in any part of Great Britain, but even here it would be impossible to draw a distinct dividing line between the agricultural labourer, as generally understood, and the small occupier of land, the general labourer, the navvy, the harvesters, haymakers, hop-pickers, and others who share with him the labour of the fields. The main interest of the inquiry must, however, centre upon the class who live by wages earned in agriculture. [illegible]

81. It is desirable to ascertain what are the numbers and the relative strength, compared with that of other industrial classes, and also with the whole order of agriculturists, of those who are included in the class of agricultural labourers, and to determine whether that class has decreased, and, if so, to what extent. It is not possible to do more than form an approximate estimate of the numbers of the class, though a Census has so recently been taken, and the comparison of the results of one Census with those of another is rendered difficult by the changes which have from time to time been made in the classification for Census Returns of persons engaged in agriculture.

82. I have prepared for the Commission some notes on the Census Returns for 1871, 1881, and 1891, and in them I have endeavoured to compare the results of these Returns by adjustments and omissions, and I shall not enter into details on this point now.† (*See* Memorandum on Census Returns.) Census Returns, 1871, 1881, 1891

I need only mention first that the nondescript or indefinite class of general labourers includes a good number of those who are engaged in agricultural work, and that there is reason to believe that a larger number of those who work on farms are now included in that designation than in former years; secondly that the Returns for 1871 include superannuated members of the class who are omitted from subsequent returns; and thirdly that the latest Census Returns exclude all those who are less than 10 years of age, while those of 1881 did not separate those who were 5 and less than 15 years of age. This last named difference in the two Returns cannot practically affect the statistics, since the employment of children of less than 10 years is prohibited by law, but the numbers of wage earners in agriculture not exceeding 10 years of age was in 1871, 3,311.

The numbers of those whom I have classed as wage earners in agriculture, that is, farm bailiffs, shepherds, agricultural labourers, and farm servants, were in 1891 as follows:—

—	Males.	Females.	Total Numbers, Census 1891.	Percentage.	
				Males.	Females.
England and Wales	774,763	24,150	798,913	96·98	3·02
Scotland	147,713	33,057	180,770	81·74	18·26
Ireland	254,043	18,041	280,096	92·1	7·9
Great Britain and Ireland	1,131,319	69,349	1,199,768	93·3	6·7

These numbers may be compared with those for 1871 and 1881, though for the reasons already stated the results of such comparison must be regarded as approximate only.

WAGE EARNERS IN AGRICULTURE.

—	1871.		1881.		1891.	
	Numbers.	Percentage of Males.	Numbers.	Percentage of Males.	Numbers.	Percentage of Males.
England and Wales	996,618	94·17	890,174	96·47	798,912	96·98
Scotland	165,186	71·08	148,761	67·19	180,770	81·74
Ireland	309,344	87·70	336,187	89·3	280,096	92·1
Total	1,471,087	—	1,375,091	—	1,189,768	—

Of the whole number at the present time two-thirds are in England and Wales, one-tenth in Scotland, and one-fourth in Ireland."

The rate of decrease which is observable in each country is shown by the following table:—

—	Decrease Per Cent.		
	10 Years, 1871–1881.	10 Years, 1881–1891.	20 Years, 1871–1891.
England and Wales	10·8	10·65	19·83
Scotland	9·3	19·1	25·8
Ireland	34·00	16·7	45·0

83. General labourers, of whom it has already been said that a considerable number are probably employed in agriculture, numbered in 1891, 780,126, or about 2 per cent. of the population, thus distributed:—

England and Wales	596,075
Scotland	66,071
Ireland	118,080

Another class of workers is not represented in the numbers given above, and it is that of male relatives residing with farmers.

In Ireland certainly, and probably in many parts of Great Britain, farm work for wages is done by young men of this class who would not describe themselves as agricultural labourers.†

84. It may be worth while to compare the number of wage earners with certain estimates of the theoretical total cost of labour which have been made by statisticians at various periods. I extract the following statement from a most valuable paper read

by Major Craigie (now Director of the Statistical Department of the Board of Agriculture) before the Farmers' Club, December 1888 :—

" The several estimates of the last 20 years have been these—the totals being for " the United Kingdom as a whole :—

		£	
" Leone Levi - - -	1866	64,800,000	In " Wages and Earnings."
" Dudley Baxter - -	1867	53,500,000	" " National Income"
" Craigie - -	1878	58,000,000	" " R. A. S. E. Journal"
" Leone Levi - - -	1884	64,500,000	" 3rd edition " Wages and Earnings."
" Caird - - -	1886	28,000,000	" Evidence Royal Commission on Trade Depression.
" Morton - - -	1886	43,500,000	" Labour on Farm (adjusted figures).

Major Craigie in his paper stated that he would roughly estimate the total in 1888 at 50,000,000*l*.

It is clear that all these estimates, except perhaps that of Sir James Caird, must include a large amount of labour which is not done by those who are enumerated in the Census under the occupations which I have classed as wage earners. They are, in fact, based upon the average cost per acre of manual labour, whether that labour is done by hired persons or by the farmer and his family.

The moderate estimate of 50,000,000*l*. would give an average earning of 16*s*. a week to every man, woman, and child included in the number of wage earners in agriculture in the three countries.

85. The proportion which the wage earners in agriculture bore to the total population at the periods of the last three Census Returns was as follows :—

—	England and Wales.	Scotland.	Ireland.	Great Britain and Ireland.
1871 - - -	4·34	4·20	9·45	5·31
1881 - - -	3·43	4·00	6·50	3·94
1891 - - -	2·75	3·00	5·85	3·18

86. It will be of interest to inquire what proportion these wage earners bear to the whole body of agriculturists, of which they form so important a section. The numbers and proportion of the agriculturists at different periods are fully detailed in my Memorandum on the Census Returns. It will suffice to say here that the agriculturists in fields and pastures were in proportion to the total population as follows :—

AGRICULTURISTS.

—	England and Wales.	Scotland.	Ireland.	Great Britain and Ireland.
Ratio of agriculturists in fields and pastures to total population	Per cent. 3·78	Per cent. 4·80	Per cent. 19·18	Per cent. 5·64

The distribution of the class is approximately one-half in England and Wales, two-fifths in Ireland, and one-twelfth in Scotland.*

87. The proportion which the wage earners bear to the agriculturists in the different parts of the Kingdom varies from about 30 per cent. in Ireland to 73 per cent. in England and Wales.

WAGE EARNERS IN RATIO TO AGRICULTURISTS.

Wage Earners.	England and Wales.	Scotland.	Ireland.	Great Britain and Ireland.
Percentage of agriculturists -	73·14	62·46	30·63	61·69

* England and Wales - - - 49·8 per cent.
Scotland - - - 8·7 "
Ireland - - - 41·5 "
100·0

These figures show most distinctly that it is in England more than in other parts of the Kingdom that the agricultural labourers are most prominent as members of the agricultural class, while in Ireland, as might be expected, they form only a small section of that class.

The numbers and per-centages given above may be misunderstood by many, inasmuch as they fail to record the numbers of those who are dependent upon the labourers for their support.

88. At first sight it might seem that a mere 3 to 5 per cent. of the population were a small and insignificant section, scarcely entitled by its numbers to the attention which it undoubtedly has received of late. A truer estimate of the relative strength of the class may be arrived at by comparing the number of males of 20 years and upwards who are classed as agriculturists and as wage earners in agriculture with the total number of the same age.

RATIO OF AGRICULTURISTS AND WAGE EARNERS TO TOTAL.

—	England and Wales.	Scotland.	Ireland.	Great Britain and Ireland.
Total number of males 20 years and upwards	7,414,234	1,006,018	1,281,121	9,706,174
Agriculturists—Numbers	810,606	127,918	691,175	1,629,694
Percentage of total	10·84	12·71	53·9	16·48
Numbers of Wage earners in agriculture	563,683	68,201	191,328	823,312
Percentage of total	7·60	6·78	15·1	8·43

It appears from this table that in Great Britain from 6¾ to 7½ per cent. of the adult males are workers in agriculture, while in Ireland the proportion is twice as great. An estimate of the number of these males who would be married and of the average number of their children which I have made upon the basis of statistics applicable to all classes brings the number of workers with the families dependent upon them to something like the same proportion of the whole population. There is no class of occupation and no single industry which includes so many persons as the one under consideration. The miners of all descriptions in England and Wales number 424,000 adult males.

89. The proportionate number of male wage earners at different periods of age in England and Wales has been calculated, and is now stated for three periods, which may be said to correspond approximately with the growth, maturity, and decline of manhood. By the time that he has reached 20 years the agricultural labourer has begun to receive full man's wages and he usually marries before he reaches the age of 21. When he has reached 55 years, although he may still be able to do in many ways as much as younger men, he cannot keep pace with them at some descriptions of work where the biggest wages are earned.

In 1891 the agricultural labourers in England and Wales were divided at the periods of age thus chosen in the following proportions:—

Under 20 years	27·25	per cent.
20 and under 55 years	54·29	"
55 and upwards	18·46	"

These proportions are a very close approximation to those of 3, 6, and 2.

I am unable to carry out the same comparison in the case of Scotland, or in that of Ireland, no break being made in the returns between the ages of 45 and 65.

In the following Table an opportunity of comparing the relative number of male wage earners of different ages in 1871, 1881, and 1891. It must be pointed out, however, that the Census Returns for 1871 include superannuated agricultural labourers in that class, while those of 1881 and 1891 exclude them. The number of these could not be sufficient to materially affect the result. It will be seen that the details with respect to ages are not so full in the case of the 1881 census as in those of 1871 and 1891; the continual changes in the form of the Census Returns interpose great difficulties in the way of any comparison between different periods of time, and necessitate the frequent reiteration of the caution that the figures submitted are approximate only.

MALE WAGE EARNERS AT DIFFERENT PERIODS OF AGE. [ENGLAND AND WALES.]

Table [illegible]

Groups of Ages	1871 Percentage of Total at each Period		1881 Percentage of Total at each Period of Age		1891 Percentage of Total at each Period of Age	
Under 15 years	10·4		8·0		8·4	
15 years and under 20 years	15·8		18·1		18·5	
Total under 20 years		26·2		26·1		27·1
20 years and under 25 years	11·0	11·0	11·8	11·8	11·9	11·9
25 " " 35 "	16·1				17·0	
35 " " 45 "	14·4				13·2	
Total 25 " " 45 "		30·5	29·8	29·3		30·2
45 " " 55 "	13·0				12·8	
55 " " 65 "	10·2				10·3	
Total 45 " " 65 "		23·2	23·8	23·8		22·4
65 and upwards	9·1	9·1	8·7	8·7	8·3	8·2
		100·0		100·0		100·0

As would naturally be expected, the Table shows a considerable falling off in the relative numbers of boys of less than 15 years of age, and a corresponding increase in the strength of those between 15 and 20, but what is most remarkable in these figures is that adult males between 20 and 25 were relatively more numerous among wage earners in 1881 than they were in 1871, and again in 1891 slightly more numerous in proportion to the total number of wage earners than they had been in 1881. In the next stage, from 25 to 35 years, there were 170 per thousand in 1891 to 161 in 1871. After the age of 45 the proportionate strength in each group declines from 1871 to 1891. The Census Returns in this respect give no support to the opinion so generally entertained that it is the young men and men in the prime of life who desert agriculture for other callings, and that the farmer has more and more to depend upon the old and incapable.

The Table to which reference has just been made gives only the relative proportions of male wage earners of different ages. In the following Table the actual numbers enumerated at the three decennial periods, and the rate of decrease in each group, are shown.

MALE WAGE EARNERS AT DIFFERENT PERIODS OF AGE.

Table [illegible]

Ages.	Numbers 1871.	Numbers 1881.	Numbers 1891.	Increase or Decrease* 1871 to 1881.	Increase or Decrease* 1881 to 1891.	Increase or Decrease* 1871 to 1891.
Under 15 years	98,029	67,299	64,620	30·6	8·5	33·0
15 years and under 20 years	148,123	156,464	146,479	5·5	7·1	2·0
Total under 20 years	246,152	224,563	211,099	8·87	6·0	14·3
20 years and under 25 years	102,998	100,041	92,104	2·81	7·9	10·5
25 " " 35 "	151,091	—	132,031	—	—	12·6
35 " " 45 "	135,038	—	102,051	—	—	24·4
Total 25 " " 45 "	286,149	249,025	234,112	13·0	6·0	18·2
45 " " 55 "	122,563	—	94,357	—	·	23·0
55 " " 65 "	95,184	—	79,710	...	—	16·3
Total 45 " " 65 "	217,738	202,014	174,087	7·0	14·1	20·0
65 and upwards	83,289	73,595	63,230	13·7	13·9	25·7
Total	938,530	849,029	771,762	9·45	9·8	17·13

This Table exhibits in another form the same facts as the previous Table. The effect of the Education Act of 1870 is seen in the group of those under 15 years. The group of those 65 years and upwards may be slightly affected by the exclusion of superannuated labourers in the two later returns. Leaving these two groups, the first and last, out of account, we see that in 20 years the decrease has been at a faster ratio in those above the age of 35 than in those below that age, and at its maximum between 35 and 45 years, though little less in the next decade of age.

It must be confessed that these are very unexpected results, and that they are entirely at variance with the prevailing opinion in the rural districts.

The proportionate number of male wage earners in agriculture who are recorded as being 65 years of age and upwards are in the three countries as follows:—

England and Wales - -	6·17 per cent.
Scotland - - -	4·28 "
Ireland - - - -	7·12 "

90. The ratio which agriculturists and wage earners bear to the cultivated area may be briefly noticed. In England and Scotland the agriculturists are almost exactly the same in number for every 100 acres, but the wage earners are relatively more numerous in the former country. In Ireland the agriculturists are much more numerous, while the wage earners are proportionately fewer. The following are relative proportions of these classes in the three countries:—

Table 89.

	Number per 100 Acres Cultivated Area.	
	Agriculturists.	Wage Earners in Agriculture.
England and Wales - - -	3·92	2·84
Scotland - - - - - -	3·93	2·45
Ireland - - - - -	6·04	1·85

It is not possible to carry this comparison of agriculturists and wage earners further in the case of England and Wales, inasmuch as the Returns as to occupations of the people are given for registration counties, while the Agricultural Returns are given for counties proper, and there is only one single instance where the two areas agree, and that is the county of Cumberland, which is one of the least representative counties in respect of its agriculture.

91. Taking the agricultural divisions or groups of counties adopted by the Board of Agriculture for statistical purposes an approximate comparison of the numbers of these classes may be arrived at.

Table 90.

Agricultural Divisions.	Agriculturists, 1891.	Wage Earners in Agriculture, 1891.
I.—E. and N.E. Counties - - -	4·58	3·79
II.—S.E. and E.C. " - - -	4·65	3·78
III.—S.W. and W.M. " - - -	3·57	2·52
IV.—N. and N.W. " - - -	3·10	2·08
England - - - -	3·09	3·09
Wales - - - - - -	3·18	1·54
England and Wales - -	3·93	2·83

These agricultural divisions are ranged in respect of the corn area, the first of them having the largest extent of those crops, and it will be seen that the wage earners diminish in number with the decrease of corn. The second division is practically identical in its relative number of wage earners with the first, and this may be accounted for by the fact that the market gardens of Middlesex and other home counties, the hop and fruit gardens of Kent, Surrey, and Sussex, and the woods and underwoods of Sussex and Hampshire are included in it.

92. It is noticeable that the number of females among the wage earners has decreased continuously, and to a large extent in England and Wales. In Scotland there was a large decrease from 1871 to 1881, followed by a considerable increase in the following decade.

The proportion which they bore to the whole number in different parts at those periods is shown below:—

WAGE EARNERS IN AGRICULTURE—FEMALES IN RATIO TO TOTAL NUMBER.

—	England and Wales.	Scotland.	Ireland.
1871 - - -	6·51	24·92	12·30
1881 - - -	4·53	18·81	10·7
1891 - - -	3·02	16·28	7·9

93. It would undoubtedly be very desirable that some classification of the labourers, in respect of their particular employment, should be made, but it cannot be said that the Census Returns throw very much light on this subject, except by distinguishing shepherds from other labourers. In 1871 the number of farm servants (indoor) was given separately from those of the outdoor labourers. In 1881 the division was abandoned. In 1891 an attempt was made to distinguish men in charge of horses from other labourers, but it is extremely doubtful whether those who have to fill up the Census papers discriminate sufficiently to make the return of much value.

And in truth the work of the farm is so varied, the different classes are so bloodied, that although there are many men whose work is definite and can be described with accuracy, there are a great many more who have no definite sphere of work.

In the north of England and in Scotland this is not the case, but over a large portion of England it is so.

It may, however, be convenient to notice some of the more prominent classes of labourers, premising that any classification is subject to much modification, and that the boundary between the different classes is not always definitely marked out. On the larger farms work is more organised than it is on smaller farms, and the labourers on them have, each of them, their own special department, at least at certain periods of the year; while on the smaller farms a man has to put his hand to every kind of work.

94. I shall deal first with the farm bailiffs or foremen. I do not include in this class men of a superior station to the labourers, who have been trained to their work or brought up as farmers, such men as are found on the home farms of large estates, but I speak of the foremen on the farms of ordinary tenant farmers.

These men mostly spring from the ranks of ordinary labourers, having shown some aptitude for the management and superintendence of other men.

On large farms where the farmer is not resident the foreman directs the work of the labourers, subject to a varying amount of control by the master, and even where the farmer is resident it is not unusual, if the farm is a large one, for the foreman to receive his orders from the master and to see them carried out by the men.

Under a farmer the bailiff is rarely called upon to buy or sell stock or corn, &c., but he generally pays the labourers their wages, makes contracts with them for piece work, measures up the work if necessary, and sees that the contract has been properly carried out. He frequently has charge of the keys of the barn and granary, and renders periodically an account of all that has been brought on to the farm or removed from it. The position is one of great trust and responsibility. It is not uncommon to find the place filled by a man who has been advanced from the rank of an ordinary labourer, who has had little advantage in the way of education at school, but one who knows how any kind of work ought to be done and how long any given piece of work should take to complete. He can take to piecoe a reaping machine, a mowing machine, a drill or other farm implement and replace any castings or fittings that are out of order; he will notice and appreciate symptoms of illness in any of the live stock of the farm, apply remedies or palliatives, and decide whether the case is or is not one for a veterinary surgeon.

The hours of a foreman are not limited, and they are necessarily long, as it is his duty to see that the men in charge of the horses have fed them before the working hours begin, and to direct all the labourers to the work which they have to do, this work being subject to constant variation at short notice by the chances and changes of the weather; and when the work of the day is over the foreman will look all round the premises the last thing at night to see that all is safe and sound. On a large farm the bailiff will have little time for manual work, his business is to see that others work, but he will not be above lending a hand wherever assistance is required, and if he is a perfect man in his position, he will never be "in the way" and never "out of the way."

In some parts of the country, and notably in Lincolnshire, Notts, and the East Riding of Yorkshire, the foreman has generally to lodge and feed several horse-keepers and farm lads, for each of whom a weekly sum is paid by the farmer. In some other counties, as in Cambridgeshire, he frequently occupies a large cottage or disused farm-house, in which he is expected to find lodging for a certain number of hired men, who receive and spend their own wages, finding their own food, and paying an agreed weekly sum for accommodation, cooking, service, and sometimes inclusive of vegetables, puddings, and condiments.

The success of a foreman under either of these systems depends very largely on the character and ability of his wife and her efforts to make the house comfortable for her lodgers. It is not less important to the farm lads who come into a foreman's house at the age of 15 to 17 years that the man should be moral, steady, industrious, and punctual.

Naturally the post of foreman is a pretty well paid one as compared with that of the ordinary labourers, and men in this position often save money and become farmers on their own account.

I have described the duties of a bailiff on a large farm. On many farms where the farmer is resident and retains the direction of the labourers in his own hands, the head carter, or perhaps the shepherd, acts as foreman in his master's absence.

95. Next to the bailiff in importance and in respect of responsibility comes the shepherd, who is often quite independent of the bailiff, and takes his orders from the master only.

On the hill farms of the North Country it is not too much to say that the success of the flock depends very largely upon the sagacity and the fidelity of the shepherd, who has to judge where suitable and seasonable herbage is to be found, when a particular hill should be grazed, where the sheep are least exposed to danger when a storm is impending, and his position demands that he should be always watchful, prepared, and untiring.

In the sheep breeding districts on the Downs of the south of England, which stretch from Dorset eastwards, and in the turnip districts of Suffolk, Norfolk, Lincolnshire, and East Yorkshire, indeed everywhere throughout the country where sheep-breeding is carried on, if the shepherd is not called upon so severely as his northern fellow may be, his work demands for success considerable skill, unremitting attention, and a hearty interest in his work.

The working hours of a shepherd are irregular or rather unlimited. At certain seasons of the year he must be about early and late, and in the lambing season he must be with his flock night and day, snatching an hour's sleep when opportunity offers; after this busy period is over his work is not very arduous generally, but if his heart is in his work he has anxious times and busy days when the sheep are struck by flies, or fall with the foot-rot, or the lambs go wrong. In the turnip districts, where large numbers of sheep are fattened or grazed, a good deal of the work of cutting the turnips, moving the folds, and feeding the sheep, is done by ordinary labourers, boys, and women. Where mixed farms prevail the shepherd who has not sufficient work to occupy his whole time is a less distinct type than in the great sheep districts, and he frequently combines some other work with that of looking after the flock. On smaller farms sheep, if kept at all, will probably be in the charge of the farmer himself.

Wherever the shepherd's business is sufficient to occupy a man's whole time the occupation is generally hereditary. The boy begins at an early age to accompany and assist his father, often long before he is employed for wages. He thus acquires gradually and intuitively that knowledge of the habits of the sheep which is so essential to him in after life, and begins to practice that observation which will enable him to distinguish each sheep of the flock of which he has the charge, and to see at a glance and, as it were, by instinct if any of them be sick or sorry.

The pay of a shepherd is generally somewhat above that of other labourers; in most counties he is hired by the year, and provided with a cottage and garden rent free.

In the Cheviot Hill district it has been in the past a custom to pay the shepherd chiefly by the keeping of a small flock of his own, but I reserve notice of the earnings of shepherds for a later section of this Report. Although the hiring is generally an annual one, it is probable that no farm servant is less given to change than a shepherd, particularly where a breeding flock is kept, and the continuity of interest is preserved.

96. Carters, horsekeepers, &c. One of the leading and important men on every farm is the head man in charge of horses. On many farms he acts as foreman. The system of management of horses varies so much in different parts of the country that the work

of the horsemen in the stables before and after field work differs greatly. For instance, in Northumberland "the hind" (that being the invariable title of the horseman) has charge of a pair of horses, which he works, tends, and feeds.

In Yorkshire and North Lincolnshire a head horsekeeper has a number of younger men and strong lads helping him and working under him; these young men are boarded and lodged at the farmer's expense, and generally in the foreman's house.

In other parts of England one man, with perhaps a boy to help him, takes charge of several horses (five to eight), and the ploughmen who work the teams have little to do with them in the stable. But everywhere the head horsekeeper is an important and trusted servant. He generally considers it his privilege to be on the road, if there is any produce to be delivered; he drills the corn, or leads the drill, works the reaping machine, and takes the foremost place amongst those at work in the cultivation of the farm, as distinguished from the care of the cattle and the sheep. In most districts, as will appear from the district reports, the carter or horsekeeper is engaged by the year, and paid in one way or another a sum which makes up to him for his additional hours, and for the lack of those opportunities of adding to his ordinary wages by contract work, or in other ways that are open to the ordinary labourer. Frequently the carter has passed the period of early manhood, and he prefers the regularity and the comparatively easy work of attending to and working the horses to the more exhausting work which the labourer has often to perform.

One essential characteristic of a good horsekeeper is a love for his team, and this is seldom wanting. A lad who has not this feeling rarely continues in the position of a horseman when he is competent to earn man's wages at other work.

The regard for his horses and his pride in their appearance often leads the horsekeeper into trouble, by tempting him to steal corn or oilcake for his team or his favourites among them. In his code of ethics there is no immorality in taking the master's corn for the master's cattle, but many a valuable horse has been killed or ruined by its being indulged with forbidden food. Worse still, the horsekeeper has had handed down to him from his seniors secrets and prescriptions of drugs which are reputed to improve the appearance of horses, and not many years ago numerous cases of poisoning by means of drugs administered by horsekeepers, with no evil intention, led to the passing of an Act of Parliament for the punishment of offenders of this character. [illegible]

In the Census Returns for 1891 an attempt has been made to distinguish this section of agricultural labourers as either horsekeepers, horsemen, teamsters, or carters, but the result cannot be considered satisfactory as the numbers of those enumerated under this head are less than one for every thousand acres of cultivated area, and less than two for every thousand acres of arable land. For Cambridgeshire 185 are enumerated, and this is about one for every 2,000 acres of arable land or one to every 50 horses used for agricultural purposes in that county.

97. In breeding districts, or wherever a herd is kept, and wherever dairying is carried on extensively the occupation of stockmen is a distinct one from that of the ordinary labourer, and unless the farmer is a working farmer a good deal of responsibility rests with them. Stockmen.

Where cattle are largely fed in the winter on arable farms a great deal of their well-being depends upon the yardman or "garthman" (as he is called in Lincolnshire and Yorkshire), or "byreman" (as he is called further north). In the south and west of England the "foggers" and milkers are frequently men who for the most part milk at night and morning, and make up the rest of the day in other work of the farm.

98. In addition to those labourers already mentioned, whose work is on a large farm of a distinct and definite character, there are a large number of labourers who are regarded as ordinary workmen, but it would be a mistake to suppose that they are all of the same grade. Other labourers.

A considerable number of them have aptitude and skill in one or more branches of farm work. One is, perhaps, hedger and ditcher in the winter, he hoes corn or roots at another season, thatches the hay and corn, and pursues throughout the year a pretty regular sequence of work in certain lines of his own choosing. Another drives an engine or takes charge of some of the more complicated machinery; a third is stacker when corn is harvested or threshed, or hay is carted. Another is always in the barn when corn is to be dressed. Thus, on a large farm, almost every man has a special function at times, either alone or in company with regular mates, but wherever two or three work together, one is the head man, or ganger, and is recognised as such by his companions, though often self-elected to the post—he sets the stroke, calls the time for meals, and takes the chief part in the striking of the bargain. On smaller farms there cannot be this division of work, and those employed have to undertake whatever kind of work has to be done, unless the farmer himself or a member of the family does it.

The general impression respecting the ordinary agricultural labourer is that of a man engaged in work which requires little intelligence, skill, or training, but in reality there are few duties which he has to perform which do not call for a certain amount of judgment, dexterity, and practice; and the training and management of horses, the art of ploughing, mowing, or sowing, the use of a spade or fork must be learned, and the labourer who had not learned to economise his forces and attack his work at the point of least resistance would be worn out very quickly.*

99. In Scotland the working staff of a farm is highly organised; the hinds, who are all of them yearly servants, have thus definite duties. The shepherds in the pastoral districts of the Highlands and the hills in the south form a very distinct class, but the Scotch labourers will be dealt with in another section of this Report.

100. In Ireland a large proportion of the labour is done by men casually employed, or by farm servants (indoor). On the demesne and home farms, and on some of the larger occupations, different classes of labourers with distinct functions exist as in England; and in the great grazing districts the herds are a particular class.

101. With these preliminary observations as to the principal classes of labourers, I proceed to notice the results of the inquiry by the Assistant Commissioners, dealing at present exclusively with the case of England, and following as closely as I can the order of subjects observed in the notes for the inquiry, the main heads being as follows:—

1. The present supply of labour.
2. The conditions of engagement of the labourers.
3. Wages and earnings.
4. Cottage accommodation.
5. Gardens and allotments.
6. Benefit societies.
7. Trade unions.
8. General relations between employers and employed.
9. The general condition of the agricultural labourer.

ENGLAND.

1. Supply of Labour.

102. From what has been already said as to the decrease in the number of wage earners, it might be supposed that the result would be a scarcity or deficiency in the supply of labour in the localities most denuded by migration, but it is a curious circumstance that the chief complaints on this score come from some of those districts where there has been an increase of population.

In a great majority of cases the Assistant Commissioners report a sufficiency of labour, at least for present requirements, with a little scarcity at exceptionally busy periods, the chief complaint being as to the quality of the labour, and not as to the quantity.

A few extracts from the Reports of the Assistant Commissioners as to different parts of the country may be given. But, before quoting from any of them, it may be well to point out that the supply varies greatly within very narrow limits of space. In one parish there is a positive scarcity, in the next a superabundance of labour, and nothing shows more clearly the want of energy and enterprise that characterises so many of the labourers than this fact.

Frequently no doubt a want of cottages creates a scarcity in a particular district, but this is not always or even generally the case; good, or at least average, cottages stand empty where workmen are wanted, when perhaps a few miles off there are too many hands for the work.

* The following quotation from a paper read by [illegible] before the Statistical Society in 1880 expresses a view which is [illegible] than the prevailing conception of the agricultural labourer:—

"The training of a good labourer commences from the time when as a boy he follows his father into the fields, [illegible] an agricultural labourer being unskilled, though [illegible], he is a [illegible] skilled workman, and to be good for anything he must be brought up to his profession from his early boyhood. It requires [illegible] qualities of mind and body to be a good labourer than to be a good carpenter, whose tools keep him [illegible] by line and by rule, &c., while the other makes parallel lines in a field with an awkward thing called a plough, and with awkward things called horses."—[illegible], Per. LXXI., [illegible].

The most positive evidence of a scarcity of labourers is perhaps that of Mr. Wilkinson with regard to Uttoxeter (Stafford and Derby)—

"Labour is decidedly scarce; men are out of work at Abbots Bromley and Newborough, but the testimony from all other parishes points to a great difficulty in getting hands. The principal difficulty is in getting cowmen. The apparent plethora at Abbots Bromley does not render it any easier for the farmers to get help."

Now Uttoxeter is a district of stationary population, where the land is almost entirely in pasture.

Again, in the case of Wetherby, where the population is now about the same as it was 20 years ago, Mr. Wilkinson says—

"The supply of labour is generally somewhat short. . . . . Many farmers have been at their wits' end this harvest to obtain extra hands."

Mr. Richards' report as to Belper, an industrial district where the agriculture is of a decidedly pastoral character, and the population is increasing, is that the supply of labour is barely sufficient, but it would seem that the complaint as to scarcity is rather that good men are not to be had than that labourers are wanting, and this is the general tendency of many Reports.

Thus Mr. Chapman says of Thame—

"There is, as a rule, a sufficiency of ordinary labourers but a deficiency of skilled labour."

And he goes on to name eight parishes in the district where the supply was in excess of the demand, 10 where the supply and demand were equal, and 15 to 18 where the supply was deficient at some periods of the year.

In many instances it is stated by the Assistant Commissioners that the supply is sufficient except at busy times.

Mr. Wilson Fox reports as to Glendale, which is one of the most highly paid districts, and where all the conditions of the labourers are more favourable than usual—

"The supply of labour seems to be scarcely sufficient."

But, with a few exceptions, the supply of labour is described as generally sufficient or about sufficient.

Mr. Bear tabulates the results of replies to his inquiries in six districts in the southern and midland counties. These replies relate to 121 parishes, in 81 of which the supply is said to be sufficient, and in only 16 is it said to be scarce or not enough. In the remaining cases some qualification is introduced, such as this, "Short at busy times"—"Short of boys."

Of all the districts visited, Godstone, which has no very distinct agricultural characteristics, appears to have the most abundant supply.

Mr. Spencer says of it—

"The supply of labour in all parts of the union seemed to be sufficient, and was generally said to be plentiful."

Mr. Wilson Fox says:—

"Doubtless the conversion of arable land into grass has been the means of dispensing with much labour."

Mr. Chapman reports:—

"Labourers say generally that the farmers are not yet 'in a fix,' but as so many labourers have left the country things are better for those who remain."

And further on—

"The effect of this decrease in the supply of labour upon the position of the farmers would have been disastrous if they had not been economising their labour during the same period. Farm staffs have generally been reduced, machinery has been adopted wherever it is possible and the farmer can afford it, mations on farms is generally neglected, and in most places the land is fuller of weeds than it ought to be, thistles are no longer pulled but cut, and hedges are not kept as I was assured they used to be 15 or 20 years ago.

"Labourers say everywhere that the land is labour starved, and farmers constantly declare that they cannot afford to do the land justice owing to bad prices."

Mr. Wilkinson takes the view that it is not so much the regular staff of the farm that has been reduced, but the casual helpers and Mr. Wilson Fox says on this point of machinery displacing labour:—

"I have consulted several large farmers both in the northern and eastern counties, ... and they agree in thinking that this is not so as regards the *ordinary staff of the farm*."

The fact that less labour is generally employed on farms cannot be disputed, and the main causes of the decrease are not in doubt. What is disputable is the share which each cause has had in bringing about the result.

105. I venture to express the opinion that a change in the system of farming in all the arable districts of the country was originated by the agricultural lock-out of 1874. Farmers were then compelled to substitute machinery for manual labour wherever possible, and they were induced to lessen the area of those crops which required most labour.

The great rise of wages which then occurred led farmers to employ fewer men and to leave undone all work which could be abandoned. The period was one of great unrest, and many labourers left their native villages and either emigrated or were absorbed in the town populations.

The wet and disastrous seasons of 1878–1881, and the fall in prices of corn, stimulated the laying down land to grass, and at the same time crippled the farmers and compelled the great majority of them to reduce their labour to the narrowest possible limits, and since that time a still lower general level of prices of cereals has augmented the difficulties of the farmers, and diminished the volume of demand for labour.

It is undoubtedly the opinion of many persons that want of employment was the cause of the labourers migration to the towns, but I venture to maintain, with Mr. Wilkinson, that the reduction of the working staff on farms was the consequence, and not the cause, of migration.

The agricultural lock-out was no doubt the result of competition for the labourers' services by employers engaged in other industries. Although it was confined to a few counties its influence was widely felt, and the competition which led to it was everywhere experienced.

106. The connection between a sudden and considerable rise in wages and a simultaneous and consequent restriction of the number of labourers employed is strikingly illustrated by a copy of a farmer's accounts of sums paid for labour from 1869 to 1892, which is appended to Mr. Wilson Fox's Summary Report. These accounts were supplied by a gentleman who is a well known and extensive farmer, whose occupation lies in Norfolk and Suffolk. They show (1) the current rate of weekly wages in the months of May and November in each year. (2.) The total sum paid for labour in each year.

The rate of wages in 1869 was 9s. a week. By May 1874 they had risen to 14s. 6d., from which point they declined again to 10s. in 1889, and they were 11s. in November 1892. The total sum paid for labour ranges from 844*l*. in 1869 to 1,164*l*. in 1878, and in 1892, the last year of the series, it was 1,020*l*.

The total cost of labour on a farm varies in different years, not only according to the rate of wages paid, but according to the crops which are grown. Unfavourable seasons may make roots a total failure, or largely increase the cost of harvest. To compare the results of certain years taken singly would be misleading; the area of crops will vary, as also the bulk of them. But if an average of four years be taken

Fen.
A. App. A

Table [illegible].

[illegible]
[illegible]

Royal Commission on Labour.

Diagram showing the rise and fall of Wages, Cost of Labour, and Extent of Employment upon an occupation in Norfolk & Suffolk during 24 years 1869 - 1892. (divided into six periods of 4 years each.) Constructed from Accounts communicated to Mr A. Wilson Fox A. C. by Mr J. Ferguson. Thetford. (Vol. I. App.)

In this Diagram 100 is taken to represent the mean rate of (1) Weekly Wages (2) the Total Cost of Labour and (3) the Extent of Employment upon a particular occupation during a period of four years (1869 to 1872) and the rise and fall in each of these during subsequent similar periods is shown by three separate lines joining the points which represent to Scale the Percentage of rise and fall from the Standard or Starting Point 100.*

Wages Black Line. Total Cost of Labour Blue Line. Extent of Employment Red Line.*

**Extent of Employment is the Expression of the result obtained by dividing the Total Cost of Labour by the mean rate of Weekly Wages (e.g. £1000 spent in Labour when Wages are 10/- a week gives employment to 2000 labourers for one week, while £1000 divided among Labourers who have 13/6 a week employs only 1482 men per week.)*

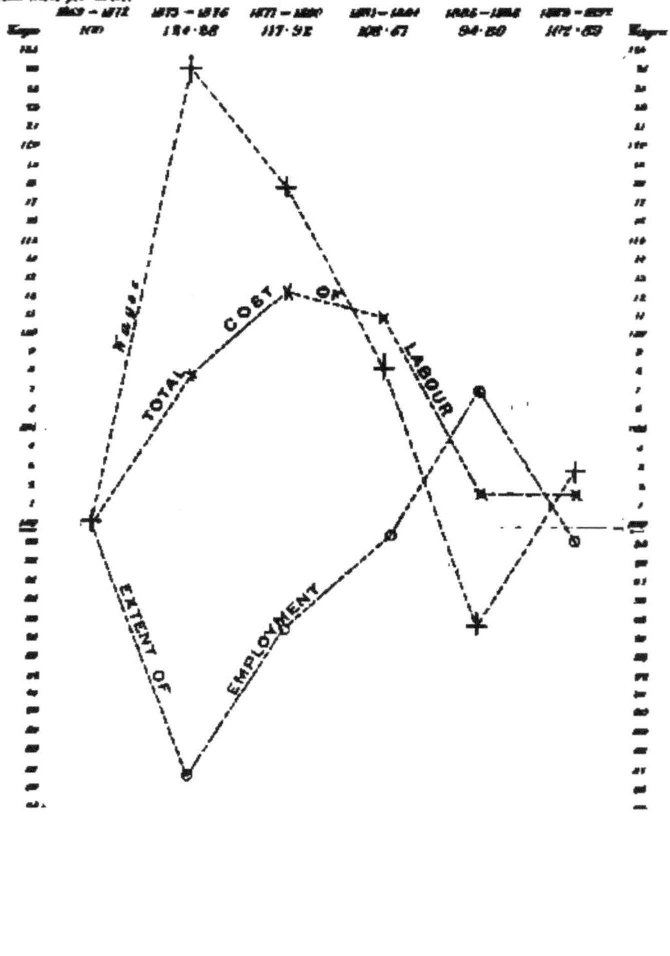

the whole farm, under the four course system, will have been under the regular rotation of crops, and the effects of any extraordinary circumstances attending a particular year will be spread over the four years.

If the whole cost of labour be divided by the mean wages of the two months May and November, the labour can be expressed in so many weeks' wages of one man at current rates; thus in 1870, when the mean rate of wages was 10s., and the total cost was 979l., that sum represents the employment of one man for 1,958 weeks, or 1,958 men for one week, and 1,958 divided by 52 will give nearly enough, for purposes of comparison, the equivalent of the number of men employed for the whole year at current wages. The accounts referred to, if treated in the manner thus indicated, show the following results:—

Fox, A. App. A, Table 3a.

FLUCTUATION IN WAGES, COST OF LABOUR AND EXTENT OF EMPLOYMENT, based on Farm Accounts supplied by Mr. Ferguson, Thetford, Norfolk, to Mr. A. Wilson Fox.

—	Periods of Four Years	Average of mean Yearly Rate of Wages	Total Amount spent on Labour	Total Number of Weeks' Work for One Man at current wages	Extent of Employment expressed in Number of Men at Current Wages	Extent of Employment expressed in Average Yearly Number of Weeks' Work for one Man
		s. d.	£			
1	1869-1872	10 9½	3,980	7,382	35·65	1,854
2	1873-1876	13 [illegible]	4,593	6,398	30·75	1,600
3	1877-1880	12 7	4,574	6,860	33·88	1,760
4	1881-1884	11 [illegible]	4,419	7,431	35·16	1,661
5	1885-1888	10 [illegible]	4,024	7,916	37·94	1,974
6	1889-1892	11 1½	4,054	7,289	35·04	1,831

If 100 be taken to represent the results of the first period, 1869-1872, the five other periods will be in ratio to it as follows:—

1	1869-1872	100	100	—	—	100
2	1873-1876	124·84	107·01	—	—	86·30
3	1877-1880	117·[illegible]	115·40	—	—	94·92
4	1881-1884	104·67	111·03	—	—	89·38
5	1885-1888	94·80	101·08	—	—	106·47
6	1889-1892	103·[illegible]	101·84	—	—	98·76

It will be seen by this Table that as wages rose employment decreased, and vice versa, when wages decreased employment increased.

The total cost of labour does not correspond exactly or closely with the increase of wages, but it exhibits a tendency in the same direction.

The results of this comparative statement are presented in the accompanying diagram, which graphically represents the effect of high wages in decreasing the extent of employment.

In the first period of four years, wages rise to the extent of nearly 23 per cent.; the sum expended, however, rises only 8 per cent., and it is divided among fewer workmen. The number of weeks' employment for one man falling from 1,854 to 1,600, or nearly 14 per cent.

In the fifth period, 1885-1888, the mean rate of wages has fallen below the starting point (though not below that of the first year in the series) by a little more than 5 per cent., and the number of weeks' work for one man has risen to 1,974, which is 6½ per cent. above the standard taken for comparison.

I will not at the present moment stop to inquire whether current weekly wages are now a less certain measure of earnings than they were 20 or 30 years ago; but if we assume for the sake of argument that earnings now are more in excess of nominal wages than they were formerly, it is clear that the decrease of employment has in this case been greater than that which is shown by the diagram.

It would of course be dangerous to generalise from a single statement; but the figures noticed do support what is a very general opinion, namely, that farmers curtail labour when wages increase. But in former years when wages were regulated by the price of corn, the consequence of a rise of wages was not so usually restrictive of employment as it is now, because the farmer was enabled to meet the higher wages with his increased receipts for corn.

Migration of labourers.

107. To return to the subject of migration from the rural districts, all the Assistant Commissioners report such migration as common, if not uniformly the same in degree. The causes assigned for this migration are several, the prominent ones being the desire

for better wages, greater prospects of advancement, a wish for a more exciting and less monotonous life. In two or three districts the attractions of Small Holdings or of work in the woods in winter, are said to act as inducements to labourers to remain.

Mr. Bear says—

"In all the districts there is complaint of the migration of the strongest and best of the young labourers."

But he notes as to Basingstoke, that there is less migration than elsewhere in his experience as an Assistant Commissioner, and he attributes this to the work in the woods, which provide employment for the labourers whose work is slack on the farm. In Melton Mowbray he says that the men leave agriculture for better paid employment in the neighbourhood, but they do not go away from the district.

Mr. Chapman finds that—

"the agricultural population continues to decrease, and that with the exception of North Witchford (Cambs), there is not much difference between one district and another. The migration from country to town is not more marked in the poor districts than it is in the more prosperous."

He assigns as contributory causes—

"The higher standard of comfort which prevails amongst labourers, the desire for a freer and less dull life, the low standard of wages, the miserable condition of many of the cottages, the absence of any prospect of making provision for old age, and the reduction of the staff upon many farms."

But he then proceeds to show that "bad cottages have very little to do with the change," by instancing North Witchford, and Oakley in the Thame district, and he concludes—

"That when Englishmen desert their homes they are seeking one or both of two things, namely, independence in tenure of house and security for old age."

Mr. Wilson Fox found that in Glendale, where the wages were much higher, and the condition of the labourer superior to that of those in Norfolk and Suffolk, the young men left the district just as much, and he is of opinion that their purpose is not simply to get higher wages, but also to lead a less monotonous life, and to rise in the social scale.

Mr. Richards reports the answer he received to a question on the subject from the spokesman for the labourers at a meeting in Nantwich:—

"The intelligent part of our rural population do not find in agriculture a sufficient interest to retain them in the district. Young people have never been taught that there is anything more in agriculture than hard work."

Mr. Spencer points out that—

"the attraction of the town as compared with the country has not only affected the labouring class but has had exactly the same effect on other classes of the community. The superior physique of lads bred in the country enables them at once to find employment in trades where strength and power of endurance are requisite, and the country thus becomes the natural recruiting ground for the town."

Mr. Wilkinson thinks that the young go away and get employment on railways or in the police force

"less for the better wages than for the lighter hours, and above all things, for the sake of being more in the stream of life."

108. In several districts where the resident population is insufficient to meet the demand for labourers at particular seasons there is a considerable migration of labourers from neighbouring districts where work is less plentiful, and also from Ireland, though in less numbers than formerly.

The Assistant Commissioners report that considerable numbers of Irishmen still go to Glendale for harvest, to Garstang and Atcham for the summer and autumn, to Uttoxeter for the hay season, and in other districts they are mentioned as assisting in the hay and harvest and at the time for raising potatoes, though in smaller numbers than formerly. A rather remarkable class of migrants is noticed by Mr. Bear as having their homes near Basingstoke. These are small holders who having put in their spring crops, lock up their houses and drive off with their wives and children to other districts where work may be found; and a similar class is mentioned by Mr. Chapman in his report on the district of Thame. The hop and fruit districts are regularly visited by families from London and the manufacturing towns of the Midlands and the Black Country.

If the use of machinery for cutting hay and corn crops, haymaking, raising potatoes, &c., has diminished the demand for outside labour, it has not yet superseded the hop and fruit pickers.

109. I have stated that in several cases where a scarcity of labourers was alleged the complaint of the farmers was rather that skilled labour was wanting than that the number of hands was insufficient, and this raises the question whether the agricultural labourer is now less efficient than he was formerly. Efficiency of labourers.

Is he less able or less willing to do a fair day's work or to do it in a workmanlike manner?

It is very generally asserted by farmers, and it is not denied universally by labourers, that as a rule men are less skilful and less industrious; that they do not care to excel or to acquire any accomplishment, even though excellence in any particular department of farm work is in demand and commands a higher price than unskilled labour.

The different views which are entertained on this subject and the various reasons which are assigned for the alleged falling off in skill may be illustrated by the succeeding extracts from reports.

Mr Bear writing in his report on Basingstoke says— Bear, IV. 13.

"According to the evidence of the majority of the employers visited, there has been some deterioration in the efficiency of the labourers in recent years.

"The most common complaint is that they do not take the same interest in their work . . . and in some districts it is said that the young men do not care to learn to thatch or to do other work involving some skill."

"Some of the best employers, however, and those who pay the highest wages, give conflicting testimony, saying that they noticed no difference in the efficiency of the men, and expressing moderate satisfaction with their work and conduct. There is no doubt that such men get the pick of the workmen, and that the satisfaction which they give by their payments tends to induce the men to satisfy them in return."

Mr. Chapman, in his Summary Report, says:— Chapman, A. 10, 41.

"It is very commonly said by employers that agricultural labourers are by no means so skilful as they used to be. This is due to the fact that the all-round sort of man who can lay a hedge, thatch a rick, make a drain, and shear sheep is becoming a thing of the past. There is no doubt of this fact, but it does not necessarily imply that labourers have lost their efficiency for the work which they are asked to do.

"The principle of the division of labour upon large farms has been so generally adopted, that each man becomes accustomed to a particular kind of work, and has little chance of learning work of another sort. Skilled work in some districts is quite as well done now as ever it was, but not so often by the ordinary staff of the farm. On the other hand, the use of machinery has called forth a fresh kind of intelligence, and it is probably true to say that the labourers are more skilful now in the use of machines and less skilful in the use of hand tools than they were.

"Considering the universal testimony that the best and most intelligent of the labourers are being drawn into the towns, it is rather wonderful that there is so little complaint about the ordinary work of the farm."

Mr. Chapman goes on to point out that skill can only be acquired by early training, and that the age at which boys now begin to work and the inability or unwillingness of the farmer to train them as apprentices increases the effect produced by the division of labour which he had spoken of before, and he adds:—

"As to industry and interest in work, the testimony is almost overwhelming that there has been a great falling off in efficiency with average labourers on average farms."

In his report upon Buntingford, Mr. Chapman quotes opinions of employers who take different views; one of them declaring that the want of skill in the men was due to the fact that "the farmers were no longer able to teach them their work," and pointing as a contrast to the example of some Cornish farmers who had come into that district, and who got their work well done because they were able to do it with their own hands. Chapman, B VI. 41.

Mr. Wilson Fox reports thus:— Fox, A. 13.

"In the two Unions in the Eastern Counties (Norfolk and Suffolk) the majority of employers agree that the men do less work, and are not so skilled as formerly.

"Some say that the cause of this is that the best young labourers go away, while others say that they now take but little interest in their work. Possibly, part of this disinclination for agricultural labour may be traced to a more educated generation shirking and resenting toil which is comparatively badly paid, monotonous, and productive of no material or social improvement.

"The evidence in the three Northern Counties (Northumberland, Cumberland, and Lancashire) was curiously conflicting on the question, but there was practically a unanimity of opinion that, as far as willingness to work was concerned, there was little or no falling off.

"Some expressed strong opinions that the men were as skilled as ever, while others, with great emphasis, gave contrary evidence."

Mr. Richards reports thus:— Richards, A. 7.

"There is an almost uniform testimony to the lowered efficiency of labour, attributed by employers to the possibilities afforded by a higher degree of education, and to the greater attractions of industrial occupations."

In his Report on Cirencester, however, he records the fact that—

"One large farmer very emphatically expressed the opinion that the labourers are much better now than formerly, that their education and the increased use of machinery had made them more useful all-round men."

Mr. Spencer says:—

"The comparative efficiency of labourers is a question which everywhere gave rise to considerable difference of opinion.

"The balance of opinion from the farmers' side is that labour has deteriorated, it being very commonly said that three men now do not do the work that two used to do, although some farmers said that they had nothing to complain of.

"Labourers, as a rule, considered that the efficiency of labour had not deteriorated, but admitted that the younger hands did not learn special crafts as their fathers before them did.

"The opinion that I formed, though with some hesitation, is that labour has not generally deteriorated to the extent supposed.

"I think, however, that the more intelligent and ambitious men leave the country, and those who are left are frequently led to look down upon agricultural work altogether, and thus become unwilling to take up and learn special branches."

Mr. Wilkinson in his final Report says:—

"It must apparently be conceded that there is a general falling-off in experience, arising from the fact that as the older men, who are generally as efficient as ever, drop off, there are few equally skilled younger men to take their place.

"It is probably true that less interest in their work, less anxiety to do it well for the sake of having it perfect, is evidenced by all, both old and young; but there is an absolute inferiority in the case of many of the younger hands, due not only to this lack of interest, but to a vague restlessness which makes them uncertain of adhering to field work in any form, and therefore disinclined to take the trouble of acquiring any of the special arts connected with it.

"It is true that machinery has superseded much of the old skilled work, and also true that many young men show great aptitude in learning the management of it; but such things as thatching, hedge cleaning or laying, drain laying, mowing, shearing, are in many parts becoming almost lost arts.

"There was hardly a district where I did not hear complaints on this score, none where I did not hear the praises sung of some exceptionally clever young fellows who had preferred to keep to agricultural life, and who could and would do well at anything that was set before them. As skill and industry are not yet prevented from receiving more reward than ignorance and idleness, it need hardly be said that these young men were in constant employment at good wages."

On the whole the balance of evidence seems to confirm what common sense would suggest that if the more active and intelligent young men of the class are drawn away by various inducements from agricultural pursuits, the average of those who are left must be lowered, and naturally if there be amongst the young men of the class a general feeling of restlessness, and a desire to escape from field work and the monotony of life on the farm, which cannot, I think, be questioned, the spirit of emulation and a desire to attain to excellence in work is not likely to be fostered. But notwithstanding all that may be said in dispraise of the present race of workmen, there is still, wherever encouragement is given, a very considerable amount of proficiency, and incompetence is not the badge of all the labourers. There is no part of the country which is without farms where a high standard of work is to be observed.

110. One point which is raised by the notes for inquiry has not received much elucidation in the Reports of the Assistant Commissioners. Everywhere the question seems to have been regarded as one which could be answered on the spot by those interested in the locality, and it is a remarkable circumstance that however severe employers may have been upon the shortcomings of the labourers, they were always free to contend that the men of their district were rather better than those of any other. This local prejudice in favour of one's own country is exemplified in Mr. Fox's Report on Wigton (Cumberland).

"The general opinion among the employers is that the Cumberland men's work will compare very favourably with other districts. Mr. Nelson, Mr. Punchard, and Mr. Walker support this view, though *the latter, who is a Devonshire man, says he thinks the Devonshire men are better.*"

A score loads of manure means 20 cubic yards in one district, and 800 cubic feet (nearly 30 yards) in another. Even thatching at per square of 100 feet is not a subject of comparison unless one knows something of the style which prevails in the different districts; and, moreover, in some of the highest wage districts there is no piece work to form the basis of comparison.

Again, the cost of labour per acre, taking a whole farm, is not a complete test; it would be a sufficient one only where the conditions as regards soil and system of farming were pretty much the same. There can be little doubt that the sum of the labour bill on farms in Northumberland is less than it is in the eastern counties, though the wages are much higher in the former county; but one reason for this is undoubtedly that a very considerable portion of the work is done by women, one of whom certainly does as much as many a man does in the latter district.

The evidence of contractors who have had experience of labourers from different parts of the country seems to show that the northern labourers are capable of doing more than those in the south, and that they are therefore worthy of higher wages.

2. Conditions of Engagement.

111. The period for which engagements are made between employers and labourers varies from a single day to a year. In by far the larger number of districts a mixed system prevails, under which horsemen and cattlemen are hired for a year, while ordinary labourers are under no contract unless the occupation of a cottage is a condition of employment.

Shepherds are almost universally hired for the year. Horsemen very generally for the same period, cattlemen less frequently so. In some districts the dividing line between yearly men and others engaged for shorter periods is that the former are boarded either in the house of the farmer or that of the foreman.

In Glendale (Northumberland) all the men are engaged by the year. The women are not really engaged at all by the farmer; the hind engages to find a woman worker, frequently a daughter, and the engagement is practically for a year.

In Dorchester—

"Ordinary labourers as well as carters, shepherds, and stockmen are hired by the year. The agreement for hiring is generally verbal, but occasionally in writing."

These are the only districts where a yearly agreement is reported as the prevailing system.

In contrast to the two districts just spoken of may be instanced Woburn, of which Mr. Bear writes thus:—

"Farm labourers are engaged by the week. I did not hear of any instance of monthly or yearly hirings, or of men being lodged and boarded in farm houses."

Similarly with regard to Buntingford, Mr. Chapman says:—

"The contract for all kinds of farm labourers is exactly the same, namely, for a week only."

And the same system prevails generally, though not exclusively, in districts in the Eastern Counties (Norfolk, Suffolk, and Essex), in the Midland Counties of Bedfordshire, Huntingdonshire, Northampton, and in the Southern Counties of Surrey, Sussex, Somerset, Devon, and Cornwall.

Thus, in 12 of the districts of inquiry the engagement is almost entirely a weekly one.

The mixed system which divides the labourers into classes in respect of their duties is found in Staffordshire, South Lincoln, Cambridge, Warwick, Oxon, Monmouth, Gloucester, Wilts, Berks, Hants, and Kent, but the relative proportion of the two classes, and the system of hiring differ considerably.

To take an example from the West of England. Mr. Richards, reporting of Cirencester, says:—

"Ordinary labourers are engaged by the week or the fortnight, the former term being the more general; cowmen, stockmen, waggoners, and shepherds are engaged by the year."

In Hollingbourn (Kent)—

"The engagement is called weekly in the case of ordinary labourers, but is in reality by the day, as it is considered that a man need not be kept on if work is impossible owing to wet weather or any other reason. Waggoners, and their mates, and stockmen, are generally hired by the year."

In North Witchford (Cambridgeshire), with almost every possible variety of practice, there is one phase not noted as occurring elsewhere. On many farms the horses are in the charge of young unmarried men and lads who lodge with the foreman, providing their own food. This is probably a survival of the old system of boarding and lodging the farm servant in the farm house.

Somewhat similar to this system and one which is a step nearer to the indoor farm servant system, is that obtaining in North Lincolnshire and the East Riding of Yorkshire, where not infrequently the young men, including horsekeepers, under shepherds, and stockmen, are lodged and boarded, or as it is called "metted" in the foreman's house.

In other parts of Yorkshire and in Cumberland, Lancashire, Cheshire, Shropshire, Hereford, Worcester, Derby, and Notts., the mixed system is one of weekly labourers and farm servants, hired by the year, and boarded in the farm house.

Mr. Chapman reports of Atcham thus:—

"The contract of service varies in this Union to a remarkable extent, being sometimes by the week, sometimes by the month, sometimes by the quarter, and sometimes by the year, and it is scarcely ever in writing. The only labourers engaged by the year are those who are hired into the house; these are always unmarried men, generally from 18 to 25 years of age, and nearly always strangers. They are usually employed as waggoners, under-waggoners, or cattle men. On the Welsh border and on small farms the practice of hiring men into the house is a common one, and rather increasing; but in the rich districts and on large farms the habit is decreasing, and it is more and more difficult to get men to engage themselves in this way."

112. The comparative advantages and disadvantages of yearly hirings are discussed by Mr. Wilson Fox in his Summary Report:—

"The Unions assigned to me afforded me the opportunity of comparing the advantages and disadvantages of long and short periods of engagement.

"In Suffolk and Norfolk the engagement of ordinary labourers is a daily one; in Cumberland it is a half-yearly one for the hired men who live in the farm houses, and a weekly one for the married men.

"In Lancashire the engagement of hired men is a yearly one, and that of married men a weekly one. In Northumberland all the men, whether married or single, are engaged by the year."

After pointing out the advantage to the men of losing no time or pay in wet weather or slack times, Mr. Fox continues:—

"Arguments are sometimes raised against the hiring system, but these come more often from the masters than from the men. I am convinced that the northern labourer is much indebted to the system which insures him regular pay at all seasons and under all circumstances."

And he then proceeds to point out that the hiring system causes men to change their situation frequently.

Mr. Wilkinson writes thus, on the same subject:—

"Great differences of opinion exist as to the comparative advantages and disadvantages of yearly engagements.

"It is curious that what is meant to secure continuity of service in the interest both of the farmer and the labourer has in some respects an opposite effect. The man is engaged fast for the year, and though the engagement is sometimes broken by him, he may be assumed generally to keep it. Yet the fact of feeling tied and not free to go where he likes makes him very frequently change when his year is up, for the mere sake of change, and it is curious that many married men are almost as apt to change as single men. The master of the school at South Elkington (Louth) complained very much of the migratory character of so many families, handicapping heavily as it does his chance of helping the children and the children's chance of learning. It was a very common complaint everywhere. This habit of constant flitting is prejudicial in many ways. It prevents interest being taken in the house or garden; it lessens the chance of cordial friendship springing up between the labourer and his master. So far, then, as the system of yearly engagements increases the inclination to move, it is productive of harm.

"It is, of course, a very great boon to the man to know that his pay is secured to him no matter what the weather may be, and it should be a boon to the farmer to be sure of a man when labour may be scarce.

"But it is not always so. If he engages a stranger he may often engage a man whom, as it turns out, it is simple vexation and loss to keep to the end of the year.

"On the whole, I incline to think that if one ignores the effect in inducing a migratory habit and the question of cottage tenure . . . the yearly engagement is more to the men's than to the farmers' interest."

Mr. Chapman describes the system of

"hiring by the week into a farm cottage either free or at a moderate rent,"

as one universal in Crediton, and to be found everywhere as

"a form of hiring which farmers, as a rule, consider the best."

But he adds :—

"on the part of the labourers there is a growing dislike to this system. They prefer to have their "cottage quite independent of their labour contract."

He then notices the system of weekly hiring, without privileges, at a regular wage, a system which he says Chapman, A. 61.

"is universal where men live in village cottages, and appears to be most popular with the men. It has "the great attraction of independence after working hours. Its disadvantages consist in the distance "from work for the labourers, the difficulty in getting a good garden with the house, and of keeping "a pig. It also means, as a rule, high rent."

It is not necessary to add much to these statements. The subject is mixed up with that of cottage accommodation and tenure, to be noticed hereafter. Upon one point there can be no dispute, namely, that the system of hiring for the year secures to the labourer the greatest boon, regular employment.

It will be found, upon examination of the Reports, that weekly engagements are most common where the supply of labourers is most abundant, and that where there is any approach to a short supply, farmers endeavour to secure at least a sufficient number of hired men to attend to the live stock of the farm.

113. The subject of the regularity or continuous nature of employment has been incidentally raised by the question previously discussed. There is no doubt from a perusal of the several Reports, that everywhere there is some risk of loss of time by ordinary labourers in wet weather or continued frost, but that a great number of farmers find work for the men during such periods. On this point, Mr. Bear says :— Continuity of work. Loss of time in wet weather.

"There is no doubt that, as a rule, day labourers in all the districts lose *a little* time in wet weather, although the farmers frequently state that they always find something for men to do who come to work, except when they are employed at piece work, which they do in their own time. Bear, A. 6.

"On the whole, my impression is that the loss of time from wet weather is very small in all my districts, except among irregular labourers, or when men are at piece work."

Mr. Chapman reports thus :—

"Apart from the nature of employment, it is curious to find that regular men who are supposed to be engaged by the week, are obliged on some farms to lose time from wet weather. This is especially complained of in Buntingford, but is occasionally the case also in Crediton, Truro, and Atcham.

"Such a loss of time involves a distinct violation of the contract, although it is usually done in a form which gives colour to the idea that the labourer has chosen to lose a day. When the labourer comes in the morning to do his work, he is told that there is nothing for him to do at the farm, and he can either stand out in the wet or go home, but if he goes home he must lose a day's pay. This amounts to treating a man as a day labourer, who has been engaged at a weekly price, and it ought not to be allowed. Chapman, A. 60.

"It probably would not pass muster if the question were tested in a court of law, and it is satisfactory to know that the majority of farmers disapprove of the practice."

The question is one of engagement. Where men are hired for the year there is no lost time; but odd men even in the northern counties, where the great majority of the labourers are hired by the year, are liable to be out of work in inclement weather; and Mr. Spencer instances Dorsetshire, where Fox, A. 16.

"the terms of hiring being yearly for all farm hands employment is regular and time is not lost in "wet weather. . . . In the other counties I visited ordinary hands occasionally lose by wet "weather." Spencer, A. 13.

Mr. Wilkinson say that— Wilkinson, A. 60.

"many farmers, and as I gather, an increasing number, do not make their men lose time for wet "weather."

A reference to the Analytical Index to Reports,* will show those districts where the habit is most marked, and a considerable number of districts where the regular men lose no time on account of weather.

114. There are only three instances in the Reports where any attempt is made to estimate what the average amount of time lost is, or the deduction from weekly earnings which is occasioned thereby. Estimates of amount of loss.

In Thingoe the labourers estimated the average loss at from 1s. to 2s. a week to those who were liable to be sent home; and in Swaffham the estimate is the same. In Pershore Mr. Spencer estimates the average loss from wet weather at about two weeks in the year, or a little less than four per cent., say 6d. a week. Appended to this Report are the details of the weekly earnings of two men during 12 months. One of these, a stockman, loses no time by wet weather, but he is absent 24 days Fox, R. I. 11, R. II 15. Spencer, R. VI, App. C.

* Vol. I., Part VII.

on account of illness, three days working on his own land, and three days visiting his friends. The other, an ordinary labourer, is only noted as having lost three days by wet weather, but he was 25½ days working on his own land during the year.

115. The deductions from pay when a labourer is absent through illness are not the subject of much remark by the Assistant Commissioners. Mr. Fox remarks upon the custom in Northumberland of paying the hinds regular wages during illness, and upon the consequent absence of any benefit societies in that part of the country; and Mr. Spencer says that in Dorchester "the farmer does not consider himself bound to "pay wages during illness," and it may, I think, be taken for granted that as a general rule this is the practice throughout the country.

The general tenor of the evidence as to continuity of employment would appear to me that farmers, or at any rate the larger farmers, keep a certain staff of men who are employed regularly throughout the year "wet and dry," the number of such staff being the minimum number required for everyday ordinary work, and that they rely for help at busy times upon casual labourers.

116. The tendency at the present time is undoubtedly to divide the labourers more distinctly than was formerly the case into regular and casual workers, the latter working for various masters as opportunity offers and inclination prompts them, and preferring the independence of such a life to any prolonged engagement. Mr. Wilkinson says on this point:—

> "I could not help noticing in almost every district how very frequently the unemployed are so by their own choice. There are scores everywhere who will not take regular work, but, because casual work at busy times is highly paid, lay themselves out for that, quite content, too, if they get such work for three or four days in a week, to do nothing for the other days. Much even of their occupied time is taken up in going about to inquire for these odd bits of work. Restlessness is often the characteristic of these men rather than laziness."

And Mr. Bear records a statement made to him by the principal spokesman of a group of labourers, whose evidence was taken at Melton Mowbray, to the effect that

> "There are some who will not take it (work) regularly, preferring to get extra pay at threshing and other jobs for three or four days in the week to working regularly at lower wages."

If the labourers should in increasing numbers choose this casual employment, it follows naturally that the farmers will employ them only just when they require their services.

117. The increasing number of allotments and the desire for them are perhaps partly the result of casual employment. If it be said that allotments fill up the time which would otherwise be lost, it may also be said that as the allotment holder's busy season is also the time when the farmer wants him most, and as the labourer chooses the best weather for doing his own work, it can scarcely be expected that the farmer will give constant employment to a man who chooses just the day when he will work for himself and when for another.

A good deal of unfair criticism of the farmer has been indulged in on this point. The Special Commissioner of the *Daily News*, in a letter subsequently published in "Life in our Villages," * describes with much indignation a case where a farmer discharged a workman who had preferred getting in his own crop to harvesting that of his master; but if the writer had realised that the absence of one man from a set of harvesters might throw the work into confusion and seriously impede half a dozen more men and as many horses he would have seen that the farmer had some reason for saying "If you are to be free to work for yourself whenever you please I can only "employ you when I require your help." In no other business than that of agriculture would it be contended that a labourer could absent himself when he chose and still retain his situation, or the certainty of employment when he had no work of his own to be done.

Hours of Work.

119. The number of hours during which a labourer works varies considerably even in the same district or parish, though in many cases the positive difference is more apparent than real. There are two ways of looking at the subject: first, with respect to the hours over which work is extended, and during which the workman, if his home is not near at hand, must be away; and second, the actual hours during which he works, allowance having been made for the intervals which are allowed or which he takes for rest and refreshment. Hours of work.

120. Each of the Summary Reports of the Assistant Commissioners contains a very full statement comparing the customs of the districts visited. It will be sufficient if in this place a general view of the limits of time occupied and the actual working hours be taken, and for this purpose it will be convenient first of all to take the ordinary labourer as an example, bearing in mind that those who have charge of stock usually add to the labourer's hours of work time at both ends of the day. The longest hours noted by any of the Assistant Commissioners are those in Nantwich where the labourers milk before and after their field work. They begin at 5.30 in the morning and do not finish before 7 in the evening. Limits of day

In Garstang (Lanc.), the few day labourers who are employed, work the same hours as the hired men who live in the farmhouses. These hours are described as from 5 or 6 a.m. to 6 or 7 p.m. In this district, as in that of Nantwich, the early and late hours are spent in milking. In both of them the men may be regarded as stockmen, and their hours must be compared with those of men in that class. It will be seen that these hours are 13 to 13½, and the intervals for meals are said to be 1½ hours in Nantwich, and 1½ to 2 hours in Garstang. Richards, B. VI. 11. Milking cows. Fox, B. II.

In 17 districts the hours are said to extend from 6 a.m. to 6 p.m., or 12 hours, with generally 1½ hour respite for meals, and two hours or more in Glendale. In seven districts the hours are from 6 to 5.30, the hours for meals being exactly the same as in the districts before mentioned. In eight other districts the full hours of attendance are only 11, as from 6 to 5, 6.30 to 5.30, or 7 to 6, with the same time allowed for meals as in former cases. In four districts the hours are from 7 a.m. to 5 p.m., with 1 to 1½ hours off for meals.

121. An examination of the localities where these different customs prevail throws no light on the causes of such variety, which, probably, is due to long usage, dating back from a time when there was some cause to account for it. If we classify the districts in accordance with the extreme limits of time that the working hours extend over, we see that the geographical distribution is apparently capricious. Local variations.

Hours of Attendance.

Table 63.

13½ to 14	12		11½	11	10
Nantwich.	Atcham.	Louth.	Belper.	Basingstoke.	Thakeham.
Garstang.	Bromyard	Monmouth.	Brixworth	Cirencester.	Thame.
	Buntingford	Pershore.	Godstone	Crediton.	Truro.
	Dorchester.	Swaffham.	Maldon.	Holbeach.	Wantage.
	Driffield.	Thingoe.	Melton Mowbray.	Pewsey.	
	Easingwold.	Uttoxeter	North Witchford.	Stratford.	
	Glendale.	Wetherby.	St. Neots.	Wigton.	
	Hollingbourn.	Woburn.	Southwell.		
	Langport.				

122. The situation of the men's homes, and the distance that they have to walk is an important element for consideration in connection with hours of work. If the journey is done in the men's time it may account for the shorter hours in some districts. Mr. Bear speaks of Woburn and St. Neots as districts where the cottages are not conveniently situated, and the men have considerable distances to walk to their work; while in Thakeham and Basingstoke they are distributed on the farms, and the men are close to their work, thus— Distance of homes from work. Bear, A. 10.

"A great contrast is offered in the Thakeham Union as compared with the St. Neots or the Woburn districts. Instead of being nearly all crowded into villages, the labourers, to a very B. II. 29.

considerable extent, live in cottages on farms, which are usually the best of the cottages, the cheapest and the best supplied with gardens. The consequence is that comparatively few men have a long distance to walk to their work."

And he speaks in very similar terms with regard to Basingstoke.

Now in Thakeham the hours are 10, in Basingstoke 11, in St. Neots 11½ and Woburn 12.

In his Report on Woburn Mr. Bear states that in some parishes where the men have to walk a long distance they are allowed to leave at 5.30 p.m. We may perhaps conclude then that the men make their journey home in the master's time.

Mr. Chapman mentions Truro and North Witchford as districts where men walk long distances to work.

Mr. Richards reports as to Monmouth that—

"unless by the merest accident, cottages are very inconveniently situated. It is quite an accident if a labourer has a cottage convenient to his work. Labourers have to walk all distances from one to five miles to their work."

Mr. Wilkinson says:—

"If there is a general rule for the hours of beginning and ending work in a district, there are many exceptions to it in various parishes or on various farms, and occupiers of adjoining farms frequently differ in the extent to which the passage to and from work is allowed to be done in their (the employers') time. I think it is most usual to require men to stay at work till the nominal hour for the work to close, but that farmers are generally pretty easy in the mornings and are content if the men leave home at the stated hour and come straight to their work. At the same time so many farmers allow the time taken in getting both to and from work to be reckoned as part of the day's work that I have not counted that time in the table below. The men to suffer most are those who live in some of the open villages among the Wolds and work on outlying farms in the same or adjoining parishes."

On the other hand Mr. Richards has, in stating the hours for some districts, added one hour to the nominal working hours on account of time spent in "walking to and from work." It seems necessary to draw attention to this difference in the method adopted by different persons in estimating the hours of work.

In Glendale where the regular labourers are all housed on the farms, the limits of time are from 6 a.m. to 6 p.m., which is considerably longer than in many other districts, but, as will be seen, when meal hours are deducted the hours of work are really shorter than in most places.

123. The ordinary meal hours and those almost universally allowed are one hour for dinner and half an hour for luncheon or second breakfast; but if the situation of the men's homes is such that they can go there for dinner they are expected to perform the journey to and from home in the hour allowed. In Glendale, however, an interval of two and half hours is allowed (from 11.30 a.m. to 2 p.m.) for absence from work for dinner and rest, and a quarter of an hour for luncheon. Work is continued in the field wherever it may be until 6 p.m. The nominal 12 hours is thus reduced to about 9¼ or 9½ hours.

Any statement of hours worked must, however, be considered as approximate only. The variations, even in the same parish, are so considerable, and it must be said the labourers' consciences are so elastic, that any statement as to fixed hours must be regarded rather as the maximum than the mean time. When it is remembered that much of the work is so scattered that the going and coming of the men cannot always be checked, and that no master or foreman can be in several places at once, it is not much to say that the total hours are often stretched and that the labourer's timekeeper is a little slow in the morning and rather fast in the evening.

124. The result of a comparison of the estimates of Assistant Commissioners of the working hours in different districts is shown by the following statement, in which the mean quantity is taken wherever there are more estimates than one.

STATEMENT showing approximately the HOURS of ACTUAL WORK in the several DISTRICTS of INQUIRY in the case of an ORDINARY LABOURER in SPRING, SUMMER, and AUTUMN, and exclusive of HAYTIME, HARVEST, or WINTER.

Table 54.

1. 11 hours and upwards.	Hrs.	2. 10 to 11 hours.	Hrs.		Hrs.	3. 9 to 10 hours.	Hrs.	4. Less than 9 hours.	Hrs.
Monmouth	12	Atcham	10½	Brixworth	10	Basingstoke	9½	Thame	8½
		Buntingford	10½	Cirencester	10	Crediton	9½	Wantage	8½
*Bromyard	11½	Dorchester	10½	Langport	10	Holbeach	9½		
Nantwich	11½	Easingwold	10½	Louth	10	Maldon	9½		
		Garstang	10½	Melton Mowbray	10	Pewsey	9½		
Selby	11	Godstone	10½	North Witchford	10	Stratford-on-Avon	9½		
		Hollingbourn	10½	Pershore	10				
		Thingoe	10½	St. Neots	10	Glendale	9¼		
		Wigton	10½	Southwell	10				
		Woburn	10½	Swaffham	10	Thakeham	9		
						Truro	9		
		Driffield	10¼						
		Uttoxeter	10¼						
		Wetherby	10¼						

* This includes one hour for walking to and from work, in addition to full hours on the farm, and is must be regarded as an extreme case.

125. The hours given in this table apply only to the spring, summer, and autumn. During the winter months, or from 12 to 14 weeks from the early part of November to the last week in February, the hours of attendance are shortened in the morning and evening, except in a few instances where barn work is carried on by lamplight, but as the usual hours are generally at that season during daylight there is less difference between the hours of different districts in winter than in the summer time. Hours in winter shortened.

126. During hay and harvest, a very varying period, work is much prolonged in the evening, but several breaks are made in the course of the day, even by men who are paid entirely by piece work. Hay and harvest.

If it be assumed that the long hours of hay and harvest balance the short hours of winter, and that the hours given in the preceding table are applicable to about the same number of workers, then the average working day would be 10 hours; but, for the reasons already given, this must be regarded as a maximum estimate. Indeed, it would not be difficult to show that some estimates are extreme, since they assume that every labourer has an hour's walk going to and returning from his work.

It is not to be assumed that the 10 hours' work, which is said to be the average time during which the agricultural labourer is employed, is all of it of a severely laborious character, though no doubt it would be such to anyone unaccustomed to it, but inasmuch as a man will readily accomplish from 25 to 33 per cent. more work when paid by the piece than he does when paid by the day, that he will complete his task in eight hours and go to work on his allotment afterwards, it is clear that he has a considerable reserve of force, and that his ordinary work does not exhaust his energies. It may be mentioned here that in many parts of the country men are not induced by piece work to spend longer hours, but that, on the contrary, they shorten the day by one, two, or three hours, except during hay and harvest. Chapman, B. III. 55.

127. If there is some difficulty in fixing even approximately the hours of an ordinary labourer, that difficulty is much increased in the case of men who have the charge of stock. Hours of stock men.

With regard to carters, waggoners, and others who have the care and working of horses, the hours vary in the same district and parish to a great extent. One farmer requires the horsemen to return to the stables after supper to rack up the horses; another divides this work among several men who take it in turn; a third turns out the horses into an open yard, and thus dispenses with the late attendance of men. In some districts men are expected to begin feeding their horses at 4 a.m., while in others they begin at 5.30 a.m.; very much depends upon the number of horses which a man Carters, &c.

has to see after. The following examples will exhibit the variety which exists. Mr. Richards in his Report on Bromyard (Hereford) gives as the extreme—

Waggoners and cowmen, 5 a.m. to 8 p.m. - -	15 hours.
Walking to and from work, one hour - - -	1 „
Total - -	16 „
Deduct meals -	1½ „
Leaving as working hours - - - -	14½ „

but he adds—

"It will very seldom happen that any cowmen or waggoner will have to walk any distance to his work, so that probably 13½ will represent the extreme of his employment."

It is, however, extremely improbable that these men work from 5 a.m. to 8 p.m. with only 1½ hours out for meals. The farmers' statement on this point was that the waggoners' hours were from 5.30 a.m. to 6.30 p.m. in summer, and from 6 or 6.30 a.m. in winter to 6.30 p.m. The mean between the statements of the men and those of the masters would give 12¾ hours in summer and 11¾ in winter.

Writing of Dorchester district, Mr. Spencer says—

"A carter has to come to the stable at 4 a.m. or 5 a.m., that is, about two hours before the teams go out, which is 6 a.m. in summer, and 7 a.m. in winter. They come in from the fields at 2 p.m. The carters are then employed for two or three hours in the stable with the horses, having done that they go home, but have to return about 7 p.m. to rack up for the night."

And he estimates the hours of labour at 11 or 11½ hours in summer, and rather less in winter.

The same gentleman describes at length the work of the waggoner and the waggoner's mate in Kent, thus—

"A waggoner and his mate, usually a young man of 17 or 18 years old, have charge of a team of four horses. The waggoner comes to the stables about 4 a.m. to get his horses ready for the day's work. At about 5.30 he gets his breakfast, and is ready by 6 a.m. to go out with the team to plough. He returns from the field at 2 p.m., has his dinner, and after dinner would have about three hours' work in the stable, and get home at 6 p.m., when his day's work is finished. The mate comes at 6 a.m. to go out with the waggoner to plough; he has his dinner on his return from the field, and works afterwards just as the waggoner does, but has in addition to return to the stable for an hour or so about 7.30 p.m. to rack up his horses for the night."

The estimated hours of work after deductions for meal-times are 12 hours for summer, and rather less in winter.

In Glendale the hours of labour of the hinds are rather shorter than elsewhere, because of a long break in the middle of the day; and also because each man has only two horses to feed and groom.

The hind and his team either leave the homestead at 6 a.m., or in some districts are in the field at that time: and they finally leave the field at 6 p.m., but they have had a break of two or three hours in the middle of the day. They have to attend their horses before and after the field work, so that their day extends over at least 14 hours, their actual working hours are estimated by Mr. Fox at 9 to 10½ hours in summer, and 7½ to 9½ hours in winter, but it is rather difficult to make this estimate accord with that of the Glendale Report previously referred to, which would seem to give some 12 hours of actual labour.

Mr. Wilkinson gives the total hours of work in summer as varying from 11½ to 12 hours in Wetherby, to 12½ to 13 in Louth and Driffield, with about an hour less in winter.

In his Driffield Report he gives a description of the horseman's hours and duties on a large and well known farm, a description which he says—

"Will hold good pretty generally, except that often a lad has only two horses to attend to. Each lad looks after three horses. He rises in the summer about 4.30 a.m., does his horses and gives them corn and water, and generally employs himself in the stables till 5.40 a.m., he then comes in to breakfast, and goes out to work at 6 a.m.

"He comes in with his horses at 12 for dinner, returning to work at 1 p.m., continuing at work till 6 p.m., when he brings the horses back to the stable and does them up, and comes in to the house for supper at 6.45 p.m.

"At 8 p.m., or a little before, returns to the stable and fodders up for the night. In winter he gets up about half-past five. Breakfast then is at half-past six.

"It will be seen that this is very far from the 16 hours, or, with the hour allowed for dinner, the 15 hours at which the horseman's day is often estimated. Still the hours are long, even if the physical work in the extra hours is not severe, and leave a lad little time to himself."

In many districts the horses are turned out to grass for the night in the summer months, and the horse-keeper's work ends nearly as soon as that of the ordinary labourer's.

Taking the several statements of the six Assistant Commissioners as to the different districts, and striking an average, the actual hours of work would fall a little short of 11½ hours. It must be remembered that these hours, though long, are not all of them spent in arduous labour. The stable work on most farms does not occupy one half of the time spent in attendance there, and much time is loitered away in the fields, as anyone who travels through the country with his eyes open must observe.

Ploughman's day's work.

128. A ploughman who has taken his team half a mile to the field, ploughed an acre of land there, and returned to the stable, will have travelled 12 miles. To accomplish this task he will occupy from 8 to 8½ hours. If half an hour be allowed for his meal and one minute be supposed to be lost by each turn at the furrow's end, two hours may be deducted from the 8 hours, and the horses will have travelled at the rate of 2 miles an hour.

Cowmen, &c.

Cowmen and stockmen have rather shorter hours than horsemen in all districts except those where a considerable number of cows are milked. Wherever milk is sent away the milking has to be done at an early hour, and where cheese is made, the day is often prolonged until 7.30 or 8 p.m.

Wilkinson, B V. 16.

Mr. Wilkinson reports that in Uttoxeter the milking in summer begins at 5.0 a.m. and is not deferred much beyond 5.30 in winter. The evening milking is often completed by 5 p.m. in winter, but goes on in summer till nearly 6.

Richards, B VI. 11. B V. 16.

Mr. Richards gives 5.0 a.m. to 7.30 or 8.0 p.m. as the hours of cowmen in Nantwich and Bromyard.

Spencer, A. 16.

In the districts reported on by Mr. Spencer the actual working hours of stockmen are said to range from 9¾ hours in Maldon to 11 hours in Pewsey.

Fox, A., App. I. A. 19.

Mr. Wilson Fox gives the summer hours of cattlemen as 11¼ in Thingoe, 11 in Swaffham, 10½ to 11½ in Garstang and Wigton; and he observes that in the last-named districts, where the masters and men are frequently on terms of social equality, the longer working hours prevail.

In many places the hours of cattlemen do not exceed those of ordinary labourers, and they are not unfrequently men who are past the prime of life, or men who are less capable of severe work than others.

Shepherds, as has been stated previously, have no very regular hours. During the lambing season they are on duty, as it were, night and day, and during the summer they should be about both early and late, but they enjoy a good deal of leisure and many easy days.

Sunday work.

129. It is only the men who have charge of stock who have work to do on Sundays, and the proportionate number of these men and the extent of their work will vary according to the quantity of live stock and the manner in which those stock are treated. Naturally the amount of employment is almost everywhere greatest in the winter, when the cattle are in the yards and sheep are, many of them, having roots cut for them.

In the milking districts the work is necessarily heavy. Whatever preparation has been made previously as regards food, the operation of milking must be performed. Accordingly we find that in Belper, Uttoxeter, Nantwich, and Melton Mowbray, from 75 per cent. and upwards of the labourers are said to have more or less of Sunday work. In Basingstoke, Godstone, Maldon, and Stratford, about half are said to be engaged. In St. Neots and Thakeham from one-fifth to a quarter are said to have work on that day. (*See* Analytical Index).*

The hours during which the men are engaged vary from two-and-a-half hours to the whole day.

Chapman, B VI 44.

In Atcham, for instance, it is said that "The Sunday work for cowmen is very "severe, being practically the same as on week days. It is the same almost for "stockmen as for milkers."

Spencer, B VI 61. B II 11.

In Peraboro, Mr. Spencer notes that stockmen work from four hours to a whole day. On the other hand, he says that in Pewsey horsemen have two to three hours, cowmen four hours' work. On larger farms, where a number of men are employed, the men share the work, and either shorten the hours of all or take turns at the work, and so set some of their mates at liberty every Sunday. On small farms a good deal of the Sunday work is done by the farmers themselves. On those a little above that

* Vol. I., Part VII.

grade the Sunday work is generally the heaviest, as the number of men among whom it can be distributed is limited. Except in the milking districts the Sunday work in summer is very insignificant in amount.

Women employed in agriculture.

130. One very marked feature distinguishing the present inquiry from any of the previous investigations of a similar character is the lessened employment of women in farm-work. In 1871 in England and Wales the female agricultural labourers and farm servants (indoor) were 5·8 per cent. of the total wage earners. In 1881 the female agricultural labourers were 4·53 per cent. In 1891 they had declined to 3·08 per cent. If it be granted that the numbers for 1871 and 1881 are not strictly comparable, those for 1881 and 1891 deal with precisely the same class, and in that decade the actual numbers for England and Wales declined from 40,345 to 24,150, or at the rate of 40 per cent. If England be taken alone, the numbers have decreased from 35,576 to 21,270, or at the rate of 40 per cent, the ratio to the total number being in England taken alone only 2·82 per cent.

In the registration districts of the northern counties,* where women are most employed, they declined in 10 years, 1881 to 1891, from 5,795 to 4,184, or at the rate of 27·8 per cent.

They were, in those counties, in 1881, 16·6 per cent. and in 1891 only 13·6 per cent. of the wage earners in agriculture.

In the county of Northumberland females were 25·2 per cent. of the wage earners in 1871, and in exactly the same proportion to the total number in 1881. In 1891 they still remained 24·1 per cent. of the class, and 28·3 per cent. of the agricultural labourers.

Percentage of age of females employed.

131. It is a little remarkable that there are now a larger proportionate number of females under the age of 15 years employed as agricultural labourers than there were formerly.

The percentage of those of different ages at the two Census periods is shown by the following comparative statement:—

Table 15.

—	1881.	1891.
Females under 15	5·09	8·95
15 and under 20	22·08	19·59
Total under 20	27·17	28·54
20 and upwards	72·83	71·46
	100·	100·

Thus it will be seen that while the proportion of adult females is larger than it was, the proportion of young girls is also greater, while the girls between 15 and 20 years of age have decreased to the greatest extent.

Observations of Assistant Commissioners on the subject.

132. On the subject of employment of women, the following observations by Assistant Commissioners may be quoted.

Mr. Bear says:—

Bear, A. 6.

"In only two of my districts, Basingstoke and St. Neots, are women commonly employed on the land. In the rest, a few of them do a little work in haytime, and help their husbands at piecework in harvest, but otherwise are rarely seen in the fields, or even in the allotments."

And in his district Report on Basingstoke he notes that:—

Bear, B. IV. 18.

"Women work in the fields to a considerable extent in the district, picking stones off the fields, weeding and doing work in the hay-field."

And as to St. Neots he says:—

Bear, B. III. 14.

"There are a good many regular workers in market gardens among the women, while a few women work on farms more or less."

Mr. Chapman writes thus:—

Chapman, A. 15.

"As to women for agricultural purposes they are extremely scarce, and except in Cambridgeshire and Berkshire very rarely employed, an evidence of improvement in the labourer's condition. The only work which women care to do in the fields now is haymaking and harvest, and even that they are not always willing to undertake."

* Cumberland, Durham, Northumberland, and Westmorland.

As to the Cambridgeshire district, North Witchford, which he visited, he says:—

"It is more difficult than it used to be to get women to work on a farm, as married women are giving it up and the bigger girls more frequently go into service, but the gang system still prevails." Chapman, B. III. 51

He describes these gangs as consisting of 15 or 20 girls and women and as—

"going from farm to farm, commencing work usually in March or April and continuing till December. They are employed to set potatoes, to hoe and weed corn, and at singling roots and hay-making; they are disbanded for harvest and afterwards begin picking and forking couch and rubbish on the stubbles, spreading manure and picking up potatoes and mangolds." Chapman, B. III. 52

Mr. Wilson Fox reports thus—

"In the Thingoe Union, Suffolk, and the Garstang Union, Lancashire, women are very rarely employed at field work, and in the Wigton Union, Cumberland, only to a limited extent, but in the Glendale Union, Northumberland, universally. In the latter union nearly all the unmarried women are regularly employed and on many of the farms, there are as many women working as men.* This custom has existed ever since the district has been under cultivation, and has proved most beneficial to the agricultural community, as it has been the means of bringing to each house the earnings of several workers instead of only one. To landlords and farmers it has also proved an advantage, to the former because the system of hiring families entails a smaller supply of cottages, to the latter because labour, almost as efficient as that of a man, is thereby obtained at a far cheaper rate. As married women do not work no question arises as to their over straining themselves when not physically fit, while the young children have the advantage of their mother's care at home, and the husband has the comfort of a tidy house and properly cooked meals. Fox, A. 12.

"Further, the women who do work make it their business from girlhood. Certainly the splendid health and cheerful spirits of the women in Glendale bear a very practical testimony to the beneficent results of an active outdoor life when combined with good feeding at home.

"A very different state of things exists in Norfolk. In that county young girls are not trained in the same way, for many only work at odd intervals. Sometimes a wife but little accustomed to it will go out into the fields, insufficiently fed, in the most unsuitable clothes and boots, to add something to the earnings of the family, if a large one, or during the illness of the husband. In such a case, the children, the household duties, and the husband's comfort are neglected, the woman's strength is exhausted, and in time she becomes prematurely old. There is no doubt that both in the northern and eastern counties women are less inclined to work than formerly.

"The labourers, with the exception of those in Glendale, are averse to the employment of women.

"Under these circumstances it looks as if the employment of women in agriculture is, at no distant date, likely to become a thing of the past."

In his Glendale Report, Mr. Fox says that hinds with daughters able to work are greatly in demand at the yearly hirings, and he thus describes the system of engagement— Fox, B. III. 8.

"Women, with the exception of cottars,† and sometimes byrewomen,‡ are not engaged directly by the farmer, but in reality by the hind, who agrees with his employer to provide so many women workers. For all practical purposes their engagement is a yearly one, as they agree to work on the farm as long as the engagement continues. The women make their own arrangements with the hinds, but as they are nearly always their daughters, probably no arrangement is made. The employers agree to pay the men so much a day for the women's work." Fox, B. III. 21.

133. The old bondage system, which was one of hiring by the hinds of women whom they boarded and to whom they paid a money wage not dependent upon the number of days worked, is said to be extinct, but the condition of finding a woman worker is one which is universal in Glendale in the engagement of hinds. In this district girls begin to work on the farm at from 10 to 13 years of age. The amount of work performed by some of these women is remarkable. Mr. Fox mentions one case of a byrewoman who attended 42 feeding cattle, as many stirk (1 store) ones, five cows, six calves, 20 pigs, and the poultry. Bondage system extinct, [illegible] B. III. 22. Amount of work performed by women in Northumberland. B. III. [illegible] note to par. 10.

134. With respect to Swaffham, Mr. Fox says:—

"Women are very generally employed in many of the parishes, and their employment usually consists in pulling and cleaning roots, stone picking, weeding corn, singling turnips, and raking after the waggons in hay and harvest times. Some of them work in gangs, which are chiefly composed of girls and widows." Nature of work in other districts. Fox, A. II. [illegible]

Mr. Richards reports:

"Where there is most arable land there is also the largest employment of women. This is found most in Stratford-on-Avon, Ibsworth, Cirencester, and Monmouth. In Bromyard such employment prevails in hop-picking season." Richards, A. 14.

And he speaks of an influx of women and children from the Black Country at that season.

In Nantwich—save for milking—and Belper he found little or no employment of female labour, and he expresses the opinion that elsewhere such employment is rapidly decreasing.

Spencer, A 17.

Mr. Spencer says:

"Women are occasionally employed at farm work in Dorset, Wilts, Worcestershire, and Surrey, and but rarely in Somerset.

"In Kent they work a good deal at fruit-picking, hop-tying, and hop-picking, but very little at the heavy kinds of farm work. In Essex they have considerable employment at pea-picking. In all districts it was said that except at such light work as pea and hop picking women work now much less than they used to do.

"The reason for this appears undoubtedly to be that the labourer is better off than previously, and can now afford to do without the extra earnings of his wife at hard field work."

Mr. Wilkinson observes that:—

Wilkinson, A 94.

"In all the districts except Holbeach there is a great decrease in the number of women who do field work. Harvest is the only form of work which is generally taken by them. . . . In Holbeach a very great number are employed in connection with potato growing, the setting, weeding, and lifting giving employment for several months in the year. Whilst the potato industry lasts they are not likely to drop what is such lucrative work for them.

"In Easingwold also, where considerable quantities of potatoes are grown, several women are to be seen in the fields at potato planting time. They are considered handier than men at that work.

"It is pretty generally conceded that the principal reason why fewer women take field work now than formerly is that their circumstances have improved, so that there is no longer the necessity."

Decrease conceded that as consequence of improved circumstances.

135. It will be seen from the foregoing extracts, that the testimony of all the Assistant Commissioners is uniformly to the effect that there has been a great decrease in female employment, which is nowhere considerable, except in Glendale, and in those districts where certain crops for which they have a special aptitude are largely grown; and further, that all are agreed as to this decrease being a consequence of improved circumstances of the labourers.

Hours of work by women. Fox, B III. App. B 1.

136. The hours of work for women in many instances are not stated. The longest hours are those of Glendale, where they leave home at 6 a.m., and cease work in the field at 6 p.m., but, as in the case of the men, the severity of the work is much lightened by a long interval of 1½ hours or 2 hours in the middle of the day. As they are all living on the farms, this gives them time to return to their homes for a hot midday meal.

Chapman, B 13.

The shortest hours are those in Wantage district, where they extend only from 8 in the morning to 4.30 in the afternoon, with an hour off for dinner.

The hours in many districts are from 8 to 5, in some instances extended to 5.30, or from 8 to 8½ hours labour.

In the hop and fruit districts, where much of the work is done by the piece, the hours are irregular, and they often work for a part of the day.

Boys working in agriculture.

137. The effect of the Education Acts has, of course, been to diminish the employment of young boys. In a Memorandum upon the Report of the Royal Commission on the Employment of Children, &c., in Agriculture,* 1867, which I have prepared for this Commission, I have drawn attention to the very early age at which boys were set to work on farms in many parts of the country, it being at that date a not uncommon thing to find children of six, seven, and eight years of age regularly at work.

In the Census Returns for 1871, 10·45 per cent. of the male wage earners in agriculture were under 15 years of age, and in 1881 only 8·0 per cent. were under that age.

Since the latter period the proportionate number of those under 15 has slightly increased, it being then 8·47 per cent., while those of the age of 15 and under 20 years are now 18·76 per cent. against 18·42 per cent. in 1881.

I have already recorded some complaints in various quarters as to a scarcity in the supply of boys, particularly in Woburn and St. Neots districts.

Difficulty in obtaining boys as indoor servants. Chapman, A 48. B VII. 26. See Desb. Final Report, 9, 11, 136, II. 44.

138. Mr Chapman speaks of the increased difficulty in getting them, if they are wanted to live in the farm house; they dislike the confinement and control which accompany such service.

They appear very generally to be taken on to work at the age of 12 or 13, and farmers complain that this is not early enough for them to begin to learn their business, while much work that would be too expensive if done by them is left undone because there are no boys available for it, but these complaints are certainly less loud and less general than they were at the time of the inquiry under the Richmond Commission.

* App., Vol. V., Part II., sec. I., A.

139. In North Witchford and Swaffham districts the Assistant Commissioner notes the existence of gangs of boys as well as those of females, and Mr. Fox gives in an appendix some interesting evidence of one who had been in such a gang, and also the evidence of a gang-master. Gangs. Lo-C. Final Report, p. 35. Chapman, B. III. 22 Fox, B. II.

140. In the appendix to his Report on Glendale, Mr. Fox prints a communication received from Mr. Cleghorn, of Millfield, Wooler, which gives a graphic description of the different grades through which a farm lad passes in his progress towards manhood and the position of a full hind. Mr. Cleghorn says:— A boy's progressive stages.

"Generally speaking, at about 11 or 12 years of age a boy is set on to work. For a year or two he does any odd jobs to which he may be put, such as herding crows from off potatoes, &c., thinning turnips, and so on, and for this he is paid at the rate of about 8d. or 10d. a day. Fox, B. III, App. C. 4.

"At about 14 he rises a step by getting the 'odd' horse and cart, and does all the small carting work about the farm. From 7s. to 8s. a week is what he earns in that capacity. In another year or two he may be given the charge of a pair of old horses still to do carting work. Gradually he is taken from step to step from doing merely carting work to sowing turnips and to ploughing.

"At about 18 years of age he is usually considered fit to take full charge of a pair of horses and to do full hind's work except, perhaps, such work as making turnip drills [ridges].

"In another year or so he is a 'full man.'"

141. The hours during which boys work are generally those of the ordinary labourer, or where, as is often the case, they are helpers in the stable or waggoners' mates, they work pretty much the same hours as the horsemen. Where they work in gangs, their hours are rather shorter, unless the work lies, as is frequently the case, at a distance from home. Hours of work for boys.

3. Wages and Earnings.

142. The subject next to be considered is one of the most important, and certainly not the least difficult to deal with, in the whole range of inquiry. What are the earnings actual and possible of the different classes of workers in agriculture, and what is the rate of the payment received by them, are questions which have been most minutely investigated by my colleagues, and they are copiously illustrated in their Reports. It will be seen on examination that there is a wide range of variety, not only by comparison of one district with another, but that within the same district, and oftentimes within the same parish, there will be found variations in the current rate of wages, and in other matters which go to make up the sum of a man's earnings, which render it exceedingly difficult for the most painstaking inquirer to estimate even approximately the average results. Wages and earnings. Wide variety.

In the Notes for Inquiry which were placed in the hands of the Assistant Commissioners investigation on the subject of Wages and Earnings was suggested under the following subheads:—

(a.) Current rate of weekly wages.
(b.) Opportunities of adding to wages by piece-work, &c.
(c.) Additions to wages by perquisites, allowances, and payments in kind.
(d.) Supplementary earnings.
(e.) Estimated annual earnings of different classes of labourers.

I shall proceed to summarise the information collected under these sub-divisions of the subject.

and indeed in some places they preserve an exact ratio to this rate, hired stockmen being paid one or two shillings a week more than the ordinary labourer's weekly wage.

Weekly wages used in former times to rise or fall with the price of wheat and bread, but of late years the rate has had no relation to the value of commodities. It is governed by the law of supply and demand, though it is often difficult to trace the connection between these two factors.

Theoretically, the farmer buys his labour as cheaply as he can; practically he is influenced by other considerations, even by the desire to give a "living wage," and an inveterate and instinctive objection to change—a disposition to keep the same men and to pay them at the same rate; to "give and take" is more characteristic of the farmer than to take advantage of every turn in the labour market.

144. It is not unnatural—it is certainly very common—to suppose that the rate of wages in different districts and different parts of the country supplies a standard by which the earnings of the labourers may be measured and compared.

A more fallacious idea could not be entertained. In some places the weekly rate is unvarying throughout the year, and with a very slight addition represents the whole earnings of the labourer. In others, it is the minimum sum paid to the least skilled labourers, engaged in the lightest work, during the time when work is least pressing. In many districts it varies with the seasons, and is augmented at different periods of the year.

145. It seems necessary at the outset of the inquiry into this subject to emphasise the distinction between *wages* and *earnings*. It will be conceded that a high rate of pay combined with irregular employment may yield smaller earnings to the worker than would be obtained by constant work at a lower rate, and that a uniform weekly payment throughout the year may be better for the labourer than payment by results (*i.e.*, by piece-work).

On the other hand a low rate of wages, regarded as a retaining fee and ensuring a man constant employment, with the opportunity, if he chooses, of adding very considerably to those wages by piece-work, may place the labourer in as good a position as that of one who is apparently receiving higher wages.

146. But whether the wages of different districts of inquiry are indicative of the earnings of the labourers or not, it is necessary that the results of the inquiry should be set out as clearly and as accurately as possible.

The Assistant Commissioners give in their district Reports details on the subject, and as a rule in their final Reports they sum up their conclusions on this point.

In the following table I have as far as possible adopted the conclusions of the Assistant Commissioners. Where a definite sum is stated I have not altered it, but where two or more rates are given I have taken the mean of the two extremes as the rate for the district.

I am aware that this method is open to criticism, but it nevertheless seems the only available course. The average which is stated at the foot of the Table is, of course, subject to any errors which may have been made in the original estimates, but it is probably a nearer approximation to the absolute truth than some of the data upon which it is founded.

No.	District.	Range as stated in Farm Report.					Estimation of A.C., or Mean.		Reference to Reports.
		s.	d.	to	s.	d.	s.	d.	
18	Louth (*Lincs*)			—			15	0	Wilkinson; A. 36.
19	Maldon (*Essex*)	11	0	to	12	0	11	6	Spencer; A. 22
20	Melton Mowbray (*Leicester*)	13	6		15	0	14	0	Bear; A. 2.
21	Monmouth (*Mon.*)	13	0		13	0	13	6	Richards; B. IV. 24
22	Nantwich (*Cheshire*)	12	0		18	0	15	0	Richards; B. VI. 15
23	North Witchford (*Cambs*)			—			12	0	Chapman; A. 71
24	Pershore (*Worcester*)	11	0	to	13	0	12	0	Spencer; A. 28
25	Pewsey (*Wilts*)			—			10	0	Spencer; A. 65
26	St. Neots (*Hunts and Beds*)	13	0	to	13	0	13	0	Bear; A. 2.
27	Southwell (*Notts*)			—			15	0	Bear; A. 5
28	Stratford-on-Avon (*Warwick*)	11	0	to	13	0	11	6	Richards; B. I. 19
29	Swaffham (*Norfolk*)			—			12	0	Fox; A. App. 2
30	Thakeham (*Sussex*)	11	0	to	13	0	12	0	Bear; A. 5.
31	Thame (*Oxon and Bucks*)	11	0		13	0	12	0	Chapman; A. 71
32	Thingoe (*Suffolk*)			—			11	0	Fox; A. App. 2
33	Truro (*Cornwall*)	13	0	to	15	0	14	0	Chapman; A. 71
34	Uttoxeter (*Stafford and Derby*)	15	0		17	0	16	0	Wilkinson; A. 29
35	Wantage (*Berks*)	10	0		13	0	11	0	Chapman; A. 71
36	Wetherby (*Yorks, W.R.*)	15	0		17	0	16	0	Wilkinson; A. 39
37	Wigton (*Cumberland*)			—			18	0	Fox; A. App. 3
38	Woburn (*Beds*)			—			12	0	Bear; A. 8

Average of 38 Districts.—13s. 5d.

148. It will be seen from this table that the rate of weekly wages current at the date of the inquiry ranged from 18s. in Garstang and Wigton to 10s. in Dorchester and Pewsey. The average of the 38 separate estimates is 13s. 5d. a week. Range of wages and average rate.

149. The geographical position of the districts having comparatively high and low rates is shown by the following table, in which the districts are arranged in agricultural divisions* and classed in order from the highest to the lowest rate. Distribution of high and low rates.

RATE OF WEEKLY WAGES.

DISTRICTS classified and arranged in the several AGRICULTURAL DIVISIONS of ENGLAND, in order from highest to lowest mean rate, 1892-3. Classification of districts in respect of weekly wages.

1st class, 16s. and upwards; 2nd class, 14s. and under 16s.; 3rd class, 12s. and under 14s.; 4th class, under 12s.

Table 37.

Rate.	I. N. and N.E. Counties.	II. S.E. and E.C. Counties.	III. W.C. and S.W. Counties.	IV. N., N.W., and N.C. Counties.
	1st Class.—16s. and upwards.			
s. d.				
18 0				Garstang, Wigton } 18s.
17 6	—	—	—	
17 0				Glendale, 17s.
16 6	—	—	—	
16 0				Belper, Uttoxeter, Wetherby } 16s.

12 4				[illegible], 12s. 4d.	—
12 0	[illegible], 12s.	—			—
12 4				[illegible], 12s. 4d.	—
12 0	North [illegible], [illegible], [illegible], [illegible] } 12s.	[illegible], Thame } 12s.		[illegible], 12s.	—
		4th Class.—Under 12s.			
11 6	Hungerford, Maldon } 11s. 6d.	[illegible], [illegible] } 11s. 6d.		—	—
11 0		Wantage, 11s.		[illegible], Langport } 11s.	—
10 6				[illegible], 10s. 6d.	—
10 0				[illegible], Pewsey } 10s.	—

150. It will be seen that the five districts in the first class, with wages of 16s. a week and upwards, are all of them in the Northern or North-western division, extending from Northumberland to Derbyshire and Staffordshire, and including districts in Northumberland, Cumberland, Lancashire, Yorks W.R., Stafford, and Derby. Of these five districts Glendale and Wigton are districts where the greater part of the work is done by hired servants living in the farmhouse, and the daymen or "darrickers," as they are called, are odd men called in on a press of work and working long hours. In Glendale, which stands third on the list, there are no ordinary labourers, the wages put down are those paid to "spadesmen"—experts with tools, who are generally paid wages in excess of the ordinary weekly sum throughout the country. In Belper mines and other industries compete severely with agriculture, and both there and in Nantwich most of the ordinary labourers share the long hours of milkmen and stockmen.

Thus the only district in the first class where the ordinary labourer, as the term is generally understood, forms a class is Wetherby, where, as will be shown hereafter, the weekly wages approximate very closely to the total earnings.

In the second class, with a rate of wages between 14s. and 16s., come districts in Yorks, Lincoln, Notts, Chester, Salop, Northampton and Leicester, Kent, Surrey, and Cornwall.

In the third class, with wages from 12s. to 14s., are districts in Norfolk, Suffolk, Cambs, Huntingdon, Bedford, Bucks, Oxon, Worcester, Monmouth, Sussex, and Devon.

In the fourth and lowest class, with weekly wages under 12s. a week, we have districts in Essex and Herts, and in Hereford, Warwick, Gloucester, Berks, Hampshire, Wilts, Dorset, and Somerset.

151. The following summary shows the results of the preceding table:—

Agricultural Divisions of England, with the Number of Districts in each Division, classed according to the Current Rate of Weekly Wages in 1892–3.

Classes in respect of Current Rate of Weekly Wages	I. N. and N.W. Counties.	II. S.E. and E.C. Counties.	III. W.C. and S.W. Counties.	IV. E., S.W., and N.C. Counties.	Total in each Class.
1.—16s. and upwards	—	—	—	6	6
2.—14s. and under 16s.	3	5	3	2	13
3.—12s. " 14s.	5	2	2	—	9
4.—Under 12s.	2	3	5	—	10
Total in each Division	10	10	10	8	38

152. Inasmuch as in all previous inquiries into the condition of the agricultural labourer considerable stress has been laid upon the weekly wage rate, it may be desirable to compare the present rates with those ascertained at other periods.

I have, in two separate papers prepared for the use of the Commission,* given the results of my investigation as to the rates of wages prevailing when the Inquiry by the Royal Commission on the Employment of Children, &c. in Agriculture (1867–1870)

* App. Vol. V., Part II., Sec. [illegible]

and by the Richmond Commission took place (1879–1881), and I have there tabulated the result of those inquiries. Mr. Kebbel, in his book on the Agricultural Labourer,* gives a table partly constructed by himself and partly by Mr. Druce, an Assistant Commissioner under the Richmond Commission, in which table the rates at the two periods are compared. My tables, independently prepared, differ in some cases from those of Mr. Kebbel's book, a circumstance not to be wondered at when the nature of the materials from which these tables are compiled is taken into account.

In constructing the following table, where there was a difference between the two sets of figures, I have taken the mean between Mr. Kebbel's estimate and my own.

153. TABLE showing approximately the RATE of WEEKLY WAGES in the several Districts of Inquiry in 1892–3, and the Rates in the several Counties within which those Districts lie in 1879–81, and in 1867–70. Table 153.

No.	Districts of Inquiry	Rate of Weekly Wages in Districts, 1892–3	Rate of Weekly Wages in Counties in which Districts are situate	
			1879–1881.	1867–1870.
		s. d.	s. d.	s. d.
1	Atcham (*Salop*)	14 0	18 8	10 9
2	Basingstoke (*Hants*)	11 6	13 0	10 9
3	Belper (*Derby*)	16 0	16 6	14 9
4	Brixworth (*Northampton*)	14 0	13 6	13 0
5	Bromyard (*Hereford*)	11 0	11 9	10 0
6	Buntingford (*Herts*)	11 6	13 6	11 0
7	Cirencester (*Gloucester*)	10 6	13 3	10 10
8	Crediton (*Devon*)	13 6	13 0	9 0
9	Dorchester (*Dorset*)	10 0	10 6	9 6
10	Driffield (*Yorks, E.R.*)	16 6	14 0	14 6
11	Easingwold (*Yorks, N.R.*)	15 6	16 6	14 0
12	Garstang (*Lancs*)	18 0	17 6	15 6
13	Glendale (*Northumberland*)	17 0	17 0	16 6
14	Godstone (*Surrey*)	14 0	14 0	13 6
15	Holbeach (*Lincs*)	11 3	13 0	13 6
16	Hollingbourn (*Kent*)	14 6	15 9	13 9
17	Langport (*Somerset*)	11 0	12 6	10 0
18	Louth (*Lincs*)	14 0	15 0	11 8
19	Maldon (*Essex*)	11 6	12 6	11 3
20	Melton Mowbray (*Leicester*)	15 0	13 0	12 6
21	Monmouth (*Mon.*)	13 6	12 0	12 10
22	Nantwich (*Cheshire*)	16 0	15 6	13 6
23	North Witchford (*Cambs*)	12 0	13 6	11 0
24	Pershore (*Worcester*)	13 0	13 0	11 0
25	Pewsey (*Wilts*)	10 0	11 9	10 1
26	St. Neots (*Hunts and Beds*)	13 0	13 6	10 0
27	Southwell (*Notts*)	14 0	14 0	14 6
28	Stratford-on-Avon (*Warwick*)	11 6	14 3	11 8
29	Swaffham (*Norfolk*)	12 0	12 6	11 0
30	Thakeham (*Sussex*)	12 0	13 6	12 7
31	Thame (*Oxon and Bucks*)	12 0	12 9	12 0
32	Thingoe (*Suffolk*)	12 0	12 6	11 0
33	Truro (*Cornwall*)	11 0	13 6	11 0
34	Uttoxeter (*Stafford and Derby*)	16 0	11 6	11 10
35	Wantage (*Berks*)	11 0	13 3	10 6
36	Wetherby (*Yorks, W.R.*)	16 0	15 6	11 10
37	Wigton (*Cumberland*)	18 0	18 0	16 0
38	Woburn (*Beds*)	12 0	12 6	11 0
	Average	13 5	13 9	12 3

154. It must be borne in mind that whereas the figures relating to the rate of weekly wages in 1892–3 are given for particular districts, those for 1879–81 and 1867–70 are given for whole counties, and they are not therefore fairly comparable, since any county average must include some parts where the influence of town employment is felt and increases wages. Lower rates not strictly comparable with county rates of wages.

The districts chosen for the present inquiry are, as has been previously shown, mainly agricultural, and as a rule districts where the wages would naturally be lower than those of the county generally.

Since the wages at any time will vary in a county by as much as 2s. a week, we may disregard those variations which are shown by the preceding table as existing between the rate of wages at

* "The Agricultural Labourer," by T. E. Kebbel. London, 1887.

later period and at that of the Richmond Commission, in those cases where the variation does not exceed 1s. a week.

Instances of apparent decrease of wages.

155. With regard to those districts where a greater difference is observable :—

There are nine districts where the district rate is now lower by more than 1s. than the rate of the county in 1879–81, and four where the rate of the district is more than 1s. in excess of that of the county at the earlier period. Stratford-on-Avon and Cirencester are districts where the discrepancy is most striking.

The foundation for the Warwickshire rate, 1879–81, is Mr. Doyle's Report to the Richmond Commission. In this there are 32 returns, in reply to questions issued by the Assistant Commissioner, in which the wages of the ordinary labourer are put by one or other of the correspondents at 10s., 11s., 12s., 13s., &c., up to 18s., but there is nothing to indicate where the different rates prevailed, and there is every reason to suspect that in many cases the possible earnings of a labourer are meant and not the current rate of wages. Similarly in the case of Cirencester and Gloucestershire, the rate of wages in the county in 1879–81 was variously stated as 11s., 12s., 13s., 14s., and 15s., without any particular district being named. A witness before the Commission from the neighbourhood of Cirencester put the wages at 11s. a week. It may be fairly argued from this, either that the rate of wages in Cirencester was below the county average, or that the wages stated were really estimated earnings.

Richmond Commission, Peile's table.

With regard to other districts it would not be surprising if the rate for the county of Herts was generally higher than in Buntingford, or that of Kent higher than the rate in Hollingbourn, and again in this case the figures are not strictly comparable. In the case of North Witchford (Cambs) I think it is clear that there is an error or misprint in Mr. Kebbel's table. Mr. Druce, the Assistant Commissioner, who reported on Cambs, gives 12s. to 13s. as the wages current at the time, and a witness from the immediate neighbourhood in evidence stated the rate as 12s. I have not taken upon myself to alter any figures in Mr. Kebbel's table, but my own reading of the Report gave Cambs a range of 12s. to 13s., with a mean of 12s. 6d.

Richmond Commission, Druce, p. 12.

Average results compared.

156. For the reasons thus given the foregoing figures as regards particular districts must not be too closely compared. It may, however, be safer to institute a comparison between the average results at the three periods, which are as follows :—

	s.	d.
Current rate of weekly wages calculated on an average of the rates for counties 1867–70	12	3
And for 1879–81	13	9
Average calculated for districts, 1892–3	13	5

It is, I think, absolutely certain that wages advanced between the first and second period much more than 12½ per cent. as these figures would seem to indicate.

It is more than probable that the rate has declined in the last ten years by more than 2½ per cent.

Wages of stockmen and shepherds.

157. The wages of stockmen, shepherds, &c. are generally so much mixed up with allowances that it is scarcely worth while at this stage of the inquiry to attempt any comparison between districts or periods of time. I shall therefore postpone the consideration of them until I have to deal with the earnings of the different classes.

Wages of women.

158. A passing notice may be given to the wages of women, though in most districts they form a very insignificant part (numerically) of the wage-earners in agriculture.

The only district where women may be said to be employed regularly in outdoor work is Glendale, where they are now paid 1s. 6d. a day in summer, 1s. 4d. to 1s. 6d. a day in winter, and 3s. a day for 20 days in harvest.

In Easingwold, Holbeach, and North Witchford, women are largely employed at the seasons for planting and picking potatoes. In the first-named district they are frequently paid 3s. a day, in the second 1s. 6d. to 2s. 6d., and in the third from 1s. 6d. to 2s. when engaged in this work. In North Witchford and Holbeach they are frequently employed in other work during the spring and summer, when they are paid usually 1s. to 1s. 3d. a day.

In Hollingbourn work in the hop and fruit gardens gives a good many women employment, and they earn from 1s. 6d. to 3s. a day, and in Maldon they earn 1s. 4d. to 2s. a day pea picking, or fruit and potato picking, while at other seasons they are paid from 10d. to 1s. 3d. a day. In Bromyard, Pershore, and Godstone the same industries are found to some extent and similar wages are paid.

In Swaffham women are much employed, and the ordinary rate of pay is 1s. per day.

In St. Neots the market gardens find regular work all the year round for a certain number of women, who earn 10s. to 15s. a week in summer.

(b.) Piecework.

159. There are two ways in which the labourer may be paid for his work. One, the ordinary mode, is by time, the other is by the amount of work performed. The latter

method has been long established and generally adopted in respect of work for which the ordinary staff of labourers on the farm does not suffice, and where quick despatch is highly advantageous, as in the case of the cutting and carting of corn in harvest; and at other seasons for work which is easily measured, such as mowing hay, hedging, and ditching; and for skilled work such as sheep shearing; but the system is capable of considerable extension, and in many parts of the country it is largely adopted, not only for work done by manual labour exclusively, but also where the work of horses or other motive power is made use of.

160. The advantages and disadvantages of the system as compared with that of payment by time have been the subject of much discussion for many years past. On the one hand it cannot be denied that payment by the amount of work done secures to the able and industrious labourer a reward superior to that of the idle and incompetent man; while the payment by time too frequently treats good and bad labourers alike, and gives the good labourer just what the average labourer is worth and no more. Again, the knowledge that the pay will be commensurate with the work induces the labourer to put his whole heart into it, and to do as much as he fairly can; and then a man engaged in this kind of work is less tied in respect of his hours of work and meals, and constant supervision and watching are less necessary than in the case of the day man. On the other hand it must be admitted that where work is paid for by the piece there is a temptation, and a disposition on the part of many labourers, to scamp work—to do it carelessly or inefficiently. Another objection which has been raised with regard to piece-work in other occupations is that men are tempted to overtask themselves in their efforts to earn large wages. It is not at all probable that many instances of such over-exertion will be found among the agricultural labourers. Advantages and disadvantages of piece-work.

The system is, of course, open to abuse, but it will not be denied that it is very advantageous where a considerable quantity of work has to be done expeditiously by a scratch team of unequally matched persons.

It is also convenient for all sorts of work where the amount can be measured without difficulty, and the quality of the work can be seen after it is completed. It is very desirable and indeed essential to the success of the system that the price of the work should be settled before it is begun upon, as a matter of bargain, and that the advantages arising from despatch and economy of time should be fairly shared by employers and employed. Where these conditions are observed payment by the piece may be the means of decreasing the cost of labour, increasing the earnings of the labourers, and encouraging among them a spirit of emulation, the lack of which is so generally admitted and deplored.

An examination of the Reports of the Assistant Commissioners will show a very great difference in the extent to which piece-work prevails in different parts of the country.

161. Upon the general policy of putting out work by the piece, Mr. Chapman, in his final Report, says:— Extract from Reports of A. C. Chapman. A. 61.

"It has great advantages where the superintendence is good and the contract is fairly made, as far as possible, before the work is undertaken. In every district men constantly complain of the price, and very often that it is not fixed until the work is over.

"The tendency is for the average workman to dislike piece-work, as it screws him up to the pitch of the best, or tempts him to scamp the work."

In another portion of his Report, Mr. Chapman summarises the conflicting opinions of masters and men on the subject. On the masters' side it is urged that the men do not like it, or care to learn special work; that they scamp the work, make short hours, and that they cannot earn enough to satisfy them. On the other side the complaints are chiefly as to price, and as to outsiders being brought in to do special work. The amount is said to be generally diminishing, and in only two out of his seven districts, North Witchford and Wantage, does he report any considerable amount of piece-work. Chapman, A. 12.

Subsequently he says:—

regularly employed. Curiously enough, Mr. Richards records a complaint made by the labourers in Bromyard to the effect that it was only in the short days of winter that the farmer put out piece-work.

Mr. Wilson Fox, in his Report on Thingoe, says:—

"Many of the best farmers give their men as much piece-work as possible. The men certainly prefer piece-work to day-work."

And again in his Report on Swaffham;

"I cannot understand why farmers do not more generally employ their men at piecework, for I have invariably found, where the system is adopted, that both employers and employed are satisfied with the results, and on farms where men can only earn day wages, they always express their desire to be given the opportunity of taking piece-work. If more farmers could see their way to put out work, I believe that by giving the men an incentive to work harder, they would overcome, in time, that lack of interest in their employment which they complain has become so general of late."

And in his final Report he says:—

"In my Reports on the two eastern counties* I pointed out the value of piece-work to the men, not only from a pecuniary point of view, but as being the means of giving them an incentive to take a greater interest in their work, and I also referred to their preference for it.

"Another advantage of piece-work seems to be that the men are rewarded in proportion to the services they render, and thus the industrious are not kept on the same level as the indolent.

"Throughout my inquiries in Norfolk and Suffolk I heard very little grumbling on the part of the men as to the prices paid by the farmers for piece-work, and they expressed a unanimous opinion in its favour as opposed to day-work.

"If farmers who employ their men exclusively on day wages could see their way to following the example of those who give their men the opportunity of earning extra money by piece-work, they would be conferring a boon upon them which very possibly might not prove to their own disadvantage."

And he quotes the evidence of several farmers to prove that work costs less when put out by the piece than when paid for by the day, while the labourers earn more.

Mr. Wilkinson, in his Summary Report, says:—

"The amount of piece-work varies much in the different districts. It appears to be decreasing everywhere except in Holbeach. The reason usually assigned for its decrease is that the ordinary wages have increased to a point which causes piece-work to add but little to them."

102. The analytical Index to the Reports of the Assistant Commissioners, Vol. I., Part VII., shows the customs of the different districts as to piece-work. These districts may be divided into two classes:—

A. Those in which the system is adopted to a considerable extent.
B. Those where little piece-work is done.

Class A.

Basingstoke (Hants).
Brixworth (Northampton).
Bromyard (Hereford).
Cirencester (Gloucester).
Dorchester (Dorset).
Driffield (Yorks, E.R.)
Easingwold (Yorks, N.R.)
Holbeach (Lincoln).
Hollingbourn (Kent).
Louth (Lincoln).
Maldon (Essex).
North Witchford (Cambs).
Pershore (Worcester).
Pewsey (Wilts).
St. Neots (Hunts and Beds).
Swaffham (Norfolk).
Thakeham (Sussex).
Thame (Oxon and Bucks).
Thingoe (Suffolk).
Wantage (Berks).

20.

Class B.

Atcham (Salop).
Belper (Derby).
Buntingford (Herts).
Crediton (Devon).
Garstang (Lancashire).
Glendale (Northumberland).
Godstone (Surrey).
Langport (Somerset).
Melton Mowbray (Leicester).
Monmouth (Monmouth).
Nantwich (Cheshire).
Southwell (Notts).
Stratford-on-Avon (Warwick).
Truro (Cornwall).
Uttoxeter (Staffs and Derbyshire).
Wetherby (Yorks, W.R.).
Wigton (Cumberland).
Woburn (Beds).

18.

The numbers are thus very nearly equal of those districts which have much and those which have little piece-work.

* Thingoe and Swaffham districts.

163. Before proceeding to notice some of the districts where piece-work is most common, it may be well to inquire what are the general characteristics of those where the system is not in favour.

Of the 18 districts in Class B. only three, Buntingford, Glendale, and Truro, are classed as distinctly arable, seven are pastoral, and nine are mixed pastoral and arable, six of the nine having more pasture than arable land. (See Table 21.)

It is easy to see that pastoral districts afford much less scope for piece-work than arable districts. In them the principal crop is hay and this is not a very suitable crop for the purpose except as regards the mowing, which is now very frequently done by machinery.

Only two of the districts are notable for the cultivation of roots, which are in many districts hoed, singled, and taken up by the acre.

Another point which may be mentioned is that in 10 out of 18 districts in Class B. the weekly wages are 15s. a week and upwards.

Of the three arable districts in this class Truro is only nominally arable, a large portion being kept down in rotation grasses. Glendale is an entirely exceptional district where the universal hiring of the men at uniform wages throughout the year, and the large and continuous employment of women who are resident on the farms, has hitherto absolved the farmers from the necessity of adopting piece-work as the means of pressing on work. Of Buntingford, the remaining district, it may be said that the land is much of it unsuitable to the growth of roots, and that the inhabitants seem to exhibit to a remarkable degree the lethargy and want of enterprise which are generally ascribed to agriculturists as a class.

164. Turning now to the 20 districts where piece-work is prevalent, 11 of the 20 are distinctly arable, and in six others the arable land is in excess of pasture. In 15 districts corn growing, and in 10 districts root growing, are conspicuous. Four out of the five hop-growing districts are also included, and of the 15 districts which have been classed previously as those of sparse population six adopt piece-work. (See Table 21.)

The various descriptions of work which are in some cases put out to contract are given in great detail in the Reports of the Assistant Commissioners.

They include work accessory to cultivation of the land, such as hedging, ditching, walling, draining, claying, in addition to acts of husbandry in connection with particular crops. Thus in one or another of the districts the following processes are paid for by the measure of work done and not by time. *The ploughing (1), sowing (1), hoeing, and weeding of corn and root crops; the harvesting, thatching, threshing, and dressing of corn (2); taking up carting and clamping of roots; and in the case of potatoes, the raising and preparing the crop for market. Hay cutting, making, and carting; manure turning, carting, and spreading; trussing hay and straw for market, and numerous operations in the hop and fruit gardens.

In connexion with animals very little piece-work is done. Sheep shearing, and the winding of the wool, is very generally paid for by "tale," as by the score, and the work has become a special one, done to a great extent by outsiders, and not by the regular labourers of the farm. Dipping sheep and smearing them is frequently paid for by number.

Occasionally a "fogger," a man in charge of a dairy of cows, is paid so much per head for feeding, attending to, and milking them; and he gets such help as he may require from members of his family or others whom he pays.

It must not be assumed that all the different kinds of work described are commonly or very generally paid for by contract; they are simply stated to show how great is the variety of work to which the system is applicable and is made use of.

165. The prices which are given for different contract jobs are stated very fully in the district reports.

The wide range of them would be somewhat remarkable if the work were always the same, but as was pointed out in an earlier portion of the Report, the character of the soil and the crop are varying factors determining the amount of work which can be done by a labourer within a given period of time. For instance, Mr. Wilkinson compares the cost of under-draining, and he shows that it varies in his districts of inquiry from less than 5d. up to 10d. per chain for each foot of depth. It may be assumed that he was speaking of the same series of operations in each case. But the prices given by

* References to the [illegible] descriptions of piece-work. (1) Thingoe, [illegible] (2) North Witchford, [illegible] (3) Thame, Thingoe.

other Assistant Commissioners show a still wider range. Mr. Chapman says that 1s. a perch is paid for tile draining 3 ft. deep, which is at the rate of 1s. 4d. for each foot of depth per chain length. But it should be stated that in some cases the piece-work in draining is confined to digging the drain only, the pipes being laid by a skilled and trusted man; in other cases the prices given may include both operations, as well as filling in the drains after the pipes have been laid.

166. Mr. Wilkinson, who compares the prices for the more common forms of piece-work, states that—

"the differences are but slight having regard to the differences of soil."

Mr. Spencer, after making a similar comparison of the prices in the districts visited by him, comes to the conclusion that they are—

"lower on the whole in Dorsetshire, Wilts, and Somerset, than in the other counties visited" (i.e., Kent, Surrey, Essex, and Worcester),

and he takes for comparison the prices paid for binding corn after the machine, and setting up the shocks, which are, in Langport and Dorchester, 3s. to 5s.; in Pewsey, 3s. 6d. to 5s.; in Pershore, 4s. to 6s. 6d.; in Hollingbourn, Maldon, and Godstone, 4s. 6d. to 7s. per acre. But a mere comparison of prices is not sufficient to determine the point, as the bulk of the crops varies greatly.

167. Mr. Bear, in his Report on the Melton Mowbray district, says—

"the rates of piece-work appear to be no higher as a rule than they are in counties in which, like Sussex or Hampshire, the ordinary weekly wages are lower."

Mr. Chapman reports a form of piece-work as existing in Crediton.

"There are several kinds of work, e.g., ploughing, raking, and harrowing, and spreading dung, at which a man does so much for a day's wage, and when he has finished it he is at liberty to return to his house and work in his own garden."

And in Buntingford he found an employer who—

"allows his ploughmen to earn money for overtime; after they have ploughed an acre in summer and ¾ of an acre in winter. He pays for overtime at the rate of 2s. 6d. an acre for the extra quantity."

168. These two examples exhibit piece-work in process of development. Custom and tradition determine what is considered to be a fair day's work for an average man, and when he has done that he is either at liberty, or he is paid an extra sum in proportion to the work done beyond his task.

In the middle ages, before service due from the villeins had been commuted for money payments, a day's work at all the ordinary operations of the farm was well known and precisely defined. The Surveys of Manors of the time of Edward I. frequently declare the customary task which represents the work of a day; the number of sheaves of wheat, barley, beans, &c., that should be threshed, the length of ditching and mounding to be completed, the quantity of land to be hoed, the number of faggots or bundles of rushes to be cut were sworn to and recorded.*

169. The ratio of the earnings at piece-work to the current rate of wages varies not only with the capacity and industry of the workman, and the hours during which he works; it is also governed by the laboriousness or irksomeness of the work, the amount of skill which is required, and the necessity for despatch; and usually the price paid includes the use of the workman's tools, which he provides for himself. In some cases, where machinery has to a considerable extent superseded manual labour, the price of the work, if done by hand, has been much enhanced.

It may be said, speaking broadly, that the money earned in a given time exceeds wages to a greater extent in the low-wage districts than where the rate of wages is higher, and is greatest in those districts where there is a press of work at certain seasons of the year, and where the constant labourers are insufficient for the work, and their force has to be recruited from outsiders.

Thus mowing grass, which is, where the crop is good, one of the most exhausting descriptions of work, has always been paid for at a comparatively high rate. It requires strength, skill, and the outfit of a scythe. This work has been, wherever the land is level, largely superseded by machinery, and the price for mowing by hand has

* For examples see [illegible], Record Commission Publications, No. 131.

increased more than some other kinds of work. Sheep shearing requires a good deal of skill, and it is highly paid work. It is, in consequence, very generally done by men who make a special business of it, going from farm to farm in the season.

Ditching is disagreeable work, which has to be paid for by a price which allows a man to increase his earnings and pay for the numerous and rather costly tools which he requires. Harvest work, or some portion of it, is very generally piece-work, and in the great corn districts, where the resident population is not nearly sufficient to supply the requirements of the farmers at that busy time, the prices are such as to allow of men earning three or four times the ordinary day's wages.

Chapman, B. III. 22

The ratio which earnings at piece-work bear to day wages in different districts may be illustrated by the following examples:—

Mr. Chapman says:—

"Everywhere men complain of the price of piece-work, which they say is calculated to make men earn little more than a day's pay with more than an ordinary day's work. It should be remembered that men who work at piece-work want more food, and expect some leisure, than ordinary workmen."

Mr. Wilson Fox gives instances of men earning 2*s*. 6*d*., 2*s*. 10*d*., 3*s*., 3*s*. 6*d*., 4*s*. 3*d*., up to 6*s*. a day in Thingoe district, where the wages were only 2*s*. a day.

Fox, B. I., App. B. 4.

Mr. Spencer says:—

"As a rule, it appears that ordinary piece-work is calculated at a rate which will enable the labourer to earn about 6*d*. to 1*s*. more than he would do at his ordinary day wages, but that at special work, such as thatching and shearing, the day wages would be almost doubled."

Spencer, A. 11

Mr. Wilkinson, writing of the high-wage districts of Yorks and Stafford, says that piece-work has decreased, because it is said to add little to wages; but he instances a man who earned 3*l*. 7*s*. 9*d*. in three weeks at turnip hoeing, and another who earned 9*l*. in four weeks; these sums would give 6*s*. to 7*s*. 6*d*. a day for a man, and a singler, probably a lad, who would probably not receive more than 1*s*. 6*d*. a day.

Wilkinson, A. 19

170. Harvest prices are, as a rule, the highest in proportion to wages, and at this point it will be convenient to inquire as to the different methods of payment adopted at that season of the year.

Harvest

In the exceptional district of Glendale, harvest brings no difference in the amount of wages of the hinds, the sum regularly paid covering any extra work to be done by them in that season. Women, however, receive by agreement double wages (5*s*. a day in 1892) for 20 days in harvest. In Wigton and Belper no increased wages seem to be paid. In the districts of Swaffham and Thingoe a number of men, sufficient for the work, agree for a lump sum varying from 7*l*. to 9*l*. in Thingoe, and from 7*l*. to 8*l*. in Swaffham for the whole of the harvest work, which usually occupies about four weeks. In addition, some employers give an allowance of malt and hops or beer, and the men receive 1*s*. when the agreement is made, and 3*s*. 6*d*. to 5*s*. for "hockey money" (for a harvest supper). Each gang of men elects its own captain or "lord," who goes first when mowing and directs his subordinates throughout the harvest. The earnings would thus be about 40*s*. a week in ordinary seasons, and 32*s*. when the work is protracted over a longer period.

Methods of payment for

Fox, L. II, II. 41.

The women in Norfolk and Suffolk take no part in the harvest.

171. In the several districts named in the following table, the harvest work is chiefly paid for by an increase of wages, either for a definite period, or while the harvest lasts. In some cases allowances of food and drink are provided, and occasionally board and lodging also. As the proportionate corn area has an important bearing on this point, the per-centage which the acreage of wheat, barley, and oats (white corn) bears to the total cultivated area is given.

Increase of payment by Day

HARVEST.

TABLE showing the MODE of PAYMENT generally adopted in certain DISTRICTS of INQUIRY.

Reference to A.C.'s Reports.	District.	Wheat Corn in Ratio to Cultivated Area.	Mode of Payment.
		P.C.	
Chapman - A. 73.	ATCHAM - - -	20·54	5s. per day for four weeks or ordinary pay with food, or 2l. or 3l. in lieu of food.
Richards B. II 27	KENILWORTH - -	20·44	Double wages for four weeks, or 5l. to 7l. Some piece-work.
Chapman - A. 73.	[illegible] - -	25·93	24s. to 30s. a week or bonus of 2l. with cider and food, or 1s. a day instead of drink.
Wilkinson - B. II 21.	DRIFFIELD - - -	43·30	Increased wages with "meat" (three good meals a day) and beer or 24s. to 30s. a week without "meat."
Wilkinson - B. III. 17.	EASINGWOLD - -	30·10	18s. to 22s. 6d. a week, with "meat" or 25s. to 30s. a week without meat. Some piece-work.
Fox - - B. VI 24	GARSTANG - - -	12·37	3l. 10s. to 4l. 10s. for the month and "meat."
Spencer - B. VII. 27.	GLENDALE - -	10·02	3s. to 3s. 6d. a day, with 9d. to 1s. a day in addition to beer. Some piece-work is arranged.
Bear - - B. VI. 23.	MELTON MOWBRAY	13·03	Waggoners and stockmen 1l. extra, others 20s., 21s., 24s., 26s., up to 28s. per week for five weeks. Some piece-work.
Richards - B. VI 13.	NANTWICH - - -	10·62	30s. to 40s. bonus with beer, or 5l. to 6l. for the month.
Chapman - A. 73.	TENBURY - - -	22·16	Double wages, or 30s. a week, or food and drink and 1l. bonus.
Wilkinson - B. V 20	UTTOXETER - -	5·68	Increased wages, or 1l. bonus, or board for one month. Some piece-work.
Wilkinson - B. IV. 21, 62.	WETHERBY - -	21·94	Increased wages for four weeks, regular men 2l. bonus. Irishmen 20s. to 25s. a week with milk.
Bear - - B. I 84.	WOBURN - - -	20·76	Double wages for a month with beer; or 1s. to 3s. a week instead. 4l. 16s. to 6l. for one month's work.

172. In the districts included in the following table a mixed system of payment with more or less piece-work is adopted.

Reference to Reports of A.C.'s.	District.	Ratio of Wheat Corn to Cultivated Area.	Mode of Payment.
		P.C.	
Bear - - - B. IV 23, 26.	BASINGSTOKE	42·10	Hired men receive wages at the year's end in respect of harvest work, and 1s. a day for beer when carting. Cutting, tying, and tucking 8s. 6d. to 17s. an acre. Tying after machine 4s. to 5s.
Richards - B. V 19, 24.	BROMYARD -	18·75	Reaping 8s. to 10s. an acre; binding and stooking 4s. to 5s. an acre, men working by day receive a bonus of 1l. and cider.
Chapman - B. VII. 58	HUNGERFORD -	15·48	8s. to 10s. an acre, or 6l. 10s. to 7l. for five weeks' wages, or by double wages and beer money.
Richards - B. III 33	CIRENCESTER	25·42	Tying after machine 4s. to 5s. an acre, cutting corn 2s. 3d. an acre, mowing 3s. 6d. to 1s. an acre.
Spencer - B. I. 9	DORCHESTER -	22·30	Cutting 3s. to 4s. an acre; tying 3s. to 3s.; extra wages 1l. to 2l., and in addition 10s. to 20s. for drink money.
Wilkinson - B. VI 87	HOLBEACH - -	34·00	Tying and stooking 6s. to 7s. an acre; mowing and tying 10s. to 14s. an acre; waggoning and stacking 9d. to 10d. for four men (two yearly men working with them).

Reference to Reports to A.C.'s	District	Ratio of White Corn to Cultivated Area	Mode of Payment
Spencer - - B. III. 22, 23	Hollingbourn - -	23·68	Cutting and tying 8s. to 16s. an acre; tying after machine 4s. 6d. to 7s.; carting by the day; overtime paid for 3d. or 4d. an hour with beer.
Spencer - - B. IV. 18, 19	Langport - - -	17·37	Binding and "stitching" 3s. to 5s. an acre; carrying done by day, lump sum 10s., 20s., or 30s. a man with cider.
Wilkinson - - B. I. 14.	Louth - - -	34·80	Tying and setting up 4s. to 7s. an acre.
Spencer - - B. V. 28, 30	Maldon - - -	33·73	Cutting and tying 7s. to 14s. an acre; not uncommon for men to take the whole of the reaping, tying, carting, and stacking at an inclusive price 14s. to 15s. 6d. an acre.
Richards - - B. IV. 25.	Monmouth -	13·91	Mowing 4s. to 4s. 6d. an acre; tying 4s. to 5s. 6d.; setting up 9d. to 1s. 6d. an acre; sickling 8s. to 20s. an acre; regular men, bonus generally 1l. and cider.
Chapman - - B. III. 41, A. 75.	North Witchford -	51·31	All by contract, except machine mowing; mowing, tying, and stooking 12s., 11s., exceptionally 20s. an acre; tying after machine 5s. to 6s. 6d. an acre; carting and stacking 6d. to 1s. an acre for each man in a set of five or six; men earn 30s. to 40s. a week, women assist.
Spencer - - B. VI. 26, 27	Pershore -	20·97	Cutting and tying 8s. to 20s. an acre; tying 4s. to 6s. 6d.; daymen 2s. 6d. and cider, or 3s. to 3s. 6d. without drink; sometimes 1l. for the season.
Spencer - - B. II. 13, 14	Pewsey -	27·98	Cutting and tying wheat 8s. to 15s. an acre; tying 1s. to 3s.; by day 2s. 6d. to 3s., with 6d. to 1s. beer money.
Bear - - B. II. 22, 23.	St. Neots -	33·03	Mowing and binding 10s. to 12s. an acre; binding after machine 4s. to 6s.; carting and stacking 3s. to 3s. 6d.; men earn 5l. to 6l. in 24 days; wives and families earning in addition.
Bear - - B. V. 24	Southwell - -	25·28	Waggoners and stockmen receive 1l. to 2l. 10s. extra, the latter frequently allowed to take piece-work; cutting, tying, ricking by piece; carting by day 4s. 6d. to 5s.
Richards - B. I. 91	Stratford-on-Avon -	19·50	Reaping 16s. an acre, or wages 25s. a week, where not set to contract.
Bear - - B. III. 18	Thingoe - -	34·64	5s., 6s., 7s. tying after machine mowing; binding and setting up wheat 12s., 14s., 16s., 17s. an acre; carting by the day 3s. 6d. to 4s. with beer; casual and stockmen double wages for a month.
Chapman - - B. I. 31	Thame -	31·94	Mowing or reaping and tying 12s. to 13s. an acre; tying after machine 3s. 6d.; carting and stacking 3s. 6d. an acre; wives and families help.
Chapman - - B. II. 29.	Wantage - - -	33·80	10s., 12s., 14s. an acre for reaping and tying; binding after machine 4s., 5s.

It will be seen that in only six districts included in this table[1] is there any mention of carting and stacking being paid for by the acre.

In many cases it is not clear whether the work is done mainly by regular labourers who receive extra pay or wages in respect of the overtime, or by companies working by the piece.

Neither is it clear in all cases whether each man works independently and is paid accordingly. Where a company of men take the job for a fixed sum for the harvest, or for an inclusive sum per acre, good and bad workmen share alike. Where their wives and families work with the men, the earnings of each family are no doubt kept distinct.

173. With respect to North Witchford, Mr. Chapman notes that not one-twentieth part of the work in harvest is done by the day. As in that district the area of white corn

[1] Cirencester, Holbeach, Maldon, North Witchford, St. Neots, Thame.

occupies more than one-half of the cultivated land, and the prices per acre are higher than those given in most districts, it will be seen that a very considerable sum is there divided amongst the labourers employed in harvest.

174. It is not necessary to inquire minutely into the system of payment adopted in haytime. It will be found that with the exception of mowing, which is very frequently done by machine, there is little piece-work. In Maldon, Thame, and Thingoe prices are given for carting or making hay.

Where water meadows exist, and high backed lands have been laid to grass, the scythe is still employed, and even on level lands many farmers prefer to use it rather than a machine if they can get men to undertake the work, and mowing grass still retains a place on the price lists of many districts.

175. Haytime is very generally recognised as a time for increased wages, both on account of the greater demand for labour then created, and because the hours of work are prolonged. The custom of paying so much an hour ($2\frac{1}{2}d.$ to $4d.$) for overtime is recognised very generally, and in spite of the Truck Act, beer or cider is usually given,* and the custom is not very likely to be put down by legislation.

176. In some districts luncheons or meals are given during haytime.†

(c.) Additions to Wages.

177. Any comparative estimate of the earnings of labourers in different parts of the country would be misleading which did not take into account such additions to wages as are given either by common usage or by agreement. Mr. F. Purdy, in a paper read before the Statistical Society in 1861, says:—‡

"The diversity of form under which the labourers obtain their remuneration renders it difficult, if not impossible, to reduce their earnings to a unity of expression in money value, and therefore renders any comparison of the weekly wages of one district with those of another liable to error if the value of the labourers' perquisites is not kept in view."

There is a general agreement in the reports of Assistant Commissioners as to these perquisites and allowances having undergone considerable diminution during recent years, the tendency being to substitute money payments for other allowances; but these money payments form an addition to ordinary and nominal wages, an addition which is frequently and indeed commonly ignored by those who profess to speak for the agricultural labourer, while the labourer himself is usually extremely reticent on the subject.

178. The principal additions to wages may be classed under one or other of the following heads: cottages, gardens, and potato grounds, either rent *free* or given at less than value; money payments; food; fuel, or free carriage of fuel.

179. The system of providing some of the labourers with a cottage, rent free, is mentioned by the Assistant Commissioners as prevailing to a greater or less extent in every district. In Glendale all the regular labourers ("hinds") are provided with houses on the the farms, but in no other district is this the case.

Very generally, however, shepherds, many of the carters and horsemen, and some of the stockmen have their cottages rent free. The proportion of the whole number thus accommodated seems to be least in Garstang, Wigton, Driffield, Easingwold, Nantwich, North Witchford, and Buntingford.

Wherever the yearly system of hiring is adopted for ordinary labourers, the custom of giving them houses rent free is general.

On the other hand where a considerable number of the men in charge of horses and cattle are either lodged or boarded by the foreman, there are fewer labourers holding free cottages.

In not a few cases cottages on farms are let at a low rent.

The estimates of the Assistant Commissioners and their informants as to the value of a cottage and garden, as an addition to wages, where no rent is paid, varies from $52s.$ to $104s.$ a year, the most usual sum being $4l.$

180. As a general rule it may be taken for granted that where a cottage is given as part of the wages, a garden is given with it. The size and value of the garden varies no doubt, and the Reports do not distinguish the gardens attached to free houses from

* In 24 districts out of 38 [illegible] beer is mentioned as being given.
† Atcham, Belper, [illegible], Garstang, Godstone, Monmouth, North Witchford, Thame, Uttoxeter, Wetherby.
‡ Earnings of the Agricultural Labourer. "Journal of the Statistical Society," XXIV., p. [illegible].

those which are rented. The gardens attached to farm cottages are spoken of several times as being better than those attached to village cottages, and as it is precisely these farm cottages which are held rent free, it is fair to suppose that the gardens held rent free are above the average in size and value.

Mr. Bear speaks of Thakeham and Basingstoke as the two districts visited by him which had the best and largest gardens, and these are districts where the cottages on farms are numerous, and many of the men are hired by the year.

Potato grounds.

181. As an addition to their gardens, potato grounds are frequently given or let at low rents, not only to hired men living on the farms in free cottages, but also to regular labourers who are nominally only day labourers.

In 22 out of the 38 districts the custom is noticed. It must not, however, be assumed that in all these cases they are given rent free.

In two districts a fixed quantity of potatoes is allowed in place of the ground in which to grow the labourers' crop.

Thus Mr. Bear reports as to Basingstoke:—

"A great number of the farmers provide a piece of ground for potatoes, for men who require it, free of charge.

"Many of them stated that they allowed the men to have all they required, and that they ploughed the land for them."

In Southwell, Melton Mowbray, and St. Neots, he found the same practice more or less common.

In Thakeham, perhaps on account of the good gardens already spoken of, it was not common to provide them.

Mr. Spencer says with regard to Dorchester:—

"Men hired by the year receive a cottage and garden and a potato ground rent free. These are generally valued as being worth 5l. and 1l. for 20 perches respectively. The potato ground varies in size from 20 to 40 perches according to the size of the family of the labourer. It is ploughed and manured by the farmer with the rest of the field, and the labourer has only the labour of planting and taking up the potatoes."

In Langport they are sometimes given in lieu of harvest money. Mr. Chapman says that in North Witchford lots of one rood are allowed to hired men on the farm free of charge.

In Crediton he says the labourers are provided with good gardens and 20 to 30 poles of potato ground, and the privilege is valued in his estimates of earnings at 1l. a year.

In Truro the same practice is reported.

On the other hand Mr. Wilson Fox found few of these potato grounds in his districts. In Glendale the usual allowance of a certain quantity of potatoes relieves the labourer of the task of cultivating them.

Mr. Wilkinson speaks of these grounds in Holbeach, Uttoxeter, and Wetherby, and Mr. Richards found them in Belper, Bromyard, Cirencester. In Stratford-on-Avon he says the system is dying out and is replaced by allotments.

Money payments.

182. The larger payments in cash, over and above weekly wages, are chiefly made to yearly men as a substitute for the opportunities of earning increased wages at piece-work or contract work in harvest; or they are of the nature of profit-sharing, being given as a bonus to shepherds and stockmen in order to quicken their interest in the well-doing of the animals under their charge. A few instances of these payments may suffice. Extra wages for harvest work are in some cases paid at Michaelmas, the end of the year of engagement, and in that case they cannot be distinguished from the allowance made in respect of extra services throughout the year; but they are not the less additions to weekly wages.

Michaelmas money.

183. In Basingstoke the Michaelmas money for carters ranges from 2l. to 7l., the most common payment being 3l. to 4l.

In Wantage there is a similar payment varying from 2l. to 5l.

In Thakeham an addition of 2l. to 3l. is made to wages of carters, &c., on account of harvest.

In Dorchester the hired men receive 1l. to 2l. for harvest, besides 1l. to 1l. 10s. for "drink money," and in Godstone 1l. to 3l. is given to carters and stockmen as harvest money.

Extra payments to shepherds.

184. Shepherds in some cases, as in Godstone, Langport, Pewsey, and Pershore, have a money allowance of 1l., 2l., or 3l. for their extra work at the lambing season.

The following are specimens of allowances to shepherds in respect of their success in rearing lambs:—

In Thingoe Mr. Wilson Fox says:—

Fox, B. I. 14. "Shepherds, in addition to their wages, are given 6d. for every lamb they rear and sometimes 9d. The lamb money, of course, depends on the size of the flock, but I find they get between 7l. and 22l. in the year."

Spencer, B. I. 7. Some farmers give a graduated payment, thus, in Dorchester:—

"A shepherd is usually given an allowance of 1d. for every lamb reared, and 6d. for all twins reared."

Others give a more liberal sum in respect of numbers alive at a particular date, as in Atcham, where a shepherd is paid 1s. a head for every lamb alive on June 1st over the number of ewes put to the ram the previous year.

Chapman, B. VI. 21. Similar allowances are mentioned as made to shepherds in 19 out of the 38 districts of inquiry.

Fox, B. III. 14, and App. B. 10. In Glendale the attention of the shepherd to his flock is still frequently, and it was a few years ago universally, encouraged by allowing him to run a limited number of his own breeding sheep with the farmer's flock.

Extra payments to stockmen. Chapman, B. VI. App. II. 185. In a few instances cowmen and stockmen receive similar allowances to those of shepherds in respect of calves or pigs reared or cattle fattened. In the Appendix to Mr. Chapman's Report on Atcham details of extra payments to labourers are given and include three payments in the course of the year to a cowman for calves reared, amounting in all to 20s. for 20 calves.

Bear, B. I. 25. In Woburn the payment is, in some cases, 6d. for each calf.

Chapman, B. III. 43. Horsemen sometimes receive from 2s. 6d. to 10s. for each foal born alive; they also receive journey money when they go off the farm to deliver corn which has been sold, or for other purposes.

Journey money. Bear, B. III. 27. 186. Mr. Bear, in his Report on Basingstoke, says:

"Journey money paid to carters usually 1s. for four horses, or 6d. for two.

"In the former case there would be a second man or lad who would probably have half the money.

"In one case brought to my notice a carter received nearly 1s. a week for journey money; but probably the average for carters and under-carters together is not more than half this amount."

Mr. Richards says as to Brixworth:—

Richards, B. II. 29. "In some districts 6d. per sack or 1s. per load is allowed to carters for all corn delivered off the farm."

In Buntingford—

Chapman, B. VII. 41. "Horsekeepers get road money varying from 6d. to 1s. a day."

These payments most probably originated when the teams had to travel long distances to deliver corn and other produce, and the men had to provide themselves with refreshment on the journey.

Payment of bonus on work. Spencer, B. IV. 26. Bear, B. I. 25. Chapman, B. III. 16. 187. Other extra money payments to men in charge of horses include a bonus of 1d., 2d., or 3d. for each acre drilled or mown with a machine, the object being twofold, that of getting a fair amount of work done, and that of rewarding the labourer for his skill and carefulness in the use of the implement entrusted to him.

Food. 188. In addition to the very common allowances of milk to certain classes of labourers, and apart from payments in kind, there lingers in some districts a custom of providing food as well as drink at certain seasons of the year, or to speak more correctly in connection with certain operations on the farm. These occasions are perhaps the relics of a custom which grew up when neighbours gathered together to assist each other in turn, and were entertained and feasted by the farmer who benefited by the labour of the visitors, and perhaps of a still older custom under which the servile tenants of a manor were fed on "boon days." In course of time the extra labour of workmen was compensated by a liberal allowance of provisions, and though in most districts this has now been abandoned, and a money payment substituted, yet it still exists in some places and is sometimes given in addition to the increased money payment.

Thus in Uttoxeter Mr. Wilkinson says:—

Wilkinson, B. V. 20. "At hay harvest a lunch is usually provided in the mid-morning and the mid-afternoon, and supper is often given too, if the men work late. . . . In corn harvest full board is very commonly given."

And in Wetherby "drinkings" (that is bread, cheese, and beer) are given during harvest at 11 a.m. and 4 p.m. The custom is also noticed as still existing in Cirencester, Godstone, and Langport.

In Driffield ordinary weekly men are "meated" with three good meals a day during four weeks in harvest.

In Easingwold and Garstang it is not unusual to "meat" or feed day labourers on the six working days, and of course to pay them less wages. In the former district the difference between the wages of men who are boarded and those who are not varies from 6s. to 9s. a week. In Garstang the difference is 6s. to 7s. a week. Of this system Mr. Wilkinson says:—

"Of course it secures any amount of good food to the head of the family, the principal and only wage earner, but it is said, and no doubt with truth, that the wife and children are less well fed than when the man receives all his wages in cash and takes his meals at home."

There are some districts in which it is the custom to find food when corn is threshed.

In Garstang and Wigton men are also "meated" in hay and harvest.

189. Beer or cider is universally provided during hay time, and to some extent in harvest, though as a rule, where men take the harvest by contract, they find their own drink. In some counties, however, the allowance of drink is by no means confined to the busy seasons spoken of. Thus in Atcham one witness says cattlemen have among other allowances two quarts of beer a day, and Mr. Chapman says:—

"Beer is very commonly allowed, from one to two quarts a day, especially on the smaller farms."

In Crediton we are told the allowance of cider is two quarts a day in summer and three quarts in winter, while in hay and harvest it is given *ad libitum*.

Mr. Spencer reports of Langport thus:—

"A daily allowance of cider is still given universally throughout the district, almost every farm having a cider orchard attached to it; the allowance is usually three to four pints a day to each man. A larger quantity is given at haytime and in harvest, and also at threshing, and at some other jobs of a long or severe nature."

With regard to Pershore Mr. Spencer reports that the custom of giving a daily allowance of cider, which was universal, has been——

"discontinued in many cases owing to the action of the authorities, who have instituted prosecutions under the Truck Act, and have this year issued a notice warning farmers against giving a daily allowance of cider."

It has already been stated that drink is given very generally at hay time, and it is not necessary to specify the districts where the habit prevails.

In Holbeach yearly married servants frequently get an allowance of from 18s. to 26s. in lieu of beer, and the same is the case in Louth and Melton Mowbray. In Thingoe malt and hops are sometimes given in order that the men may brew their own beer for harvest.

190. The allowance of milk is generally restricted to cowmen or stockmen, but in Atcham, Brixworth, Driffield, Southwell, and Truro it is reported to be given pretty freely to all classes of regular labourers resident on farms. The most liberal instance is perhaps that of three labourers employed on a farm in Driffield, who received three to four pints of milk daily, and three times a week the same quantity of soup.

In Easingwold and Louth the foremen who board the young horsemen have a cow kept for them, and occasional instances are found of cows being provided for shepherds all the year round.

In Glendale farmers keep a cow for the labourer for 3s. a week, which is much less than the cost of keeping the animal, but the hinds take much less advantage of this privilege than formerly. The farmers deprecate the decreasing number of cows kept by labourers, and the hinds themselves confess that it is a mistake.

Mr. Wilson Fox estimates the clear gain to the labourer of a cow kept for him at this price as fully 6*l*. a year.

191. Before leaving the question of food provided, it will be necessary to notice some other payments in kind which are still made in a few of the northern districts.

In Mr. Wilkinson's Report on Louth district will be found several examples of payments in kind to different classes of labourers.

In the following passage from the Report the nature of these payments is described:—

Wilkinson, B. I. 14

"'Confined' men 'almost invariably have house and garden rent free . . . they also receive, as a rule, 30 stone of pork (occasionally rather more), four to six sacks of wheat or flour, 30 to 40 kids of faggots, and 40 to 60 stone of potatoes, while some receive beer money, and shepherds often some coal at lambing time."

B. VI. App. C.

And appended to his Report on Holbeach, Mr. Wilkinson gives particulars of the wages and allowances of 31 confined labourers in that district. Of these 30 have a house rent free; 12 have from 20 to 25 stones of pork; 11 have from 4*l.* to 6*l.* in lieu of pork; 3 have money (1*l.* to 2*l.*) for harvest; 19 have money (16*s.* to 36*s.*) in lieu of beer; 7 have milk; 6 have potato ground; and 2 have a certain quantity of coals provided.

Diminishing extent of payment in kind in Northumberland.

102. In Glendale, at the time of Mr. Henley's Report to the Royal Commission on the Employment of Children, &c. in Agriculture (1867), the hinds were paid mostly in kind. Mr. Wilson Fox, alluding to this fact, says:—

"Since that time there has been an entire change in this respect, and it is now the custom of the country to pay the hinds in cash."

But he adds—

Fox, B. III. 84, App. B 10, 11, 13.

"They get house—1,000 to 1,200 yards (running) of potatoes and coals led free."

In the appendix to his Report he gives some instances of kind-payments to shepherds and stewards. In the former case the cash payments are only about 25 per cent., and in the latter from 70 to 77 per cent. of the earnings.

Wilkinson, B. I. 11, B. II. 87. Fox, B. IV. 93, B. V. 17, note.

In a few districts men servants are boarded by the farmer either in the farmhouse or at the foreman's house. The character of the provision made for them is described by Mr. Wilkinson in his Reports upon Louth and Driffield, and by Mr. Wilson Fox in his Reports upon Wigton and Garstang.

Fuel provided or carted.

103. Another occasional though not very common form of allowance to men on farms is that of fuel, either faggots, or in some few instances, coals. In Basingstoke, Dorchester, Godstone, 100 to 150 "bavins" or faggots are very generally allowed, and in Crediton and Truro, Louth, and other districts, some of the labourers have them. In Maldon a certain quantity of coals are found for the horsekeepers, and in some districts shepherds are supplied with them partly on account of the lambs which he has to see to, and partly because he must for his own comfort, during the lambing season, keep a fire burning night and day.

The haulage of fuel is much more common than the provision of it. It may be taken as a universal rule that cottagers on farms can have their coals carted for them free of charge. In many places this will be a very small privilege involving little cost to the farmer, and saving the labourer only a few shillings in the year; but in remote districts, at a long distance from the railway, the advantage to the labourer is very considerable.

It is scarcely necessary to describe in detail many of the petty pickings which the labourer enjoys, such as the faggot or the bag of chips which a hedger takes home every night, by a sort of customary right tacitly acknowledged by his employer; the straw provided for the bedding of the pig and ultimately for the manuring of the garden or allotment; the allowance for every rat or stoat or mole that he kills. Enough has been said to show that a very great variety of allowances and perquisites add to the labourers' wages, and that in order to institute any comparison between the position of those in different parts of the country the value of these additions must be taken into account.

Piece-work or perquisites.

104. Speaking broadly it may be said that piece-work adds largely to the wages of the ordinary labourer, and that perquisites are enjoyed chiefly by the hired men.

Some of the best workers are attracted by the opportunities afforded by piece-work for obtaining a full reward for their own individual exertions; while some are content to take, and indeed prefer, the security of more regular wages with some additions, as rewards for diligence or skill, and some allowances, which it is convenient to them to receive, in lieu of money.

The task is by no means a simple one. In many cases my colleagues, having before them an amount of detailed information which could not be fully given in the limits of their reports, have hesitated to give any decided expression of opinion on the point, and frequently they allow a very wide range between the maximum and the minimum amount which renders it extremely difficult to fix upon any definite sum as fairly representative of average conditions. Any attempt to compare the receipts of labourers in different parts of the country must therefore be considered as only a rough approximation.

196. Before considering the earnings of the larger classes into which the labourers are divided, a brief notice of the earnings of bailiffs or foremen who occupy the first rank among wage-earners may be offered. It is not proposed to consider the pay of farm managers or stewards, whose remuneration runs up to 200*l.* or 300*l.* a year, but that of men who are working foremen. This class is scarcely noticed by some of the Assistant Commissioners, and in many districts they are no doubt a limited class, but wherever large farms exist there are men who fulfil the office of overlooker, and their rate of pay is greater than that of mere manual labourers. Bailiffs or foremen. Bear, A. 6.

With regard to Glendale, a district of large farms, Mr. Wilson Fox says:—

"The annual earnings of stewards, including all allowances, may be stated from 54*l.* to 74*l.* 10*s.*, and that of ploughmen-stewards" to be 54*l.* Fox, R. III. 35.

These sums would represent a weekly earning of 20*s.* 9*d.* to 28*s.* 8*d.*

Mr. Spencer gives only one instance, the earnings being in that case 52*l.* 3*s.* 9*d.*, or 1*l.* a week. Of this, 44*l.* 13*s.* 9*d.* was paid in cash, and the remainder is accounted for by the value of the house, garden and potato ground allowed rent free; but this man must have lost some time either by sickness or some other cause, as his money wages were at the rate of 18*s.*, with 3*l.* in addition, or 19*s.* 2*d.* a week in cash. Spencer, R. I. 8.

Mr. Bear gives a range of from 20*s.* to 30*s.* and up to 40*s.* a week, not including farm managers or stewards on farms held in hand by landlords. Bear, R. II. 88, III. 88, IV. 88, V. 78, VI. 10.

Mr. Wilkinson gives particulars of the payments and allowances made to foremen in the district of Louth, where the horsekeepers are boarded at the foreman's house. In this case the man receives in money wages:— Wilkinson, R. I. 14.

	£	s.	d.
10s. a week - - - -	26	0	0
And in lieu of beer - - -	0	15	0
	£26	15	0

In addition he receives on his own account 40 stone of pork, 100 pecks of potatoes, loan of a cow, and house and garden rent free. For each servant living with him he gets 30 stone of pork, two quarters of wheat, 24 pecks of potatoes, 1*s.* a week for beer, and 7*l.* 10*s.* in cash.

Mr. Wilkinson does not attempt to put a money value upon these allowances or to estimate the income of the foreman, but as the allowance in respect of each servant is not of less value than 24*l.* a year, or more than 9*s.* 2*d.* a week, it may be safely assumed that there is a good margin for profit on each boarder, which goes to reward the foreman's wife for her work in attending upon the young men.

In Driffield, however, the earnings of foremen under similar circumstances appear to be considerably in excess of those in Louth. Mr. Wilkinson gives three instances where the earnings, apart from allowances of from 7*s.* to 9*s.* a week for each servant boarded, are 73*l.* 4*s.*, 74*l.* 14*s.*, and 94*l.* 15*s.* a year. These sums are equivalent to 28*s.* 1*d.*, 28*s.* 9*d.*, and 36*s.* 5*d.* a week. Wilkinson, R. II. 35.

In Easingwold estimates of the value of the foreman's place ranged from 60*l.* to 65*l.* a year, or from 23*s.* to 25*s.* a week. Wilkinson, R. III. 27.

In Wetherby, however, the earnings of this class of men is said to be from 45*l.* to 50*l.*, or 17*s.* 3*d.* to 18*s.* 10*d.* a week, the farms being of smaller size and the duties and responsibilities of the foreman much less than in the districts previously mentioned. R. IV. 33.

In Holbeach the earnings of foremen, frequently only the head horsekeepers, are estimated at 48*l.* or 49*l.*, or from 18*s.* 5*d.* to 18*s.* 10*d.* a week. R. VI. 33.

I have given rather full details as to the remuneration of the headmen on farms in different parts of the country, because the places which they fill are open to and are generally filled by men who have been ordinary labourers.

Mr. Wilkinson says on this point :—

"Valuable as these places are, it seems certain from the evidence that a steady waggoner would not have to wait many years before he could get one."

But these remarks can only apply in full force to those parts of the country where large farms abound, and the system of boarding the horsemen in the foreman's house prevails.

197. The next class of labourers to be considered is that of the shepherds. I have tabulated the results of a careful examination of the several Reports (see table 62), which show a range of earnings of from 15s. to 25s. a week, excluding a few cases of exceptional earnings by men in charge of pedigree flocks.

The average of the whole number of examples given would be about 18s. a week. As might be expected the higher rates are paid in the great sheep-breeding districts, where the shepherd often earns considerably more than the stockman or horsekeeper. A few instances may be quoted showing the different forms which payment takes.

In Glendale, which is one of the highest wage districts, many of the shepherds are paid partly in kind and partly by the keep of a flock or shepherd's pack. Mr. Wilson Fox gives the particulars of the wages and allowances in two cases. In the first case the cash wages are 18l. a year, and the whole value of the emoluments is estimated at the prices of stock in 1892 as amounting to 152l. 11s. 2d., out of which he has to pay and keep two assistants who cost him 100l. He has thus 52l. 11s. 6d. a year for himself. But the average return from the same head of stock is estimated to leave him 73l. 8s., or 28s. 2d. a week after paying his two men.

In another case the earnings for 1892 are reckoned at 62l. 8s., or at the rate of 24s. a week. In the first of these two cases the shepherd has 35 ewes and four fat sheep running in his master's flock. He has also the keep of two cows, the value of which keeping is put at the extremely moderate sum of 3s. a week for each cow. Then he has certain quantities of oats, barley, beans, wheat, and potatoes.

In the second case the shepherd has the keep of 12 ewes and five young sheep; and also that of a cow. His cash receipts are 16l., or about one-fourth of his total earnings. The result to the shepherds of the system of payment of kind is, that he loses with the farmer from a depreciation of prices, and Mr. Wilson Fox points out that if the present low prices continue the shepherds of Glendale, who still cling to the old system, will no longer be content to receive what is in money less than hinds can earn.

Mr. Fox puts the average earnings of shepherds in Glendale at 21s. to 28s. a week. In no other district of England does the same system of payment exist.

Mr. Bear estimates the average earnings of shepherds in Thakeham at 15s. to 25s. a week. The larger sum is made up by allowances of so much for each lamb reared, and can only be obtained where a large flock is kept. Though the details as to the extra earnings are not given, the actual sum paid in cash in one instance was said to be 63l. 1s. 2d., in addition to which the shepherd had a cottage rent free and valued at 8l. 18s. a year.

In the Report on Basingstoke an example is given of weekly wages 14s., with firing, beer-money, and lamb-money, bringing up the earnings to 52l. a year.

Mr. Spencer gives the actual cash receipts of a shepherd in Pewsey district, whose weekly wages were 12s., as 60l. 9s. 5d., in addition to which he had cottage and garden, potato ground and firing, valued together at 6l. 5s. This man's average earnings were 1l. 5s. 7½d. a week. In the same district, however, two shepherds stated that their total earnings only amounted to 15s. 9d. and 16s. 10d. a week respectively.

Mr. Fox gives the actual earnings of shepherds in Thingoe district as ranging from 17s. to 24s. 8d. a week, to which must be added the value of a cottage rent free and some allowance of firing; this would make the minimum rate at least 17s. 6d. a week.

On the Wolds of Louth and Driffield, the pay of shepherds does not appear to exceed that of the southern or eastern counties; indeed, no instances are given of wages that equal those of Thingoe, Thakeham, and Pewsey already quoted.

In his Summary Report Mr. Wilkinson gives the range of earnings of shepherds in Driffield as 43l. to 52l., and in Louth as 43l. to 51l., but I suspect a misprint of 43l. for 48l., as the average of the instances given of actual earnings in Driffield is 54l. 17s., and in Louth 50l. 13s. 6d.

The lowest rate of earnings by this class of labourers appears to prevail in Langport, where a minimum of 13s. 6d. a week is reported. The highest reported earnings of a shepherd are those of one in the Atcham district, who received in one year 95l. 4s., or an average weekly earning of 36s. 7d.

The most remarkable features to be noticed with regard to the earnings of shepherds are the very wide differences existing within a district, and the near approach to an equality in respect of the earnings of highly paid shepherds throughout the whole country.

198. The annual earnings of men in charge of horses seem to vary from 14s. a week in Langport to 20s. 9d. in Glendale, the mean between those two sums being almost exactly the same as the average of all the districts, viz., 17s. 3½d. or 17s. 4½d. a week. Carters and others in charge of [illegible].

It must, however, be pointed out first that in this class there are included in several districts young horsekeepers, lads of 17 to 20 years of age; and secondly that in some districts the horsemen are boarded servants. Pursuing the same course as I have done previously, I shall give a few examples showing the manner in which the payment is made up. Taking Glendale first as the district of highest payment, Mr. Wilson Fox, after referring to a statement of Mr. Henley's in his Report on the district, dated 1867, that it was then "the custom of the country to pay the labourers mostly in kind" says:—

"Since that time there has been an entire change in this respect, and it is now the custom of the country to pay the hinds in cash.

"The money wages, however, do not represent all the payment a hind receives for his services, and the following statement shows pretty accurately the position of a man who lives alone, or who is the head of a house— Fox, B. III. [illegible]

	£	s.	d.
Weekly wages (say 17s. a week)	44	4	0
House	4	5	0
1,000 to 1,200 yards of potatoes	4	0	0
Coals led free	1	4	0
Total	£53	13	0

This is equal to an average weekly earning of 20s. 7½d.

In his summary Report, Mr. Fox estimates the average earnings at 20s. 9d.

In Wigton the majority of the men in charge of horses are indoor servants, receiving wages of 14l. to 15l. per half-year, if young and second-class, and 16l. to 17l. if good well-known men. Allowing 7s. a week for board and lodging, Mr. Fox estimates the earnings at from 19s. 3d. to 20s. a week. Fox, A. App. B. IV. [illegible]

In Godstone Mr. Spencer reckons the earnings of carters and stockmen at 19s. to 1l. a week, the items of receipt being: wages, 15s., the value of a cottage (2s. 6d. or 3s. a week), and 2l. harvest money. The extra value of a cottage in a residential district is here counted as increasing the earnings of the occupant. It is not that the cottage is one whit better than some of those which are counted as adding only 1s. 6d. or 1s. 8d. to the man's earnings. Spencer, B. VII. [illegible]

Mr. Richards puts the earnings of cowmen and waggoners in Belper at from 48l. to 52l. a year, which is equal to 18s. 5d. to 1l. a week. Richards, A. 14.

In Hollingbourn Mr. Spencer's estimate of waggoners and stockmen's weekly average receipts is from 18s. to 20s. Spencer, B. III. [illegible]

In Southwell Mr. Bear credits waggoners with receiving from 18s. to 21s. 7d., and stockmen from 16s. to 21s. a week. Bear, B. V. [illegible]

And in Melton Mowbray he puts both classes at 17s. to a little over 1l. a week. B. VI. [illegible]

Mr. Chapman gives Atcham as the district of highest earnings of carters and cattlemen coming under his notice, the ascertained earnings of waggoners ranging from 17s. 7d. to 19s. 1½d., and those of cattlemen from 18s. 6d. to 18s. 11d., the average of the two classes being about 18s. 6d. In these estimates the value of cottage and garden is taken at 2s. a week. Chapman, A. [illegible] B. VI. [illegible]

Mr. Wilkinson estimates the earnings of horsemen and stockmen in the six districts visited by him as ranging from 42l. to 48l., the latter sum being reached in Holbeach and Louth. The districts in question have a number of boarded servants who are, many of them, under age. Mr. Wilkinson reckons their board as worth 8s. a week, as against 7s. allowed by Mr. Fox. On the other hand he only charges 4l. 10s. for the value of the cottage. Wilkinson, A. [illegible] B. VI., App. C.

Having noticed some instances of the higher wage districts we may now contrast the earnings in some districts where they are apparently much lower.

Mr. Spencer estimates the annual earnings of carters and stockmen in the Langport district at 13s. to 15s. a week. In this amount, harvest money, cider, and house rent at 1s. 6d. a week are included. Spencer, A. [illegible] B. IV. [illegible]

Mr. Chapman gives several estimates of horsekeepers' earnings in North Witchford; these range from 14s. 3d. to 14s. 10d. It should be mentioned that these are the earnings of young unmarried men. Stockmen's earnings in the same districts are estimated at from 14*s.* 9*d.* to 16*s.* 2*d.*, the average of the two classes being 15*s.* 1*d.* a week.

In the district of Pewsey Mr. Spencer puts the earnings at from 15*s.* to 16*s.* a week, and in Dorchester from 15*s.* 6*d.* to 16*s.*

Mr. Bear estimates the average earnings of horsemen in Woburn at 15*s.* to 16*s.* 6*d.*, and of stockmen in the same union at 15*s.* to 16*s.*

In a subsequent table I have shown the range of earnings, and an estimated average of earnings of these and other classes of labourers in the different districts of inquiry.

199. In the table to which reference has just been made, I have attempted to estimate the average earnings of day labourers who form the rank and file of the class. Any statement of the kind must, however, be regarded as a mere approximation based upon a number of estimates supported by a limited number of ascertained facts. A few words are necessary in order to explain the method which I have adopted for arriving at a definite figure which I have set down as an estimated average. Where one of my colleagues has made an estimate of the maximum and minimum earnings under ordinary circumstances, eliminating from the calculation very exceptional cases, and where the difference between the maximum and minimum is not great, I have been content to assume that the Assistant Commissioner has weighed the evidence, has taken into account the proportionate number having the opportunity of earning on the higher and lower scales, and I accept the figures given and strike a mean between the two extremes for the average. For instance, Mr. Bear in his Summary Report gives estimates of earnings which do not in any case vary to a greater extent than 2*s.* 6*d.* a week for any class of labourers. Indeed, sometimes, the maximum or minimum differ by only 6*d.* a week. But the same course is not adopted by all the Assistant Commissioners, and I have, therefore, scrutinised the reports and the evidence as to earnings and calculated the average after bringing all the instances under consideration.

200. In another table the several districts have been grouped in respect of the assumed average rate of earnings by each of the chief classes of labourers.

In the first of these groups I have placed in order from highest to lowest rate all those districts where the rate of earnings is 19*s.* a week or more. In the second those where it is 17*s.* and under 19*s.* In the third those from 15*s.* to 17*s.*, and in the fourth group those districts where the average weekly earnings would appear to be less than 15*s.* a week.

It is not pretended that any statement such as this can be put forward as accurate. It is at best an approximation. It must be confessed that for the purpose of comparing one district with another it leaves much to be desired. In one district the earnings are regular and nearly uniform, by which I mean that fixed inclusive wages are paid whatever the character of the work or the season of the year, and the additions to money wages are given in a form which renders them measurable with tolerable accuracy. In another district the wages fluctuate during the year; they represent the minimum sum paid to a regular labourer; they are augmented by special allowances, or by opportunities of earning additional sums by piece-work, and these additional earnings depend so much upon the skill, strength, and industry of the labourer that the amount earned varies enormously even where men are working under precisely similar conditions.*

It may, I think, be taken as a general rule, that where piece-work is much resorted to, there is a much wider variation in the earnings than elsewhere, and therefore the maximum sum which a skilled labourer receives exceeds the average by much more than where payment is chiefly by time.

201. Although the Reports of the Assistant Commissioners give a large number of ascertained earnings of individual labourers, and a still larger number of estimates of gross earnings, there are but few instances which show exactly how the total amount is made up, but in a few cases full particulars are given.

Mr. Bear, in his Report on Woburn, gives a full account of the receipts of a skilled labourer during 12 months, May 1891 to 1892. Wages varied from 12*s.* to 13*s.*, the total amount earned was 39*l.* 3*s.* 3½*d.*, or at the rate of 15*s.* 0¾*d.* a week. Of the whole amount 29*l.* 0*s.* 2*d.*, or 74 per cent., was earned in weekly wages, and 26 per cent. was paid either for piece-work or in the shape of extras for exceptional work. But this man was absent from work 17½ days, of which 6 were due to illness, 6½ were spent at work on

* I have known young men working side by side in the harvest field with men much older than themselves earn only 2*s.* 6*d.* a day, while the older men earned from 3*s.* to 7*s.* in the same number of hours.

his allotment, and 5 on pleasure. The sum earned is therefore payment for 49 weeks work, at the rate of 15*s.* 11½*d.* a week. In another case of an ordinary labourer in the same district, the cash received was 36*l.* 7*s.* 8*d.*, and the value of the beer allowed during hay and harvest is put at 30*s.*, making an average earning of 14*s.* 7*d.* a week.

Mr. Bear's estimate of the average earnings is from 14*s.* to 15*s.* a week, and I have taken 14*s.* 6*d.* as the mean and approximate average earnings.

Again, in the Thakeham district an individual labourer's earnings are given as 46*l.* 5*s.* 4*d.* for 49½ weeks' work; this is at the rate of 17*s.* 9½*d.* a week for the whole year, but it is 18*s.* 8*d.* a week for the full time worked.

In this case, 46 per cent. of the whole sum earned was received as weekly wages.

Mr. Chapman, in his Report on Atcham, gives a detailed account of the money paid to an ordinary labourer in that district. The man received in addition to his standing wages of 15*s.* a week 6*l.* 6*s.* 6*d.* in 1892, and 4*l.* 10*s.* 4*d.* in 1891, the average total for the two years being 44*l.* 0*s.* 7*d.*, or at the rate of 16*s.* 11*d.* a week.

Mr. Wilson Fox gives in the Appendix to his Thingoe Report what are said to be the ascertained earnings of 15 ordinary labourers supplied by 12 employers, but the even sum at which these earnings are put down shows, I think, that some of them are estimates. It would be a curious fact if the payments to six men should be exactly 36*l.*, 36*l.* 10*s.*, 37*l.* 10*s.*, 38*l.*, and 39*l.* Of course it is possible that fractions have been omitted. If these cases be disregarded the average earnings of the remaining nine were 40*l.* 9*s.* 4*d.*, which is 15*s.* 7*d.* a week, while that of the whole 15 equals 15*s.* a week.

The range of earnings is from 13*s.* 0½*d.* a week, earned by a man who did not choose to work regularly, to 17*s.* 4*d.*

A similar statement with regard to labourers in Swaffham district is open to the same observations with regard to the remarkable evenness of the sums. One statement is that the average earnings of 19 labourers on one farm were 15*s.* a week; again, we may suppose that fractions have been omitted. The average of all the instances given is 14*s.* 11*d.* weekly earnings.

202. Mr. Spencer gives some very full and interesting specimen accounts of actual earnings. In his Report on Dorchester the receipts and allowances of five ordinary labourers are given. Including house rent, potato ground, and firing, these amount to 13*s.* 9*d.*, 14*s.* 5*d.*, 14*s.* 8*d.*, 16*s.*, and 16*s.* 9*d.* respectively, the average being 15*s.*

In Pewsey, the earnings given range from 12*s.* 7½*d.*, received by a single man 30 years of age, to 18*s.* 10*d.* earned by a man of 56 years, who may be assumed to be a highly skilled workman, as it is stated that he is generally engaged at piecework.

In the Report on Hollingbourn there is a detailed statement of the sums received by an ordinary labourer in each week of the year, distinguishing payments by time from those by the piece. The total sum for the whole year is 40*l.* 14*s.* 2*d.*, of which 11*l.* 4*s.* 9*d.*, or 27·6 per cent., is for piecework, which augments his receipts on 22 weeks out of the 52. The man was absent about 13 days, when he was often engaged in beating for game. The receipts average 15*s.* 5½*d.* a week for the whole year, but if calculated for the time actually at work they are equal to 16*s.* 3*d.* a week.

A similar account is given in the Appendix to the Malton Report. As in this case the earnings are considerably below those of several others mentioned in the same account, it may be presumed that they are those of a man with no special skill. Piecework represents 33 per cent. of the total sum earned, which is on the average 13*s.* 5½*d.* a week.

In another case, where the earnings average 16*s.* 2*d.* a week, the percentage of the sum paid in excess of wages on account of piece-work is 32·7 per cent.; of this sum, however, 9*l.* 5*s.* is earned in four weeks of harvest, and the remainder, 4*l.* 9*s.* 9*d.*, is to be spread over the remaining 48 weeks. In this case the nominal wages of 12*s.* a week are augmented by piece-work to 13*s.* 10½*d.*, while for the four weeks of harvest they are 46*s.* 3*d.* a week.

Other examples are given by Mr. Spencer in his Pershore Report.

In Mr. Wilkinson's Report on Driffield there are given epitomes of payments to labourers of a somewhat different character to those hitherto exhibited. In the first of these the men are at fixed wages for 45 weeks; for 40 weeks wages are 15*s.* a week, and for five harvest weeks they are 21*s.*

During these five weeks "meat" (that is "board") is provided, the value of which is estimated at 2*l.*, the total receipts per week during harvest being 29*s.* During seven weeks of turnip hoeing the earnings are 12*l.*, or at the rate of 34*s.* 3½*d.* a week. Here the extra earnings by piece-work are 6*l.* 15*s.*, and the extra earnings in harvest are 3*l.* 10*s.* As the whole amount is 49*l.* 5*s.*, the extras are only about 21 per cent., while piece-work represents only 13·7 per cent.

In contrast with this district, Mr. Wilkinson reports two cases of disengaged men in Holbeach, where a large amount of piece-work is done; the total earnings in these cases were 42*l.* 13*s.* 7½*d.* and 37*l.* 4*s.* 8*d.*; of the latter sum, 17*l.* 0*s.* 7*d.*, or 45·7 per cent., was earned by the piece.

253. In the following comparative table, which shows the range of earnings and the assumed average earnings of (1) shepherds, (2) carters and stockmen (men in charge of horses or cattle), (3) ordinary labourers, it will be seen that, taking an average of the whole number of districts, the earnings of stockmen are only about 1*s.* 3*d.* a week more than those of ordinary labourers.

This result, which can hardly be correct as regards men of equal age and capacity, is probably due to the fact that, among the class engaged in the care of horses, there are many young and immature lads, and, as has been already said, many of the horsemen are boarded servants, whose earnings are largely paid in food, and where, as in some districts the value of bed and board is taken at only 7*s.* a week, the estimate of earnings is a low one.

It must be repeated that the figures given are not to be regarded as absolutely correct. Compiled as they have been with the greatest care, they are only rough estimates. They represent what appear to be the earnings of average men who work regularly and diligently throughout the year.

In making these estimates the ordinary risks of loss of time by bad weather or sickness are taken into account. In some districts, and, indeed, wherever there is much contract work the statements given fall far below what is within the reach of a skilled worker or an exceptionally industrious man.

TABLE showing for the several DISTRICTS of INQUIRY the MINIMUM, MAXIMUM, and ESTIMATED AVERAGE EARNINGS of certain CLASSES of LABOURERS.

No.	Districts.	Shepherds. Range of Earnings. Minimum.	Maximum.	Approximate Average.	Carters, Cattlemen, and others in charge of Stock. Range of Earnings. Minimum.	Maximum.	Approximate Average.	Ordinary Labourers. Range of Earnings. Minimum.	Maximum.	Approximate Average.
		s. d.	s. d.	s. d.	s. d.	s. d.	s. d.	s. d.	s. d.	s. d.
1	Alcester	19 5	22 0	20 8	17 1	19 1	18 8	13 2	16 8	17 6
2	Basingstoke	16 0	20 0	19 5	14 0	18 0	16 5	11 0	16 0	15 0
3	[illegible]	—	—	—	15 5	20 0	19 4	13 5	20 0	18 6
4	Brixworth	—		20 0	—	—	18 1	15 0	18 7	15 9
5	[illegible]	—		—	14 6	17 3	14 10	12 6	17 7	14 9
6	Buntingford	16 6	22 6	19 8	16 0	20 0	18 9	11 6	18 10	14 4
7	[illegible]	—	—	21 5	14 7	21 6	17 9	11 0	16 0	13 0
8	[illegible]	15 5	17 0	16 3	11 7	16 6	13 10	15 11	16 1	13 0
9	Dorchester	13 6	21 4	15 9	15 6	17 11	16 2	13 9	18 8	16 0
10	Driffield	16 6	20 0	20 8	16 9	19 1	17 1	20 8	17 6	17 3
11	Easingwold	18 2	17 [illegible]	16 11	16 2	17 3	18 5	15 6	17 6	16 11
12	Garstang	—	—	—	18 6	20 10	18 8	19 8	21 2	19 0
13	Glendale	21 0	25 0	22 6	—	—	20 7	—	—	20 9
14	[illegible]	—	—	20 0	15 0	21 0	18 4	15 0	17 0	16 0
15	Holbeach	16 6	18 6	17 6	16 11	18 5	17 6	15 0	16 0	15 6
16	[illegible]	18 0	19 0	18 9	18 0	20 0	18 0	15 0	18 0	16 4
17	Langport	11 6	15 6	14 0	13 0	15 0	14 0	11 8	15 6	13 6
18	Louth	14 6	20 0	18 1	16 11	18 5	17 8	—	—	16 0
19	Maldon	16 0	18 0	17 0	18 0	18 0	17 0	15 6	19 0	16 6
20	Melton Mowbray	21 0	19 0	18 0	17 0	20 0	18 8	15 6	18 0	16 8
21	Monmouth	—	—	—	15 0	15 11	16 4	13 6	18 0	15 4
22	[illegible]	—	—	—	18 9	13 3	15 6	12 9	18 5	11 8
23	North Witchford	16 0	20 0	17 7	15 0	16 0	15 8	11 0	16 2	14 10
24	Pershore	—	—	11 9	11 0	18 0	16 1	12 5	15 6	12 4
25	Pewsey	15 9	17 10	16 10	11 0	20 0	10 8	10 4	16 0	14 8
26	St. Neots	16 0	19 0	17 0	16 0	18 0	17 0	15 0	15 6	15 5
27	Southwell	19 0	21 0	20 0	17 0	20 0	18 6	15 0	17 0	16 5
28	[illegible]		—	11 0	—	—	17 0	13 10	15 1	16 7
29	Swaffham	17 0	22 0	19 1	14 0	20 0	17 0	11 6	11 0	15 0
30	Thakeham	15 0	16 0	15 10	14 5	18 0	16 3	15 0	16 0	15 0
31	Thame	—	—	16 1	15 9	18 0	16 0	13 6	16 1	15 0
32	Thingoe	18 6	20 3	18 10	14 4	18 4	16 0	14 0	17 4	15 0
33	Truro	—	—	18 0	17 0	18 0	14 5	11 9	16 10	14 3
34	Uttoxeter	—	—	—	16 11	18 1	18 0	16 0	18 0	17 0
35	Wantage	—	—	16 0	15 6	20 0	17 5	18 6	16 0	14 0
36	Wetherby	—	—	—	18 0	18 1	17 3	18 0	19 0	19 0
37	Wigton	—	—	—	17 9	20 0	18 10	19 0	20 0	20 1
38	Woburn	15 0	16 6	15 8	15 0	16 6	15 8	14 0	15 0	16 4
	Average	—	—	—	—	—	17 8	—	—	15 11

204. It will be seen from this table that in Stratford-on-Avon the earnings of men in charge of stock are put down at 17s., while those of ordinary labourers are put at 14s. 7d. a week, the difference being 2s. 5d. a week.

Again, in Hollingbourn district, Mr. Spencer states the earnings of stockmen as ranging from 16s. to 20s., and those of ordinary labourers at from 15s. to 20s. With regard to the first of those classes, I have taken the mean 18s. as the average, but with regard to the second, I have taken the average of the stated earnings in individual cases, which is 16s. 4d., or 2s. 6d. less than the stockman's earnings.

Again, in Swaffham, there is a difference of 2s. 6d. a week between the estimated earnings of stockmen and ordinary labourers. In this case the estimates are based upon an unusually large number of statements of actual earnings.

It is not difficult to understand those cases where a waggoner's or cowman's earnings exceed those of the ordinary labourer by 2s. or 2s. 6d. a week; the difficulty arises where these classes of men appear to earn no more, or, as in some cases, actually less than ordinary labourers.

The most noticeable instance of this is Nantwich, where Mr. Richards puts the earnings of cowmen and waggoners at 15l. to 24l. with board and lodging; a mean of 19l. 10s. with an allowance of 8s. a week for cost of board would make the average 15s. 6d. a week; or if the maximum wages be taken, the amount is only 17s. 3d. a week. Against this the earnings of the labourers are said to range from 42l. to 50l., the mean of which is 46l., or 17s. 8d. a week, a difference of 2s. 2d. a week in favour of the ordinary labourer, whose maximum earnings would be 19s. 3d. But it must be noted that this is a dairy district, and the men who are spoken of as ordinary labourers come to milk at 3.30 a.m. and stop till 7.30 p.m.; and a large proportion of them are engaged in Sunday work. This explains their comparatively high rate of wages, but it does not account for those who are called cowmen and waggoners being content with less than the others get.

In Wigton Mr. Wilson Fox gives the earnings of horsekeepers as from 16s. 3d. to 20s., and those of cattlemen as from 17s. 9d. to 18s. 3d.; these estimates are made on the basis of 7s. a week, being the value of the bed and board in the farmhouse. The mean of the two extremes is 18s. 10½d., while the mean of the ordinary labourers' earnings is 20s. 3d.

I have not altered Mr. Wilson Fox's estimate of the value of board, but if 8s. a week be taken as that value, the difference between the earnings of the different classes is reduced to 4½d. a week. Here again it must be noted that the average earnings of the farm servants are probably brought down by the class including those who are not of full age.

Easingwold is another instance where ordinary labourers appear to earn more than men in charge of stock. In this case the stockmen are generally boarded, or "mealed," as it is called.

In Driffield, Glendale, and Garstang, the estimated earnings of ordinary labourers appear to be exactly the same as those of stockmen. In the first and third of these districts the boarding system prevails. In Glendale there is a general uniformity of wages and work, in fact the ordinary labourer scarcely exists, and Mr. Wilson Fox has to cite the earnings of "spade hinds" in order to get a quotation of earnings by labourers who are not in charge of stock.

In Bromyard, Crediton, North Witchford, and Wetherby the difference between the estimated earnings of the several classes is very slight. In Bromyard, piece-work in hop-gardens; in North Witchford the large amount of piece-work done by ordinary labourers, and the comparative youth of many of the horsekeepers are, perhaps, the explanation of the circumstances.

But after all has been said it is clear that there is on the average no great difference between the earnings of men in charge of stock and those within the reach of the ordinary labourer who works for a less number of hours on six days of the week and has his Sunday entirely free.

The reason for this apparent want of correspondence between work and pay is no doubt that many men prefer the certainty and regularity of work which a carter or stockman usually secures to the more arduous toil and precarious earnings of the ordinary labourer.

205. In the following Table the districts are arranged in order according to the estimated average earnings of different classes.

Earnings of Agricultural Labourers of Different Classes.

Districts of Inquiry classified and arranged in Order from Highest to Lowest Estimated Average Weekly Earnings.

Shepherds.			Carters, Cattlemen, and others in Charge of Stock.			Ordinary Labourers.		
No.	District.	Weekly Earnings.	No.	District.	Weekly Earnings.	No.	District.	Weekly Earnings.
			1.—19s. a week and upwards.					
		s. d.			s. d.			s. d.
1	Glendale	22 6	1	Glendale	20 7	1	Glendale	20 0
2, 3	Thakeham	21 10	2	Garstang	19 [illegible]	2	Wigton	20 0
	Thingoe	21 10	3	Belper	19 [illegible]	3	Garstang	19 6
4	[illegible]	21 5	4	[illegible]	19 0			
5	Maldon	20 4						
6, 7, 8	[illegible]	20 [illegible]						
	[illegible]	20 [illegible]						
	Southwell	20 [illegible]						
9	Swaffham	19 [illegible]						
			2.—17s. and under 19s. a week.					
10	Buntingford	18 [illegible]	5	Wigton	18 10	4	Belper	18 0
11	[illegible]	18 [illegible]	6	Atcham	18 [illegible]	5	[illegible]	17 [illegible]
12	Driffield	18 [illegible]	7, 8	Melton Mowbray	18 6	6	Atcham	17 [illegible]
13	Truro	18 [illegible]		Southwell	18 6	7	Driffield	17 1
14	Louth	18 [illegible]	9	Truro	18 [illegible]	8, 9	[illegible]	17 0
15, 16	[illegible]	18 [illegible]	10	[illegible]	18 1		Wetherby	17 0
	Melton Mowbray	18 [illegible]	11, 12, 13	Holbeach	17 [illegible]			
17	North Witchford	17 [illegible]		Louth	17 [illegible]			
18	[illegible]	17 [illegible]		Swaffham	17 [illegible]			
19, 20, 21	Maldon	17 [illegible]	14	Uttoxeter	17 [illegible]			
	St. Neots	17 [illegible]	15	Wantage	17 5			
	[illegible]	17 [illegible]	16	Wetherby	17 [illegible]			
			17, 18	Buntingford	17 [illegible]			
				[illegible]	17 [illegible]			
			19	Driffield	17 [illegible]			
			20, 21, 22	Maldon	17 0			
				St. Neots	17 0			
				Stratford-on-Avon	17 0			
			3.—15s. and under 17s. a week.					
22	[illegible]	16 11	23	Thame	16 9	[illegible]	[illegible]	16 11
23	[illegible]	16 10	24	[illegible]	16 [illegible]	[illegible]	Southwell	16 6
24	[illegible]	16 3	25, 26, 27	[illegible]	16 [illegible]	[illegible]	[illegible]	16 [illegible]
25	Thame	16 1		[illegible]	16 [illegible]	[illegible]	Melton Mowbray	16 [illegible]
26	Wantage	16 [illegible]		Thingoe	16 [illegible]		Truro	16 [illegible]
27, 28	[illegible]	15 [illegible]	28	Monmouth	16 [illegible]	[illegible]	[illegible]	16 [illegible]
	[illegible]	15 [illegible]	29, 30	[illegible]	15 [illegible]		Louth	16 [illegible]
				Thakeham	15 [illegible]	17	[illegible]	15 [illegible]
			31	[illegible]	15 [illegible]	18	[illegible]	15 [illegible]
			32	Pershore	15 [illegible]	19, 20	Holbeach	15 [illegible]
			33	[illegible]	15 10		Maldon	15 6
			34	[illegible]	15 9	21	Monmouth	15 [illegible]
			35	[illegible]	15 6	22	St. Neots	15 [illegible]
			36	North Witchford	15 [illegible]	[illegible]	[illegible]	15 [illegible]
							[illegible]	15 [illegible]
							Swaffham	15 [illegible]
							Thakeham	15 [illegible]
							[illegible]	15 [illegible]
							Thingoe	15 [illegible]
			4.—Under 15s. a week.					
29	Pershore	14 9	37	[illegible]	14 10	[illegible]	North Witchford	14 10
30	Langport	14 [illegible]	38	Langport	14 0	[illegible]	[illegible]	14 [illegible]
							[illegible]	14 [illegible]
							Wantage	14 [illegible]
						[illegible]	[illegible]	14 [illegible]
						[illegible]	[illegible]	14 [illegible]
							[illegible]	14 [illegible]
						[illegible]	[illegible]	14 [illegible]
						[illegible]	Pershore	14 [illegible]
						[illegible]	Langport	[illegible]

209. It will be seen from this table that some of the districts occupy a very different position in respect of the earnings of different classes of labourers.

Thus Thakeham and Thingoe, which rank 2nd and 3rd in respect of shepherds' earnings, are 25th and 29th in respect of earnings of stockmen, and 23rd in respect of those of ordinary labourers, and while Buntingford is bracketed 17th in order of earnings by stockmen, it stands 36th in respect of earnings by ordinary labourers. Swaffham is 11th in one list and 23rd in another. Wantage stands 15th in earnings of stockmen, and 30th in those of ordinary labourers.

On the other hand, there are districts which have been already noticed, which stand high in the scale as regards earnings of ordinary labourers, while the stockmen appear to earn less than in districts of lower wages.

207. If Tables 62 and 63 are compared with Tables 56 and 57 which show the mean rate of weekly wages, it will be seen that as a rule the wages in districts where the rate is low are augmented by some means or other to a much greater degree than is the case in districts of higher nominal wages, and the fallacy of the test most usually applied, viz., that of current weekly wages, will be apparent. Weekly wages and earnings compared.

In the following table the several districts are classed as in a previous table, in respect of the mean rate of weekly wages; the estimated weekly earnings of ordinary labourers are also given, and the ratio of earnings to wages is stated.

ORDINARY LABOURERS.

DISTRICTS in Order from HIGHEST to LOWEST RATE of WEEKLY WAGES, with ESTIMATED WEEKLY EARNINGS and the RATIO of those EARNINGS to CURRENT WEEKLY WAGES.

Table 64.

No.	Districts.	Weekly Wages.	Weekly Earnings.	Ratio of Earnings to Wages.*	Average Augmentation of Wages in each Class.
	Class 1.—Wages 16s. a week and upwards.				
		s. d.	s. d.		
1, 2	Garstang	18 0	19 8	109·3	11·4 per cent.
	Wigton	18 0	20 3	112·5	
3	Glendale	17 0	20 2	118·6	
4, 5, 6	Belper	16 0	18 6	115·6	
	Uttoxeter	16 0	17 0	106·3	
	Wetherby	16 0	17 0	106·3	
	Class 2.—Wages 14s. a week and under 16s.				
7, 8	Driffield	15 6	17 1	110·2	12·4 per cent.
	Easingwold	15 6	16 11	109·1	
9 to 13	Godstone	15 0	16 3	108·3	
	Louth	15 0	16 0	106·6	
	Melton Mowbray	15 0	15 9	105·0	
	Nantwich	15 0	17 8	117·7	
	Southwell	15 0	16 6	110·0	
14	Hollingbourn	14 6	16 4	112·6	
15	Halstead	14 3	16 3	114·0	
16, 17, 18	Atcham	14 0	17 6	125·0	
	Brixworth	14 0	15 9	112·5	
	Truro	14 0	16 3	116·1	
	Class 3.—Wages 12s. a week and under 14s.				
19	Crediton	13 6	15 8	116·0	21·8 per cent.
20	St. Neots	13 0	15 9	121·2	
21	Monmouth	12 6	15 4	122·7	
22 to 28	North Witchford	12 0	15 10	131·9	
	Pershore	12 0	13 6	112·5	
	Swaffham	12 0	15 0	125·0	
	Thakeham	12 0	15 0	125·0	
	Thame	12 0	15 0	125·0	
	Thingoe	12 0	15 0	125·0	
	Woburn	12 0	14 6	120·8	
	Class 4.—Wages under 12s. a week.				
29 to 32	Basingstoke	11 6	15 0	130·4	33·4 per cent.
	Hungerford	11 6	14 4	124·6	
	Maldon	11 6	15 6	134·8	
	Stratford-on-Avon	11 6	14 7	126·8	
33 to 35	Bromyard	11 0	14 9	134·1	
	Langport	11 0	12 6	113·6	
	Wantage	11 0	14 9	134·1	
36	Cirencester	10 6	12 6	119·0	
37, 38	Dorchester	10 0	14 6	145·0	
	Pewsey	10 0	14 9	147·5	
	Average	13 3	15 11	119·2	19·2 per cent.

* Wages taken as 100.

Average ratio of earnings to wages.

208. It will be seen from this statement that the estimated earnings of ordinary labourers are in ratio to current weekly wages as 119·2 to 100, taking all the districts together, but that this ratio varies from 147·8 in Pewsey to 106·3 in Uttoxeter and Wetherby, and that as a rule the ratio increases as the districts are classed in a descending scale. Thus in the districts where wages are below 12s. a week earnings are, on the average, 33·4 per cent. in excess of wages. Where wages are over 16s. a week, earnings are, on the average, 11·4 per cent. above wages.

Earnings in 1867–70.

209. In a memorandum* upon the Reports of the Commission on the "Employment of children, &c. in agriculture," I have given an estimate which I compiled from those Reports, showing the estimated earnings of labourers in several counties at that date. In the following statement the results of the present inquiry are compared with those obtained from the former inquiry. But it must be remembered that the earlier figures refer to counties at large, and the later figures refer to selected districts only.

TABLE comparing the ESTIMATED WEEKLY EARNINGS in DISTRICTS OF INQUIRY in 1892, with those of the COUNTIES in which such DISTRICTS lie in 1867–70.

Table 44.

No.	District.	Estimated Weekly Earnings, in 1892.	Estimated Weekly Earnings, 1867–70.	Counties.
		s. d.	s. d.	
1	Atcham	17 8	12 3	Salop.
2	Basingstoke	15 0	14 0	Hants.
3	Belper	18 6	15 6	Derby.
4	Brixworth	15 0	15 3	Northampton.
5	Bromyard	14 0	12 9	Hereford.
6	Buntingford	14 1	13 6	Herts.
7	Cirencester	15 0	12 9	Gloucester.
8	Crediton	15 8	12 6	Devon.
9	Dorchester	14 6	11 6	Dorset.
10	Driffield	17 1	17 6	Yorks.
11	Easingwold	16 11	17 6	Yorks.
12	Garstang	19 6	17 9	Lancaster.
13	Glendale	20 8	17 6	Northumberland.
14	Godstone	16 0	17 8	Surrey.
15	Holbeach	15 6	16 3	Lincoln.
16	Hollingbourn	16 4	17 0	Kent.
17	Langport	17 6	12 3	Somerset.
18	Louth	16 0	16 3	Lincoln.
19	Maldon	13 5	12 3	Essex.
20	Melton Mowbray	16 3	15 5	Leicester.
21	Monmouth	15 4	13 6	Monmouth.
22	Nantwich	17 8	—†	
23	North Witchford	14 10	—†	
24	Pershore	13 6	13 5	Worcester.
25	Pewsey	14 9	10 0	Wilts.
26	St. Neots	15 3	11 3	Hunts.
27	Southwell	16 6	—†	
28	Stratford-on-Avon	14 7	13 0	Warwick.
29	Swaffham	13 0	14 9	Norfolk.
30	Thakeham	13 0	16 8	Sussex.
31	Thame	15 0	13 6	Oxon.
			14 8	Bucks.
32	Thingoe	15 0	—†	
33	Truro	16 3	12 6	Cornwall.
34	Uttoxeter	17 0	14 0	Stafford.
			15 6	Derby.
35	Wantage	14 9	13 6	Berks.
36	Wetherby	17 0	17 6	Yorks.
37	Wigton	20 3	—†	
38	Woburn	14 6	11 3	Beds.

Increase or decrease since 1867.

210. This statement shows that in 23 districts out of 33 for which estimates are available, there was an increase ranging from a few pence to 5s. 3d. a week, the most conspicuous increase being in Atcham, Truro, Glendale, Belper, Crediton, and Dorchester. In nine districts the estimated earnings are now less than they were in the counties where those districts lie at the earlier period. This decline is most conspicuous in Godstone and Thakeham, and it seems probable that the apparent decrease is due to the fact that for this inquiry rural districts of less than average wages have

* App., Vol. V., Pt. II., Sec. I., A.

† [illegible] not available.

been selected. Three of the districts where earnings appear to be less than in 1867–70 are in Yorkshire and two in Lincolnshire, one in Kent and one in Warwick. In all these cases a similar explanation may probably be offered to that suggested in the case of Surrey and Sussex.

Distribution of [illegible]

211. In so far as these figures can be relied upon they show that the earnings have increased most in the pastoral counties. Taking the agricultural divisions of England as adopted by the Board of Agriculture, there is only one district in Divisions I. and II., the most distinctly corn-growing divisions, where the increase of earnings appears to have been at the rate of 10 per cent. or upwards, and that is Melton in Leicestershire, which is chiefly pastoral in character. In that district the increase is about 20 per cent. In the Third Division, which extends from Salop to Dorset and westwards to Cornwall, every district except Langport shows a considerable increase. In Atcham it is 42·5 per cent., in Truro 30·0 per cent., in Dorchester 26·1, in Crediton 25·3 per cent. In the Northern Division the rate of increase is less marked, but as I have shown previously the average earnings of labourers were, 20 years ago, and still are, on a higher scale than in other parts of the country, and except for the Yorks districts the earnings have increased. Speaking broadly the average increase in Division I., including E. and N.E. Counties, is 1·1 per cent. In Division II., comprising S.E. and E.C. Counties, it is 1·9 per cent.; in Division III., which includes the W.M. and S.W. Counties, it is 18·4 per cent.; and in the remaining Division IV., including N. and N.M. Counties, it is 9·3 per cent.

Pastoral counties show greatest increase.

212. The conclusion to be formed from these comparative statements appears to be that there has generally been an increase of earnings, such increase being most marked in the south-west and west of England and in those districts where the rate of earnings was lowest; and that the increase has been least in the great corn-growing counties of the country, in some of which it seems doubtful whether there has not been a decline.

Hitherto the question of the remuneration and earnings of the labourer has been considered exclusively with regard to the money value received. It will, however, be necessary in a subsequent section of this Report, when examining the present condition of the labourer as compared with that of previous periods, to inquire as to the purchasing value of the money which he receives, and as to the share of the gross produce of the land which is appropriated to the reward of the labourer.

Casual labourers.

213. It is not possible to form an estimate of the total annual earnings of casual labourers or catch men. They very generally prefer the big wage which may be earned at exceptionally busy periods, and the additional wages which many farmers are willing to pay to men who are employed only when they are required, to the lower rate of wages paid to those who are regularly and constantly employed, and many of them supplement their earnings on farm work by employment in other industries.

Boys.

214. It is not easy to arrive at any very definite conclusion as to the wages and earnings of boys, as the class may include males of any age between 12 and 18 or 20 years. No doubt the rate of payment to them varies generally with that made to men, but this is not invariably the case. Where it is the custom to work many of the teams by young lads, and to employ them in the stables, they are more highly paid than where the horses are entirely worked by men.

Wages at starting.

215. In several of the district reports the wages paid to boys when they first go out to work are stated. The following statement extracted from the reports shows the starting point of wages paid to boys who are day labourers in some districts:—

Table [illegible].

From these starting points wages gradually increase until manhood is attained. In some districts a lad receives full man's wages at 18 (as in Glendale, St. Neots, &c.); in others he does not reach that standard until he is 20 years of age. Perhaps the difference which is here shown, where it is not in accordance with the scale of men's wages, may be accounted for by the difference of age at which boys commence work. Mr. Wilkinson, in his Report on Holbeach, says that in that district 1d. for each year of age may be taken as the daily rate of pay for boys—this would give to a boy of 14 a weekly wage of 7s. These wages are in corn districts subject to considerable increase in harvest. In North Witchford boys, at that season, when not working at contract work with their fathers, where they can earn 2s. to 3s. a day, are paid double wages.

216. Not infrequently the family income is substantially increased by the wages of two or three boys who are regularly employed, and though these boys cost a good deal for food and clothing (or, as the Cambridgeshire people say, "billing and filling"), a good housewife finds it far easier to provide for a large family with the united earnings of three or four members of the family, than it was to provide for a small household with only one wage-earner to rely upon.

217. In some districts boys are very commonly hired and taken into the farmer's house, or boarded and lodged at the cost of the employer in the foreman's house, and in all such cases, if the board and lodging be taken into account at its full value, the lads are more highly paid and better fed than where they work for weekly wages. The following statement shows the scale of payment reported as prevailing in certain districts, with average weekly earnings, inclusive of diet at lodging, which I have calculated at 7s. a week.

Districts.	Wages.	Average Weekly Earnings, inclusive of Board and Lodging.
Atcham	4l. 10s., rising to 15l. and 18l.	8s. 9d., 12s. 9d., 14s.
Driffield	(2l. less than number of years) lad of 14 gets 12l.; lad of 16 gets 14l.	11s. 6d. — 12s. 4d.
Easingwold	5l. and upwards	8s. 11d.
Garstang	5s. to 7s. 6d. a week	12s. — 14s. 6d.
Louth	10l. to 14l.	10s. 10d. — 12s. 5d.
Uttoxeter	7l. to 18l.	9s. 8d. — 14s.
Wetherby	Boys at 11, 6l. to 10l.	9s. 4d. — 10s. 10d.
Wigton	Young lads, 6l. to 7l.	9s. 4d. — 9s. 8d.
	Older, 8l. 10s. to 10l.	10s. 3d. — 10s. 10d.

218. The wages received by women and girls have been already stated (par. 188). It is only in a few of the districts of inquiry that any considerable number of females work, and the materials for estimating what are their aggregate earnings in the course of a year are not forthcoming, except in the case of Glendale.

Mr. Wilson Fox gives, in an Appendix to his Report on this district, the actual payments and other receipts of 12 women employed on Mr. Albert Grey's farm at East Learmouth. Of these 12, two appear to be "cottars" (women householders engaged to work on the farm and provided with a house), and their average earnings were, in 1890–91, 26l. 10s. 10½d., or at the rate of 10s. 2¼d. a week. Of this 8s. 4¾d. a week was received in cash. The 10 "women workers" received on an average 17l. 17s. 1d., or 6s. 10d. a week; the extreme range being from 10l. 12s. (= 4s. 1d. a week) to 22l. 8s. 11d. (8s. 7½d. a week).

In an estimate of the amount of wages paid at different periods to women on a large farm in the same district, workers are estimated to work 40 weeks out of 52. The annual earnings at different periods, are compared in the following table:—

219. The Reports of the Assistant Commissioners supply a few examples of the united earnings of the members of a family living under the same roof and clubbing their resources, and attention may be drawn to some of the instances recorded. Family earnings.

220. Mr. Wilson Fox, in his Summary Report, refers to the system which prevails in Northumberland, of sons and daughters of the hinds working on the same farm with their father, and living with their parents, and he remarks upon the advantages of this family arrangement. He gives, in the Appendix to his Glendale Report, an instance where the family income was 213*l.* 4*s.*, and another where it was 199*l.* 10*s.*; but these must be regarded as somewhat exceptional cases. In the first of these cases there were three men, three women, and a boy; in the second, two men, a boy, and four daughters. There are few labourers' cottages which could decently accommodate such families as these. Two statements more interesting than those just mentioned are to be found in Appendix A. of the same Report, where the expenditure of the family income is given in minute detail. At the present moment I shall only refer to the amount of the income at the disposal of the family, which consists of man, wife, four sons (æt. 21, 16, 11, 3 respectively), and one daughter (æt. 14). The three workers (two men and the boy of 16 years) earn 114*l.* 9*s.* a year. In the second case, the family includes man, wife, son a full man, three boys of 17, 12, and 4 years, and a girl aged 15. Here, again, there are three persons employed whose earnings are put down at 111*l.* 13*s.* in 48 weeks only (Jan. 1 to Dec. 1, 1891). If given for the whole year, they would amount to 119*l.* 13*s.*

Family system of Northumberland. Fox, A. 5. Fox, B. III., App. B. 10. B. III., App. A. 10.

221. Mr. Bear says, in his Report on Southwell, that "there must be many instances "of family earnings amounting to 130*l.* or more, and 120*l.* cannot be a very "uncommon sum to come into the cottage of even a day labourer's family in the course "of twelve months." His estimate is made on the assumption that a waggoner receiving 50*l.* a year has two sons who are paid 6*l.* and 10*l.* as wages, with board, for which the waggoner receives 26*l.* in each case.

Examples from other districts. Notts. Bear, B. V. 38.

222. Mr. Chapman gives, in his Report on North Witchford, particulars of the sums earned by some families in that district. In one case a working foreman, receiving a nominal wage of 14*s.* a week, is paid in cash for his own services, and those of two sons and two daughters 161*l.* 2*s.* 9*d.*, while the value of his perquisites and the produce of his land add 42*l.* 10*s.* to the earnings, making the total income 203*l.* 12*s.* 9*d.* It is a fact worthy of notice that if the four wage-earners of this family were employed full time at the wages stated the whole sum received would have been only 131*l.* 16*s.*,† out of 161*l.* 2*s.* 9*d.*, so that nearly 30*l.* must have been added to wages by piece-work or extra payments.

Cambs. Chapman, B. III., App. B.

Other instances of family earnings in the same district are given. They are as follows: 100*l.* 10*s.*, 93*l.* 19*s.* 1*d.*, 93*l.* 6*s.*, 73*l.* 7*s.* 1*d.*, 64*l.* 17*s.* 7*d.*, and 46*l.* 0*s.* 5*d.*

223. Mr. Richards, in his Bromyard Report, gives particulars of the earnings of a family consisting of father, mother, and two sons. The total amount is 109*l.* 9*s.* 6*d.*; one of the sons was absent from work 35 days and the other for 31 days. In another case the income is 90*l.* 19*s.*, and in a third 64*l.* 17*s.* 7*d.*

Hereford. Richards, B. V., App. 10 and 12.

Mr. Bear, again, in his Report on Basingstoke, has given examples of family earnings amounting to 82*l.* 4*s.*, 80*l.* 4*s.*, 79*l.* 4*s.* 6*d.*, and 74*l.* 17*s.* 5*d.*

Bear, B. IV., App. 4.

It is not necessary to adduce further proof that in many labourers' cottages the income available for the support of the family compares favourably with that of a city clerk or a poor curate.

(d.) Competing Industries and Supplementary Employment.

224. In a few of the districts of inquiry, the supply of labour and its value are materially affected by local industries, such as mines, quarries, railway works; but the greater number are free from such influence in their immediate locality, though all have been to some extent depleted of their younger and more active men, who have

Local industries.

* [illegible]

† [illegible]

	£	s.	d.
52 weeks at [illegible]	124	16	0
Foreman's wages in lieu of harvest	7	0	0
	£131	16	0

been attracted by higher wages to be earned in employment of this character. In some districts industries exist side by side with agriculture, and usefully supplement the earnings of the labourers when farm work is least abundant, or provide constant employment for some members of their families.

In about one-third of the whole number of districts there appears to be no noticeable employment but that of agriculture.*

225. On the other hand, in Belper, Monmouth, Nantwich, Truro, and Uttoxeter, there are industries which have an important influence on agriculture.

Mr. Richards says, in his Belper Report:—

"Belper is so entirely surrounded and intersected by mineral industries . . . . . that there is both a constant and large volume of demand for labour of a suitable class, and a supply of such labour in the neighbourhood. There is, however, a constantly varying quantity not employed, which is always available for the farmers. The farmers say that such labour is, under these circumstances, of little use to them, except for hitting the harvest. . . . . They require good all-round men."

Of Monmouth he says, that—

"The Forest of Dean . . . . and the very important iron and coal industries of Ebbw Vale, Tredegar, and their neighbourhood, which are very accessible from the western parishes, largely influence the agricultural labourer in the Monmouth Union."

"The young men will not learn agricultural work, but are 'off to the hills,' as they say when they go to the mines or the iron works. . . . . . Consequently the work has to be done by the middle-aged and older men, and as these die off they are not replaced."

Mr. Richards also speaks of the railway works at Crewe as having a very powerful influence on the labour market in Nantwich.

Mr. Chapman reports thus of Truro:—

"The proximity of the mines offers the agricultural labourers a chance of work, with shorter hours, more liberty, and more pay whenever they quarrel with their masters; so that the miners have the effect of creating great independence, and very often dissatisfaction with the ordinary routine work of the farm. On the other hand, when mines are in a depressed condition, and miners are thrown out of work, they increase the supply of unskilled labour beyond the demand, and cause a certain number of jobbing men to be out of employment."†

226. Among the supplementary industries open to the agricultural labourer none is, perhaps, more beneficial to him than that of work in woods.

Mr. Bear, writing of Basingstoke, says:—

"The retention of a great area of woodlands in the district must, undoubtedly, be considered an important advantage under existing circumstances.

"Apparently, the woods and coppices are now the most profitable portions of many estates, and the great amount of work which they afford must be regarded as one of the chief advantages enjoyed by the labourers of the district. During the winter, work in the coppices is found for a large number of men, while in the spring the barking and felling of trees gives further employment. Owing to the demand for labour in the woodlands during the slackest agricultural periods of the year, it has been very rare to find many men out of employment."

Work of various kinds in the woods is mentioned in the reports on Bromyard, Crediton, Driffield, Hollingbourn, Langport, Maldon, Monmouth, Pershore, Pewsey, Stratford, and Thakeham.

227. Market gardens and fruit farms are mentioned as affording considerable employment in Godstone, Holbeach, Hollingbourn, Pershore, St. Neots, Southwell, Thakeham.

The wages earned in them are generally in excess of that on farms. Watercress beds are mentioned in the Basingstoke report, and women are said to earn 15s. a week bunching the produce for market.

Osier beds and rod peeling are described as supplementary employments in Langport, St. Neots, and Southwell. Fishing, long-shore or oyster dredging, are to some extent carried on by casual agricultural labourers in Louth, Maldon, and Truro. The wives and families of agricultural labourers earn money in slop work, shirt and collar making in Langport and Thingoe; in glove making in Crediton and Langport; in lace making in Thame and Woburn; but the two last-named industries are said to be dying out.

There is very little evidence as to the aggregate earnings of labourers or their wives and families engaged in any of the occupations which have been named as

* These are the districts (13 in number) referred to:—Bromyard, [illegible], Cirencester, Dorchester, Driffield, [illegible], Glendale, Holbeach, North Witchford, Pewsey, Swaffham, Wetherby, [illegible].

† Mines, railway works, or quarries are referred to in the following districts:—Atcham, Belper, Brixworth, Garstang, [illegible], [illegible], Maldon, Monmouth, Southwell, Stratford, Thakeham, Truro, Uttoxeter, Wigton.

supplementary to that of work on the farm. The work which has to be done by men is, of course, only open to those who are unattached or engaged for short periods. It may be assumed that generally a labourer can earn more money in these occupations while working for a shorter day than that of the ordinary agricultural labourer. On the other hand, the employment is less continuous, and therefore somewhat more risky.

4. Cottage Accommodation.

228. Following the order in which the subjects are arranged in the Notes for the Inquiry, I have next to deal with the subject of the housing of the agricultural labourers, which has been investigated very thoroughly by my colleagues, who devote considerable portions of their reports to a detailed description of the nature and condition of the cottages in the districts which they visited. Heads of inquiry.

The four principal heads under which information was desired were these:—

(a.) Supply.
(b.) Situation.
(c.) Condition and construction.
(d.) Ownership and tenure.

I propose to summarise the results of the Inquiry under each of these heads. In the Analytical Index* to the Reports a full digest of the evidence is presented.

(a.) Supply.

(a.) Supply.

229. The general effect of all the Reports is that cottages are sufficient in number for the present population, but that they are unevenly distributed and consequently redundant in some places and scarce in others.

Mr. Wilson Fox and Mr. Spencer seem to have had the least reason to conclude that there was anywhere a deficient supply.

Mr. Wilson Fox says:—

"In all the five unions there was but little complaint as to the quantity of the cottages." Fox, A. 24.

Mr. Spencer reports thus:—

"In respect of number, there is no deficiency of cottages, as owing to the diminution of population more cottages are now available for a smaller population, but comparatively few new ones have been built within recent years." Spencer, A. 10.

Mr. Wilkinson found some scarcity in parts of Wetherby and Holbeach districts, where, however, there were cottages to spare in the villages. In Driffield, Uttoxeter, and Louth the number was ample. Wilkinson, A. 46, 64.

Mr. Bear says:—

"The supply of cottages is sufficient in all the districts for the existing population, though not in all parishes of each district." Bear, A. 18.

and in his Woburn report he specifies—

six parishes in that union where there is an insufficiency, attributing this in one case to the immigration of the large staff of a printing establishment, but generally to "the demolition of old and "bad cottages without a corresponding erection of new ones." One parish is named where five cottages have taken the place of 24. "Wretched hovels," "uninhabitable old dwellings" had been in many places swept away, excellent cottages had been built, but not in sufficient numbers. In one parish a long lease having fallen in, the owners were making some progress in replacing the old cottages by excellent new ones. Bear, B. I., 31.

The chief deficiency is said to be in respect of cottages on the farms.

"The consequence being that labourers have frequently long distances to walk to their work."

Mr. Chapman says on this point:—

"The statistics of population and houses show that, if people could be mathematically arranged for, there would be a house for every five persons at least in each district. . . . In some places it appears that cottages have been allowed to fall into decay or have been pulled down without any new ones being built in their place. This is not now the rule. . . . In almost all close villages the evidence is that new cottages have been recently built or are being gradually supplied, and compared with the past the diminution in the number of cottages has not kept pace with the loss of population. Cases, however, occur where young men who wish to be married have to leave a village because there is no cottage for them." Chapman, A. 26.

* Cottage accommodation. 1. Supply, number. 2. Condition, construction, accommodation. 3. Ventilation, drainage, water supply. 4. Ownership, tenure, rent, rates. Vol. I., Part VII.

Mr. Richards reports thus :—

"In every district there is a mixture of conditions in regard to the supply of cottages. Of all it is probably correct to say that in those villages which are 'close,' i.e. the property of one owner, the supply is deficient, while in 'open' villages it is abundant. Where there is one owner, upon one person only rests the obligation to repair or pull down cottages which have become decayed. Owing to the decreased acreage of arable land the demand for cottages has naturally decreased, and advantage has been taken of every opportunity of getting rid of an investment which often brings more trouble than profit. In most of the open villages there are found a number of life leasehold cottages, which, having no permanent present holder, are often allowed to run to decay. Such cottages will not be occupied while better can be had at the same rent, and such tenantless cottages often give an appearance of an abundance which really does not exist. . . . I do not remember many district having found a good cottage vacant, while in many villages it has been said that, on the event of a marriage, the newly married couple would have to lodge with the parents of one until a cottage should become vacant. As compared with the past there are everywhere fewer cottages, but in proportion to the population more. . . . Cirencester is perhaps the only union visited by me in which there is throughout a deficiency in cottage accommodation. Here in all the villages, whether good or bad, there is a deficiency, and in no part of it, except at Hatherop Castle and in the town of Cirencester, is there any attempt made to build new or replace the old."

290. These are the summary conclusions of the Assistant Commissioners as to the supply. An examination of the district Reports will show that the supply as regards numbers is described as (1) more than sufficient or ample in three districts; as (2) sufficient or fairly sufficient in 22; as (3) generally sufficient, with some qualification, in 11; as (4) barely sufficient or deficient in two districts.*

291. Of the districts where the supply is said to be barely sufficient, or distinctly deficient, one, viz., Cirencester, has already been noticed. With regard to Nantwich, another of these districts, it appears that the deficiency is occasioned by the number of resident artisans who are engaged in neighbouring industries, and the test of sufficiency applied, and regarded as fair by the Assistant Commissioner, is that if a couple wished to be married, they would have to go into lodgings until a cottage should become vacant.

292. In the 22 districts which are classed as having generally sufficient, with some qualification, the reservation is, as a rule, that there is an allegation of scarcity in some parts of the district. In some districts, however, the complaint is that the farms are badly supplied with cottages. We have previously quoted Mr. Bear's remarks on this point, which may be further examined under the subject of situation.

(b.) SITUATION.

293. In far the larger number of districts a large proportion of the labourers' dwellings are concentrated in villages or hamlets, though there are few places where some farm cottages are not to be found, and in some instances the majority of the labourers, as distinct from the unmarried farm servants, are housed on the farm. As these districts are exceptional, it will be easier to notice them than the larger number where village life prevails.

In Glendale alone, of the whole number of districts, can it be said that the whole of the regular staff of labourers is accommodated on the farm; that is an essential condition of the hiring system, which is universally adopted there, and as a consequence every man is tolerably near to his work.

In Basingstoke, Crediton, and Thakeham, the farms generally have cottages sufficient for the housing of the carters, stockmen, and shepherds employed on them.

Of Basingstoke Mr. Bear remarks that :—

"The cottages are remarkably well distributed, and except in one instance, I heard of no complaints of men being compelled to walk a long way to their work . . . as a rule, there are sufficient cottages on farms, or close to farms, for the accommodation of carters, stockmen, and shepherds."

And with regard to Thakeham, he says :—

"Instead of being nearly all crowded into villages, the labourers, to a very considerable extent, live in cottages on farms, which are usually the best of the cottages, the cheapest, and the best supplied with gardens."

* 1 More than sufficient or ample.—Buntingford, Driffield, Louth.
2 Sufficient or fairly sufficient.—Atcham, Basingstoke, Belper, Brampton, Crediton, Easingwold, Garstang, Glendale, Langport, Monmouth, Maldon, North Witchford, [illegible], [illegible], St. Neot's, Southwell, Stratford-on-Avon, Swaffham, Thakeham, Thingoe, Ulverston, Wantage.
3 Generally sufficient, with some qualification.—[illegible], Dorchester, Godstone, Holbeach, Hollingbourne, Melton Mowbray, Thame, Frome, Wetherby, Wigton, Woburn.
4 Barely sufficient.—Nantwich.
5 Deficient.—Cirencester.

Mr. Chapman says that in Crediton "it is only the catchmen or jobbing labourers who live in the villages." Those three districts are rather marked types. In several others a mixed system prevails, and farm cottages are fairly numerous, as in Atcham, Brixworth, Godstone, Holbeach, Hollingbourn, Maldon, and Pewsey. In some counties of ancient settlement, and where the parishes are generally small, the bulk of the labourers live in villages and hamlets, and not infrequently the villages are sufficiently numerous and widely spread to make them convenient for the habitations of the labourers. But very generally where cultivation has been greatly extended in modern times, and wolds and heaths, and downs and fens have been brought under the plough, the expansion of house accommodation has not kept pace with that of cultivation, and considerable hardship is sometimes experienced by those who have to add a walk of several miles to each day's work.

234. As an instance of the influence of the past upon the present the district of North Witchford may be cited. Mr. Chapman says of this district :—

"The villages were originally built upon islands in the Fens, which were few in number, so that as more land was reclaimed they became the centre of an increased population, and though there are a great many farms in the Fens there are thousands of acres unprovided with cottages, and the large majority of the labourers live in the villages at a considerable distance from their work."

The Yorkshire wolds supply a similar instance. Mr. Wilkinson writes thus of Driffield :—

"The cottages, as a rule, are collected in long village streets. Many of the villages have outlying townships, almost the only houses in which are farm houses, the labourers who are employed on the farms living in the principal village, two or three miles away. In other cases the farm houses are in the heart of the village, but the parishes are large, and the more distant parts of the farm will be often far off. In the former case the men must regularly, and in the latter must occasionally, have some distance to go to their work."

With regard to Brixworth, Mr. Richards notes an increasing tendency to build cottages on farms, though the parishes are there so numerous and compact that "in all cases the cottages are conveniently placed." In Godstone, Holbeach, and Hollingbourn, there are said to be a considerable number of cottages on farms. With the exception of the districts already named the great mass of the labourers are housed in villages.

Complaints as to distance from work are noted with regard to Buntingford, Malton, Monmouth, North Witchford, St. Neots, Stratford, Truro and Woburn.

235. The most serious complaints as to the situation of the labourers' cottages is, however, made by Mr. Richards with regard to Monmouth district, of which he writes thus :—

"The cottage question is regarded, and justly so, by the labourers as the burning question of the district. There are not two opinions as regards their situation. Unless by the merest accident, they are very inconveniently situated. They are so scattered, dotted up and down on the hill sides that it is quite an accident if a labourer has a cottage convenient to his work. The few cottages that may happen to be near a mansion or a large farm are occupied by the personal retainers of the owner or resident, while the labourers have to walk all distances from one to five miles to their work."

236. In many places efforts have been made to remedy the inconvenience which both farmers and men suffer from the want of farm cottages, and notwithstanding the unremunerative nature of an investment in cottage building, more would probably have been done were it not for the unfortunate prejudice which exists and prevails in an increasing degree against living on a farm away from the village. On this point Mr. Bear, writing of St. Neots, where some men have to walk two miles to their work, says :—

"It is to be noticed, however, that many of the cottages on the farms are empty, because the labourers, or more often their wives, refuse to live in them on account of the attractions and conveniences of village life. I heard of instances where men refused cottages on farms, with good gardens, rent free, and chose to pay 3*l*. or 4*l*. a year in villages or towns, without gardens, although they had to walk one or two miles to and from their work in consequence."

237. Mr. Bear attributes this preference for village life to the influence of association and bringing up, and he thinks that—

"If in the first instance most of the cottages for agricultural labourers had been built on the farms the difficulty in filling them would probably not be experienced."

It is not clear when the initiative ought to have been taken or when the opportunity occurred for making a fresh departure. The district in question has probably been in cultivation for many centuries, though there are other districts, no doubt, where more cottages might have been built when the prices of corn were sufficiently high to stimulate the inclosure and reclamation of wastes.

238. That the feeling against living in farm cottages is not peculiar to one part of the country is sufficiently evident from the frequent reference to the subject in the Reports. Mr. Bear found it common in Southwell and Melton Mowbray. Mr. Chapman speaks of excellent estate cottages unoccupied because the labourers chose to live in villages. And in Buntingford he said that "men frequently walk a mile or a "mile and a half rather than live in a farm cottage," and exactly the same state of things is reported as to Thame and Truro.

239. The present distribution of cottages is, no doubt, the result of causes which have been long in operation, though some of them have, no doubt, been less potent of late than they formerly were. Apart from the circumstances which led to the early settlers choosing fertile spots near running water, and clustering their habitations together for mutual protection and safety, the agrarian system of open commonable fields which prevailed over a large part of the country up to the early years of the present century must have been a great barrier to the distribution of cottages. In those parishes where the largest proportion of owners of land was to be found, there was no land outside of the village ring available for cottage sites, all the arable land being held subject to the common right of grazing in the fallow year and at other periods, and the grass was lotted meadow or common pasture, which the owner, as a tenant of the manor, could not enclose. The lord of the manor could, of course, build on his demesne, but he had no particular object in doing this, if the increasing population of the village supplied the labour required by the farmer; but he could permit, and did frequently allow, squatters to build huts on the waste of the manor, though he could not make an inclosure for the purpose of building. Thus, very generally, where the open field system existed, the increased population had to be located on the homesteads in the villages or in hamlets on the fringes of the open commons.

240. One great cause for the irregular distribution of cottages was the system of parochial responsibility for pauperism, which existed until 1865. Owners of close parishes had up to that time a strong motive for restricting the number of the resident population of those parishes to that of the barest minimum required for the constant service of the farmers, thus avoiding, as much as they could, the burden of pauperism. The restriction in the number of cottages in the close parishes stimulated the building of them in neighbouring parishes in which the labourers had to congregate. The Union Chargeability Act of 1865 removed the great obstacle to cottage building by estate owners, and there can be little doubt as to its having led to a considerable improvement; but the effects of the old system are still observable in many districts. At the present moment the dislike of the labourer to life in an isolated spot, and his objection to tying himself for a period to a particular employer, are facts to be taken into consideration in discussing the question of situation.

(c.) Condition and Construction.

241. As regards the present condition of the labourers' cottages, a general conclusion, which will apply, with very few exceptions, to all the districts of inquiry, may be briefly stated in these terms:—In every respect, whether as regards the present condition, the original construction, or the amount of accommodation provided, there is everywhere an extreme variation in the character of the houses occupied by labourers. As a rule, where a village belongs entirely or chiefly to one landowner, the cottages compare very favourably with those of "open" villages, where the property is divided and no one person has a feeling of paramount responsibility with respect to the village. Again, cottages which form part of the general equipment of a landed estate, provided by the landowner for the accommodation of those employed in the cultivation of that estate, are almost invariably superior, and are kept in better order than those which are held without any connection with farms, and hired of owners who depend to some extent upon their cottage rents for their living. Invariably the worst specimens of cottages are those which have been built by squatters on "wastes," cottages which are leaseholds, and those which belong to the parish.

242. Very generally an improvement has taken place, and is still in progress, but this is chiefly on the estates of large proprietors, and it is to be feared that a large proportion of the cottages inhabited by labourers are below a proper standard of what is required for decency and comfort, while a considerable number are vile and deplorably wretched dwellings.

The following extracts from Reports of the Assistant Commissioners may be quoted in support of the conclusions thus stated :—

243. Mr. Chapman says— Cottages classed.

"The cottages available for agricultural labourers are very unequal in the different districts and in the different parishes ; they may be roughly described as follows :— Chapman, A. 98.

(i.) Good cottages of modern construction, with proper regard to air space, ventilation, warmth and other requirements for proper sanitation. Mr. Chapman's views.

(ii.) Fairly good cottages of old construction without special regard to the rules applicable to ventilation and sanitation.

(iii.) Thoroughly bad cottages, ill-constructed, out of repair, and deficient in proper accommodation of every kind."

With regard to the first of these classes, he says that "there has been a steady improvement," that "they are gradually increasing in number, and are generally found upon estate farms or in close "villages ; they are seldom or rarely met with in districts like North Witchford, where there are no "resident proprietors."

Those of the second class "are found everywhere. They are made of all kinds of material and "differ one from the other principally in their state of repair. As a rule these cottages are com- "fortable enough, and no complaint is made of them, although they must be overcrowded at times."

The third class "are to be found in open villages where men have bought or built houses for "speculation, and on waste land where labourers have built houses for themselves. The latter are "almost invariably the worst of all."

Mr. Wilson Fox states that in the five districts which he visited there was little complaint as to the quantity of the cottages, though there was a good deal as to their structure and condition. Comparing the cottages of the North of England with those of the Eastern Counties, he says that "the worst and the best are to be found in Suffolk and Norfolk, the worst being chiefly in open "villages, where impecunious owners or small and greedy speculators are frequently the landlords, or "where 'Sicholds' are numerous. The best are nearly always situated on farms or in close villages, "belonging to landed proprietors who build them without expecting a direct return for their "money." Mr. Fox. Fox, A. 91.

Mr. Richards contrasts the condition of cottages on some estates which he names, where they are excellent, with those of open villages, "where cottages are owned either by independent cottage "owners or by life leaseholders," where there is "a large percentage of poor and dilapidated "property" and an "absence of all necessary conveniences." Mr. Richards. Richards, A. 17.

Mr. Spencer reports thus :— Mr. Spencer.

"The cottages in the best condition and affording the best accommodation are undoubtedly, as a rule, those belonging to resident landowners, or situate on large estates where there is a good agent who carefully attends to the cottage property. On most of the large estates which I saw cottages are exceedingly well kept up. Those belonging to independent owners of small means are frequently in a bad state and so too are cottages belonging to labourers themselves. These last are in many cases built on the roadside waste, of poor materials and afford indifferent accommodation. Some of the worst cottages are those held on Sichold tenure in the West of England, but this form of tenure is becoming gradually extinct." Spencer, A. 23.

Mr. Wilkinson, after describing in detail the result of his observations in each district visited, observes that "it is the same tale everywhere. Everywhere we have a considerable number of good "and even excellent cottages, and everywhere a much larger number of indifferent cottages." Mr. Wilkinson. Wilkinson, A. 47.

244. I must refer to the several Reports of my colleagues for details as to particular districts, and to the Analytical Index[1] to those Reports, which summarises the information contained in them, and content myself with a notice of a few districts which may be regarded as typical. Typical districts.

In his Summary Report Mr. Bear speaks of Southwell as, on the whole, the best in respect of labourers' dwellings, and in his Report on the district in question he says that—"Although the district "is not as remarkable for model cottages as the portion of the Woburn district where the Duke of "Bedford is the principal owner, there are fewer bad cottages in the Southwell Union than I have "seen in any district of the country in which I have travelled extensively." . . . "Nearly all the "cottages are constructed of brick and tile, and, as a rule, they are commodious" . . . "In all the "parishes visited the cottages appeared to me to be generally good. I was informed that there were "a few bad ones in two or three of the villages which I did not visit, but I can only speak of the 31 "parishes through which I passed." Bear, A. 16. Good. Bear, B. V. 33.

And with regard to Thakeham, Mr. Bear reports :—

"On the whole the cottage accommodation in the Thakeham Union is good, and in some parishes it is excellent." Bear, B. III. 38.

Mr. Spencer writes thus of Hollingbourn :—

"As regards repair, the cottages I saw struck me as being in a decidedly better state than most of those I had visited in Wiltshire and Dorsetshire. The standard is apparently considerably higher in Kent than in either of those counties, and even where belonging to persons of small means they are generally pretty well kept up. Spencer, B. III. 39.

Many old farmhouses have in recent years been converted into cottages, and give superior accommodation. B. III. 37.

[1] Vol. I., Pt. VII.

"The cottages are constructed usually either of brick or weather-boarding with tile roofs; some older ones are built of wattle and dab, that is lath and plaster; on the chalk hills they are sometimes constructed of flint. They have, as a rule, two rooms downstairs and two upstairs, but the newer ones are generally furnished with three upstairs rooms."

245. These are instances of districts exhibiting the most favourable characteristics. In the following cases the extreme variety which is frequently presented within a small area is exemplified.

Mr. Richards reports that:—

"Stratford-on-Avon presents the widest variety of cottage accommodation. Nothing could be better than the excellent houses built by the Marquis of Hertford and Mr. West, and had I not visited Ireland since, I should have added nothing could be worse than a few of the hovels found at Wellesbourne, Bearley, Wootton, Wawen, and Kineton."

And in Brixworth similar contrasts are spoken of as existing between the cottages on the estates of Earl Spencer, Lord Clifden, and Lord Wantage, and those of the open villages as already stated.

Mr. Wilson Fox, in his Report on Thingoe district, says:—

"There is a marked difference between the cottages in the 'open' and those in the 'close' villages. The lot of the labourer in the latter is very different to that of one in the former. On estates such as the Duke of Grafton's, the Marquis of Bristol's, and Lord Cadogan's, the cottages are well built and kept in excellent repair. In the 'open' villages the cottages are commonly owned by small tradesmen, who have bought the property as an investment, men without means to carry out improvements or to effect necessary repairs, and whose one object is to get as high a rent as possible. This class of property is frequently mortgaged, and in some instances there is no margin available for outlay even if the owner had the desire to improve it." *

Appended to Mr Fox's Reports on Thingoe and Swaffham are tabulated statements as to the ownership and the condition of cottages in a large number of parishes. The following is as fair a summary of the general results of those statements as can be presented in so small a compass.

246. I must refer those who wish to pursue the subject further to the valuable and interesting statements which Mr. Fox has compiled:—

COTTAGES in CLOSE and OPEN VILLAGES in the Unions of THINGOE and SWAFFHAM classified in respect of REPAIR, GENERAL CONDITION, &c.

Condition	District	Close Parishes		Open Parishes		Total in each class
Very good, excellent	Thingoe	7		—		
	Swaffham	6	13	—	—	13
Good, pretty good, or above average	Thingoe	18		2		
	Swaffham	9	27	3	5	32
Fair generally	Thingoe	—		—		
	Swaffham	2	2	3	3	5
Bad	Thingoe	—		10		
	Swaffham	1	1	1	11	12
Very bad	Thingoe	—		2		
	Swaffham	—	—	1	3	3
						65
Ownership mixed and condition varied or undefined	Thingoe 9, Swaffham 4					13
						78

The information upon which these statements were based was given by sanitary officers. It will be seen that out of 65 villages for which sufficiently definite information is given 45 are described as "above average" or "very good," and that 40 of these are

* In App. B. 19 to the Thingoe Report some instances of ownership are given; in one of them a poor widow [illegible] from the [illegible] ownership of a row of houses, and this is her whole source of livelihood.

close villages; on the other hand, 15 are classed as "bad," or "very bad," and only one of them is a close village.

247. As an instance of the worst type of district is Mr. Richards' description of the cottage accommodation in the Monmouth Union, that district having already been noticed as one where great complaints as to the situation of the cottages were made. Mr. Richards says: "During five days of "driving I did not see more than half-a-dozen really good cottages. . . . Some of the farmers "described as good cottages which are very bad as compared with, for example, the model "cottages found in some of the villages in Warwickshire, Northampton, and Gloucestershire. The "standard of such cottages is three rooms upstairs, one room 10 feet by 10 feet, and two rooms "rather smaller, ceiled and a fireplace in at least one of the bedrooms, and two rooms down, one "a good room at least 12 feet by 12 feet, and a good back kitchen or parlour, and good washing and "outdoor conveniences. I did not find one cottage up to this standard, though there were perhaps "about six having the standard number of rooms.

"The average number of rooms is placed as two up and two down, but this can only be arrived at by counting as a room what is at least a small lumber room or pantry, opening from the side or back of the living room, as a rule the cottages are in bad repair. . . . They are mostly built of stone, with rough slate roof, though some old mud and thatch cottages are found here and there, the thatch is all cases very poor and thin, as compared with that usually put on cottages in the north. The rooms are small and entirely devoid of the usual conveniences."

Worst type of district. Richards, B. IV. 52, 58.

248. Another district of inferior accommodation is that of North Witchford in Cambs, of which Mr. Chapman speaks in the following terms:—

"The cottage accommodation is the worst feature of the Union. The majority of cheap cottages are bad, and a great many of them appear to me quite unfit for habitation. This is especially the case in the Fens, but even in the towns and villages there are still a great many with only one bedroom which is approached by a ladder through a hole in the floor without a trap-door to cover it. The fen cottages and cottages built upon the waste are usually built of what is called mud and stud, and are remarkable for the low pitch of the doors and ceilings. Most of the cottages are in the hands of small proprietors, who depend upon them for profit, and there is no resident squire or large proprietor to set an example to his neighbours by building new agricultural cottages or improving the old ones."

Another district of inferior accommodation. Chapman, B. III. 43.

249. Mr. Spencer, in his Report on Dorchester, quotes from a Report made by the late Hon. E. Stanhope to the Royal Commission on the Employment of Children, &c., 1867, some very severe strictures on the state of the cottages in Dorsetshire, and the impediment which leases for lives presented to improvements, and he says:—

Leases for lives an impediment to improvement.

"These remarks I have no hesitation in endorsing with regard to many of the cottages in the "district. In Charminster there are 130 labourers' cottages of which 18 have more than two "bedrooms, and three one bedroom only; 50 of these cottages are owned by large landowners and "let with farms of 300 to 600 acres, four are let with a farm of 70 acres, 11 belong to the County "Asylum, one is the freehold property of the labourer who inhabits it, and the remainder belong to "independent owners. . . . The repair is, according to my observations, bad in almost all of "these without much distinction of ownership." . . . And later on Mr. Spencer says, "I was "informed that many of the houses had probably had little done to them since they were visited by "Mr. Stanhope on the occasion of the former Commission."

Spencer, B. I. 6.

But even in this district is able to state that—

"Speaking generally, it appears to me that in many places considerable improvement has been effected in the cottages in recent years, but . . . a large number of the cottages are still bad."

250. The following attempt to classify the different districts in accordance with the Reports of the Assistant Commissioners must be regarded as a tentative effort to arrange them in respect of their general characteristics:—

Districts classified.

Table III.

1. Good generally	2. Fair	3. Varying from Good to Bad	4. Bad generally	5. Very Bad
Crediton.	Basingstoke.	Atcham.	Buntingford.	Bromyard.
Godstone.	Belper.	Brixworth.	Dorchester.	Cirencester.
Hollingbourne.	Garstang.	Glendale.	Driffield.	[illegible]
Southwell.	Louth.	Holbeach.	Maldon.	Monmouth.
Thakeham.	Melton Mowbray.	Langport.	North Witchford.	St. Neots.
Woburn.	Uttoxeter.	Nantwich.	Pewsey.	
	Wetherby.	Pershore.	Thame.	
	Wigton.	Stratford-on-Avon.	Truro.	
		Swaffham.		
		Thingoe.		
		Wantage.		
6	8.	11.	8	5.

Census Returns as to tenements.

251. Information as to the general character of the cottage accommodation in the districts of inquiry may be supplemented by some notes on Returns collected at the Census of 1891 on the subject of tenements of less than five rooms. In the General Report of the Commissioners the results for the whole country are given, and those for the urban and rural districts are separately stated. In Vol. II. the particulars for each sanitary area (urban or rural) are given. Table 6 in each divisional Report gives the total number of tenements in each district, the number of tenements having one, two, three, or four rooms respectively, and the number of tenements in each of those classes having one, two, three, &c., up to 12 or more occupants.

Tenement defined.

Census Returns, Vol. IV., p. 30.

252. The Commissioners state that in the instructions given to the enumerators a tenement for the purposes of the Return was defined as "*any house or part of a house separately occupied either* "*by the owners or by a tenant.*" They state that notwithstanding this plain instruction the term tenement was a cause of much confusion, houses and tenements being in some cases treated as equivalent terms, while on the other hand hundreds of flats were returned as separate houses. Errors of this kind would obviously be less likely to occur in rural districts, such as those with which we have to deal than in big towns. Another opportunity of confusion which is everywhere presented is with regard to the definition of a "room."

Possible misconceptions.

253. The Commissioners say on this point, "The term room is very elastic, and can be stretched by "those who please, to cover a landing, a lobby, a closet, or any other more or less distinct space "within a dwelling. . . . It is possible that the want of precision in the use of the term may "account for some of the extraordinary differences in regard to house accommodation which will be "shown to exist between different counties and different towns."

Number and proportion of tenements in five classes.

254. The Summary Tables given in the General Report show the number and proportion of tenements in five classes, containing respectively one, two, three, four, and five or more rooms, the number and proportion of the occupants of each class of tenements, the average number of occupants per room in each class, and further particulars with reference to the evidence of the figures in question on the subject of overcrowding. These tables deal with England and Wales as a whole, and then with the urban and rural districts separately, a very marked difference being exhibited between these two divisions of the country. Thus as regards the percentage of the population in each group of tenements, the figures of the three tables are as follows:—

Table for

255. I have examined the Returns for the several districts of inquiry, with a view to comparing them with each other, and with the general or average conditions of the country. These districts are almost entirely of a rural character, there being only five of them which contain a town of 10,000 inhabitants,* although many of them include within their boundaries what are technically classed as Urban Sanitary Districts. I have, therefore, in the following tables taken the percentages applying to the rural districts of England and Wales as the standard of comparison. It happens, however, that in most cases the urban portions of the districts of inquiry the conditions are more favourable than they are in the rural parts of the district, in this respect differing widely from the results which have been shown to prevail with regard to urban and rural districts generally, results which are produced by the overcrowding which is common in large towns, but is apparently less common in small country towns than in villages and the surrounding rural districts.

It would be impossible within any fair limits of space or time to thoroughly investigate the statistics as to habitations in the districts of inquiry. I propose to give with regard to all of them, some information on the subject, and then to select for more minute inquiry a few of the more striking instances of departure from the average conditions of the country.

256. In the following table the proportionate number of tenements which have from one to four rooms, and the proportionate part of the whole population in each district inhabiting tenements with the maximum accommodation of four rooms, is given both for the Rural portions of the districts, and also where Urban areas are included in the district of inquiry for the whole district, Urban and Rural together.

TABLE showing HABITATIONS for the several DISTRICTS of INQUIRY, the PER-CENTAGE of the WHOLE NUMBER of TENEMENTS which have less than Five Rooms, and also the Percentage of the whole population Occupying such Tenements.

Percentage of Total Number of Tenements with less than Five Rooms		Districts of Inquiry.	Percentage of Total Population, Composed of Tenements of less than Five Rooms	
Rural and Urban Districts together	Rural Sanitary Districts only		Rural Sanitary Districts only.	Rural and Urban Sanitary Districts together
[illegible]	[illegible]	1. Alston	[illegible]	[illegible]
[illegible]	[illegible]	2. Basingstoke	[illegible]	[illegible]
[illegible]	[illegible]	3. Belper	[illegible]	[illegible]
—	[illegible]	4. Bosworth	[illegible]	—
. .	[illegible]	5. Bromyard	[illegible]	. .
. .	[illegible]	6. Buntingford	[illegible]	. .
[illegible]	[illegible]	7. Cirencester	[illegible]	[illegible]
[illegible]	[illegible]	8. Crediton	[illegible]	[illegible]
[illegible]	[illegible]	9. Dorchester	[illegible]	[illegible]
[illegible]	[illegible]	10. Driffield	[illegible]	[illegible]
—	[illegible]	11. Easingwold	[illegible]	—
—	[illegible]	12. Garstang	[illegible]	—
—	[illegible]	13. Glendale	[illegible]	—
. .	[illegible]	14. Godstone	[illegible]	—
[illegible]	[illegible]	15. Holbeach	[illegible]	[illegible]
—	[illegible]	16. Hollingbourne	[illegible]	—
—	[illegible]	17. Langport	[illegible]	—
[illegible]	[illegible]	18. Louth	[illegible]	[illegible]
[illegible]	[illegible]	19. Maldon	[illegible]	[illegible]
[illegible]	[illegible]	20. Melton Mowbray	[illegible]	[illegible]
[illegible]	[illegible]	21. Monmouth	[illegible]	[illegible]
[illegible]	[illegible]	22. Nantwich	[illegible]	[illegible]
[illegible]	[illegible]	23. North Witchford	[illegible]	[illegible]
—	[illegible]	24. Pershore	[illegible]	—
. .	[illegible]	25. Pewsey	[illegible]	—
[illegible]	[illegible]	26. St. Neots	[illegible]	[illegible]
. .	[illegible]	27. Southwell	[illegible]	—
[illegible]	[illegible]	28. Stratford-on-Avon	[illegible]	[illegible]
[illegible]	[illegible]	29. Swaffham	[illegible]	[illegible]
—	[illegible]	30. Thakeham	[illegible]	—
[illegible]	[illegible]	31. Thame	[illegible]	[illegible]
—	[illegible]	32. Thingoe	[illegible]	—
[illegible]	[illegible]	33. Truro	[illegible]	[illegible]
—	[illegible]	34. Ulverston	[illegible]	. .
[illegible]	[illegible]	35. Wantage	[illegible]	[illegible]
. .	[illegible]	36. Westbury	[illegible]	—
[illegible]	[illegible]	37. Wigton	[illegible]	[illegible]
—	[illegible]	38. Woburn	[illegible]	—
	[illegible]	Average Rural Districts, England and Wales	[illegible]	

about 55 per cent. of their population in tenements of one to four rooms; then follow Brixworth, Swaffham, and Buntingford, with 50 per cent. or upwards similarly housed. It so happens that 19 districts out of the 38 in England have more than the average proportion of small tenement population than the rural districts of the country have as a whole, while 19 have in their rural parts an over average proportion of the number of tenements of less than five rooms. Of the 38 districts Garstang has the smallest percentage of population (less than 25 per cent.) in small tenements. Godstone and Thakeham have about 27 per cent; Hollingbourn, Uttoxeter, Easingwold, have from 28 to 31 per per cent. thus housed.

Low percentage of small tenements.

Details further examined.

258. It is not, however, enough to inquire how many people in each locality have to put up with limited accommodation. A district with 60 per cent. of its population in houses of less than five rooms might be a poor one, but its inhabitants might be more comfortably housed, and there might be much less crowding if a large proportion of the small tenements had four rooms, than another district with a comparatively small number of small tenements, which were mainly of one room. I will, therefore, proceed to examine in greater detail the statistics relating to some districts which I select because in the previous list they exhibit a considerable departure from the average conditions of the rural districts.

Districts of high percentage of population in small tenements.

259. There are five districts of enquiry where the population inhabiting one to four-room tenements are 25 per cent. in excess of the average.

In the following Table particulars as to the population in tenements of each class in those districts are given, the districts being arranged in order from the highest to lowest proportion which the total of these four classes bears to the total population (col. 5):—

Table 74.

Selected Districts	Percentage of Population who are Occupants of Tenements containing less than Five Rooms. A Rural Districts. Tenements with					B Urban and Rural Districts together. Tenements with				
	1 One Room	2 Two Rooms	3 Three Rooms	4 Four Rooms	5 One to Four Rooms	6 One Room	7 Two Rooms	8 Three Rooms	9 Four Rooms	10 One to Four Rooms
1. Glendale	16·16	36·65	17·[illegible]	[illegible]	7[illegible]·81	—	—	—	—	—
2. Wantage	0·[illegible]	7·10	16·45	30·45	58·[illegible]	0·[illegible]	9·03	16·[illegible]	27·21	53·53
3. Thame	1·18	8·70	13·22	53·72	75·[illegible]	0·10	7·34	11·30	31·10	50·10
4. Pewsey	0·19	6·00	30·77	21·13	58·09	—	—	—	—	—
5. Thingoe	0·37	1·99	19·54	30·61	51·39	—	—	—	—	—

In this Table the remarkable characteristics of the Glendale district are exhibited, no less than 52·81 per cent. of the whole of the population being crowded into tenements of one or two rooms.

Districts of low percentage.

260. There are, as it happens, five other districts where the population occupying the small tenements is 25 per cent. below the average number for the rural districts of England and Wales, and the details of the proportionate number in each class of tenements are given in the following table:—

Table 75.

Selected Districts.	Percentage of Population who are Occupants of Tenements containing less than Five Rooms. Rural Districts. Tenements.				
	1 One Room.	2 Two Rooms.	3 Three Rooms.	4 Four Rooms.	5 One to Four Rooms.
1 Garstang	0·41	1·65	6·17	16·[illegible]	2[illegible]·65
2 Godstone	0·[illegible]	[illegible]	3·[illegible]	18·[illegible]	[illegible]
3 Thakeham	0·13	0·81	[illegible]	[illegible]	2[illegible]·67
4 Hollingbourn	0·10	0·75	[illegible]	2[illegible]	[illegible]
5 Uttoxeter	[illegible]	[illegible]	[illegible]	[illegible]	[illegible]

262. Taking the rural districts of England and Wales again as the standard of comparison, the following Table shows the average per-centage of all small tenements in each of four classes, and the average per-centage of the occupants of these tenements who are in each class:—

Percentage of Total Number of Tenements of less than 5 Rooms		England and Wales (Rural Districts)	Per-centage of Total Number of Occupants of Tenements of less than 5 Rooms	
One to two rooms	1·97	One room	1·40	One to two rooms.
19·03	17·06	Two rooms	13·[illegible]	14·[illegible]
	24·[illegible]	Three rooms	23·7[illegible]	
	56·[illegible]	Four rooms	61·[illegible]	
	100·00		100·00	

On the average, about one-fifth in number of the small tenements contain only one or two rooms, while about one-seventh of the small tenement population is housed in these two classes of accommodation.

263. In the following Table particulars as to the numbers and population in one and two room tenements are given for eight districts, which in either one category or another exceed [in] their rural districts the average proportion of the rural districts of England and Wales. The districts are arranged in order of highest to lowest per-centage of all occupants of small tenements. I have in this Table and in the selection of these districts, taken a high per-centage of small tenements and of occupancy in the classes containing only one or two rooms as indisputable indications of a low class of accommodation as regards comfort and decency. Whatever extenuating circumstances may be urged on the ground of the rooms being large, it cannot, I think, be denied that tenements of two rooms inhabited by families lack some of the requirements of comfort and decency. A few habitations of this class inhabited by married couples without children might prove a convenience rather than otherwise, but wherever one cottage out of five contains less than three rooms, or one cottage occupant out of seven has to live in tenements of this character, the standard of accommodation must be considered deplorably defective. I have used the word cottage in the preceding sentence, because in rural districts the terms cottages and tenements are practically the same thing.

TABLE showing DISTRICTS selected as exhibiting a large PER-CENTAGE of small TENEMENTS or of the OCCUPANTS of such TENEMENTS containing less than THREE ROOMS.

	Percentage of Small Tenements having One, Two, Three, or Four Rooms respectively									
	Rural Parts of Districts. Tenements having					Urban and Rural Parts of Districts. Tenements having				
	1. One Room.	2. Two Rooms.	3. One or Two Rooms.	4. Three Rooms.	5. Four Rooms.	6. One Room.	7. Two Rooms.	8. One or Two Rooms.	9. Three Rooms.	10. Four Rooms.
Glendale	[illegible]	[illegible]	[illegible]	[illegible]	9·[illegible]	—	—	—	—	—
Garstang	[illegible]	[illegible]	[illegible]	[illegible]	[illegible]	—	—	—	—	—
Truro	[illegible]	[illegible]	[illegible]	[illegible]	[illegible]	[illegible]	[illegible]	[illegible]	[illegible]	[illegible]
Axbridge	[illegible]	[illegible]	[illegible]	[illegible]	[illegible]	[illegible]	[illegible]	[illegible]	[illegible]	[illegible]
Thame	[illegible]	[illegible]	[illegible]	[illegible]	[illegible]	[illegible]	[illegible]	[illegible]	[illegible]	[illegible]
Driffield	[illegible]	[illegible]	[illegible]	[illegible]	[illegible]	[illegible]	[illegible]	[illegible]	[illegible]	[illegible]
Wantage	[illegible]	17·[illegible]	[illegible]	[illegible]	[illegible]	[illegible]	[illegible]	[illegible]	[illegible]	[illegible]
Average for Rural Districts of England and Wales	1·97	17·06	19·03	[illegible]	[illegible]	—	—	—	—	—

PER-CENTAGE of OCCUPANTS of small TENEMENTS in each CLASS of TENEMENTS having ONE to FOUR ROOMS.

—	1. One Room.	2. Two Rooms.	3. One or Two Rooms.	4. Three Rooms.	5. Four Rooms.	6. One Room.	7. Two Rooms.	8. One or Two Rooms.	9. Three Rooms.	10. Four Rooms.
Glendale	[illegible]	[illegible]	[illegible]	[illegible]	[illegible]	—	—	—	—	—
Garstang	[illegible]	[illegible]	[illegible]	[illegible]	[illegible]	—	—	—	—	—
Axbridge	[illegible]	[illegible]	[illegible]	[illegible]	[illegible]	[illegible]	[illegible]	[illegible]	[illegible]	[illegible]
Truro	[illegible]	[illegible]	[illegible]	[illegible]	[illegible]	[illegible]	[illegible]	[illegible]	[illegible]	[illegible]
Driffield	[illegible]	[illegible]	[illegible]	[illegible]	[illegible]	[illegible]	[illegible]	[illegible]	[illegible]	[illegible]
Thame	[illegible]	[illegible]	[illegible]	[illegible]	[illegible]	[illegible]	[illegible]	[illegible]	[illegible]	[illegible]
Wantage	[illegible]	[illegible]	[illegible]	[illegible]	[illegible]	[illegible]	[illegible]	[illegible]	[illegible]	[illegible]
Average for rural districts of England and	[illegible]	13·31	[illegible]	[illegible]	[illegible]	—	—	—	—	—

Overcrowding

242. There is one other aspect in which the statistics now under consideration may be regarded, and that is with respect to the average number of occupants per room in each class of small tenements. The average conditions in the rural districts of England and Wales are stated in the General Report of the Census Commissioners to be as follows:—

Average occupants per room in tenements of one room - - - 2·16
" " " two rooms - - - 1·58
" " " three rooms - - - 1·23
" " " four rooms - - - 1·10

In the following Table I have, I believe, included every district of inquiry where the average numbers above stated are exceeded in any of the four classes of tenements. The Census Commissioners treat as cases of overcrowding in the classes of tenements under consideration all those where there are more than two occupants per room.

AVERAGE NUMBER of OCCUPANTS per ROOM in TENEMENTS of different CLASSES.

Table 79.

	Rural Parts of Districts.				Urban and Rural Parts of Districts.			
	1. One Room.	2. Two Rooms.	3. Three Rooms.	4. Four Rooms.	5. One Room.	6. Two Rooms.	7. Three Rooms.	8. Four Rooms.
Atcham	[illegible]	[illegible]	[illegible]	[illegible]	[illegible]	[illegible]	[illegible]	[illegible]
Driffield	[illegible]	[illegible]	[illegible]	[illegible]	[illegible]	[illegible]	[illegible]	[illegible]
Garstang	[illegible]	[illegible]	[illegible]	[illegible]	—	—	—	—
Glendale	[illegible]	[illegible]	[illegible]	[illegible]	—	—	—	—
Louth	[illegible]	[illegible]	[illegible]	[illegible]	[illegible]	[illegible]	[illegible]	[illegible]
Pewsey	[illegible]	[illegible]	[illegible]	[illegible]	—	—	—	—
Average for Rural Districts in England and Wales	2·16	1·58	1·23	1·10	—	—	—	—

It will be observed that in five out of the six districts named this number is exceeded, though in Atcham the excess is very small, and in that district as well as in Garstang and Louth, the over-crowding is confined to one-room tenements. The overcrowding occurs in two-room tenements in Glendale, and in four-room houses in Driffield; and in the former district the average proportions for the country are exceeded in each of the four classes. Pewsey exceeds the average in only one class, that of three-room tenements, and the excess is so small that the district may be dismissed from consideration in this connection, since 1·35 persons per room in a three room tenement means only a fraction over an average of four persons per tenement. This Table must be read in connection with others which have been previously given. It has been shown in Table 72 that in Garstang only 0·48 per cent. of the population live in one-room tenements, and as a matter of fact there are only 17 of these tenements with 38 occupants in the district, so that it would be unfair to brand the district as an overcrowded one on the strength of these few instances. Louth, again, has only 14 tenements of one room out of 2,300, so that overcrowding is not there very common. Atcham has 33 tenements of this class, and 800 of three rooms with above the average number of occupants. Driffield has in its rural districts 75 one room tenements, with 267 inhabitants, or an average of 3·56 occupants for each room, but in all the other classes the number of inhabitants per room is not exceptional.

[illegible]

243. Glendale remains by the process of elimination which has been pursued the most conspicuous instance of limited accommodation affecting a very large proportion of the population. The figures already relating to this district which have appeared in previous Tables may be be usefully collected and supplemented by others which have not yet been stated.

GLENDALE, a rural sanitary district; acreage, 147,816. Total population (1891), 10,156; (1881), 10,[illegible]. Houses, inhabited, 2,0[illegible]; uninhabited, 168; building, 9. Tenements, 2,133; ratio of tenements to inhabited houses as 10[illegible] to 100.

of overcrowding as defined by the Census Commissioners, including in it tenements of one room with more than two occupants, those of two rooms with more than four, those of three rooms with more than six, and those of four rooms with more than eight occupants.

Table 8[illegible]

Number of Occupants of Tenements.	One Room. Tenements.	One Room. Occupants.	Two Rooms. Tenements.	Two Rooms. Occupants.	Three Rooms. Tenements.	Three Rooms. Occupants.	Four Rooms. Tenements.	Four Rooms. Occupants.	Less than Five Rooms. Tenements.	Less than Five Rooms. Occupants.
Three	68	204	—	—	—	—	—	—	68	204
Four	61	244	—	—	—	—	—	—	[illegible]	[illegible]
Five	44	[illegible]	[illegible]	[illegible]	—	—	—	—	[illegible]	[illegible]
Six	[illegible]	[illegible]	[illegible]	[illegible]	—	—	—	—	[illegible]	[illegible]
Seven	[illegible]	[illegible]	[illegible]	[illegible]	[illegible]	[illegible]	—	—	[illegible]	[illegible]
Eight	16	[illegible]	[illegible]	[illegible]	[illegible]	[illegible]	—	—	104	[illegible]
Nine	11	99	[illegible]	[illegible]	[illegible]	[illegible]	[illegible]	[illegible]	[illegible]	[illegible]
Ten	3	[illegible]	7	70	[illegible]	[illegible]	—	—	19	[illegible]
Eleven	5	55	[illegible]	[illegible]	[illegible]	[illegible]	[illegible]	[illegible]	[illegible]	[illegible]
Twelve or more	—	—	6	[illegible]*	[illegible]	[illegible]*	[illegible]	[illegible]*	[illegible]	[illegible]*
	[illegible]	[illegible]	[illegible]	[illegible]	[illegible]	[illegible]	[illegible]	[illegible]	[illegible]	[illegible]

* Number taken at 12, but it may be more.

266. It is certainly a remarkable fact that in so far as the house accommodation in the districts of inquiry can be tested by the Census Returns, Glendale, which is a district of comparatively high wages, and one in which, if any other standard than the one under consideration be applied, the great majority of the agricultural labourers stand upon the highest level, compared with England generally, should exhibit such a deplorable condition of affairs, and it is no less remarkable that of the six districts included in Table 75 in which overcrowding, as defined by the Census Commissioners, is found, only one, Pewsey, can be classed as a district of comparatively low wages or low earnings (see Tables 57, 63).

267. There are, however, many other points of view from which the cottage accommodation of different districts may be regarded, besides those of condition, construction, and number of rooms. It may be urged with reason that the size of the rooms is a very important consideration, and that a two or three-roomed tenement of one district may compare very favourably with a four or five-roomed tenement in another part of the country; and, as regards cubical space, it is no doubt true that the larger size of the rooms in the northern districts does mitigate the conditions, and, if no considerations of decency and the proper separation of the sexes in their sleeping apartments were involved, it would be possible to present a much more favourable view of the housing of the labourers in Glendale, as compared with other parts of the country; but this plea cannot be urged in justification of the one and two-roomed tenements in which so large a number of families have to live, as has been proved to be the case, in the district of inquiry in Northumberland, by the figures submitted.

Size of rooms

With regard to the size of rooms and the cubical space of cottages in different districts, the Reports of the Assistant Commissioners, and particularly those of Mr. Fox and Mr. Spencer, give a very large amount of information, and a few examples may be selected as exhibiting the different types of cottages which exist.

268. Mr. Bear gives in an Appendix to his Report on the Woburn district details as to the dimensions of cottages provided by the Dukes of Bedford on the Woburn estate at different periods, viz., 1845, 1850, 1865, and 1870, with particulars as to outhouses, &c., and cost of construction. The cottages of 1870, which are markedly in advance of those of previous periods, contain living room, kitchen, pantry, three bedrooms, two of which are provided with fireplaces, with detached washhouse, coal barn, earth-closet, and soft water tank. Cottages of this class are let, with gardens of 40 perches, at 1s. 7d. a week, or 4l. 2s. 4d. a year. The cubical contents of the rooms in these houses are about 6,100 feet, while the rooms in cottages built about 1850 contained only about 3,600 cubic feet of room space. In his Report on Thakeham, Mr. Bear gives some particulars as to cottages on the Duke of Norfolk's estate, which contain two downstairs rooms, each 12 by 12, and pantry, and three large bedrooms. He also describes some on Lord Leconfield's estate, with living room, kitchen of good size, and four bedrooms. Mr. Spencer gives particulars of some cottages in Hollingbourn, built by a resident landowner, containing two downstairs rooms, 14 by 14 and 13 by 13 respectively, a pantry and three bedrooms 14 by 14, 10 by 7, and 13 by 13, all 10 feet high; the cubical space of the rooms in this instance is 8,000 cubic feet, without taking into account the pantry, the dimensions of which are not stated.

269. The cottages already described represent the highest type of labourers' houses, such as are found on many of the large estates throughout the country. The great

Spencer, B. IV. 33, and App. Richards, A. 37. Chapman, B. II. Fox, B. I. Chapman, A. 96 (k). Spencer, A. 33.

majority of the labourers have to live in cottages of very inferior character to those already noticed. Mr. Chapman gives a description of what he calls old-fashioned, moderate cottages, which are, he says, to be found everywhere.

"They contain, as a rule, one sitting-room of fair size, about 12 feet square and 7 feet high, and two bedrooms, which have not separate access. They often have no fireplace in a bedroom, and the windows are upon the floor level, so that there is no proper escape for the foul air. They have back kitchens, with no coppers or proper fireplaces." Mr. Spencer describes an ordinary two-storied cottage thus:—

"Downstairs there is usually a living room, in size about 12 by 12 by 8, and a small back kitchen, scullery, or pantry; upstairs in an old cottage there will be one good-sized bedroom, and one smaller one, into which the staircase often leads; more often than not neither bedroom has a fireplace."

Wilkinson, A. 65.

Mr. Wilkinson speaks of a fairly good four-roomed house as containing "a principal room, 14 by "13 by 8 (which is larger than the average), with a bedroom of the same dimensions over it, and a "back kitchen or scullery of say 11 by 8 by 8, with a bedroom over it. One or other room will "have a considerable space taken out of it by the staircase. The back bedroom will generally have "a sloping roof, coming sometimes to the floor itself, and generally to within two or three feet "of it."

Fox, B. III. 31.

Mr. Wilson Fox describes the cottages in Glendale thus—

"The houses are generally built on one floor, and go by the name of 'two end houses.' Although "some new ones are now being made with a storey above, many 'two end' ones are still being built, "as they usually prefer them, partly perhaps from habit, partly because they dislike the trouble "of going up and down stairs, and also because they only necessitate the burning of one fire. "A 'two end' house usually consists of a good sized kitchen, which is used both as a living room and "a sleeping room, often about 21 by 16, and one other smaller room, a small pantry or back kitchen, "and a loft above the kitchen and communicating with it by a ladder, in which some of the family "often sleep." In the Appendix to the Report he gives particulars as to 24 cottages in the district; only one of these can be described as having five rooms. It has two rooms downstairs, each of them 16 by 12, and two above which are 16 by 9 and 12 by 9 respectively. The cubical contents of these rooms would be nearly 3,000 feet. There are also a small loft and a pantry. This cottage is perhaps hardly a labourer's dwelling, as it is held with four acres of land. Another type of cottage has three ground-floor rooms, 21 by 16, 12 by 9, and 12 by 9, with a loft, the cubic space of the three rooms being 1,416 feet. A third type has one room 18 by 18 by 8 on the ground floor, and two bedrooms 15 by 9 by 9 and 18 by 12 by 8 respectively, the cubical space being 5,835 feet. Then there are two-room cottages containing about 3,300 cubic feet, and in the lowest class one-room cottages, of which the worst specimen seems to be fourth on the list, the room being 18 by 12 by 7 (1,512 cubic feet), this room being inhabited by a man, his wife, a son aged 15, and two girls, aged 21 and 17.

Worst types of cottages.

270. If we compare the last-named cottage with some of a bad type in other parts of the country, we shall see that as regards space the Glendale cottages are by no means the worst specimens, of which a few instances may be culled from the Reports:—

Bear, B. II. 22.

Mr. Bear describes a pair of cottages in Little Stoughton as containing a living room about 11 by 10, with a bedroom over it of the same measurements. There is no ceiling in the bedroom between the floor and the thatch, and the tenant has put up an apology for a ceiling consisting of paper.

Chapman, B. III. 45.

Mr. Chapman describes a few cottages of the old type which he found—

"Occupied by a labourer who farmed four acres of land and had nine children. It had one sitting room with roof sloping to four feet, doors about 5 feet 6 inches high, two bedrooms, one bad in pantry, all on the ground floor."

And in his final Report he gives a general description of the faults which characterise the worst class of cottages.

Chapman, A. 96.

"Rooms 6 feet high below or between the rafters, where they should be 7 feet 6 inches or 8 feet. In the Fens the height is sometimes even less than that, and the occupants are in danger of striking their heads against the beam which supports the ceiling. The room is often only nine feet square. . . . one bedroom only, or one bedroom and an alcove upon the landing, each of them containing only about half the cubic air space for two adults which should be allowed for one. A small ladder reaching to the bedroom instead of a proper staircase. One bedroom window about a fourth of the proper size, on the floor below the wall plate or on the floor, corner wise, instead of two windows against the ceiling. No fireplace in the bedroom. Walls built of half brick nogging instead of the thickness of a brick and a half. Roofs of thatch instead of tiles or slates, in places where the occupiers are dependent upon rain water for the supply of the house, draught without ventilation, and smoky chimneys, no back kitchen or coppers."

Spencer, B. V., App. C.

Mr Spencer gives in the Appendix to his Report on the Maldon district some extracts from a recent official Report on the Housing of the Working Classes in the Chelmsford and Maldon Rural Sanitary District, by Dr. Thresh (D.Sc., M.B.), Medical Officer of Health to the Sanitary Authorities of those districts. As there is reason to believe that many other districts contain a considerable number of cottages such as are there described I venture to reproduce a part of the quotation from the Report.

EXTRACTS from the REPORT of JOHN C. THRESH, D.Sc., M.B., &c., on the HOUSING of the WORKING CLASSES in the CHELMSFORD and MALDON RURAL SANITARY DISTRICTS.

The Construction and Condition of Cottages.

"The character of the cottages themselves varies very considerably in the different villages. In some there are very few dilapidated houses, very few of the old lath and plaster cottages roofed with thatch, few without ample gardens. In others the cottages are crowded together and a large proportion of them are so old or so structurally defective that they are really unfit for human habitation. * * * * * In nearly every parish there are so-called houses which are so structurally defective that they can never be converted into comfortable healthy dwellings, and which are becoming so decayed from age and neglect that they are really unfit for habitation. In many such instances neglect rather than age has been the cause of the dilapidated condition. In cottages, as with men, neglect leads to premature decay. These old places are built of a timber frame-work, studded outside with laths, and daubed over with plaster, or with a mixture of clay and chopped straw. Many of them have not been lined with lath and plaster inside, and consequently are fearfully cold in winter. The walls may not be an inch in thickness, and where the laths are decayed the fingers can easily be pushed through. Every time also a piece of plaster falls off outside the interior is exposed. The floors downstairs usually are of brick, laid directly on the ground, and are almost invariably damp, often indeed reeking with moisture. The bricks also get broken, the floor becomes uneven, and the bare earth may be exposed. To obtain some slight degree of comfort bits of board are laid down and several thicknesses of sacking and mats are laid upon the floor. These have to be renewed periodically, as the damp causes them to rot and become useless.

"The roof is of thatch, which, if kept in good repair forms a good covering, warm in winter and cool in summer, though doubtless in many instances it serves as a harbour for dirt, for vermin, for the condensed exhalations from the bodies of the occupants of the bedrooms, and where persons suffering from the various fevers are nursed therein, possibly also for the infectious material which propagates such diseases.

"The bedrooms in such houses are almost invariably in the roof, and if there be more than one, the one is usually entered from the other. The windows are small, formed of small panes of glass let into a leaden framework. These windows are usually of the most rickety description, and often do not open, but the defect is atoned for by the ease with which the air can obtain access to the rooms around the sides of the defective frame. The utmost care has to be taken when cleaning them to avoid pushing them out. In fact, in many cases I do not know how the housewife contrives to rub the panes without someone is pushing against them outside to prevent a catastrophe. Where a leaded window has been so pushed out the opening is usually found covered over with a piece of matting. The doors are of the rudest description. Probably when originally made there was some pretence to 'fitting,' but there is none now. To keep out the draught bits of listing or pieces of wood have been nailed along the edges or over the cracks, but the result is rarely satisfactory. The fireplace also, and usually there is only one in the whole house, is of the most primitive character. A few iron bars are set in the brickwork, and as if further to prevent any economy in fuel, the bricks at the back crack and crumble away and rarely get replaced. The chimney corners are large and the chimneys wide, admitting sometimes of freer ingress for the external air than of egress for the air inside and the smoke from the fire.

"Complaints are made of the draughtiness of even the best of these cottages. Often in winter the candle or lamp is said to be blown out, and yet it is impossible to tell where the draught came from. The ceilings are usually not underdrawn, and when the bedroom floor is in holes one can see into the room below. To prevent this, or to avoid the foot of the bed going through when moved, pieces of wood or of old iron are nailed over the apertures. I came across an old man who tripped over one of these holes (or a piece of wood which had been nailed over it, I forget which), and broke his leg, an accident which I only wonder is not more common.

"Very few of these cottages have more than two bedrooms, many of them have only one, and usually, from their being placed in the roof, it is only possible to stand upright in the middle. The living rooms are low, many only from 6 ft. to 6 ft. 6 in. in height, yet the floor space is usually larger than the majority of the more modern cottages.

"Apparently at the time when they were erected such conveniences as ovens, coppers, or sinks, were considered luxuries which the poor man could very well dispense with, but it is difficult to conceive how the tenants get along without them. Sometimes a bakehouse with brick oven has been provided for a group of cottages, but these are now little used, or used only as storerooms for wood, &c., if, indeed, they are not too dilapidated even for such a purpose. In many cases an attempt has been made to render these dwellings more habitable by putting down a wooden floor to the living rooms and substituting modern sash windows for the old leaded ones. Without an occasional coat of paint these window frames rapidly decay, and in many cases they are now nearly in as bad condition as the ones they displaced. The floor boards are usually laid upon or within a few inches of the damp earth beneath, without ventilation under, and they speedily rot. To have raised them some inches above the level of the ground outside would have caused the rooms to be too low for an average adult to stand upright in, and to have removed some inches of the sodden earth and have laid a bed of concrete before putting in the floor would have entailed too great an expenditure, hence the present condition of things.

"When these cottages were erected there were no sanitary authorities to prevent their being built anyhow and anywhere, and consequently we often find them in the most unlikely and most unsanitary positions, in old gravel or marl pits, on ground which is constantly waterlogged, and far from any source of water supply except as can be obtained from polluted ponds and ditches."

It is unnecessary to add anything to this graphic description of a state of things which is too prevalent.

271. Almost every district would probably supply instances of good, bad, and indifferent cottages, the difference between the districts being more in respect of the numerical proportions which good and bad cottages bear to each other. I have already extracted from Mr. Fox's Reports some statistics as to the general condition of village cottages in open or close parishes (see Paragraph 246), and I now propose, with a view to throwing some light upon the relative amount of accommodation given in different classes of houses occupied by labourers, to avail myself of the very copious information which that gentleman has obtained and tabulated in his Reports on the Swaffham and Thingoe districts. In these Reports Mr. Fox gives as the result of his own personal investigation extended particulars on various points with respect to 171 cottages.

272. For the purpose of classification I have take the number of rooms as the basis, putting in the first class the few labourers' cottages which contain six rooms, and in the second class houses of five rooms, and so on in a descending scale. Happily it was unnecessary in dealing with these two districts to form a class of cottages containing only one room. But within each of the classes thus formed there is a considerable difference in the size and character of the rooms, and in additional accommodation, such as a pantry or cellar, or out-houses used for wash-houses or bake-houses. I found it impossible, however, to classify in respect of size of rooms, and the information as to out-houses was too general to be taken into account. I have therefore sub-divided the several classes in respect of differences in the indoor accommodation. I have assumed that a scullery means some sort of room inferior to what is classed as a kitchen, and that a kitchen is not equal to what is described as a sitting or living room.

The tables which have been compiled show in addition to the number of houses in each class the state of repair under five different degrees, (1) very bad, (2) bad, (3) fair, (4) good, and (5) very good; they also indicate the number of cottages which have separate provision of closets, and those which have no such sanitary necessity, the number which have gardens attached, and the maximum, minimum, and average rental of those cottages which are rented in each class.

I have selected these returns given by Mr. Fox because, though they are not the only ones contained in the Reports, they deal with a large number of cottages, and they contain rather fuller information than those of other Assistant Commissioners; but I shall take the opportunity of referring to some similar tables given by Mr. Spencer.

TRURO DISTRICT.—CLASSIFICATION of COTTAGES reported upon by Mr. A. WILSON FOX in respect of ACCOMMODATION, STATE of REPAIR, CLOSETS, GARDENS, and RENT.

Class	Sub-Class	Living Rooms	[illegible]	Pantries	Bed Rooms	No. in Sub-Class or Class	Very Bad	Bad	Fair	Good	Very Good	No Particulars Given	Separate Use	Joint Use	None	[illegible]	[illegible]	[illegible]	Average Size	[illegible]	None	[illegible]	Rent Free	Rented	Maximum	Minimum	Average
I. Six rooms	I a	Two	[illegible]	[illegible]	Four	[illegible]	[illegible]	[illegible]	[illegible]	[illegible]	[illegible]	[illegible]	[illegible]	[illegible]	[illegible]	[illegible]	[illegible]	[illegible]	[illegible]	[illegible]	[illegible]	[illegible]	[illegible]	[illegible]	[illegible]	[illegible]	[illegible]
	„ b	Two	[illegible]	[illegible]	Three	[illegible]	[illegible]	[illegible]	[illegible]	[illegible]	[illegible]	[illegible]	[illegible]	[illegible]	[illegible]	[illegible]	[illegible]	[illegible]	[illegible]	[illegible]	[illegible]	[illegible]	[illegible]	[illegible]	[illegible]	[illegible]	[illegible]
Total for Class I.						[illegible]	[illegible]	[illegible]	[illegible]	[illegible]	[illegible]	[illegible]	[illegible]	[illegible]	[illegible]	[illegible]	[illegible]	[illegible]	[illegible]	[illegible]	[illegible]	[illegible]	[illegible]	[illegible]	[illegible]	[illegible]	[illegible]
II. Four rooms	II a	Two	[illegible]	[illegible]	Two	[illegible]	[illegible]	[illegible]	[illegible]	[illegible]	[illegible]	[illegible]	[illegible]	[illegible]	[illegible]	[illegible]	[illegible]	[illegible]	[illegible]	[illegible]	[illegible]	[illegible]	[illegible]	[illegible]	[illegible]	[illegible]	[illegible]
	„ b	Two	[illegible]	[illegible]	Two	[illegible]	[illegible]	[illegible]	[illegible]	[illegible]	[illegible]	[illegible]	[illegible]	[illegible]	[illegible]	[illegible]	[illegible]	[illegible]	[illegible]	[illegible]	[illegible]	[illegible]	[illegible]	[illegible]	[illegible]	[illegible]	[illegible]
	„ c	Two	[illegible]	[illegible]	Three	[illegible]	[illegible]	[illegible]	[illegible]	[illegible]	[illegible]	[illegible]	[illegible]	[illegible]	[illegible]	[illegible]	[illegible]	[illegible]	[illegible]	[illegible]	[illegible]	[illegible]	[illegible]	[illegible]	[illegible]	[illegible]	[illegible]
	„ d	Two	[illegible]	[illegible]	Three	[illegible]	[illegible]	[illegible]	[illegible]	[illegible]	[illegible]	[illegible]	[illegible]	[illegible]	[illegible]	[illegible]	[illegible]	[illegible]	[illegible]	[illegible]	[illegible]	[illegible]	[illegible]	[illegible]	[illegible]	[illegible]	[illegible]
	„ e	One	[illegible]	[illegible]	Three	[illegible]	[illegible]	[illegible]	[illegible]	[illegible]	[illegible]	[illegible]	[illegible]	[illegible]	[illegible]	[illegible]	[illegible]	[illegible]	[illegible]	[illegible]	[illegible]	[illegible]	[illegible]	[illegible]	[illegible]	[illegible]	[illegible]
	„ f	One	[illegible]	[illegible]	Three	[illegible]	[illegible]	[illegible]	[illegible]	[illegible]	[illegible]	[illegible]	[illegible]	[illegible]	[illegible]	[illegible]	[illegible]	[illegible]	[illegible]	[illegible]	[illegible]	[illegible]	[illegible]	[illegible]	[illegible]	[illegible]	[illegible]
Total for Class II.						[illegible]	[illegible]	[illegible]	[illegible]	[illegible]	[illegible]	[illegible]	[illegible]	[illegible]	[illegible]	[illegible]	[illegible]	[illegible]	[illegible]	[illegible]	[illegible]	[illegible]	[illegible]	[illegible]	[illegible]	[illegible]	[illegible]
III. Four rooms	III a	Two	[illegible]	[illegible]	Two	[illegible]	[illegible]	[illegible]	[illegible]	[illegible]	[illegible]	[illegible]	[illegible]	[illegible]	[illegible]	[illegible]	[illegible]	[illegible]	[illegible]	[illegible]	[illegible]	[illegible]	[illegible]	[illegible]	[illegible]	[illegible]	[illegible]
	„ b	Two	[illegible]	[illegible]	Two	[illegible]	[illegible]	[illegible]	[illegible]	[illegible]	[illegible]	[illegible]	[illegible]	[illegible]	[illegible]	[illegible]	[illegible]	[illegible]	[illegible]	[illegible]	[illegible]	[illegible]	[illegible]	[illegible]	[illegible]	[illegible]	[illegible]
	„ c	One	[illegible]	[illegible]	Two	[illegible]	[illegible]	[illegible]	[illegible]	[illegible]	[illegible]	[illegible]	[illegible]	[illegible]	[illegible]	[illegible]	[illegible]	[illegible]	[illegible]	[illegible]	[illegible]	[illegible]	[illegible]	[illegible]	[illegible]	[illegible]	[illegible]
	„ d	One	[illegible]	[illegible]	Two	[illegible]	[illegible]	[illegible]	[illegible]	[illegible]	[illegible]	[illegible]	[illegible]	[illegible]	[illegible]	[illegible]	[illegible]	[illegible]	[illegible]	[illegible]	[illegible]	[illegible]	[illegible]	[illegible]	[illegible]	[illegible]	[illegible]
	„ e	One	[illegible]	[illegible]	Three	[illegible]	[illegible]	[illegible]	[illegible]	[illegible]	[illegible]	[illegible]	[illegible]	[illegible]	[illegible]	[illegible]	[illegible]	[illegible]	[illegible]	[illegible]	[illegible]	[illegible]	[illegible]	[illegible]	[illegible]	[illegible]	[illegible]
	„ f	One	[illegible]	[illegible]	Three	[illegible]	[illegible]	[illegible]	[illegible]	[illegible]	[illegible]	[illegible]	[illegible]	[illegible]	[illegible]	[illegible]	[illegible]	[illegible]	[illegible]	[illegible]	[illegible]	[illegible]	[illegible]	[illegible]	[illegible]	[illegible]	[illegible]
Total for Class III.						[illegible]	[illegible]	[illegible]	[illegible]	[illegible]	[illegible]	[illegible]	[illegible]	[illegible]	[illegible]	[illegible]	[illegible]	[illegible]	[illegible]	[illegible]	[illegible]	[illegible]	[illegible]	[illegible]	[illegible]	[illegible]	[illegible]
IV. Three rooms	IV a	One	[illegible]	[illegible]	Two	[illegible]	[illegible]	[illegible]	[illegible]	[illegible]	[illegible]	[illegible]	[illegible]	[illegible]	[illegible]	[illegible]	[illegible]	[illegible]	[illegible]	[illegible]	[illegible]	[illegible]	[illegible]	[illegible]	[illegible]	[illegible]	[illegible]
	„ b	One	[illegible]	[illegible]	Two	[illegible]	[illegible]	[illegible]	[illegible]	[illegible]	[illegible]	[illegible]	[illegible]	[illegible]	[illegible]	[illegible]	[illegible]	[illegible]	[illegible]	[illegible]	[illegible]	[illegible]	[illegible]	[illegible]	[illegible]	[illegible]	[illegible]
	„ c	Two	[illegible]	[illegible]	One	[illegible]	[illegible]	[illegible]	[illegible]	[illegible]	[illegible]	[illegible]	[illegible]	[illegible]	[illegible]	[illegible]	[illegible]	[illegible]	[illegible]	[illegible]	[illegible]	[illegible]	[illegible]	[illegible]	[illegible]	[illegible]	[illegible]
	„ d	Two	[illegible]	[illegible]	One	[illegible]	[illegible]	[illegible]	[illegible]	[illegible]	[illegible]	[illegible]	[illegible]	[illegible]	[illegible]	[illegible]	[illegible]	[illegible]	[illegible]	[illegible]	[illegible]	[illegible]	[illegible]	[illegible]	[illegible]	[illegible]	[illegible]
	„ e	One	[illegible]	[illegible]	One	[illegible]	[illegible]	[illegible]	[illegible]	[illegible]	[illegible]	[illegible]	[illegible]	[illegible]	[illegible]	[illegible]	[illegible]	[illegible]	[illegible]	[illegible]	[illegible]	[illegible]	[illegible]	[illegible]	[illegible]	[illegible]	[illegible]
Total for Class IV.						[illegible]	[illegible]	[illegible]	[illegible]	[illegible]	[illegible]	[illegible]	[illegible]	[illegible]	[illegible]	[illegible]	[illegible]	[illegible]	[illegible]	[illegible]	[illegible]	[illegible]	[illegible]	[illegible]	[illegible]	[illegible]	[illegible]
V. Two rooms	V a	One	[illegible]	[illegible]	One	[illegible]	[illegible]	[illegible]	[illegible]	[illegible]	[illegible]	[illegible]	[illegible]	[illegible]	[illegible]	[illegible]	[illegible]	[illegible]	[illegible]	[illegible]	[illegible]	[illegible]	[illegible]	[illegible]	[illegible]	[illegible]	[illegible]
	„ b	One	[illegible]	[illegible]	One	[illegible]	[illegible]	[illegible]	[illegible]	[illegible]	[illegible]	[illegible]	[illegible]	[illegible]	[illegible]	[illegible]	[illegible]	[illegible]	[illegible]	[illegible]	[illegible]	[illegible]	[illegible]	[illegible]	[illegible]	[illegible]	[illegible]
Total for Class V.						[illegible]	[illegible]	[illegible]	[illegible]	[illegible]	[illegible]	[illegible]	[illegible]	[illegible]	[illegible]	[illegible]	[illegible]	[illegible]	[illegible]	[illegible]	[illegible]	[illegible]	[illegible]	[illegible]	[illegible]	[illegible]	[illegible]
Grand Total						[illegible]	[illegible]	[illegible]	[illegible]	[illegible]	[illegible]	[illegible]	[illegible]	[illegible]	[illegible]	[illegible]	[illegible]	[illegible]	[illegible]	[illegible]	[illegible]	[illegible]	[illegible]	[illegible]	[illegible]	[illegible]	[illegible]
Percentage of Total Number						—	[illegible]	[illegible]	[illegible]	[illegible]	[illegible]	[illegible]	[illegible]	[illegible]	[illegible]	[illegible]	[illegible]	—	—	[illegible]	[illegible]	—	—	—	—	—	—

273. It will be seen that in respect of the number of rooms in cottages the district of Thingoe stands higher than Swaffham, but that as regards the state of repair, the provision of closets, and the possession of gardens, the conditions of Swaffham are superior, while the average rent is, in every class of cottages, higher in the latter district than in the former. In Swaffham only about one out of 16 of the cottages visited was held rent free, while in Thingoe one in eight was so held.

The following Table gives in a more succinct form the comparative results of the former Tables. Taking the two districts together, about three per cent. of the cottages inspected had six rooms, 10 per cent. had five rooms, 41 per cent. had four, about 36 per cent. had only three, and 10½ per cent. had two rooms only.

In respect of the state of repair, 38 per cent. were bad or very bad, 33 per cent. were in fair order, and the remainder were described as good or very good. Three per cent. of the houses were absolutely unprovided with sanitary closets, and 83 per cent. had gardens, though some of these were, as will be seen from the former tables, of very limited dimensions.

COTTAGE ACCOMMODATION.

SUMMARY CLASSIFICATION of COTTAGES in SWAFFHAM and THINGOE, reported upon by Mr. A. WILSON FOX, A.C. See B. I., App. A.; B. II., App. A.

Class.	Number: No. in each Class.	Number: Percentage of Total in each Class.	State of Repair: Very Bad or Bad.	State of Repair: Fair.	State of Repair: Good or Very Good.	Closets: Provided.	Closets: Not Provided.	Gardens: Provided.	Gardens: Not Provided.	Rent: Average Rent.	Rent: No. held Rent Free.
I. Six Rooms.										s. d.	
Swaffham -	—	—	—	—	—	—	—	—	—	—	—
Thingoe -	5	4·5	1	—	4	5	—	5	—	94 6	1
Total -	5	2·9	1	—	4	5	—	5	—	Mean 94 6	1
II. Five Rooms.											
Swaffham -	6	9·8	3	1	2	6	—	5	1	89 6	—
Thingoe -	11	10·1	1	5	4	7	1	11	—	74 5	—
Total -	17	10·0	5	6	7	15	1	16	1	Mean 82 5	—
III. Four Rooms.											
Swaffham -	26	42·7	6	12	6	24	—	17	7	76 0	3
Thingoe -	44	40·1	15	16	18	44	2	41	1	69 7	8
Total -	70	41·0	21	28	24	68	2	58	8	73 10	11
IV. Three Rooms.											
Swaffham -	22	37·1	14	15	1	22	1	16	6	81 6	3
Thingoe -	38	34·9	11	18	10	38	1	26	9	71 10	3
Total -	61	35·7	24	34	18	58	2	46	14	76 3	6
V. Two Rooms.											
Swaffham -	9	16·3	6	2	1	9	—	7	2	66 10	—
Thingoe -	9	8·2	4	2	—	8	1	6	3	37 0	—
Total -	18	10·5	10	4	1	17	1	13	5	52 [illegible]	—
I.–V.											
Swaffham -	60	100·0	26	27	11	61	1	47	15	76 [illegible]	4
Thingoe -	109	100·0	40	29	37	103	4	84	15	71 [illegible]	13
Grand total -	171	100·0	66	56	48	164	5	130	27	Mean 74 9	17
Percentage of total	—	—	38·1	33·3	28·6	97·0	3·0	83·0	17·0	—	10·0

Statistics from Mr. Spencer's Reports.

274. I have extracted from four of Mr. Spencer's Reports particulars of the number of cottages (among those inspected by him) containing from two to six rooms and I have tabulated the results side by side with those which have been obtained from the Reports of Mr. Fox. The four districts to which the statistics apply lie widely apart, in Essex, Wilts, Somerset, and Worcester. It will be seen that Langport and Maldon compare favourably in respect of the number of rooms with Swaffham and Thingoe; Langport has more than 38 per cent. and Maldon about 31 per cent. of cottages (as sampled by the Assistant Commissioner) with five or six rooms, while Swaffham has less than 10 per cent. and Thingoe has less than 15 per cent. in these two classes. Pershore and Pewsey are decidedly inferior in character, as evidenced by these returns, than Langport or Maldon, and somewhat below Swaffham and Thingoe.

COTTAGE ACCOMMODATION, COMPARATIVE STATEMENT, showing the NUMBER OF COTTAGES inspected in Six Districts, containing 1, 2, 3, 4, 5, or 6 Rooms.

Table [illegible].

Class and Number of Rooms.	Spencer.								Fox.			
	Langport. R. IV., App. C.		Maldon. R. V., App. B.		Pershore. R. VI. App. B.		Pewsey. R. II., App. B.		Swaffham. R. II., App. A.		Thingoe. R. I., App. A.	
	No.	Percentage of Total.	No.	Percentage of Total.	No.	Percentage of Total.	No.	Percentage of Total.	No.	Percentage of Total.	No.	Percentage of Total.
I. Six rooms	7	9·4	1	3·1	—	—	—	—	—	—	5	4·0
II. Five rooms	[illegible]	[illegible]	8	[illegible]	1	4·2	7	17·2	4	3·7	11	10·1
III. Four rooms	[illegible]	[illegible]	19	27·6	4	15·4	13	31·7	[illegible]	[illegible]	16	[illegible]
IV. Three rooms	16	22·6	5	20·1	16	51·6	10	[illegible]	[illegible]	47·1	[illegible]	34·0
V. One room	4	5·6	1	6·1	6	19·4	2	4·9	9	14·0	5	4·2
	71	100·	[illegible]	100·	31	100·	41	100·	[illegible]	100	[illegible]	100·

If the six districts are taken together the result will be as follows:—

—	Number	Percentage.
1st Class.—Cottages containing 6 rooms	8	2·3
2nd " " " 5 "	49	17·0
3rd " " " 4 "	117	[illegible]·7
4th " " " 3 "	101	35·0
5th " " " 2 "	31	9·0
	348	100·0

Sanitary condition of cottages.

275. The sanitary condition of the labourers' dwellings, the drainage, the supply of water, are subjects which have been minutely investigated by the Assistant Commissioners, whose Reports contain several communications from sanitary officials* as to the present condition of the districts with which they are connected, and the improvement which has been effected by the action of the sanitary authorities.

It would be impossible to condense within moderate limits of space the information which is contained in the Reports on this point. The Analytical Index† which has been issued summarizes the facts with regard to each district as a whole, but almost every one of those districts presents a great variety of conditions. For instance Mr. Richards appends to his Report upon the district of Nantwich a statement by Mr. Davenport, C.E., as to the cottages, drainage, and water supply in 71 villages in that district. In 38

* References to communications from sanitary officials:—Bear, R. II. [illegible]; IV. [illegible]; VI. [illegible]. Chapman, R. I. [illegible], II. [illegible]; III. [illegible], IV. [illegible], V., App. C.; VI. [illegible]; VII. [illegible]. Fox, R. I.,* App. A.; II., App. A.; IV. [illegible]; V., App. B.* [illegible] Richards, R. III., App. A.; V., App. B.; VI., App. B.* Spencer, R. I.* [illegible]; IV., [illegible]; V.,* App. C.; VIII. [illegible]. Those marked * are [illegible] full and [illegible].
† Vol. I., Part VII.

cases out of 71 the statement as to drainage is sufficiently definite to permit of its being classed, with this result—

Drainage bad	-	7 villages.
" not good, defective, indifferent, unsatisfactory	-	10 "
" capable of improvement	-	3 "
" fair, moderate, above average	-	12 "
" good	-	4 "
" good and bad	-	2 "

With regard to water supply the same Report, out of 53 cases, the report is—

Bad		in 11	villages.
Not good		9	"
Capable of improvement		4	"
Moderate or fair		7	"
Good	1		
Supplied by main	19		
		20	"
Good and bad		1	"
		52	

I have quoted from this particular Report because it supplies evidence of a very vigorous effort having been made by the local authorities and private owners to overcome the difficulty which arises as regards water supply from the geological formation on which the district lies. Mr. Richards says:—

"The inherent difficulties of the water supply lie in the fact that the whole district is situated on a bed of marl some 900 feet in thickness in which there is no water; here and there where there are sand drifts water is found, but it is unfortunately often so brackish as to be unfit for use." Richards, B. VI. 19.

Fortunately for the district the main which carries water from the Vyrnwy to Liverpool passes through it.

"The means adopted for carrying out the supply by mains to a scattered population are by a combination of voluntary efforts with a charge upon the rates." Richards, B. VI., App. B.

276. Of the great majority of country districts it may probably be said that little has been attempted in the way of drainage from the houses; that the sanitary arrangements are in many respects defective; that the closet accommodation is insufficient in supply and very bad in character; and that the water supply is inadequate and far from pure. Drainage little attempted generally.

Mr. Chapman observes on these points:—

"Except in towns and some large villages drainage, in the strict sense of the word, is unknown in a country district, though much more attention is now given to the subject than used to be the case. Surface water and house refuse are carried to the brooks or compounds in open gutters, but in every district schemes for some improvement are being discussed or put in force where the guardians will admit of them, and the people are alive to the necessity for efficient measures being taken. The number of privies are being generally increased, though in such places instances occur where one privy is shared by three or four cottages, and in Truro it is a common thing to find a whole row of cottages without any privy accommodation at all." Chapman, A. 33.

. . . . One of the great difficulties of an agricultural labourer's life is the absence of good water; it is a matter of frequent contention. "In the fens particularly it is true that there is 'Water, water "everywhere, but not a drop to drink.' Cottages with thatched roofs depend upon the rainfall, and "when that is insufficient the occupiers must buy water from their neighbours or drink what they "can get from the dykes, brooks, or ponds. In most villages there are shallow wells which are liable "to contamination from surface water, and such contamination is very frequent in agricultural "districts, from surface manure and from the excreta from the houses. A cesspool and a well are "often close to each other."

Mr. Wilson Fox says:— Fox, A. 20.

"Any system of drainage, particularly in the northern counties, is generally conspicuous by its absence; . . . . I have in my reports commented on the insufficiency of closets provided in many districts. In some villages the supply is totally inadequate, and it seems a reprehensible state of things that the inmates of four or five houses containing twenty or more men, women, and children should provided with but one between them. I fail to see why sanitary authorities should not insist on owners providing one to each house."

Richards, A. 31.

Mr. Richards reports that in Monmouth,

"no provision is made for a water supply. If the cottage happens to be near a spring, well and good. If not, cottagers must go for the water. At Gurway, Tregare, and other villages, the labourers have to go from half to three-quarters of a mile for good water or use any impure water, which may be more convenient."

Mr. Spencer says:—

Spencer, A. 17.

"It is much, I think, to be desired that it should be made compulsory that every cottage should have a separate privy. It is common throughout the parts that I visited to find one privy doing duty for two or sometimes for three cottages.

Privy accommodation defective.

"The water supply is not good in some parts, but considerable attention to this important particular is now being paid by the sanitary authority in the districts.

"I have shown in Tables what numbers of the houses which in Swaffham and Thingoe were inspected by Mr. Fox had a separate provision of closets, many had only the joint use of one, and how many were unprovided; but of course such a summary statement does not disclose those cases of inadequate provision where one privy only is provided for six or seven houses, instances of which are to be found in the Schedules attached to Mr. Fox's Reports. In Glendale, 13 only of 84 cottages visited by Mr. Fox had absolutely no provision of this necessary character. In Wigton, four out of seven were similarly unprovided. In Truro the Medical Officer of Health reported that in certain parishes 20 per cent. of the houses had no closet accommodation at all; and 50 per cent. had only a share in a closet common to two or three houses."

Chapman, B. V., App. C.

Water supply.

It would be easy to quote from many of the Reports passages to show that there is a great and general deficiency in the supply of good water, and the difficulties which the sanitary authorities experience in making any great improvement. Mr. Bear quotes the following passage from the Report of Mr. Wright, the Medical Officer of Health for the St. Neots Union:—

Bear, B. II. 11.

"We are confronted by difficulties which it is impossible to combat, there being no practicable means of securing a good and adequate supply for the various villages without incurring such an expenditure as could not possibly be met, and all that can be done is to watch the condition of the shallow wells which, in the majority of instances, afford the water supply, and guard them, as far as may be, from all possible sources of contamination."

In his Reports upon Thakeham, Basingstoke, Southwell, Melton, Mr. Bear quotes from Reports of Medical Officers of Health unfavourable opinions as to the water supply.

Action of sanitary authorities.

Chapman, B. IV. 79, B. VI. 69, B. III. 38; Spencer, A. 28; Richards, B. V. 30; Fox, B. II. 34.

277. The Assistant Commissioners report very generally that the sanitary authorities have made considerable efforts to improve the condition of the cottages,[1] although, in a few instances, they express an opinion that the authorities have been somewhat supine. Some suggestions are offered with a view to an increase of energy and activity in the work of sanitary reform, and this will be a convenient place for bringing these suggestions under notice. But before doing this I may call attention to some of the difficulties which an active Medical Officer of Health has to encounter.

Difficulties experienced by sanitary officers.

278. The following passage which is extracted from the Appendix to Mr. Richards' Report on Cirencester shows the practical difficulties which are met with in putting in force the provisions of the Housing of the Working Classes Act, 1890.

EXTRACT from REPORT of FRANCIS T. BOND, M.D.

(Gloucester, March 26, 1892).

Richards, B. III. App. A.

"House Accommodation.—The work of gradually closing dilapidated and defective dwellings has gone on in various parts of the district much as usual. Whenever an opportunity has occurred by the death or departure of the occupant of a dwelling which did not come up to reasonable sanitary requirements, occasion has been taken to prevent it from being re-occupied. As I have frequently indicated in previous reports, the worst cases of this kind are, as a rule, those in which the occupier is the owner, and so poor as to be unable to put the premises in which he lives in a proper state of repair. These are most difficult cases to deal with. It is a striking comment on the difference which there is between making laws and enforcing them, that the 'Housing of the Working Classes Act,' which was specially designed to deal with this evil, is practically so difficult of enforcement, in consequence of the complexity of the machinery which has to be worked to give effect to its provisions, and of the doubts involved in the initial step which is required to set that machinery in motion. The Act provides that 'where any representation is made to any rural sanitary authority or medical 'officer of health respecting any dwelling as dangerous and injurious to health as to be unfit for 'human habitation,' certain steps, which are specified by the Act, may be taken to close or demolish the dwelling in question. It might naturally be supposed that nothing would be easier than to find an abundance of dwellings in most rural districts which are so far below the standard of fitness for human habitation as to deserve closing or demolition. But although this is so, directly the medical

[1] Reference to statements on the subject.—Bear, B. III. 33, VI. 27. Chapman, B. I. 31, III. 38, VI. 79. Fox, B. II., App. A. 6. Richards, B. III., App. A. Wilkinson, A. 62, B. I. 14, II. 58.

officer of health proceeds to take action in this direction, he finds his path full of all sorts of obstacles. There is first the question of proving that beyond doubt the premises are 'dangerous or injurious to health,' not merely to the health of the inmates, who could avoid the danger by leaving them, but to that of the public at large, and then one must also prove that they are so defective that they cannot be amended by repair. These points have often to be established against a defendant in the person of the incriminated owner of the property, who may have secured the services of a shrewd lawyer, by a medical officer of health who has no special aptitude for contentious business of the kind, and is unprovided with any legal assistance to enable him to avoid the pitfalls which his legal opponent will not be slow to construct for him. Then when he has succeeded in obtaining his closing order, he has before him a pleasing vista of indefinite complications between the county council and the local sanitary authority, in regard to which he will have to keep pegging away for months to turn out people who will not only give him no thanks for so doing, but will, in all probability, when put into the witness box, declare that they are quite content to be let alone. Decidedly the work of the medical officer of health who embarks on this course of procedure is by no means an easy one.

But the greatest difficulty which the sanitary authorities themselves have to confront is that if they were to close all insanitary dwellings a considerable number of people would be houseless and unable to find a home in the district where their work lies. Spencer, B IV. 41.

Another formidable obstacle to progress is the heavy expenses which fall upon the ratepayers, who in agricultural districts are little able to bear any additional burdens. Bear, B. V. 37.

279. And a further hindrance to improvement, and a discouragement to its promoters, is the want of appreciation on the part of the labourers of better and more sanitary dwellings, and the total absence of any active assistance by them in the work of the amelioration of their homes. Want of assistance from occupants.

Where good and roomy cottages are provided, it is only by stringent regulations and constant supervision, that the tenants are prevented from taking in lodgers if they have the opportunity. Mr. Chapman speaks of two cottages constructed to hold one family each, in which "no less than nine male lodgers were taken in, four in one house "and five in another." Mr. Wilson Fox reports that in Glendale, where closets have been provided, there is the greatest difficulty "to induce the people to utilise them, and "in many instances the new ones have been turned into hen houses and lumber sheds by the tenants," and a similar course seems to have been taken in Crediton. Chapman, B IV. 78. Fox, B III 44. Chapman, B IV. 14.

280. Upon the subject of overcrowding, a suggestion made by Mr. H. Lee Warner, and reported by Mr. Wilson Fox, who thinks it a practical proposal, may be noticed:— Suggestions by Assistant Commissioners. Overcrowding.

"As regards the number of the rooms and condition of the cottages, I should like each cottage to be licensed to hold a certain number of residents, and no more, and the local board to be obliged to issue byelaws. It would be an immense boon to our small local boards if the Local Government Office could draw up simple and shorter specimens of byelaws, and fix a minimum area on which cottages should be built, so as to secure fresh air and decent outhouses." Fox, B III. 55.

With a similar object in view, Mr. Chapman suggests that local authorities should keep a register of the cottages in every parish. Chapman, A 91.

Mr. Wilson Fox himself suggests that it would be a practical plan of ensuring cottages being kept in better repair, &c., if all owners of cottages with a rental under 10*l*. were compelled to make a return to a local authority every year stating the number of persons in each cottage, their sex and age, whether the house is provided with a proper water supply and a closet, and whether the premises are in good repair. Repairs of cottages.

281. One of the most practical proposals supported by several of the Assistant Commissioners is that the medical officers of health should be appointed by some other public body than a local sanitary authority (urban or rural), and that he should be paid such a salary as would enable him to give up the whole of his time to the work of his office and absolve him from the necessity of private practice. Mr. Spencer says:— Medical officers of health appointment and salary.

"It is to be regretted that the medical officer of health has not in every district, as he has in some, a salary sufficient to enable him to be independent of private practice and devote the whole of his time to the duties of his office." Spencer, A 36.

Mr. Chapman says:— Chapman, A 91.

"The evils connected with cottage accommodation are great and require constant attention, but it is doubtful whether the law requires alteration. It certainly requires more frequent application, and for this purpose it is most important that the responsible medical officer and sanitary inspector should, as far as possible, be independent of the guardians. It is very difficult for men who are paid by the guardians to risk their appointments by recommending necessary changes, which will involve an increase of the rates, and their work would probably be better done if they were responsible to a more central authority."

Mr. Chapman further suggests that it is desirable to give greater publicity as to the names of the public officials and their duties.

"It is a common thing for villagers to have never heard of a nuisance inspector, and I think it would be useful to have a list of local officials, with a short account of their duties, on every church or chapel door in each district. There are plenty of statutes passed for the benefit of villagers which they never hear of."

282. Mr. Richards in his Report on Stratford-on-Avon, says:—

"There has been a considerable amount of discussion in this union in regard to the appointment of a medical officer. To appoint a competent man might be a serious burden upon one union; and to introduce an outsider acting under a central authority in the county or in London might lead to a conflict of authorities; but for some reasons it would seem highly desirable that he should be absolutely independent of any pressure. His task is often a difficult one, even under the most favourable conditions. If he condemns property as not habitable, he disobliges owners who are often influential in the neighbourhood, and often linked closely with those who are to be judges of the complaint. Often too, a tenant will tolerate any amount of discomfort and dilapidation rather than leave a house which may have been his home for many years, or run the risk of having to leave the neighbourhood, a not uncommon risk."

And in a subsequent Report he expresses the opinion that sanitary inspectors should be appointed by some outside authority:—

"Were quite independent of pressure. From what I have seen and heard in both Monmouth and Bromyard, it would seem desirable that sanitary inspectors should not be placed in the very invidious position they now occupy. Where such an officer receives a salary of only 60*l.* to 80*l.* per annum he is not likely to be in a very independent position when dealing with matters affecting his masters—the guardians. A hint from a guardian—a property owner—that a salary will be docked 10*l.*, or the appointment taken away, is a serious inducement to withdraw, or not to press a complaint against insanitary or overcrowded property belonging to such owner. In both places I was informed that such fears are not without foundation, and that duty and interest are not infrequently brought into collision with each other. This suggests that such appointments should be made by an authority of wider jurisdiction, or more remote from local and personal influence."

Mr. Wilson Fox says:—

"It has been suggested that in order to ensure an unbiassed supervision free from all local influences and prejudices there should be a periodical Government inspection of cottages, and further, that a sanitary inspector should be paid a salary which would enable him to devote the whole of his time to the service of the union."

283. Mr. Wilkinson suggests legislation with a view to prevent the erection of any new cottages with inadequate accommodation.

"Though I do not see how people can be prevented from letting or hiring cottages which are not in an insanitary condition, I do not see why the Legislature should not interfere with respect to cottages hereafter to be built, and enact that each such cottage should (unless special leave to the contrary were given) have at least three bedrooms (two of them with separate access) proper offices and a fair sized garden or garden allotment attached to it. More than one labourer thought that such an enactment would do good. Leave to build smaller and cheaper houses might be coupled with permanent conditions as to the number of their inmates and otherwise."

But in his Summary Report, in referring to his previously expressed opinion upon this matter, he adds:—

"It would be long, however, before this had much effect. Unless they could be built to pay, there would not be many built, and, as now, it would be only on the large estates that one would see good cottages rising, and there they are doing so without legislative interference."

284. Mr. Chapman suggests with regard to the supply of water that the powers of the sanitary authorities should be enlarged.

"The Act of 1875 (Public Health Act) enables a sanitary authority to prevent any cottage from being built without a proper water supply, but it does not enable them to deal with an old cottage. If a house may be closed because its drainage is unsanitary it might surely be within the discretion of authorities to close a house because the water supply is dangerously bad. It may be assumed that the power would not be exercised unless there was some means of supplying the defect which the owner was neglecting."

(d.) Ownership and Tenure.

285. The owners of cottages may be broadly divided into four classes—

1. Estate owners or landowners whose cottages are primarily intended for the accommodation of those employed on the property of the owner.
2. Private owners who hold cottages like any other description of property yielding an income, and let them on commercial principles at the best rent that they can obtain.
3. Leaseholders or lifeholders who very generally have either built the houses themselves or acquired a title from the original builders and copyholders.

4. Occupying owners: as a rule, however, where labourers own the cottages they are leaseholders.

The extent to which the ownership by each of these classes prevails differs greatly in different districts, but as a rule, by far the larger number of cottages occupied by agricultural labourers belong either to the first or second of the above-named classes.

In some of the districts of inquiry large estates with numerous cottages exist, in others, the ownership, apart from any connection with the land, is the rule, and the estate cottage the exception; but there is not one in which both classes are not represented. The Reports of the Assistant Commissioners do not afford the materials for discriminating those districts in which estate cottages are most numerous from those of detached ownership, and even if they did, any comparison between the two might be misleading. It has been already stated that the general condition of the cottages in "close" villages is superior to that of "open" villages, and there is throughout the Reports overwhelming testimony to the effect that estate cottages are far superior to all others. Among the cottages owned by others than landowners there is no doubt a great variation in condition; but the general average state of them is low. The cottages held by leaseholders or lifeholders are perhaps the worst of all.

Mr. Spencer in his Report on Maldon says:—

"The majority of the cottages are owned by small independent owners, and some of the worst in "the district are copyhold property. The extreme poverty of the owners is frequently the cause of "the dilapidation of the cottages." As to this, Dr. Thresh says:—"In several instances I have "found that the rents from one or two old cottages constituted the sole income of the owners, who, "under such circumstances, could not find the money to put them in repair were a repairing order "made; and, if closed, the owners, and in some cases the tenant also would be thrown upon the "Union. Sometimes, the owner himself lives in one of these cottages. Two of the most tumble-"down, wretched pair of cottages known to me are owned by aged men. Each lives in one and "lets the other and with the rent, a few shillings earned at odd times, and the produce of a garden, "they contrive to eke out an existence without becoming paupers." In other cases the owners are non-resident in the district, and probably have never seen their property, which is left to the mercy of agents, whose interest it is to remit the rents with as small deductions as possible for repairs. The cottages situated on and let with farms are usually in comparatively good condition.

286. Mr. Richards notices the miserable condition of leasehold cottages in Cirencester and Belper and of those held by squatters on a "cot-rent" in Monmouth.

Mr. Chapman writing of Truro says:—

"In small villages cottages are nearly always the property of small owners, who require to make a profit out of them, and are obliged to charge a market price for them. The leasing for lives is a system which still prevails very largely, but is gradually dying out, and is not applied even to building leases now. The bad character of the cottages in this district is in a great measure distinctly traceable to this system."

Mr. Wilson Fox says:—

"In the open villages they are constantly owned by small tradesmen who have bought the property as "an investment, men without means to carry out any improvements or to effect any necessary "repairs, and whose one object is to get as high a rent as possible." Another quotes the evidence of witnesses on this point.

287. The tenure upon which the labourers hold their cottages varies with the class of ownership; the system of management adopted by the estate owner; and the usual customs of the district. Where the cottages belong to another than a landowner the labourer hires without any condition as to where he shall work. The term for which the hiring is made varies from a week to a year. Where the cottages belong to an estate the occupier of a cottage is supposed to work upon the estate if he is not actually under any obligation to do this, but in many cases his cottage is held, either rent free or not, as may be agreed, conditionally upon his working on a particular farm. Upon large estates there are three different systems of management:—

(i.) Cottage held directly from the estate owner with an understanding that the labourer will work on the estate.

(ii.) Cottage held by labourer from estate owner upon the nomination of the tenant of a farm for the service of which the cottage has been provided or allocated.

(iii.) Cottage held under the farmer upon condition of working for him.

288. The first system is undoubtedly the most popular with the labourers, and commends itself to the estate owners and to outsiders also. It gives the labourer a greater security in his home and a better chance of having it kept in repair.

289. The second system is a compromise between the first and the third. It recognises, partially, the necessity which a farmer experiences of having at his disposal house room for some of those men whose services are indispensable for the care of his horses, his herd, and flock.

290. The third system is, except in a few districts, applied to a part of the estate cottages only. In Glendale, however, the cottages are almost universally let with the farms, the labourers occupying them rent free. They are hired for the year, and at the end of that period both parties consider themselves free to make fresh arrangements. It is the custom of the district, and there is no evidence of its being distasteful to the labourers. In many other districts farmers demand as a condition of holding farms the control of a certain number of cottages, the number depending very much upon the situation of the farm with respect to a village population. Where the farmer's homestead is in a village, as it frequently is, the occupier has some chance of supplying the place of a carter or cowman who for some cause or other quits his employment, but when the farm lies remote from a village or hamlet it is essential to the proper conduct of his business that the men in charge of stock who occupy farm cottages should hold them as a condition of service, and vacate them when they cease to do the work for which they have been engaged in order to make room for one who will do that work.

291. An examination of the Reports shows that farm cottages let with the farms and sub-let to the labourers are found to a greater or less extent in 25 districts out of 38, while in 14 districts estate owners generally retain the control of the cottages. In some districts the number of landowners' cottages is relatively very small. A few instances of various prevailing conditions may be given.

In Basingstoke, Mr. Bear says:—

"Probably more than half the cottages are let through the farmers, who need them for their hired servants. Those on farms are always so let, and a good many in the villages as well. Others are let by the landlords to the occupiers directly."

As to Woburn, he says:—

"Nearly all the cottages are held direct from the owners, farm servants in some instances having the privilege of nomination when a cottage is vacant. Except where farmers own land and cottages, I did not hear of any instances in which they had the power of turning out the occupiers."

Mr. Spencer reports as to Pewsey:—

"There are generally some cottages let by landlords with each farm. The farmer puts his yearly servants into these cottages rent free, but charges rent to any ordinary labourers that he supplies with a cottage. The number of cottages held by farmers would be about one, or sometimes more, to every hundred acres, and probably more are let in this way by landlords than was the case formerly. In Collingbourn Ducis this was the chief subject of complaint by the labourers, who said that the letting of cottages to the farmer placed the labourer too much in his power, and had the effect of keeping down wages. They said that if a labourer 'had words' with his master he turned him out of his cottage at a week's notice. I suggested to them that it was essential to a farmer for profitably carrying on his business that he should be able to find cottages for his carters, shepherds, and stockmen. They agreed to this, but said that a farmer should not have cottages for his ordinary labourers, but that these should hold straight from the landlord or from independent owners."

In Dorchester also the ordinary labourers are generally housed in cottages let to the farmer, and held rent free during service.

In Swaffham, Mr. Wilson Fox reports—

being built on a farm expressly for the accommodation of the shepherd and stockman, "but nobody "could be persuaded to take them, and they remained vacant for more than a year. Eventually, "they were hired by labourers who were employed upon another farm, and the men who were "employed upon this farm hired cottages elsewhere."

Mr. Richards reports that—

"In Monmouth there has been the strongest possible repugnance to living in farm cottages, and it "is not often that labourers are so housed." And that in Nantwich, "Landlords set themselves "against the practice of letting cottages go with the farms." "On Lord Tollemache's estate, where "a cottage is vacant, and a farmer is in want of one for a labourer, he may nominate the labourer "for a cottage. If there is no solid objection to the man, the nomination is accepted, and the "labourer installed in the cottage. Once there, however, his employer has no further say in the "matter of his cottage, and should he obtain employment elsewhere, he would still hold the cottage. "This would not be the case if such employment were on some other estate." Richards, A 14

292. With regard to the condition sometimes imposed by landlords that the occupant of an estate cottage should work on the estate, the justification for such a restriction is briefly stated by Mr. T. Fair, Lytham, in a communication to Mr. Wilson Fox, thus— Conditions of occupation.

"I stipulate that the tenant of the cottages or some of their family must work on the estate if I let "them a good house, which costs 200*l*., and a garden of from a quarter to half an acre for a "rent of 5*l*." Fox, B V

293. Mr. Wilkinson discusses the whole question of letting the cottages with the farms, or independently, at some length. He thinks the labourers' objection more sentimental than valid; points out that farmers living far from a village and having cottages for men in charge of stock would have difficulty in finding any one to replace these men if they threw up work and he had no cottage to offer. He comes to the conclusion, that where a homestead is in a village independent hiring from the landowners is the best system. Policy of letting cottages with farms. Wilkinson, A 77

294. A few particulars as to the number of cottages on some large estates and the system pursued by the owners with regard to them may be gleaned from the Reports. Statistics as to large estates.

In the Woburn district the Duke of Bedford has 290 cottages and 12,378 acres of land. This is an average of 2·34 cottages per 100 acres, or one cottage to 42¾ acres of land. It is not to be assumed that all these cottages are occupied by agricultural labourers. The practice on this estate is to let directly to the labourers; some of the paternal regulations imposed are said to be disliked by the occupiers. If a man's family is too large for a cottage, he has to move, an arrangement which will commend itself to every one; but, if from any reason his family becomes too small for the cottage, he has to move, and of this men complain; but, as Mr. Bear observes, large cottages cannot be found for large families, if couples without families are allowed to occupy them.

On the Savernake estate (Wilts) there are 1,020 cottages, [not including those let with small holdings of from two acres up to ten acres]; 322 of these are let with farms, and the remainder (698) are let directly to the labourers. The number let with farms has not increased in the last 10 years.

"In NORFOLK. Lord Walsingham lets 192 cottages out of 196 direct to labourers.

"Lord Leicester lets all of his (over 1,000) direct to the labourers.

"Lord Amherst of Hackney, lets one or two cottages with each farm, and retains control of the rest.

"In SUFFOLK. On the Duke of Grafton's property, there are 235 cottages, 55 of which are let with the farms, and 180 direct to the labourers.

"On the Marquis of Bristol's property, there are 250 cottages, 130 of which are let directly to the labourers.

"On Lord Cadogan's estate there are 215 cottages, 209 of which are let directly to labourers."

295. Before leaving the subject of estate cottages and the management of this kind of property, I may draw attention to the conditions upon which the Duke of Norfolk lets his cottages to labourers and to farmers for the use of labourers. It will be seen that precautions are taken against sub-letting by the farmer to any but those employed on the farm; that a maximum rent is prescribed; that repairs are provided for; and that the farm tenant is made responsible for preventing overcrowding. Where the labourers are themselves the tenants strict regulations are made against overcrowding, and the tenant covenants to give up possession when the family increases beyond the number specified as permissible. Conditions of letting on Duke of Norfolk's estate. See Bear, B III. App. VIII.

296. Mr. Bear records, in his Report on Melton Mowbray, an interesting fact, which illustrates the relations frequently existing between estate owners and their cottage tenants, though the bond between them is not generally so definite as in the instance given. "The cottages on the Duke of Rutland's estate descend under the system of "primogeniture, the eldest son of the late occupier having the first offer; or, if there "is no son, or he does not require the cottage, it may be taken by some other member "of the family."

In the same district there are said to be a good many cottages owned by the occupiers, with a little land attached to them, but it is not clear that these occupiers are agricultural labourers.

297. In the Reports on 16 districts labourers are mentioned as owning cottages, but in several of these the statement is either that there are a few or that there are not many.

In Basingstoke there are squatters' cottages at Pamber, "queer-looking dwellings, "with high-pitched thatched roofs, reaching within about four feet of the ground; "but most of them appeared fairly comfortable, as the occupiers can generally afford "to keep them in repair"; but these squatters are really small holders.

In Southwell Mr. Bear reports "some miserable old cottages built by squatters on the "waste;" but these, he was informed, had been condemned by the sanitary authority.

Mr. Chapman thus describes some cottages built by the labourers themselves on the waste or common land in some villages in Thame.

"They are usually made of mud, with thatched roofs, and are erected on patches of ground without any margin for a garden. The result is, very small, ill-constructed rooms, and a very bad state of repair."

It may be safely inferred that the number of cottages owned by labourers is small, and that the general character of such cottages is very inferior.

Mr. Spencer records some recent purchases of cottages by labourers in the Pewsey district.

"In Ludgershall there has recently been a sale of cottages, and some of the better class of labourers have become owners."

This is, I believe, a solitary instance in the Reports.

298. The rent paid for cottages hired by labourers varies from 9d. to 7s. a week, the most usual sum charged being apparently about 1s. 6d. a week or 4l. a year. It is abundantly clear from the evidence that the amount of rent has no relation to the character or condition of the cottage, the accommodation given, or the financial position of the occupant. It is determined by the ownership and the terms upon which the occupation is held. Estate cottages are on the average not only better in every respect than village cottages, but they are let upon much easier terms as regards rent than others, and cottages hired by farmers as part of their farm take are, wherever rent is paid, let for less money than any other class of dwellings.

The following summary statements embody the results reported by Assistant Commissioners:—

Mr. Bear says—

Mr. Spencer tabulates the rents of cottages in the districts visited by him thus :— Spencer, A. 38.

Dorchester, 5*l.* a year	1*s.* 11*d.* a week.
Godstone	2*s.* to 1*s.* a week.
Hollingbourn	3*s.* to 3*s.* a week.
Langport, 4*l.* to 5*l.* a year	1*s.* 6½*d.* to 1*s.* 11*d.* a week
Maldon, 3*l.* 10*s.* to 6*l.* a year	1*s.* 4*d.* to 1*s.* 11*d.* a week.
Pershore	2*s.* a week.
Pewsey	1*s.* a week.

Mr. Wilkinson gives the range of rents in his districts of inquiry as follows :— Wilkinson, A. 61-64.

Driffield, 1*s.* a week to 5*l.* 5*s.* a year.
Easingwold, 1*s.* a week, 3*l.*, 4*l.*, 5*l.* a year.
Holbeach, 3*l.* to 6*l.* a year.
Louth, 9*d.* to 1*s.* a week for an old two-roomed cottage with no garden ; 5*l.* for a four-roomed cottage with a fair garden.
Uttoxeter, 3*l.* to 5*l.*
Wetherby, 2*l.* 10*s.* to 6*l.*

299. Mr. Wilson Fox has not given a summary statement of rents in his final Report, but I have already referred to, and made use of, the statistics which he has collected on the subject of cottage accommodation in the districts of Swaffham and Thingoe. In one of the three other districts which he visited, namely Glendale, the question of rent paid by agricultural labourers hardly arises as the men are provided with cottages on farms rent free. In Garstang a considerable number of the workers are boarded in the farm houses, and there are consequently few farm cottages. In Garstang the average rents are said to be between 4*l.* and 5*l.* a year. In Wigton they are said to be from 3*l.* to 5*l.* Particular comparisons as to cottages. Swaffham, Thingoe. Fox, B. V. 40. B IV. 44.

With reference to both these districts Mr. Fox makes the following remarks :—

The accommodation provided or the state of repair cannot be measured by the rent paid, for a very inferior cottage is often let at the same rent as a new one with good airy rooms, a large garden, and all the necessary outhouses." B. V. 40.

I have in Tables 78, 79 given the extreme range, and the average rental, of each class of cottages in Swaffham and Thingoe, and a reference to these tables will supply conclusive evidence as to the want of correspondence between rent and apparent value in these two districts, and they tend to confirm what is stated by each one of the Assistant Commissioners as the result of his experience.

In Table 80 the average rent in each class of houses is given for each district, and the mean of the two districts is stated. The rents of 154 cottages which are let are stated. The results are as follows :— Table 80.

—	Average. Swaffham.	Average. Thingoe.	Mean. —
	s. *d.*	*s.* *d.*	*s.* *d.*
1st Class.—Six rooms	—	93 6	—
2nd " Five rooms	90 6	74 0	82 3
3rd " Four rooms	75 0	69 9	72 10
4th " Three rooms	81 0	71 10	76 5
5th " Two rooms	86 10	37 8	62 3
Average for district	78 8	71 3	74 9

It will be seen that in both districts the average rent of a three-roomed cottage is greater than that one with four rooms, while the mean rent of five-roomed houses in the two districts is only 1*l.* a year more than that of two-roomed cottages—a difference of 4½*d.* a week for the accommodation of three extra rooms.

The details as to accommodation, repair, provision of outhouses, gardens, &c., supply the means of close comparison. In the following comparative statement I have selected from the list of the cottages described in the Thingoe district examples bearing the maximum and minimum rent in each of the first four classes into which I divided the houses, and an instance of maximum rental in the class of cottages containing two rooms only, and I have shown the character of the cottage, the amount of accommodation, the size of garden, and, in fact, everything except situation, which goes to make up the value for which rent is paid.

COTTAGE RENTS.—SELECTED INSTANCES of MAXIMUM and MINIMUM RENTALS of COTTAGES of different CLASSES in THINGOE DISTRICT, with PARTICULARS as to ACCOMMODATION, GARDENS, STATE of REPAIR, &c.

—	FIRST CLASS Six Rooms		SECOND CLASS Five Rooms		THIRD CLASS Four Rooms		FOURTH CLASS Three Rooms		FIFTH CLASS Two Rooms
	Maximum.	Minimum.	Maximum.	Minimum.	Maximum.	Minimum.	Maximum.	Minimum.	Maximum.
No.	1.	2	3	4.	5	6.	7.	8	9
Rent	[illegible]	[illegible]	[illegible]	[illegible]	[illegible]	[illegible]	[illegible]	[illegible]	[illegible]
Rooms, living	Two, with good back-kitchen.	Three.	Two, and scullery	One and kitchen; good larder	One, and small scullery.	One, and small kitchen.	One	One.	One
Rooms, bed	Three	Three	Two.	Three	Two	Two.	Two.	Two.	One
Outhouses	[illegible] in bakehouse and wash-house; pig-stye	A shed.	Small.	An outhouse.	Good shed	An outhouse	An outhouse	An outhouse	—
Closet	Separate	Separate	Joint use of [illegible]	Separate.	Joint use.	Separate	Joint one	[illegible]	Separate
Garden	15 perches.	16 perches	9 perches	20 perches	7 perches.	25 perches	15 perches	30 perches	4-5 perches
Water supply	Well	Well	Well	Well.	Pump	A well.	Good	Well	Good.
Materials	Stone, brick, slate	Brick.	Plaster and tiles.	Plaster, wood, and tiles.	Lath, plaster, tiles.	Stone and slate	Lath, plaster, thatch	Brick	—
State of repair	Very good	Good.	Fair.	Good	Bad	Good	Bad	Good	—
Inhabitants	Man, wife, six children	Man, wife, and three children.	Mother, daughter, son-in-law, two children	Man, wife, and baby	Man, wife, and two children	Man, wife, and daughter.	Man, wife, six children	Three	Man, wife, and one child.
Reference, Page	51	[illegible]	[illegible]	48	43.	49	41.	50.	43.
Name of Occupier	Granger	Frost	Ellington	A. Sharp	James Byford	Garrod	Parsons.	Raffe	Talbot.

Naturally, I have selected for contrast extreme instances of good accommodation and bad. In the first class I was, however, unable to find an instance of a bad cottage at a high rent. In this class the lower rented cottage (No. 2) is not in all respects equal to the higher rented one (No. 1), but it contrasts favourably with No. 3, with a rent of 5*l.* 5*s.*, and still more favourably with Nos. 5 and 7, rented at 4*l.* 10*s.* each. In the second class, No. 4, at 2*l.* 12*s.*, is in every respect superior to No. 3 at twice the rent, 5*l.* 5*s.* In class 3, No. 6, at a rent of 2*l.* 2*s.*, has the same internal and external accommodation, is in good repair, and has 25 perches of garden, while No. 5, at 4*l.* 10*s.*, has only two perches of garden, and is in bad repair. It is not necessary to point to further instances showing the want of correspondence between rent and value. It may, however, be noted that though the examples given were selected with the object previously stated, and with no other purpose than that of contrast, it so happens that Nos. 4, 6, and 8, which are instances of cottages of different classes, but good of their kind and rented at a low sum, are all of them situated in the village of Little Saxham, which is described, in Appendix A. (4) to Mr. Fox's Report, as a close village belonging to the Marquis of Bristol, one of several landowners in the district whose cottages are spoken of in most favourable terms.

300. With regard to the proportionate number of cottages held at different rates of rent the following statement shows the result of an examination of the statement so frequently referred to.

Proportionate number of cottages at different rates of rent.

COTTAGE RENTS.—Cottages inspected in Thingoe district graded in respect of Rent.

Table 60.

	Annual Rent.		Weekly Rent.		Number.	Average Annual Rent.
	Exceeding	Not Exceeding	Exceeding	Not Exceeding		
	£ s. d.	£ s. d.	s. d.	s. d.		£ s. d.
I.	—	2 12 0	—	1 0	30	2 10 10
II.	2 12 0	3 5 0	1 0	1 3	16	3 0 3½
III.	3 5 0	3 18 0	1 3	1 6	23	3 12 6½
IV.	3 18 0	4 11 0	1 6	1 9	*20	4 3 7½
V.	4 11 0	5 4 0	1 9	2 0	4	5 0 0
VI.	5 4 0	—	2 0	—	*3	5 10 0
		Total rented			95	3 11 3
		Free or particulars not stated			14	
		Total			109	

It appears from this statement that rather more than one half of all the cottages are let at a rent not exceeding 1*s.* 6*d.* a week, while only seven out of 109 are let at more than 1*s.* 9*d.* a week.

The minute particulars given with regard to the cottages in this district seemed to invite a close examination, but there is every reason to believe from the Reports of other Assistant Commissioners that a similar variety of conditions, and a similar want of connection between rent and value, is general, if not indeed universal.

301. It may be worth while before leaving the subject of rents of cottages to contrast the rental in districts of comparatively large earnings with those of the districts where the earnings are on the lowest scale. In Table 63 the several districts of inquiry are classed in respect of average earnings. In the column referring to ordinary labourers there are nine districts in the two highest classes and ten in the fourth class. I proceed to compare the rents in these different districts. I have arranged the information which the Reports afford with respect to the districts under the heads of (i) General Statements; and particular statements as to (ii) Estate or Farm Cottages and (iii) Village Cottages.

Districts of high and low earnings compared.

* [illegible]

	Districts in numerical order (of Table 43.)	1. General Statements.	2. Estate or Farm Cottages.	3. Village Cottages.
36	Langport	-	3l. to 4l.	3l.-4l.
37	Pershore	2s. a week	1s. 6d. a week	In one village they run up to 7l. or more; statements given of rents 4l. to 8l.
26	Buntingford	Average 4l. with garden, 3l. without	On farms 3l. to 4l. Estate 1s.-1s. 3d. a week.	—
31, 32	Dorchester	1s., 2s., or 3s. a week. Average 5l. a year.	On farms usually rent free.	—
	Woburn	6d. to 2s. 6d. 1s. to 1s. 6d. the usual figure	6d., 1s. 6d.	—
33	Stratford-on-Avon	Extremes 30s. to 160s., general average 70s.-80s.	1s. 3d., 1s. 3d., a week	—
30, 32	Wantage	Average 1s. 6d. a week	1s., 1s. 3d.	2s., 2s. 6d. a week.
	Pewsey	9d.-1s. 6d. average about 1s.		
	Hungerford	4l. to 6l.	-	—
20	North Witchford	Average 104s. for two-roomed cottage. 1s. 3d. to 1s. 6d. a week for cottage with one chamber.	Farm 1s. a week	110s., 180s.

It is clear from this comparative statement that cottages which are rented of those who are not estate owners are frequently let for as much money in districts of low earnings as in those of higher earnings, and that the rents of estate or farm cottages vary very little as between districts of high and low earnings.

I have discussed the question of rent in its relation to accommodation and to the financial ability of the labourer, because it seems to me that rent is the crux of the problem. How is the cottage accommodation of the agricultural labourers to be improved?

302. The district Reports contain numerous statements as to cost of building good cottages. Many of these refer to estates of noblemen or wealthy proprietors who build with taste and provide more than is absolutely necessary. The cost will of course vary with the supply of materials on the spot, as well as with the substantial construction of the building. One of the lowest figures given is that of 200l. for a pair of cottages on Lord Savile's estate in Southwell.

Mr. Spencer says that in Langport the cost would be from 100l. to 150l., and he gives an estimate by Sir M. Hicks-Beach's agent, of 150l. as the cost of a good cottage in Pewsey.

Mr. Fox says that in Garstang the cost of building a pair of useful cottages is between 200*l.* and 400*l.*

Mr. Chapman gives a full description of excellent cottages on Lord Wantage's Estate in Berks, which cost from 240*l.* to 300*l.* a pair.

I have quoted the lowest prices and estimates given. I could have given numerous instances of 200*l.* being spent upon a single cottage, and some of 300*l.* or even 350*l.*, but these exceptional instances are not material. What is desired is the minimum cost of a well-built cottage containing the necessary accommodation and sanitary appliances. The necessary accommodation for a full sized family cottage must comprise three bed-rooms, a pantry, a living room, kitchen and washhouse, a closet and coal house. The average cost of a cottage of this description properly constructed and fully equipped cannot be put at less than 125*l.*, exclusive of the value of the site. If a garden of 20 perches be added—and it is most desirable that this should be done wherever circumstances permit—an addition of 5*l.* will be a very moderate one to make, and the capital outlay will stand at 130*l.* This sum, at the simple interest of 4 per cent., represents a rental of 2*s.* a week, and a very large number of landed proprietors would no doubt be very glad to accept such a return for their money, if the tenant undertook to pay rates and bear the cost of repairs and insurance: as a matter of fact they accept on an average 4*l.* a year and pay the cost of repairs, and, very generally, the rates. The return for their capital is thus reduced to about 3*l.* as interest secured on a perishable investment of 130*l.*, which is at the rate of 2*l.* 6*s.* 2*d.* per 100*l.* It is only a matter for astonishment that so many good cottages should have been built of late years under conditions such as those described, for it must be remembered that the case assumed is that of minimum expenditure with an average rental, whereas in most cases of estate cottages the expenditure has been considerably in excess of the assumed sum, while the rent has been less than the average amount.

Cottage building does not pay.

303. A conclusion which may be drawn from the facts submitted is that cottage building, for agricultural labourers does not pay directly as a commercial undertaking. Large or wealthy landowners may continue from philanthropic motives and from a sense of duty to indulge in unremunerative investments, but the ordinary owner of land cannot follow their example, and a great and general improvement of cottage property cannot be anticipated until some means are devised for making cottage building directly remunerative as an investment.

Possible adjustment of outlay and return.

304. There are three directions in which it would seem to be possible to approach to a more satisfactory adjustment of outlay and return :—

I. To reduce the original cost by the adoption of the best plans for economising space and construction and the use of materials most readily available.

II. By loans at a low rate of interest.

III. By an adjustment of rent in proportion to the character and amount of accommodation afforded.

IV. By the attachment of larger gardens, than are now usual, to cottages where such a course is practicable.

Reduction of cost.

305. (I.) Time and space forbid my entering upon the first of these subjects, further than to say there is still great scope for improvement in the arrangement of cottages and perhaps for a considerable saving in the proper use of materials locally available.*

Loans for cottage building.

306. (II.) Government loans to landowners, at such a rate of interest as would secure the State from loss, might diminish the difficulty which many proprietors experience in keeping down the interest on loans for cottage building. Under present circumstances, if expenditure of this kind is undertaken upon a loan advanced by one of the land companies, the proprietor has for thirty years to pay from 5·65 to 6·51 per cent. on the outlay in order to provide for the repayment of principal and interest. At the present time the State lends to local authorities in Ireland upon terms which involve an annual charge of 4·825*l.* per annum for 35 years, and if the period of repayment be extended to 50 years, the annual instalment is reduced to £4·40 per cent.

Increased rent.

307. (III.) The payment of an increased rent by the labourer would however facilitate the provision of new and better cottages more than anything else. It is worth while to

* I may, in passing, mention that I have recently had the opportunity of seeing some cottages and other buildings erected by [illegible]

consider whether such an increase is practicable? If it can be shown that agricultural labourers do already pay in many instances, and in many districts a rent which would be a sufficient inducement to landowners to build cottages, can there be any impossibility in their doing so generally? I have shown that in Garstang, where wages are 18s. a week, and earnings may be estimated at 19s. 8d., cottage rents are on the average no higher than they are in Pershore, where wages are 12s., and estimated earnings are 13s. 6d. It might not be easy for the Pershore labourer to pay another 1s. a week for his cottage; but it ought not to be difficult for the Garstang labourer, if he had a sufficient appreciation of the value of a good and healthy cottage, to pay the commercial value of that cottage.

308. At the present time, the landowner or the farmer or the two parties conjointly really pay the labourer who occupies a cheap cottage, more than he believes that he is receiving. The provision of a cottage at the rent of 1s. a week, which could not be built by the greatest exercise of economy for less than 100*l*., must be equivalent to a bonus on wages of at least 1s. a week, but it is not so regarded by the labourer, who unfortunately prefers to pay a high rent for a bad cottage in a village rather than a low rent for a good cottage on a farm.

309. Some of my colleagues do, however, express a belief that the labourer does appreciate and would be prepared to pay a higher rent for additional and better accommodation. Thus Mr. Wilkinson, in his Final report, says:—

"It is not uncommon to hear it stated that labourers do not often care to have three bedrooms, and will not use the third if they have it. I certainly saw it used in several cases as a granary, a lumber-room, or anything but what it was intended for, and it is also true that many like being packed together for the sake of the warmth, and see no indelicacy in the most objectionable arrangements. But I am convinced that the desire for houses which do not necessitate such arrangements is becoming more and more widespread and stronger in intensity."

Mr. Wilson Fox, in his Report upon Swaffham, says:—

"I have sometimes heard it said 'If there were better cottages, the men would take them.'"

And again in his Final Report, he says:—

"If a good class of cottages were built, with a sufficient garden attached, some labourers could and would pay a higher rent than they do at present."

Mr. Chapman expresses the opinion that:—

"As the standard of comfort and decency rise, labourers will more and more appreciate extra accommodation."

And again:—

"There is nothing which old labourers comment upon more frequently than the improved sanitary condition of their houses."

310. These expressions of opinion are not very conclusive, and when they are set against the fact that the highest paid districts in England are precisely those where the labourers' cottages are most overcrowded, that good cottages on farms are deserted for bad ones in villages, that increased accommodation is too frequently either misused or unused,* it seems impossible to acquit the agricultural labourer of some share in the blame for the present condition of cottages.

311. (IV.) Another means by which the rent of cottages may be somewhat increased is by attaching to them a garden somewhat larger than is now usual. This course is often in villages impossible, but wherever new cottages are built and land is available it is, I think, highly desirable that a good garden should be attached. I would even go so far as to recommend 40 poles as not too large for ordinary labourers.†

312. As a rule, cottages let by an estate owner or held under a farmer are held clear of rates, and this is also frequently the case with village cottages held of independent owners. Occasional instances are, however, found where, as a matter of principle, the occupiers of cottages pay directly the rates assessed upon their cottages, and thus have an interest in the proper administration of local funds.

* Mr. Fox mentions a case where "in a cottage [illegible] by a farm bailiff, a most respectable man, I found sleeping in the same bedroom two sons, aged 16 and 1[illegible], and two daughters, aged 2[illegible] and 1[illegible]. As it happened this state of things was quite unnecessary, as there was a second room on the ground floor [illegible] which was unused." B. I. 75.

† If I may venture to give my own experience on this point, I may say that for [illegible] years past all the labourers' cottages on the farm in my occupation have had one rood of garden attached to them, and I believe that the result has been very beneficial to the occupiers.

Mr. Chapman, in his report on Atcham, says :—

"On the Powis estate, and on Sir Baldwyn Leighton's, the occupants of the cottages pay the rates, except when they have the cottage rent free. Sir Baldwyn Leighton says the Small Tenements Act is a very bad thing, as it prevents the labourer from realising the meaning of rates and his own responsibilities as a householder." Chapman, B. VI. 81.

Mr. Bear says :—

"The Southwell Union is the only rural district hitherto visited in which the rates are almost invariably paid by the tenants, except where the cottages are supplied to the labourers rent free." Bear, B. V. 81.

Other districts in which mention is made of rates being borne by the cottage occupants are Belper, Cirencester, Crediton, Driffield, Garstang, Langport, Melton, Pershore, Uttoxeter, Wetherby, Wigton, Woburn, but in all these cases it appears to be an exception rather than the rule for them to do so.

313. I have reviewed the whole of the evidence connected with the housing of the agricultural labourer at considerable length, because I am convinced that in the whole field of survey of the conditions under which that class have to live there is no darker spot than it. To recapitulate in brief what I have endeavoured to deduce from the Reports which are before the Commission, I venture to submit the following conclusions :— Recapitulation and summary of conclusions.

The supply of cottages is not now generally defective in respect of numbers, owing partly to the decrease in the rural population, and partly to the large number of cottages which have been built by large landowners and others who can afford to build without an expectation of a profitable return for their outlay.

The distribution of cottages is irregular, and their situation often very inconvenient for the inhabitants.

The accommodation provided in respect of the number, size, and comfort of the rooms, the sanitary condition, and the water supply are lamentably deficient generally and require amendment.

The action of the local sanitary authority, though vigorous in some districts, is in many places ineffective, and it is everywhere impeded and sometimes arrested by the knowledge that the owners of insanitary dwellings have not the means to remedy the defects, and that the consequences of closing such dwellings would be to make the present inhabitants homeless.

The rent which is received for cottage property in rural districts is not sufficient to make the building of good cottages directly profitable.

That rent has generally no relation to the size of the cottage, the cost of its construction, the accommodation which it affords, its condition as regards repair or sanitary arrangements, or to the earnings of the occupier.

Under these circumstances I venture to submit to the Commission that the subject is one which deserves the gravest consideration, with a view to the suggestion of remedial action.

314. I have reported certain suggestions as to amendments of the sanitary laws, which have been made by the Assistant Commissioners or reported by them as proceeding from other purposes. In more than one instance no legislation is required to effect the change proposed. It is neglect and indisposition to use powers which sanitary authorities already possess, or can obtain, rather than the want of power that stands in the way of reform. Recommendations.

315. There is no doubt, in addition to the general indifference and indisposition to achieve reform, a very prevalent want of knowledge on the subject, and the powers of sanitary authorities are latent and unused, because so few people are acquainted with the existence of them. I have taken some pains to ascertain what are the powers which rural sanitary authorities possess, either absolutely or potentially, with regard to cottages, their structure, accommodation, sanitary condition, and arrangements. The subject is too complicated for anyone who is not an expert to deal with fully. I can only attempt to point out the nature of the powers which rural sanitary authorities may exercise. General want of knowledge in exercise of sanitary authorities.

316. Under the Public Health Act of 1875 the Local Government Board could, upon an application from a rural sanitary authority or from a certain number of ratepayers representing a definite proportion of the rateable property, invest that authority with some of the powers which urban authorities possessed with regard to the building of houses, and many rural sanitary authorities availed themselves of this opportunity. Public Health Act, 1875.

317. The Public Health Acts Amendment Act, 1890, gives to all rural sanitary authorities, *if they choose to adopt* so much of Part III. of the Act as is made applicable to rural districts, powers with respect to new buildings, but with this condition: "If " the authorities adopt at all, they must adopt all the sections thus made applicable. " They cannot adopt some of these sections without adopting the others, nor can they " adopt for a portion of their district only."

Under this part of the Act, if adopted, a rural sanitary authority is enabled to make byelaws—

(*a*) with respect to the structure of walls and foundations of new buildings for purposes of health;

(*b*) with respect to the sufficiency of the space about buildings to secure a free circulation of air, and with respect to the ventilation of buildings;

(*c*) with respect to the drainage of building to water-closets, earth closets, privies, ash-pits, and cesspools, in connexion with buildings, and to the closing of buildings or parts of buildings unfit for human habitation, and to prohibition of their use for such habitation;

(*d*) with respect to the keeping water-closets supplied with sufficient water for flushing, and

(*e*) with respect to the structure of floors, and the height of rooms to be used for human habitation.

The byelaws thus indicated apply to new buildings only, but byelaws relating to the drainage of buildings, and to water-closets, earth closets, privies, ashpits, and cesspools, &c., may be made so as to affect buildings erected before the Act was put into operation.

318. The Housing of the Working Classes Act, 1890, enables the rural sanitary authority to close insanitary dwellings, to compensate the occupier at the expense of the owner for compulsory disturbance, and in the event of the defects not being remedied, to demolish, without any further compensation to the owner than the proceeds from the sale of the materials minus the expenses of demolition and removal.

319. If the rural sanitary authority are remiss in their duty after complaint or representation, the county council may themselves take the necessary proceedings with the object of closing and demolishing insanitary dwellings.

Under the same Act a rural sanitary district desiring to adopt Part III. of the Act, which authorises the building of houses for the working classes, may apply to the county council, who, after public inquiry, may issue a certificate, after which the rural sanitary authority may put in force the powers conferred by the Act. It is under these provisions of the Act that the West Suffolk County Council have sanctioned the action of the rural sanitary authority of Thingoe in building cottages at Ixworth,* to which reference is made by Mr. Wilson Fox in his Report on that district.

320. One other provision of the Housing of the Working Classes Act, 1890, may be noticed. By section 75 it is provided that "in any contract made after the 14th August " 1885 for letting for habitation, by persons of the working classes, a house or part of " a house, there shall be implied a condition that the house is, at the commencement of " the holding, in all respects reasonably fit for human habitation.†

It would appear, then, that even the rural sanitary authorities may exercise very considerable powers with regard to the construction, accommodation, and arrangements of new buildings, that they can close absolutely insanitary dwellings, and that they can acquire powers to deal with drainage and the sanitary conveniences of existing houses.

321. It would, I think, be desirable to carry out Mr. Wilson Fox's suggestion that the owners of all houses let at a rental of less than 10*l.* a year should make a return to the sanitary authority every year, stating the number of persons in each cottage, their sex and age, whether the house is provided with a proper water supply and a closet, and whether the premises are in good repair.

322. I think it very desirable that the medical officer of health should not be engaged in private practice, that he should give up his whole time to the duties of his office, and that he should not be removable from his office without the consent of the Local Government Board. In order to secure a properly qualified man under these conditions it would be necessary to offer such a salary as would be a heavy tax upon many small sanitary districts—while such districts would not afford sufficient work to occupy the whole time of the officer; but this difficulty would be overcome by combining two or more sanitary districts, and the independence of the officer would be increased if he were appointed by the county council, subject to the approval of the Local Government Board. Medical officer of health, appointment, &c.

323. I have already recommended that loans should be advanced to landowners, at the lowest rate of interest which would secure the State from loss, for the purpose of building cottages. Such loans might be made subject to express conditions as to the character of the cottages and the arrangements, the valuation, the provision of attached gardens, and the maximum rent to be charged. Loans for cottages to landowners.

324. It will probably be expected that I should give some reason why, with the example of Labourers Acts, Ireland, in view, I do not propose the adoption of similar means for providing adequate and proper house accommodation for agricultural labourers in England. Reasons for not recommending action similar to that taken in Ireland.

In the first place I would urge that any general application of the principle of providing house accommodation by local popularly elected bodies would open the door to an unlimited amount of jobbery, favouritism, and corruption which might find scope in the choice of sites, the allocation of houses, the rents charged and enforced, and for these reasons it is only as an ultimate resort, and after the failure of all other possible means of supplying decent accommodation, that recourse should be had to a system of building largely by local authorities; the adoption of the system would put a stop to all private enterprise in supplying cottages unless the rents charged were such as to secure the ratepayers from loss. It is clear from the evidence with respect to the working of the Labourers Acts in Ireland that every house which is built under the provisions of these Acts is the cause of a considerable annual loss to the ratepayers, even if the rents are regularly collected, which is not the case. The knowledge of this fact, and the objection to increasing the burdens of the ratepayers, have prevented a large number of local authorities in Ireland from taking any action in the matter, and a demand is now made that these authorities shall be compelled to exercise the powers which they possess.

But, further, it seems very doubtful whether local authorities are capable of judging dispassionately whether it is desirable, or even possible, to retain the present number of inhabitants in the rural districts. If corn prices remain at the level which they have now reached, it is certain that large tracts of land will go out of cultivation, and employment will be much more restricted than it is now. If good houses had been supplied in all the rural districts 20 years ago, it is certain that many of them would now be unoccupied.

And, lastly, any action by a local authority in the way of purchasing land and building must, in the interest both of the ratepayers who have to bear the risk, and also of those individuals who may be injured by the action of the board, be subject to such an amount of control and formality that the cost of the work accomplished must be materially increased.

325. On the other hand if a loan be made to landowner, the executive of the State has only to consider whether the property to be charged is a sufficient security for the advance. The applicant acts upon his own judgment as to the number of cottages which are required, and what is the best situation for them. If he makes a mistake, he or his successors are the only sufferers. The security being sufficient, the comparative simplicity of the process of dealing with an individual instead of a representative body is obvious. Comparative simplicity and safety of loans to individuals.

326. But I must again repeat what I have already said, and express my firm conviction that no great and lasting improvement will be effected in the housing of the agricultural labourer until his sense of self-respect, and his regard for his family, impel him to demand better cottages and inspire him to make some sacrifice in order to obtain them. No great improvement until labourers desire better houses.

3. LAND HELD BY LABOURERS.

327. I have already, in dealing with the subject of cottage accommodation, given some information as to the supply of gardens attached to cottages, but it may be desirable to treat the subject separately, and to exhibit, by extracts from the Reports, the variety which exists both as to the supply and demand for them.

It may be stated as a general rule that estate or farm cottages, and those in close villages, are supplied with gardens, and that in open villages, if gardens exist, they are generally too small to be of much use. In the North and also in some dairy districts there is little demand for gardens, while in some of the low wage districts the position of the labourer is considerably ameliorated by the possession of a good garden, particularly in those districts which are adapted to fruit growing, either as standard trees or bush fruit or "berries." The area which can be cultivated by a labourer without taking him from his ordinary work and sacrificing wages, is the subject of much difference of opinion amongst employers and owners of estates.

With regard to the supply and size of gardens Mr. Bear, in his final Report, says :—

"The best and largest gardens are those in the Thakeham and Basingstoke Unions, and generally they are the best stocked with fruit trees. Melton stands far below other Unions in supply and size of gardens, and there are a great many cottages in the Southwell neighbourhood with no gardens or very small ones. This is also the case in some of the Woburn and St. Neots villages; but the general prevalence of large allotments in these two Unions makes up to a great extent for any deficiencies in the provision of gardens."

Mr. Chapman says on the same subject :—

"Good gardens are a great compensation to an agricultural labourer, and when they can be provided of sufficient size they take the place of allotments or potato grounds. For example, at Crediton, where the labourers live almost entirely in farm cottages, the size of gardens vary from 15 to 40 poles. They often contain a small orchard, and I have known one woman estimate her filbert border alone to be worth 1l. a year to her. In Atcham, also with farm cottages, gardens are from 1 to 3 roods, and with the village cottages from 7 to 10 poles. In some places these gardens contain plum trees, the value of which men estimate at 2l. per annum. In neither of these districts are allotments wanted. In Thame, gardens are very general of from 5 to 20 poles, except where cottages have been built on the waste. These gardens are not large enough to make up for allotments but they are much appreciated. In Truro, except on the farms, men make nothing of gardens. In the close villages of Wantage and elsewhere good gardens are often a feature of the place, but in North Witchford, where open villages are the rule, there are either no gardens at all or such small ones as to be of no practical use.

"To be of any value a garden ought to be half a rood in extent to a rood or more if the land is poor. There should, at any rate, be enough land to provide garden stuff for the family for a year, and enough for a pig with the addition of a little meal."

Mr. Wilson Fox reports :—

"On the whole Norfolk and Suffolk labourers are better off, both as regards the number and the size of the gardens than the Northumberland, Lancashire, and Cumberland men, though in the open villages in the two former counties there is frequently a scarcity of them.

"To an eastern counties' labourer a good garden is a great boon and is much appreciated by him . . . . In most cases where men are provided with gardens of from 20 rods to a quarter of an acre, they seldom desire to take an allotment, and it is generally stated that a garden of about a quarter of an acre, certainly not more than half an acre, is sufficient to occupy all a man's spare time, and to provide a man with all the potatoes and vegetables he requires.

"In Cumberland and Lancashire it may be said that on the whole the people are fairly supplied with them, and that they are satisfied with what they have got, but in these counties comparatively little interest is taken in gardens, partly because potatoes are given as perquisites, and also because they would rather buy potatoes and vegetables than work in their spare time.

"In Glendale everybody has a small garden ranging from one-twentieth to one-tenth of an acre, and sufficient vegetables are grown in them for the use of the family . . . . potatoes being provided as part of their wages."

Mr. Richards says :—

both in the same Union and throughout the whole of them. In the open villages . . . . . the houses are closely built . . . . In such places there are no gardens, or none worth mentioning.

"Monmouth and Hereford have very much in common both as to cottages and gardens . . . . Both are to a considerable extent apple-growing districts, and most of the gardens attached to the cottages are in reality orchards, as a rule, well stocked with fruit trees. The size of such gardens or orchards varies considerably, but the produce often pays the rent."

Mr. Spencer gives the following brief summary of his observation:—

"In the great majority of cases cottages have gardens attached to them which are included in the rent paid. The size of the gardens varies from 2 or 3 perches to a quarter or half an acre. They are the smallest in large villages where the houses are built near together, and most ample in the case of detached cottages and those outlying on farms. The dimensions are so various that it is difficult to draw conclusions as to their comparative sizes in various counties, but, roughly speaking, cottages in Wilts, Somerset, and Dorset seemed to be better supplied with gardens than those in Kent, Surrey, and Essex." Spencer, A [illegible]

Mr. Wilkinson reports thus:—

"It is impossible to say generally of any district whether or not the gardens are adequate, hardly any two parishes being at the same level; and the range being great I think on the whole Uttoxeter is the best supplied, though no district is without many cottages with capital gardens." Wilkinson, A [illegible]

A few extracts taken from district reports may perhaps be admitted. As an example of good conditions as regards gardens Basingstoke may be taken. Of that district Mr. Bear says:—

"With the exception of the parishes of Basingstoke, Basing, and Worting, the cottage gardens throughout the district are generally large, in many cases extending to a quarter of an acre, and some to a larger size. As a rule they are more or less stocked with fruit trees and bushes, and I was informed that a good many of the occupiers were able to pay their rents from the sale of fruit. The cultivation of some of the gardens is not all that could be desired. Possibly the frequent changes of tenancy, incidental to the yearly hiring system, may partly account for the neglect of gardens which is noticeable in many instances." Bear, B. IV [illegible]

For a less favoured but fairly supplied district, Driffield may be cited.

"The cottages are, on the whole, fairly supplied with gardens. In Cranswick some cottages hardly habitable have at least half an acre of garden. At Kelham over 30 cottages have no gardens, and in other cases the gardens are very small . . . . There is hardly a parish without some houses gardenless . . . . . but the majority are either sufficiently supplied or are within easy reach of available garden allotments. On the estate of Mr. F. Quintin . . . . in or round Lowthorpe, the gardens run from three-quarters of a rood to a rood." Wilkinson, B II [illegible]

Taking another district of mixed, good, and bad conditions, I may refer to Thingoe, as to which I have already given particulars in a table in connexion with cottage accommodation. Mr. Fox says:— See Table [illegible]

"The gardens vary very much in size. In many places, especially in the open villages, there is a want of them, but on the large properties in the close villages, and at the farms as a rule, they are plentiful and of a good size, often from 15 rods to a quarter of an acre. Most men are quite satisfied with a quarter of an acre." Fox, B I [illegible]

328. I have shown in Tables 82 and 83 that of 171 cottages inspected by Mr. Fox in the two districts of Thingoe and Swaffham, 118 had gardens of a specified size and 25 more had gardens of some sort; 27 are described as having no gardens, and as regards 0 the particulars are wanting. The average size of the gardens in Thingoe, in cases where it is stated, was 10½ perches while in Swaffham it was 18 perches. Size of gardens.

Mr. Spencer also gives in several of his reports particulars as to the size of gardens attached to a number of cottages which he visited. From the two sets of returns compiled by these gentlemen I have prepared the following table, which deals with 331 cottages in six different counties. To a certain extent the returns are defective, as in some places where a blank is left it is not clear whether it is intended to indicate that there is no garden or that a note was not taken. In other cases it is definitely stated that there is no garden. In some the expression used is "small" or "good." I have placed all those instances where there is a positive statement in one column (c), and all the doubtful cases with those where the expression is indefinite in another column (d). I have also classified gardens according to size, and shown how many of those for which particulars are given there are in each class, the average size of the whole number and the extreme range. I should mention that I have omitted to include one or two cases where the size is one acre or more, inasmuch as the inclusion of such instances would unduly increase the average size of cottage gardens.

PARTICULARS as to the GARDENS attached to COTTAGES personally inspected in SIX DISTRICTS of INQUIRY by Messrs. WILSON FOX and A. SPENCER.

Districts.	Number. a Total No.	b With Gardens of definite size.	c Without Gardens.	d Indefinite or unascertained.	Size. 5 Perches.	5 and not exceeding 10 Perches.	10 and not exceeding 20 Perches.	20 and not exceeding [illegible] Perches.	Exceeding [illegible] Perches.	Average size. Perches.	Maximum and Minimum size. Perches.
[illegible]	[illegible]	15	2	—	[illegible]	4	[illegible]	1	—	14½	[illegible]
Langport	[illegible]	[illegible]	[illegible]	[illegible]	[illegible]	[illegible]	[illegible]	[illegible]	—	17½	[illegible]
Pershore	[illegible]	[illegible]	1	[illegible]	[illegible]	[illegible]	7	[illegible]	—	[illegible]	[illegible]
Pewsey	[illegible]	[illegible]	[illegible]	1	[illegible]	11	[illegible]	[illegible]	[illegible]	[illegible]	[illegible]
Swaffham	[illegible]	44	1	[illegible]	[illegible]	7	[illegible]	[illegible]	1	[illegible]	[illegible]
Thingoe	[illegible]	[illegible]	[illegible]	[illegible]	[illegible]	[illegible]	[illegible]	[illegible]	—	[illegible]	[illegible]
Total	[illegible]	[illegible]	[illegible]	[illegible]	[illegible]	[illegible]	[illegible]	[illegible]	[illegible]	—	—
Percentage of Total		[illegible]	[illegible]	[illegible]	[illegible]	[illegible]	[illegible]	[illegible]	[illegible]	—	—

It will be seen that of the whole number 75½ per cent. have gardens of a specified extent, while 11½ per cent. are absolutely without them; but nearly one-fifth of the cottages have gardens which do not exceed 5 perches, an area which is almost too small to be of any practical use; another one-fifth have gardens between 5 and 10 perches, while only a little more than one-third of the whole number have more than 10 perches. No doubt a considerable number of the cottages visited were in villages where it is often extremely difficult to attach good-sized gardens, and in many cases the occupants have land in the shape of allotments or detached gardens.

329. Taking the general statements of the Assistant Commissioners, the several districts may be roughly classed in respect of the provision of gardens thus:—

Districts.	No.
Supply good generally.—Atcham, Basingstoke, Bromyard, Crediton, Dorchester, Langport, Louth, Monmouth, Pershore, Pewsey, Thakeham, Uttoxeter, Wantage, Wetherby	14
Supply fair.—Driffield, Easingwold, Hollingbourne, Maldon, Thame	5
Mixed conditions; supply partially good, partially insufficient.—Brixworth, Cirencester, Godstone, Stratford-on-Avon, Swaffham, Thingoe, Woburn	7
Supply insufficient.—Buntingford, Holbeach, Melton Mowbray, North Witchford, St. Neots, Southwell	6
Demand not great.—Belper, Garstang, Glendale, Nantwich, Truro, Wigton	6

The Allotments Compensation Act, 1887, however, defines an allotment for the purpose of the Act thus: "Allotment means any parcel of land of not more than two "acres in extent held by a tenant under a landlord and cultivated as a garden or as a "farm or partly as a garden and partly as a farm," and this definition is repeated in the Allotments Rating Act, 1891.

In a memorandum upon the Reports,* &c., of the Commission upon the Employment of Children, &c., which I have laid before the Commission, I have epitomised the information which is given in the Report as to the history of allotments previous to the period of inquiry (1867-1870).

331. It appears that the system of providing allotments for the labouring class has existed for more than 100 years. It probably originated in private efforts to ameliorate the condition of the poor, but about the beginning of the present century it became usual to insert in private Inclosure Acts provisions for securing a portion of the lands to be inclosed to be set out in "field gardens." In 1845, a general Inclosure Act provided that in the inclosure of any waste or land, subject to rights of common, *not limited by number or stints*, there should be an appropriation of such an allotment for the labouring poor as the Inclosure Commissioners should think necessary. Under these provisions no great quantity of land appears to have been appropriated for allotments. Mr. H. S. Tremenheere, one of the two members of the Commission already referred to, estimated that between 1845 and 1869, out of 320,000 acres inclosed, only 2,119 acres had been assigned as garden allotments; but the evidence given before a Select Committee on the Inclosure Act, 1869, rather modified this statement, which was an estimate not strictly authenticated, and based apparently upon the quantity inclosed, whether that land comes under the definition as to common rights given above or not.

The Commons Act of 1876 may be said to have made the provision of land for labourers a condition of any future inclosure. It has been stated by Mr. Mark Jeans (F.S.I.), in a paper upon allotments and small holdings read before the Surveyors' Institution in 1887,† that this proviso "practically put an end to inclosure unless in "exceptional cases, there having been only 21 orders for inclosures under the Act "up to the end of 1885."

332. The Acts which have been named, and many others which were passed between 1845 and 1863, dealt with allotments as an incident of the inclosure of commons or wastes, but some efforts which were made by the legislature in the earlier half of the present century to place small plots of land within the reach of the labourers may be noticed.

In 1819 an Act empowered churchwardens to purchase or take on lease a limited quantity of land for the purpose of letting to poor and industrious labourers. In 1831 an amending Act extended the powers of the parochial authorities in this respect, and also authorised them to inclose a limited quantity of waste for this purpose. In 1832 another Act, which deserves notice as a precedent of the Allotments Act of 1882, enabled trustees of allotments which had been made under Inclosure Acts for "the "benefit of the poor, chiefly with a view to fuel," to let such allotments in "portions "of not less than a quarter of an acre and not exceeding one acre as a yearly occupa- "tion (and at such rent as land of the same quality is usually let for in the same "parish), to such industrious cottagers of good character, being day labourers or "journeymen legally settled in the parish and dwelling within or near the bounds of "the parish."

In 1882 the Allotments Extension Act, which is by its preamble essentially an amendment of the Act of 1832, imposed upon the trustees of land, vested in them for the benefit of the poor, the rents or produce of which were distributed in doles, the obligation of setting apart such land (with certain exceptions) for allotments to "cottagers, labourers, and others." It empowers the trustees, where the lands which they owned were inconveniently situated, to let them, and to hire, in lieu thereof, other lands more conveniently situated.

The rent at which the lands in question were to be offered was, by the provisions of the Act, to be a rent "free of all charges, that is to say, tithe, tithe rentcharge, rates, "taxes, and outgoings whatsoever . . . . and such rent as land of the same quality "is usually let for in the same parish with such addition as is necessary to satisfy the "said charges."

The Allotments Act of 1887 must be regarded as a new point of departure in legislation for providing allotments. Up to that time Acts had been passed enabling

* App., Vol. V., Pt. II., Sec. I. A.

† "Transactions Surveyors' Institution," Vol. XX., Pt. II.

public bodies to provide allotments thus giving to the labouring poor a claim to the occupation of land left or set aside for the benefit of their class. This Act imposed upon the local authorities the duty of inquiry as to the provision of allotments required, and, where other means failed, of supplying them either by purchase or hire. In the event of the sanitary authority being unable to acquire sufficient land, power was given to the county authority (the county council under the Local Government Act, 1888) after inquiry, to make a provisional order authorising the sanitary authority to take land compulsorily under the provisions of the Lands Clauses Consolidation Act for the purpose of providing allotments.

Those for whom allotments may be provided under this Act are "persons belonging "to the labouring population resident in the district or parish for which the allotments "are provided, and desiring to take the same"; but the sanitary authority may make regulations (subject to confirmation of such regulations by the Local Government Board) defining the "persons eligible as tenants." The size of the allotment or allotments held by one person under this Act was limited to one acre.

Another Act relating to allotments was passed in 1887 with the object of securing to allotment holders compensation for growing crops, labour, and manure expended in anticipation of a crop, and, where the previous consent of the landlord has been obtained, for fruit trees or bushes, drainage, and buildings. The principle of compensation is extended to cottage gardens and to holdings of not more than two acres "cultivated as a garden, or as a farm, or partly as a garden or as a farm."

I may conclude this brief sketch of the legislation for the purpose of providing allotments by stating that the Local Government Act of 1894 gives to parish councils power to hire and, with the consent of the county council, to acquire, compulsorily, by hiring, for a term of years, land for allotments, the size of which is, apparently, unlimited, except in cases where the land is hired compulsorily, when the size must not exceed four acres.

333. There are no official statistics available for determining the number or extent of allotments set out under the provisions of Inclosure or Commons Acts, or those of the Allotments Extension Act of 1882, or of other Acts which have been mentioned; but it is clear that a large proportion of the allotments in existence have been provided by private individuals. The Act of 1887 had, no doubt, a great effect indirectly in stimulating the supply of these privately owned allotments, but the number of allotments already in existence before the passing of that Act was very considerable, as will be seen by reference to three Parliamentary Returns made in the years 1873, 1886, and 1890. These Returns, though not precisely on the same lines, show the number of allotments under one acre detached from cottages in England, Wales, and Scotland, and in each county of Great Britain at the respective periods.

Taking England alone, the following results are shown:—

Date.	Number of Allotments.	Increase since 1873.		Increase since 1886.	
		Number.	Rate per Cent.	Number.	Rate per Cent.
[illegible]	[illegible]	—	—	—	—
[illegible]	[illegible]	[illegible]	[illegible]	—	—
[illegible]	[illegible]	[illegible]	[illegible]	92,159	[illegible]

Thus, in 13 years, between 1873 and 1886, the rate of increase was at the rate of 45·8 per cent., while in the next period of only four years it was at the rate of 20·4 per cent. It must be borne in mind that these Returns do not include allotments of one acre, of which there are, no doubt, a considerable number, and that there were in addition to these allotments 25,680 small holdings of a quarter of an acre but under one acre in England in 1891.

A Return to the House of Commons, dated 20th June 1892, gives particulars as to the number and extent of allotments acquired under the provisions of "The Allotments Act, 1887." It appears from this Return that 56 rural sanitary authorities had acquired land either by hire or purchase to the extent of 1,120 acres. In two cases, however, land having been acquired was abandoned as the rent demanded was considered by the applicants too high. Four county councils had acquired land for 198 tenants. The whole quantity thus acquired by local authorities under the Act was, up to the period of the Return in question, two years after the date of the Return previously alluded to, about 1,207 acres, occupied by 2,891 tenants. As the increase in the number of allotments between 1886 and 1890 was upwards of 92,000, and less than 3,000 were obtained directly under the powers of the Act, it is clear that a very large proportion of the whole number must have been provided by private arrangement, though in many cases the Act has no doubt facilitated such arrangements.

In 17 counties of England and in all the counties in Wales no land has been acquired by sanitary authorities for allotments.

234. Within the several counties of England there exists a very wide difference in respect of the supply of allotments, and no doubt in respect to the demand or desire for them. For the purpose of comparison it is not easy to find a satisfactory basis. Attempts have been made to find this in the number of agricultural labourers, but it is notorious that in the neighbourhood of some large towns a very large number of allotments are held by artisans and others. The total population forms no satisfactory basis of comparison, since there must be in the more populous counties a vast proportion of the people who do not want allotments, and the total area of a mountainous county is no measure of the possible requirements in this respect. The extent of cultivated area and the number of allotments in proportion to that area may however give some indication as to the relative supply of allotments in different counties. Distribution in counties.

In the following Table those counties which have the greatest and least number of allotments in proportion to the extent of their cultivated area are shown.

Allotments under One Acre in 1890; Number for each 100 Acres of Cultivated Area.

Table 53.

A.—Counties having more than twice the Average Number					B.—Counties having less than one-half of the Average Number				
		Number per 100 Acres of Cultivated Area					Number per 100 Acres of Cultivated Area		
No.	County	Under ¼ of an Acre.	¼ but under 1 Acre	Total under 1 Acre	No.	County	Under ¼ of an Acre.	¼ but under 1 Acre	Total under 1 Acre
1	Bedford	2·67	3·16	5·83	42	Cumberland	0·10	0·01	0·11
2	Leicester	4·31	0·43	4·74	41	Hereford	0·25	0·02	0·27
3	Northampton	3·03	1·43	4·46	40	Salop	0·27	0·09	0·36
4	Nottingham	4·15	0·51	4·66	39	Westmorland	0·35	0·01	0·37
5	Oxford	3·17	1·18	4·35	38	Cornwall	0·36	0·04	0·40
6	Buckingham	2·30	1·45	3·75	37	Northumberland	0·41	0·04	0·45
7	Warwick	2·33	1·25	3·58	36	Yorks E. R.	0·15	0·34	0·49
					35	Lancashire	0·51	0·03	0·54
					34	Cheshire	0·50	0·10	0·60
					33	Monmouth	0·61	0·11	0·72
					32	Devon	0·70	0·16	0·86
	Average for England					1·75 per 100 acres.			

Of the seven counties in column A., Bedfordshire is the only one in which the number of allotments of one quarter of an acre and under one acre exceeds that of allotments under one rood, but it may be noted that in Cambs, Huntingdon, Lincoln, Norfolk, Suffolk, and Worcester (counties not included in column A.), the larger allotments exceed in number the smaller ones, and probably if allotments of one acre and above had been included in the Return these counties would have ranked higher in respect of allotments in ratio to cultivated area than they do under the Return of 1890.

It may be supposed that in those counties where the number of allotments is comparatively small their place is supplied by gardens or small holdings. According to the Return of 1890 there is not one of the counties in column B. of the above Table where the number of allotments under one acre, and small holdings of a quarter of an acre and under five acres in proportion to cultivated area, is equal to the average proportions of such allotments and small holdings for all England. With respect to gardens, however, there is in some counties a considerable compensation for the scarcity of allotments in the number and size of the gardens attached to cottages. The statistics as to allotments for 1890 give no information on this point, and the latest available Return is that of 1886, where it is given for each Poor Law Union (C.—4,974, 1887). The Agricultural Returns for 1886 contain similar information with regard to each county.

It may be stated here that in Wales the number of allotments per 100 acres of cultivated area is only 0·26. The geographical position of the counties in column A. of the preceding Table is in a compact central group, extending from Notts in the north to Bucks and Oxon in the south, Beds lying on the east and Warwick in the west. The counties in column B. all lie in the north or west with the exception of the East Riding C.—4974, 1887.

of Yorks. Other counties having less than the average number are Yorks North and West Ridings, Stafford, Lincoln, Norfolk, Essex, Kent, and Sussex. Those counties not enumerated in column A., which have more than an average number in proportion to cultivated area, lie with the exception of Durham round and about the group of midland counties given in column A. They are Rutland, Hunts, Cambs, Suffolk, Herts, Middlesex, Surrey, Berks, Hants, Wilts, Dorset, Somerset, Gloucester, Worcester, and Derby.

335. The general purport of the reports of the Assistant Commissioners on this subject is that as a rule the supply is equal to the demand, though some parishes and districts are mentioned where this is not the case.

Mr. Bear, in his final report, compares the six districts which he visited thus:—

"Woburn and St. Neots stand far ahead of the other districts in the supply and sizes of allotments. In proportion to population the ratios given in the several reports are one to 8·8 in Woburn, one to 7·3 in St. Neots, one to 11·6 in Melton, one to 16 in Southwell, one to 91 in Basingstoke, and one to 71·3 in Thakeham."

With regard to Basingstoke, one of the districts where the allotments are comparatively few, Mr. Bear says that his informants unanimously—

"declared that there was no demand for them. Few as there are in many parishes, some are unoccupied, and it is said that the men could easily obtain more if they wanted them. Having, as a rule, sufficient garden ground, it was added, few of the men cared for allotments. The labourers who were questioned upon the point generally confirmed these statements. A few of them said that more allotments would be gladly accepted, but admitted that no effort had been made to obtain them."

As to Thakeham, he writes:—

"Few districts are worse supplied with allotments, in proportion to population and area, than Thakeham Union, just as few counties in England are less supplied than Sussex is."

Mr. Bear says he received evidence generally to the effect that there was no demand, and he gives instances where land had been offered for the purpose and not accepted, and of allotments having fallen out of use, and he came to the conclusion—

"that the majority of the labourers of the district are either too comfortable or not sufficiently energetic to desire land in addition to their gardens."

Mr. Chapman reports thus:—

"Of allotments it is satisfactory to be able to report that in most places the supply is equal to the demand, and, except in Thame, I met with no case in which it was necessary to have recourse to the Allotments Act to satisfy the labourers' wants. . . . Speaking generally of that Union, it is a rare thing to find a labourer who does not take an allotment when it is offered. The same may be said of North Witchford, where almost every man possesses an allotment from 20 poles up to three acres in extent. In Crediton and Atcham they are not wanted, because of the gardens or potato grounds, except in two or three places. In Wantage there are sufficient. In Truro there is very little demand for them, except from people who are not agricultural labourers, and in Wallingford they are rather in excess of the demand."

Mr. Wilson Fox found in the northern districts visited, viz. Glendale, Wigton, and Garstang, no demand for allotments. He says "I believe in all the three Northern Unions a great many labourers would not have them as a gift." In the eastern counties a very different feeling prevails.

"On the whole the supply of the allotments in the Swaffham Union of Norfolk and the Thingoe Union of Suffolk is sufficient, though there are exceptions.

"In the latter county a return is made to the County Council every year from each parish of the number of allotments, their size, rent, and other particulars, an example which, perhaps, might with utility be followed by other county councils. There is no doubt that in these two Eastern Unions the allotments are much valued by the men, and those who see them cannot fail to be struck with the care their owners bestow upon them."

Mr. Richards says:—

"It is somewhat difficult to determine whether or not in any given place the supply of allotments is equal to the demand. It is always necessary to consider what is the position of the ground offered for allotments, what is its quality, and what is the rent. Probably only in the [illegible] Union could it be said that, having a due regard to all these conditions, the supply is equal to the demand. It was estimated that 80 per cent. of the agricultural labourers were allotment holders. . . . In Stratford-on-Avon there was a wide difference of from 3 to 75 per cent. . . . In Cirencester piece-work, especially in the larger farms, is very general, and those who would be industrious enough to work at allotments make long days on the land . . . . In the Cotswold portion of the Union, where there is more grazing, about 80 per cent. of the labourers have allotments, and they are well worked while at Fairford and Marston Meysey Hampton, where there are large farms with piece-work, allotments have been given up. Monmouth and Bromyard are both unfavourably placed with regard to allotments. The villages, with a few exceptions, are very scattered. . . . In both unions also there are large garden orchards, which in many cases occupy all the time the labourer can give. In Monmouth I heard of only one parcel of allotments at Garway, though it was stated by the men at the Llangattock meeting that they would gladly take some allotments if they could have them at a fair rent; there was a strong feeling in their minds that this would be extremely improbable. In Bromyard the minds of the labourers are bent more on small holdings than on allotments. . . . . This preference is still further developed in Nantwich and Belper. . . . Of Monmouth, Nantwich, and Belper it may be said that the conditions are on the whole not favourable to allotments, that the actual demand is met by the supply, and that it would require very favourable conditions to create or increase the demand."

Mr. Spencer reports thus:—

"In all the counties that I visited, allotments are common, and in many cases have been in existence for a great number of years, though they have certainly increased in number since the passing of the Allotments Act, 1887. There is a good deal of difference in different counties with regard to the demand, supply, and size of allotments. In some districts they do not appear to be much sought after; in others the demand and competition for allotments is keen. In Dorsetshire, Wiltshire, Somersetshire, and Worcestershire, I did not come across any parish that had not allotments. In Kent, Essex, and Surrey I found that in several parishes there are no allotments at all, as for instance at Purleigh, Essex, there appeared to be no demand for them, partly because perhaps the heavy land is not particularly suitable for garden crops, and partly because the earnings being comparatively high in these districts there is not the same eagerness among labourers to supplement them by means of allotment cultivation as there is in low-wage districts. Speaking generally, the supply of allotments seems most ample where the rate of earnings is lowest. In Worcestershire, where the soil is admirably adapted for gardening and fruit-growing, and where there are great opportunities of disposing of garden crops, the demand for allotments is keen and the supply is plentiful, though not equal to the demand."

Mr. Wilkinson says—

"Allotments are generally plentiful, or rather the supply is equal to the demand. In some parts there is no demand for them, and, where they have existed for many years, they have often been gradually given up. Holbeach is abundantly supplied, and I should fear that in some places almost too many have been provided, and that they will prove rather a burden than otherwise before long."

He then gives particulars of some parishes in different districts where more are desired, of some where the situation of them was complained of, and of others where they had been given up. He remarks as to the occupants—

"It is difficult to say what proportion of the allotments is in the hands of the labourers. It is not uncommon to find fields originally laid out as allotments for the convenience of labourers, but from which they have gradually retired, which are now occupied by two or three tenants, of whom not one will be a labourer. . . . . . If I might hazard a general statement, I should say that in Holbeach fully three-quarters of them are in the hands of labourers no matter what the size; and that in other districts rather more than half are in the hands of labourers where small plots still prevail, but that where by original plan or through consolidation from want of applicants the size runs to an acre or upwards, comparatively few are held by them."

336. If the district reports of the Assistant Commissioners be examined in detail, it will appear that in 15 districts out of 38 the supply of allotments is sufficient. In 7 other districts there is a partial insufficiency. In one, namely Melton Mowbray, there appeared to be a general complaint both as to the number and the size of them. In no less than 15 districts it is estimated that there is little or no demand for them. Of these districts, 9 are situated in the Northern or Western Counties, viz., Glendale, Wigton, Garstang, Nantwich, Atcham, Bromyard, Monmouth, Crediton, and Truro; Uttoxeter, Belper, and Southwell are in the North Midlands; Godstone, Basingstoke, and Thakeham are in the south-east.

337. Evidence of the abandonment or relinquishment of allotments is given with regard to Thakeham, Basingstoke, Cirencester, Wetherby, but in almost every case, it will be found either that the land is unsuitable or badly selected, or else that the provision of large gardens or small holdings is considerable.

338. It would be possible, if time permitted, to ascertain the number of detached allotments under one acre in extent, in the several districts of inquiry in 1890, but as the returns are given for individual parishes the difficulty of doing this would be considerable. I have, however, compiled the statistics contained in the following Table, which shows the number of allotments and the ratio which that number bears to that of the inhabitants in 10 selected districts of inquiry, and I have compared the number of allotments in 1886 with those of 1890 in those districts. In selecting these districts I chose those where the number of allotments in 1890 was greatest in ratio to the population as ascertained in 1891. I have also added to these statistics the number

of inhabited houses in 1891 and the number of gardens of one-eighth of an acre and upwards attached to cottages held by labourers or working men in 1886. It may, I think, be taken for granted that these gardens have not diminished in number since that period. It must be remembered that allotments of one acre, and what are described in the returns of 1890 as small holdings, are not included in column 1 of this table. I have given in the table as a contrast to these districts, where allotments are numerous, particulars as to two other districts, Thakeham and Atcham, where very different conditions prevail.

ALLOTMENTS in PROPORTION to POPULATION in certain selected DISTRICTS of ENGLAND in 1890.

Districts, Poor Law Unions.	1. Allotments (detached) under 1 acre, 1890.	2. Population, 1891.	3. Inhabited Houses, 1891.	4. Allotments per 100 Inhabitants.	5. Inhabitants to each Allotment.	6. Allotments (detached) under 1 acre, 1873.	7. Gardens attached to Cottages of and exceeding 1/8 of an acre, 1886.
Brixworth	[illegible]	12,166	2,679	18·83	5·31	1,658	488
Woburn	1,734	9,803	2,294	16·92	6·16	1,612	330
Pewsey	1,774	11,711	2,618	14·16	6·60	1,377	727
Thame	1,911	13,099	[illegible]	14·52	6·86	1,695	530
Pershore	1,979	14,005	3,151	14·16	6·93	1,786	720
St. Neots	2,168	15,317	3,469	17·97	7·49	1,197	317
Wantage	1,887	16,517	3,612	12·20	8·10	1,688	401
Thingoe	1,377	13,747	3,149	9·16	10·84	1,185	271
Chesterton	1,388	20,396	4,384	6·80	11·77	1,327	688
Langport	936	11,139	3,348	6·80	11·89	1,494	878
Thakeham	114	5,073	1,210	1·88	51·8	163	673
Atcham	199	16,196	3,211	1·03	97·04	279	1,000

The first 10 districts in this Table are all of them distinguished for the large supply of allotments in proportion to population. They are almost entirely rural in character.

In Brixworth, which heads the list, there are on an average 188 allotments per 1,000 persons of all ages, or 10 allotments for 53 persons, or about 10 average families; for every 120 inhabited houses there are 100 allotments, and if we include the cottage gardens, there are 10 allotments or gardens to 45 persons.

In Langport, which stands tenth on the list, there are 10 allotments for 146 persons, or about one for three families.

If we contrast these conditions with Atcham, we find there little more than one allotment for 100 persons or only about one for 20 houses; but if cottage gardens be taken into account there is either one or the other for 19 or 20 persons.

It may be worth while to examine in detail the statistics as to allotments, small holdings, and gardens in two districts representing those where the supply of allotments is most liberal, and in contrast with them in two districts of small supply. The Returns for 1890 do not give particulars as to gardens; for this purpose we have recourse to the Returns for 1886. The following Table gives the number of allotments under a quarter of an acre and between a quarter of an acre and an acre, the number of small holdings a quarter of an acre, and under one acre, and between one and five acres. It will be seen that in Brixworth there are for every 100 inhabitants 23 of these holdings, while in Atcham there are less than seven. It must be pointed out that a considerable proportion of the inhabitants of Atcham are townspeople. Thakeham is, however, entirely rural, and in that district there are less than nine of these plots for every 100 persons. Looking at the relative numbers of different sized allotments and small holdings a great difference is observable. In Brixworth allotments of a quarter of an acre and under an acre form nearly one-half of all the plots included in this Table. In Woburn, Thakeham, and Atcham, smaller allotments are the most numerous.

In ratio to population small holdings between one rood and five acres are most numerous in Brixworth and next in Thakeham, while gardens are only about one-seventh of the holdings under consideration in Brixworth, and about one-eighth in Woburn; they are two-thirds of that number in Thakeham and Atcham.

* Return [C.—[illegible]] 1890.

Table 64.

	Brixworth.			[illegible]			Thingoe.			[illegible]		
	Number.	Ratio to 100 Inhabitants.	Percentage of Total.	Number.	Ratio to 100 Inhabitants.	Percentage of Total.	Number.	Ratio to 100 Inhabitants.	Percentage of Total.	Number.	Ratio to 100 Inhabitants.	Percentage of Total.
Population, 1891	[illegible]	—	—	[illegible]	—	—	[illegible]	—	—	[illegible]		
Allotments (detached) 1/8 acre and under	[illegible]	[illegible]	[illegible]	[illegible]	[illegible]	[illegible]	[illegible]	[illegible]	[illegible]	[illegible]	[illegible]	[illegible]
Over 1/8 and under 1 acre	[illegible]	[illegible]	[illegible]	[illegible]	[illegible]	[illegible]	[illegible]	[illegible]	[illegible]	[illegible]	[illegible]	[illegible]
Total under 1 acre	[illegible]	[illegible]	[illegible]	[illegible]	[illegible]	[illegible]	[illegible]	[illegible]	[illegible]	[illegible]	[illegible]	[illegible]
Small Holdings Over 1 and under 5 acres	[illegible]	[illegible]	[illegible]	[illegible]	[illegible]	[illegible]	[illegible]	[illegible]	[illegible]	[illegible]	[illegible]	[illegible]
Over 5 to 50 acres (with or without)	[illegible]	[illegible]	[illegible]	[illegible]	[illegible]	[illegible]	[illegible]	[illegible]	[illegible]	[illegible]	[illegible]	[illegible]
Total, 1 and above 1 acre	[illegible]	[illegible]	[illegible]	[illegible]	[illegible]	[illegible]	[illegible]	[illegible]	[illegible]	[illegible]	[illegible]	[illegible]
Gardens of and exceeding 1/8 of an acre, attached to cottages	[illegible]	[illegible]	[illegible]	[illegible]	[illegible]	[illegible]	[illegible]	[illegible]	[illegible]	[illegible]	[illegible]	[illegible]
Total of Allotments, Small Holdings, and Gardens per 100 inhabitants	[illegible]	[illegible]		[illegible]	[illegible]	—	[illegible]	[illegible]	—	[illegible]	[illegible]	—

339. There can be little doubt that if allotments of one acre or more had been included in the Returns for 1890, the numbers would in some districts have been considerably increased. In no less than seven districts they are said to run up to two acres and in some to three or even five acres, but probably these large allotments are returned as small holdings. In five other districts they are said to run up to 1 acre. At the other extreme will be found allotments of 5, 6, or 7 perches, and in the neighbourhood of towns, even as little as 100 square yards or about one-forty-eighth part of an acre is found. Size.

340. The rents vary from a mere nominal sum to 4s. per 100 square yards, which is about 9l. 13s. 6d. an acre. This rent is paid for the small plots previously mentioned as lying near to towns. Rents. Chap. II. VI. App. D.

With regard to the rent charged for allotments Mr. Spencer makes the following observations:—

"The rent of allotments varies greatly. Sometimes it is as low as 1l. an acre, sometimes as high as 8l. About 3l. or 4l. per acre is a very common figure. The rent is usually higher than that of the neighbouring land let to a tenant farmer, and labourers frequently complain that the allotments are rented too highly. It is, of course, only reasonable that a somewhat higher figure than for farm land should be charged, for the allotment holder does not pay rates, taxes, or tithes, and takes a small piece of accommodation ground, but I think that even taking these circumstances into consideration the rent of allotments is frequently much too high. I think that in many cases the comparatively high rental would be reduced if it were properly brought to the notice of the proprietors, but while it remains as it is, it causes a considerable feeling of discontent on the part of the labourer, who thinks that he is not being treated fairly as compared with the farmer." Spencer, A. 44.

Mr. Chapman speaks in very similar terms as to the rents which are sometimes charged, and the feeling of injustice created in the labourers' minds thereby. Chapman, A. 163.

Mr. Wilson Fox says that the rents in Swaffham and Thingoe generally vary from 1l. to 2l. an acre, though there are instances where the rents were high and the land not very accessible. Fox, A. 76.

Mr. Richards says the prevailing rent is at the rate of 2l. an acre, but accommodation ground at Stratford was let at 3l. and 6l. per acre. In his Report upon Brixworth Union, he gives the rents charged in a considerable number of parishes. They range from 17s. to 130s. an acre. Richards, A. 28.

In the following list the several districts are classed according to the maximum rents which are reported:—

Maximum Rent per Acre	Districts
Up to 40s.	Buntingford, Louth, Swaffham (36s.).
Above 40s. and not exceeding 60s.	Atcham, Easingwold, Thrapston (53s. 4d.), Uttoxeter, Wetherby (50s.).
" 60s. " " 80s.	Basingstoke, Bromyard, Cirencester, Garstang, Hollingbourn, Thakeham, Truro, Woburn.
" 80s. " " 100s.	Driffield, Holbeach, Langport (92s.).
" 100s. " " 120s.	Dorchester, Pershore, Pewsey, Southwell, Thame.
" 120s. " " 160s.	Brixworth (160s.), Oakham, Maldon, North Witchford, St. Neots, Stamford, Wantage.
" 160s.	Crediton, Melton Mowbray.

It must be understood that these maximum prices are frequently exceptional, and they are probably charged in every case for small plots of detached garden ground near to a town. In every district there are a number of allotments at much lower rents than the maximum prices given above.

Thus, in St. Neots, where 6*l.* is a common price near a village, and 7*l.* is paid in some cases, there are allotments let at 15s. and 20s. an acre. Again, in Melton, where allotments near the town run up to 9*l.* 12s. an acre, there are allotments on large estates let at 26s. 6*d.* an acre; and in Crediton, though some few are said to let at 1s. 7*d.* a pole (12*l.* 13s. 4*d.* an acre), the usual rent is 2*l.* 13s. 4*d.* per acre.

In Thakeham there is an instance of 10s. an acre being charged.

The advantages of allotments to ordinary labourers are generally admitted, though some prejudice of the farmers against the system is reported. Mr. Chapman insists upon certain conditions as necessary for their success: the first being such working hours as will leave the labourer leisure for their cultivation; the second is a reasonable rent; the third a convenient situation and suitable soil. The last-named conditions are precisely those which tend to increase the rent above that of the average paid for a whole farm.

341. As regards the size of an allotment which a labourer can cultivate without neglecting regular work, Mr. Spencer says:—

"It seemed to be the better opinion that about half an acre is the most which a man in regular employment should undertake . . . . In Worcestershire and other counties there are frequent instances of men who hold one acre or more . . . but such men do not work as regular labourers."

The Holcot Association, whose rules are given *in extenso* in the Appendix to the Report referred to, elects a committee of management from among its members, who pay 1*s.* as an entrance fee. Presumably the members, with the exception of the president, trustees, and other officers of the society, are persons who desire to obtain allotments. Richards, B II. App. 46.

Land hired by the Association is taken in the name of the trustees. A vacant allotment is offered to members in order of priority of election. Each member on becoming an allotment holder signs a form of agreement. A valuable provision in the rules enables a man to negotiate with the Committee for the surrender of a part of his holding at short notice. The Committee are not bound to accept this surrender, but it is easily conceivable that circumstances might arise where an arrangement of the land might be desirable, and its accomplishment facilitated by means of a committee mainly constituted of allotment holders and persons desiring to procure allotments.

It is not clearly stated whether the Committee are bound to let at a rent which gives them no profit over and above the expenses of management, though this condition may be implied by clause 6 of the agreement with the landowner.

It is obvious that an association such as the one which has been noticed can hire land on advantageous terms, because it gives the landowner security for his rent and protects him from annoyance to which he might otherwise be subject. On the side of the tenant Mr. Richards says:—

"The interposition of such syndicates gives to the men a feeling of security otherwise lacking, and removes the accident of any dispute, which might arise, from the individual to the Committee." Richards, ib.

344. In some parts of the country a labourer is enabled to keep a cow by the opportunity of obtaining a summer's run for it either on a common, in a park, or a green lane, or a pasture appropriated for the purpose by an estate owner, but in order to provide for the cow during the winter he must either have the opportunity of hiring a plot of grass for mowing hay, or some arable land for growing straw and roots. The system, if that which takes such various forms can be called a system, differs from that of small holdings in that the owner of the cow does not become the tenant of the land; he buys the herbage for the year. In some cases the right attaches to a cottage, in others, however, it is a right conceded to a cottage tenant; in another instance it is merely an opportunity which a man may avail himself of if he chooses year by year. Cow pastures.

It is mainly in the northern counties that cow pastures or cow gates proper are found.

Mr. Wilkinson says on the point:—

"A cow pasture proper is a field kept for the use of cow owners and let to them at so much a cow. . . . . Wherever there are wide grassy roads, as in Driffield, the 'lanes,' as in this connexion the roads are generally called, are almost always let, sometimes by the lord of the manor, sometimes by the overseer, the rent going in reduction of the local highway rates . . . . Sometimes, as at Bainton (Driffield), the tenants of certain 'cottages' have a prior right to take gates on a cow-pasture, in which case they mow their separate pieces for hay and graze their cows in common in the pasture. At other times, as, for instance, at North Dalton (Driffield), there are certain grass fields in which a man can hire mowing gates, and others, strictly cow-pastures, in which he can take grazing gates. Either could be hired independently of the other, though, in practice, this of course would not often happen." Wilkinson, A 83.

Instances are given of the rents paid for the different classes of accommodation described: for a cow-pasture 2*l.* to 3*l.* a cow is given; for a cow-run in the lanes 1*l.* is paid in Driffield, and 7*s.* or 8*s.* a cow in Wetherby; each cowkeeper, in addition, contributes to the wages of a "tenter," an old man or boy, who collects the cows, looks after them, and brings them back in the evening.

Mr. Wilkinson's Report on Driffield gives instances of different opportunities available to labourers and others for keeping cows, thus—

"At Bainton there is a cow-pasture to which the tenants of certain cottages have the first claim. These cottages are often occupied by labourers, and many of them keep cows." Wilkinson, B III 19.

"At Beeford is a cow-pasture of 48 acres, let for 85*l.* For each cow-gate, that is for each cow for which an owner hires a right of pasturage, 52*s.* 6*d.* is paid. If there are more cows than required for paying the rent the surplus is either held over to the next year or paid back to the people taking gates.

At North Dalton about 20 acres are let as cow-pasture by Lord Hotham, while some mowing gates are let in certain small detached grass fields. Several labourers have cows, but most of the gates are taken by men not labourers. The lanes here are let at 14*s.* a cow."

"In one small parish five out of eight cows running in the lanes belonged to labourers. I asked an old widow in this parish how things were managed. She said that in her husband's life they kept two cows. They hired an acre or a little more and grew what turnips and corn they could

The turnips, with bran and straw and a little hay, kept one cow during winter. In the spring they bought a cow near calving, sold the calf in two or three weeks, made butter for market, finding the spare milk very useful to feed pigs, had the cows tended in the lanes from May-day to Michaelmas, and at Michaelmas sold one of the cows. They always lost on re-sale, but it was not easy to keep two through the winter. Where they can have, say, three acres of grass, half for mowing, half for grazing, and still more where lanes are to be hired, so that no other grazing is wasted, I think it is clear that labourers can keep cows to advantage."

344a. Mr. Bear, in his report on Melton Mowbray, gives particulars of cow-runs or cow-plots in that district. These appear to be let with cottages. He says:—

"Some of these cow-plots are 3½ acres in extent, and their holders are allowed to keep only one cow, as three or more of them occupy a pasture in common, having a portion of their 3½ acres each year to mow and another portion to feed. The rent, including cottage and garden, is 10l. . . . As an example of the advantage which a cow-plot may sometimes be to a labourer and his family, I may mention the case of a widow who has 3½ acres and a very good cottage for 10l. per annum. Last year she had an exceptionally good cow, and she sold milk at the rate of 6d. a gallon, amounting to 15l. 10s., following a calf which sold at 4l. 10s.; altogether the return was 20l., besides what milk was consumed in the cottage. . . . In addition to the rent these small holders spend 3s. a month for cake."

Mr. Chapman reports that in North Witchford "a great many small owners or "labourers keep cows and hire from the local authorities the grass at the sides of the roads."

In other districts small grass holdings enable labourers to maintain themselves with cows with considerable advantage to themselves and their families. This is the case in Atcham, Brixworth, Holbeach, Melton Mowbray, and Nantwich. In the latter district Mr. Richards says:

"A very large percentage of the labourers, probably about 40 per cent., own cows, being in possession of cottage allotments."

Upon Lord Tollemache's Peckforton estate there are 255 labourers' tenements of "three acres and a cow." Of these about 179 are in Nantwich Union.

345. In Glendale it was in the past a very general custom for the farmer to keep a cow for each of the hinds on his farm; but the desire on the part of the labourer to receive his wages in cash has led to a very great diminution in the number. Mr. Wilson Fox says:—

"Most farmers will keep a cow for a man for 3s. a week all the year round, deducting this sum from his wages. The cow is kept out all the summer on grass, and during the winter the farmer agrees to give it two loads of hay or 5 cwt. of linseed cake."

It is estimated that under these conditions a cow will leave to the labourer a net profit of 6l. a year, but, nevertheless, it appears that the number of hinds who have cows steadily diminishes, though some farmers will provide the cow as well as its food where a man is unable to find the money for the purchase of one.

In Truro a system of letting cows to labourers at 9l. or 10l. a year is not uncommon.

346. Though pigs are still largely kept by labourers, they are less numerous than formerly. The sanitary authorities very properly prevent them being kept in villages under conditions where they may prove a nuisance, and not unfrequently where cottages are upon the farms the masters object to the pig on the ground that the labourers have opportunities and temptation to steal corn or other food for it.

347. Small holdings are a marked feature in some districts, particularly in Atcham, Melton Mowbray, Nantwich, and Southwell, where they are chiefly devoted to the keeping of cows; in St. Neots, where market gardening is carried on; in Thakeham and Pershore, where fruit as well as vegetables are cultivated; and in North Witchford, where ordinary farm crops with a large quantity of potatoes, carrots, and other roots, but not so much green produce, are grown. In Wigton a number of small farms supply an opportunity to farm servants who have saved money in service to make a start as farmers. In Truro there are a great number of these small holdings in the occupation of miners, who reclaim plots of 4 or 5 acres of moorland on the security of leases for lives, and build houses for themselves; but the ordinary agricultural labourers are rarely found in possession of such holdings. In the northern part of Basingstoke, a district which differs very widely in its geological character from the southern part of that district, where large farms on the chalk formation are found, a kind of settlement of small holders has been established. Mr. Bear made their case the subject of special investigation, and he gives the following account of the settlement:—

"One reason of the number of small holders found in the Pamber and Tadley districts is that there was originally a great common there which has now been enclosed. Some men squatted on the common, built houses and cultivated a little land around them, with or without the consent of the lord of the manor; but the majority hired their land after the common was enclosed, from the late Col. Beach, who was very anxious to improve the condition of the labourers. The district was particularly favourable, as the present Mr. Beach points out, for the success of small holders, because there is a great area of woodlands close by, and the men find profitable employment in the woods in winter, while in the summer they go to work in many parts of the county, and in the hop districts of other counties, the market gardens near London, and even to a small extent in the fruit districts of Kent. The men who settled in Pamber and Tadley appear to have been always a migratory race, and men, moreover, of great industry and considerable skill in farm and wood work. . . . Mr. Beach charges them only 1*l.* an acre for their land, and Mr. Wallington, his agent, informed me that they paid their rents to a day. Six or seven years ago he was authorised by Mr. Beach to offer 100 acres of additional land in one-acre plots. It was to be taken by lot, at the rent of 1*l.* an acre, and in an hour every lot had been taken, and not a single man refused the allotment which fell to his share.

"Mr. Wallington also stated that in Pamber or the adjoining parish he has taken opportunities of dividing large farms into holdings of from 20 to 50 acres. . . . The 20-acre men work in the woods, and, therefore, do not obtain their living entirely from the land which they occupy, but those who have 50 acres do not work for others. They get their living by growing corn, keeping pigs, doing a little dairying, and selling hay. As a rule, they pay about 15*s.* an acre free of tithe, and their rents are paid quite as punctually as those of larger farmers. A great majority of the small holders at Pamber and Tadley, the migratory labourers whose case is the most interesting, hold only from two to three acres of land. . . . They always drive to their work, and the farmers who employ them keep their ponies for them. They take their wives and children to haymaking, harvesting, hopping, and fruit-picking, but not generally when they go to hoeing. They frequently sleep in barns, and do not take off their clothes for weeks at a time. . . . A witness, who was formerly shopkeeper in a neighbouring parish, stated that the Pamber and Tadley men nearly always paid in gold, as distinguished from the ordinary labourers, who usually paid in silver; and it is also said that most of the men are able to buy a piece of land if they want it. It is quite clear that they do not make much money from their small holdings, as they leave them too long during the summer to cultivate them to the greatest advantage; but they are able to grow all the vegetables they require on the land, while they earn their money chiefly by working for others."

There are many other districts, besides those which have been named, where there are a considerable number of holdings of less than 20 acres.

Mr. Wilkinson appends to each of his Reports a table, giving from independent research the number of holdings of various sizes. Unfortunately, for the purpose of comparison, these tables are not constructed on uniform principles, but they are sufficient to show that there is in each district a gradation of holdings. The number of small holdings is really determined to a great extent by conditions of soil, situation with regard to markets, and population.

In many cases the small occupations are held by tradesmen and other villagers, and not by agricultural labourers.

Mr. Richards, in his Report upon the Nantwich district, gives detailed particulars as to the size of occupations on five estates, including those of Lord Crewe and Lord Tollemache. On the latter of these estates, in addition to 255 cottage holdings of "three acres and a cow," there are 19 holdings below 5 acres, 38 between 5 and 10 acres, and 21 between 10 and 20 acres, or 78 occupations of less than 20 acres. As to the occupiers of the middle-class lettings, as those below 40 acres are termed, they are said to be—

"Held by people following a great variety of occupations. Among these are the following:—Publican, grocer, carpenter, brickmaker, gentleman, wheelwright, road surveyor, potato and hay dealer, shoemaker, clerk, farmer, drainer, butcher, telegraph contractor, cattle dealer, mason, relieving officer, engineer, engine driver, timber dealer, mechanic, plumber, livery stable keeper, saddler, surgeon, provision dealer, retired innkeeper, carrier, horsebreaker, baker, pig dealer."

As to the quantity of land which is required to find employment for a man and sufficient to support a family, and as to that which an agricultural labourer can manage without giving up regular work for wages under another, opinions vary widely, and, indeed, it depends to such a great extent upon the character of the land and the use to which it is put that it is impossible to lay down any rule.

Upon the first point Mr. Bear says:—

These holdings are, of course, pastoral in character.

[illegible] N.T. App. VI. Mr. R. W. Wordsworth, agent to Earl Manvers, upon whose estate in North Notts half the holdings are less than 30 acres, expresses the opinion that 40 or 50 acres is the least a man should farm to bring up his family upon it, and that a man cannot bring up a family on 20 acres farmed in the ordinary way.

Mr. Spencer says:

Spencer, A. [illegible] "In Worcestershire and other counties there are frequent instances of men who hold one acre or more of allotment land, but such men do not work as regular farm labourers but do farm work intermittently. The least amount of land a man can make a living out of widely appeared to be four or five acres in the case of land growing fruit or garden produce, or about 20 acres of mixed arable and grass."

[illegible] 339. The direct and economical advantages or disadvantages of small holdings may be a subject of dispute between those whose experience is limited to a particular district, and those who collect facts to support previously-formed conclusions. The evidence which proves that where the land is in pasture, or the soil is easily cultivated, and is adapted for the growth of roots, vegetables, or fruit, an industrious man with a family to assist him can, and does, succeed is by no means convincing that under other and less favourable conditions the system is possible.

Fox, A. [illegible] It is clear that in many cases the small holder and his family sacrifice much for a better social position than that of the labourer, but it cannot be doubted that the existence of such occupations which a labourer may hope to secure does retain among the ranks of the labourers some of the younger and smarter men who might otherwise be drawn away from agriculture at an early age. There is said to be among farmers a general prejudice against these small holders. Probably if their feelings were better understood it would be found to be chiefly a reluctance on their part to admit that another class would succeed better than they themselves do, and a considerable number of the larger farmers would admit that a gradation of holdings, by which a man can rise by successive steps from the position of a labourer to that of a considerable farmer, is not merely beneficial to the labourers as a class but also to the farmers, inasmuch as it keeps up a supply of skilled labour available in an emergency, and acts as a recruiting ground for young agricultural labourers.

6.—BENEFIT SOCIETIES, INSURANCE CLUBS, &c.

[illegible] 340. The reports of the Assistant Commissioners show that very generally a considerable proportion of the labourers, and particularly the younger men, avail themselves of the opportunity of insuring against loss of wages by sickness and disablement. The most striking exception to that rule is the district of Glendale where the hinds being hired men who receive their wages whether they are able to work or not (for a period of six weeks), find it unnecessary to insure. With regard to two other districts, Melton Mowbray and Monmouth, the statements on the point are less positive than in other cases.

Mr. Chapman is of opinion that:—

Chapman, A. [illegible] "striking an average (in the seven districts (visited)) it will be fairly correct to say that more than half belong to some club or other."

Mr. Fox reports that in all the districts visited by him except Glendale—

Fox, A. [illegible] "Substantial benefit societies are very largely supported by the agricultural labourers."

Mr. Spencer says:—

Spencer, A. [illegible] "Agricultural labourers are fully alive to the desirability of joining a benefit society, and the majority are members of some one or other."

(a.) *The Area of Operations.*

351. First of all rank those large national societies, such as the Foresters, the Oddfellows, and many others, which attract the younger labourers not only by the greater security which they offer, but because of the facilities which they give to the transfer of members, who are looking forward to moving about the country, to affiliated branches. Next to these may be ranked the county clubs, which are philanthropic in character and are managed to some extent, if not entirely, by gentlemen of position. *Area of operations. National or General.*

Mr. Bear, in his report upon the Basingstoke district, refers at length to the Hampshire Friendly Society. It numbered in 1891 11,257 members, made up of 5,458 assurance members, 2,429 deposit members, and 370 juvenile members, including girls. The capital of this Society amounted at that time to 111,077*l*. on the assurance branch; the contributions of ordinary adult assurance members being in that year 7,104*l*. *County clubs. Bear, B-IV. 40.*

Mr. Spencer gives in full the scale of payment and the rates of allowance of the Essex Provident Society.

There are, next, district clubs, which do not confine themselves to particular areas, but they differ little from the parochial clubs in character, management, or objects. *Spencer, B-V. App. C.*

Mr. Chapman gives some particulars of the Buntingford Union Association which appears to be a very favourable specimen of a district club. Out of a population of 5,106 in certain parishes there are no less than 676 members or one to every eight persons.

The small local clubs, including public-house clubs, are very numerous and they are described generally in unfavourable terms, and many of them have been broken up. Mr. Bear speaks of them as "wretched traps for poor men's savings." *B-VII. 69. Local clubs. Bear, B-I. 64.*

Mr. Spencer says:—

"The third class (village clubs) includes some very good societies which are registered and well managed by the local gentry or clergy, *e.g.* the Charlton Friendly Society . . . It also includes some less satisfactory societies known as 'village clubs,' 'break-up clubs,' 'public-house clubs,' 'two-penny clubs,' 'slate clubs' whose rules are not registered and whose solvency is often doubtful." *Spencer, A. 10.*

Mr. Richards, in his final report, alludes to these local clubs in the following terms:—

"Agricultural labourers appear to be recovering from the shock and loss which many of them have experienced through the failure of local benefit clubs. These having in many cases come to an end, and others dragging out a precarious existence, there are in almost every district a number of the older men unprovided for." *Richards, A. 77.*

Mr. Wilkinson says on the same subject—

"There are also several free gift and dividing clubs. These last are becoming increasingly popular, owing, no doubt, to the many frauds or to the gross incompetence brought to light of late years in the management of too many of the clubs conducted on the old lines. Sometimes the incompetence was shown not so much in want of prudence of investments and general management, as in an ignorant want of actuarial experience, so that payments were made beyond what the funds of the society, which seemed inexhaustible when the members were mostly young, could possibly stand when there were many aged members to depend upon them. The dividing club is managed on the principle of dividing all the funds in hand at the end of the year among the members, a plan which is a safeguard against any serious loss through the defalcations of a treasurer." *Dividing clubs. Wilkinson, A. 20.*

Mr. Bear mentions estate clubs as existing on the properties of the Duke of Portland and Earl Manvers in Notts for the benefit of labourers on those estates. The first of these divides the balance in hand at the end of the year among its ordinary members and carries on the contributions of honorary members to a reserve fund. The second divides the surplus funds every year and carries the amount due to the account of each member to provide a fund for sick pay extended beyond the ordinary period. *Estate clubs. Bear, B-V. 41.*

(b.) *The Objects of Insurance.*

352. As has been stated previously the principal object with which labourers join benefit societies is that of insuring payment of an allowance during sickness. But it is very usual to add to this the insurance of a certain sum to cover funeral expenses at death, and very commonly the assurance of a similar though smaller allowance on the death of the insurer's wife. *Objects of clubs.*

The scales of contributions and allowances vary immensely. It is not necessary to give them in great detail, but a few typical instances may be quoted.

353. The Buntingford Union Association has been already alluded to—

This society was "established in 1857 for two purposes: (1) the providing of a weekly allowance "during sickness up to the age of 65 years, and (2) an annuity of 5s. per week after that age, *Old age pensions. Chapman, B-VII. 92.*

"together with a payment of 8l. at death. All members up to 1858 used to contribute for both these "benefits; after that time a certain number ceased to insure for the annuity, and since 1871 *the "practice of assuring for an annuity had entirely ceased*, which is greatly to be regretted. Members "now join for an allowance in illness, varying from 10s. to 15s. per week and 8l. at death. Of the "older members who joined previous to 1874, 44 are at present in receipt of a weekly annuity of 3s., "4s., or 5s., principally 5s., and there are 73 more who are assured for an annuity when they reach the age of 65. . . .

"It is worth noting that this Association is almost exclusively managed by the clergy of the district, "who are elected by the members as directors for their different parishes. . . . . The funds "of the society amount to about 35,000l., and of course the society is registered."

354. In the appendix to his Report, B. VII., Mr. Chapman gives full particulars of the scale of contributions and benefits, the former being properly graduated in respect of the age at which membership commences.

In Crediton it is said that—

"The larger clubs cost 5d. or 6d. a week as a rule, with a benefit of 10s. The village clubs are cheaper, some 2s. 6d. a quarter, others 3d. or 4d. a week, with benefits of 8s. in bed,* 4s. walking,* 6l. at death, and 4l. for widow, or 6s. in bed,* 3s. walking.*"

Mr. Spencer gives the following account of the Charlton Society in Langport district:—

"The Charlton Society is registered and managed on the bank system, with a capital of 7,381l., belonging to the members' several banking accounts. An average holding will be about 9l. Members pay 1s. 8d. a month. They receive 6s. a week sick pay for eight weeks, then 4s. for another eight weeks, and 3s. afterwards. In case of death of a member, each surviving member pays 1s. to his representative."

The allowances made by a club in Stratford-on-Avon are somewhat different to those generally adopted. Mr. Richards says:—

"In the Alcester Society, which may be taken as representative, the members contribute 6d. per week, and in case of sickness a member is entitled to receive 8s. per week for eight consecutive weeks; after this he is suspended for eight weeks, and then receives eight weeks' pay at 8s. a week as before. But in no case may a member . . . . . receive more than 26 weeks' pay during the year."

In the following table various rates of subscriptions and benefits are shown:—

Reference to Report.	District.	Contributions.	Sick Pay per Week.	Duration of Sick Pay.	Pension per Week.	Payment at Death: Member.	Payment at Death: Member's Wife.	Remarks.
[illegible]	[illegible]	[illegible] and under [illegible] years, [illegible] a month	[illegible]	[illegible]	[illegible]	[illegible]		Payments graduated according to age at entrance.
[illegible]	[illegible]	[illegible] per year	[illegible]	[illegible]	—	[illegible]	[illegible]	
[illegible]	[illegible]	[illegible]	[illegible]	[illegible]				
[illegible]	[illegible]	1s. 6d. a month	[illegible]	[illegible]	—	[illegible]	[illegible]	[illegible]
[illegible]	[illegible]	[illegible]	[illegible]	—		[illegible]	—	[illegible]
		[illegible]	[illegible]	—	—	[illegible]	—	
[illegible]	[illegible]	[illegible] a month	[illegible]		—	[illegible]	[illegible]	[illegible] Benefit Society.
[illegible]	[illegible]	[illegible] a quarter	[illegible]	[illegible]	—	[illegible]	[illegible]	Graduated according to age.

It will be seen that in these cases the great majority of the labourers join clubs with the object of making temporary provision during sickness, and for burial, and that few provide against old age.

355. In some districts the practice of labourers insuring their own lives and those of their children is noticed. In Glendale, where the ordinary benefit clubs are not required, some of the hands insure their lives. In two labourers' budgets given by Mr. Wilson Fox, "life insurance premium appears among the items of expenditure."

* The distinction between "in bed" and "walking" is not explained, but it may be assumed to differentiate cases of total and partial disablement.

Mr. Wilkinson reports that: "In Yorkshire the practice of insuring their own "and their children's lives is increasing. I was informed at Bedford that the majority "of those present at a labourers' meeting held there had effected insurances with the "Prudential Life Assurance Company." Canon Bury, in a passage already quoted, speaks of the agents of the Prudential Life Assurance calling every week at almost every cottage, and we may infer from this that a considerable business is carried on by them. Wilkinson, A. 97.

356. In his Report upon the Atcham district Mr. Chapman draws attention to the high average of membership of benefit clubs in that union, and says that one of the causes assigned for this was the strictness with which the Poor Law was administered. Provident clubs stimulated by strict administration of Poor Law.

"The refusal of outdoor relief in almost every case has compelled the people to protect themselves." Chapman, A. VI 90.

And the evidence of Canon Bury with reference to the Brixworth Union is to the same effect.

But it is curious to observe that the district of Buntingford, which was visited by Mr. Chapman immediately after Atcham, is one where the amount of outdoor relief is described by a local landowner as "*something dreadful*," and where a very large proportion of the labourers are members of benefit clubs.

In his final Report Mr. Chapman draws the following conclusions from these apparently conflicting cases:—

"The examples of Atcham and Buntingford teach two lessons. The first, that a strict system of administering the poor law encourages men to make provision for themselves; and the second that provident habits are, like other elements of character, matters of education and can be created even in districts where every other circumstance seems to be against them." Chapman, A. 103.

One other point in connexion with benefit clubs may be noticed, and it is that many employers actively encourage their labourers to join these societies, and in some cases they insist upon membership of a club as a condition of employment. Chapman, A. 109. B II. 54a. B IV. 149.

357. In Uttoxeter, two women's clubs are noticed. In one of these the contribution is 1s. a month, the benefits 5s. per week during illness, with 5*l*. on death. Women's clubs. Wilkinson, &c. B V 26.

Mr. Chapman notices branches of the Odd Fellows Women Friendly Societies in Crediton, and a branch of the Foresters enrols women members in Atcham. Chapman, B IV 92.

In addition to provident clubs of the character already noticed, there are numerous other clubs which have been formed with the object of promoting thrift and protecting the labourer from the terrible disaster which may befall him from the ordinary accidents of life. Many a young labourer with a wife and children depending upon him has been demoralised by incurring a doctor's bill which he had not the means of paying. He gets into debt for the first time, for an object which the sternest moralist cannot condemn. Forbearing and considerate as the great majority of the profession are, the country doctor, not too well paid in any case, cannot cancel all the obligations of those who profess inability to pay him what is fairly his due. One man will struggle for years to discharge his debt, another, less honest, will shift his quarters, and finding himself unable to pay the whole bill will deliberately refuse to pay any part of it. Chapman, B VI 72.

358. The clubs and societies which have been hitherto noticed do, in many cases, provide for medical attendance to the member probably the head of the family; but they do not provide for the wife and children in this respect. It is to supply the place thus vacant that medical clubs and dispensaries have been formed. Medical clubs.

Mr. Wilson Fox mentions one of these medical clubs as existing in Glendale for the purpose of affording medical and surgical aid *gratuitously* to the *necessitous poor*. Admirable as the objects of this institution may be, it does not answer the requirements. It is a charity, and only removed by one step from medical relief under the poor law. Clubs of a similar character, supported to some extent by contributions from charitable persons of larger means than the ordinary labourers are noticed by the Assistant Commissioners in the reports on Truro, Atcham, Stratford, Maldon. Canon Bury, a well known authority on the administration of the poor law, in a communication to Mr. Richards with reference to Brixworth Union, says:— Fox, B III. 64.

"Medical clubs for women and children, which were almost unknown 20 years ago, are now universal, and a man or woman who is not in some way insured against sickness is very rare. Life insurance is provided chiefly by the Prudential, whose agents call every week at almost every cottage in the union. One result is, that medical relief through the poor law is a thing of the past, and a pauper funeral is almost unknown." Richards, B II. App. C. (84)

Having failed to discover in any of the reports before me exact details as to the contributions required to secure to whole families medical attendance when required, I venture to insert the following scale of subscriptions to a club which has been very successfully carried on for several years in the parish where I live.

The club is confined to agricultural labourers and their families, and female domestic servants. It is self-supporting, and is managed by the vicar, who acts as secretary and treasurer.

The subscription for adults is 5s. a year; for two children living at home with their parents, 5s. Where the children are more than two, a subscription of 10s. is paid. Thus, a man, his wife, and five children can be assured of medical attendance including medicines, for 20s. a year. Attendance at delivery and surgical operations of a serious character are not covered by the subscription.

359. Clothing clubs and coal clubs, which fund periodical payments of small sums from labourers, and add to the aggregate amount a substantial bonus derived from charitable contributions, are so commonly distributed throughout the country as to require little remark. These clubs are generally parochial, but in some instances they are private estate clubs. An example of the latter class is described by Mr. Richards in his Report on Monmouth:—

"All the labourers on this estate (The Hendre), whether they work for Lord Llangattock or not, are allowed to join his private charity club. It is divided into clothing, coal, and shoe; each member pays 1s. or 6d. or 4d. into one or two, or even all three every month. At the end of the year 50 per cent. is added as a bonus, and an order card is given for the total amount on a tradesman."

In a few districts where cows are kept by labourers, clubs for insuring against loss by death have been established, as in Atcham, Truro, Nantwich, Easingwold. Small holders are often glad to join these clubs and reduce their risks. No definite particulars are given in the Reports as to the terms and conditions of membership of any of these clubs.

360. Co-operative stores are found in some districts, but they do not appear to be numerous. The system appears to have had the greatest success in the Brixworth district.

Canon Bury, in his communication to Mr. Richards, which I have several times referred to, says:—

"Co-operative stores are found in nearly all the larger and many of the smaller villages. As a rule they are very prosperous. . . . The dividends paid on the amount of goods purchased by members bring 2s. or 3s. in the £, thus adding 2s. or 3s. to the weekly income. At Harlestone the whole trade of the village is co-operative in the hands of one management, two co-operative shops, a co-operative dairy association, and, the only instance in the county, a co-operative public-house."

Mr. Chapman reports thus on the subject:—

"Co-operative stores are not by any means so frequent as they should be. They exist in every town, but I have only found three examples in villages, one at Shirburn in Thame, one at Ardington in Wantage, and one at Buckland in Buntingford. The result in each case is highly satisfactory. Goods are better and cheaper. Labourers are obliged to pay ready money. A dividend of at least 5 per cent. is earned for the shareholders, and profits are divided besides. The best example will be found at Buckland, where all the conditions of the village are of the simplest and most ordinary character. There is an excellent clergyman, but no resident squire. The population is 375. The annual sales at the co-operative store have varied from 277l. . . in 1883 to 640l. . . . in 1892. The sales to labourers average in amount from 10l. to 14l. a week, and have not changed since 1879. There has been a falling off in the sales to farmers."

A memorandum on the subject of these stores states that out of 97 houses in the parish of Buckland 84 are occupied by labourers. In 1876 the store was started under the advice of Mr. Albert Pell with a capital of 60l., held by 50 shareholders. It is said that—

"Twenty years ago, when the times were good and the wages higher, labourers' families presented a poverty-stricken appearance, shabbiness and rags abounded even on Sundays. Nearly everybody was in debt at the shops and the shops hopelessly in debt to the wholesale dealers. . . . Shabbiness and rags are rarely seen now, and drink and debt are the exception, not the rule."

361. With the view of attaching the labourer to the soil and of stimulating his energy and skill, the system of co-operative agriculture, or to speak more correctly that of profit-sharing, has been frequently recommended. In the past many such schemes have been started, and some of them have for a time succeeded, but very few have held their ground for more than a short time, and it is said that the only co-operative farm which has stood the test of many years, viz., the Assington, is one in

which no agricultural labourers are shareholders or profit-sharers. The District Reports contain notices of a few experiments in this direction which are now being made and a brief notice of these may be given here.

362. Mr. Wilson Fox in his final report describes one of these schemes thus:— Mr. Albert Grey's profit-sharing scheme.

"In the Glendale Union . . . . . an interesting experiment is being made by Mr. Albert Grey, with the object of increasing the zeal of the labourers by giving them a share in the profits."

In his Glendale Report Mr. Fox gives a full account of this experiment which has been in operation at East Learmouth since the year 1886. The farm contains 821 acres, 122 being pasture and the remainder arable. Fox, A. 16. Fox, B. III. 68.

"Mr. Grey's method is shortly this. After rent has been paid and interest on capital at the rate of 4 per cent., 25 per cent. goes to a reserve fund, 25 per cent. for the reward of management, that is as a bonus to the manager, the steward, and the herd, 25 per cent. to capital, and 25 per cent. to labour." Fox, A. 16.

The one-fourth of the net profit put aside for the extra reward of labour is apportioned in ratio to the ordinary earnings of each person; those who have made two complete years' service receive their portion in cash; but the shares of those who have had only one year's service are carried to the reserve fund which may be drawn upon in bad years to make up rent and interest, but which, it is hoped, will serve as a fund for superannuation allowances for aged and disabled servants. The results of the experiment during five years from May 1886 to May 1891 are thus stated by Mr. Albert Grey:—

"The rent of 1,431l. and interest on capital at the rate of 4 per cent. have been paid with unfailing regularity, 163l. 5s. 11d. has been given in bonuses to the employees on the farm, 118l. 2s. 7d. has been paid as additional interest on capital, and a reserve fund has been formed which at the present time amounts to 182l. 8s. 4½d." Fox, B. III. 68.

In the Appendix to the Glendale Report particulars as to the earnings and bonuses of each individual labourer on the Learmouth Farm in 1891 are given. In addition to the manager, steward, and head shepherd who received between them bonuses amounting to 47l. 18s. 7d., there were nine hinds, an under shepherd, two boys, and 12 women workers. Of these six hinds, two boys, and six women were qualified; the remainder who had not made two years' service were not qualified to receive a bonus.

The total average earnings of the six hinds receiving a bonus were 48l. 5s. 6d., and in addition they received an average bonus of 3l. 1s. 2d., making up a total of 51l. 6s. 8d.

The two boys averaged 21l. 11s. 0d., and their average bonus was 1l. 7s. 3d. The six women who had bonuses earned on an average 18l. 10s. 5d., and they received a bonus of 1l. 3s. 5d.

Mr. Fox reports that the labourers were "unanimous in praise of the profit-sharing system." The bailiff however says that in his opinion the work of the labourers has not appreciably improved under the profit-sharing system, but thinks it may do so in time. Fox, B. III. 68.

It must be remembered that this experiment is being tried in a district where the labour of the farm is almost entirely performed by a regular staff of labourers hired for the year, and that the conditions are so far favourable. Where a considerable share of the work is done by casual labourers it would be impossible to carry out the principle of division of profits, and the interest of the regular labourers in the success of the farm would be *pro tanto* diminished. It is however rather remarkable that the love of change which characterises the Northumbrian hinds does not appear to have been overcome by the chances of profit-sharing. In this case one-third of the hinds and half the women workers had served for only one year, and they had taken the places of those who had quitted the service the year before, notwithstanding the fact that a bonus of 5½ per cent. had been paid in that year.

363. I am indebted to the Rev. Canon Bury (Chairman of the Brixworth Board of Guardians) for some information respecting the Harlestone Co-operative Farming Association which is casually mentioned in a communication to Mr. Richards. Upon my application the reverend gentleman sent me all the published Reports of the Association, and in correspondence he very kindly replied to my queries on the subject. The Association was formed by Lord Spencer in 1887, "with a view to afford an "incentive to the co-operators, and to provide a test as to the efficacy of co-operative "farming." Harlestone Farming Association. Richards, B. III. App. C. Scheme, report, and balance sheet, 1887.

A farm of about 300 acres which had been previously hired by Lord Spencer was placed by him under a manager, to be assisted by a committee of management, with the object of the business being carried on for the benefit of the regular labourers who were by the scheme nominated as co-operators.

Capital for working the farm was found by Lord Spencer. By the scheme it was stipulated that after payment of rent, rates, and taxes, and interest at the rate of 4 per cent. upon the capital employed, the net profits of each year should be carried to a reserve fund for the repayment of the original capital, and the creation of a surplus, for which purpose 75 per cent. was to be set aside. The remaining 25 per cent. of the net profits was to be carried to the divisible profits fund, out of which each of the co-operators should receive a share in proportion to the wages earned by him during the year. It was "provided, nevertheless, that in case a loss should be sustained "in any year's operations, the divisible profits fund shall thenceforth be carried to "the reserve fund till such loss be made good, and the amount (if any) drawn from "the reserve fund to meet such loss replaced."

The original co-operators were eight in number, and the manager, in addition to them, ranked as a co-operator entitled to a share of the divisible profits. Conditional powers were given to the co-operators to fill up vacancies and to increase their number; and Lord Spencer reserved to himself the power to appoint the manager, and to determine the connexion of any co-operator or manager with the scheme. The scheme contains provisions for an annual valuation of the tenant right, and of the live and dead stock, and for a proper audit of the farm accounts. It is sad to find that owing to the disastrous times this interesting experiment has at present met with no success. The co-operators (seven out of the original eight are still on the farm) have had regular employment at wages which are said to be slightly higher than those in the district, but there have been no divisible profits. The balance sheets for the first four years show a loss in three years, and I am informed that in the two following years the loss was nearly equal to a half year's rent.*

364. Besides the two experiments in profit-sharing which have been already noticed, there is only one other instance mentioned in the District Reports. Mr. Chapman says in his Final Report:—

"I have not met with a single example of a co-operative farm in the strict sense of the term, but Lord Wantage has for some time been working the large farm of 3,000 acres on the plan of giving his labourers a bonus based upon the profits of the farm. He finds this system extremely valuable as an incentive to good work, and there is no doubt that he has attracted to himself the best labourers in the district."

In his Report on Wantage Mr. Chapman states that the bonus given to men who had worked on the farm for more than a year was in 1892 3l.

7.—TRADE UNIONS AND STRIKES.

365. It does not appear that Trade Unions have enrolled or retained as members any considerable proportion of the agricultural labourers of the country, but in a few counties which are mainly in the east and south-east of England some of these associations claim to have a large number of members, and no doubt if the demand for labour were more active than it now is their strength would increase and they might be able to exercise more influence than they do at present. In only six of the districts of inquiry are Unions of this character recognised as in existence.

366. In Hollingbourn, the London and Southern Counties Land and Labour League exists but it is said that "not many agricultural labourers belong to it."

In his report upon Maldon, Mr. Aubrey Spencer says:—

"The National Agricultural Labourers' Union has a number of members in Essex but not many in the Maldon Union, nor so far as I heard have there been any strikes there."

As regards Langport Mr. Spencer says:—

"A Trade Union has been formed in this district called the West of England and Somerset Labourers' Union. Mr. George Mitchell is the president, and Mr Fred Weston the secretary. It

* Profits and Losses, 1887-1890

	Loss	Profit

was started in the early part of 1892 and about 1,000 members joined it. The payment for membership is 1d. a week, but as I understood many of those who joined are not regular subscribers. There are local agents in several of the villages that I visited, and it is claimed by the organisers of the Union that wages went up in Allar and other places 1s. a week in the spring (1892) in consequence of its formation. This, however, is denied by the farmers who say the two was unconnected with the Union. In Barrington a letter was sent in the spring demanding a rise of wages and a strike was threatened, but it came to nothing. . . . . . In many villages there seemed to be no labourers who were members of the Union, and from the statement made to me by the president I gather that it is not in a particularly flourishing condition."

Mr. Richards in his Final Report says :—

"I have not found outside Stratford-on-Avon any trace of any Agricultural Labourers' Union, and here it is only an echo of the past. Wellesbourne in this Union is the place in which Mr Joseph Arch, M.P., commenced the Agricultural Labourers' Union, and though here and there a few continue to subscribe it has practically ceased to exist so far as this district is concerned. The permanent result of the strike which followed almost immediately on the formation of the Union, was a rise in wages of 3s. to 4s. per week. After making all allowances for a reduction in the number of labourers, resulting from the constant drift into other employments of the more active and able-bodied men, it is probable that the position of the labourer has been improved to the extent of 2s. per week. The establishment of this Union and the extortion, from their standpoint, of the higher pay stimulated the farmers to adopt all the means in their power to supplant or diminish the necessity for labour. Machinery was bought where possible, and the rate of putting down land to permanent pasture was accelerated. . . . . . Wages have risen in sympathy with wages throughout the other industries in the country, and in consequence of the constant withdrawal of the agricultural labouring class into the towns. There is nothing, in fact, which suggests that the results flow from any other cause than supply and demand." Stratford.

Mr. Wilson Fox reports on the subject in the following terms :—

"In Northumberland, Cumberland, and Lancashire Trade Unions are unknown, while in the two Eastern counties (Norfolk and Suffolk) they have a good many adherents among the agricultural labourers. The Union in Suffolk is called the Eastern Counties Federation, and that in Norfolk the National Agricultural Labourers' Union. Fox.

"Opinions as to the effect of the Unions differ widely. A great number of people say their effect has been to strain the friendly relations between employers and employed, while others assert they have been the means of raising the rate of wages. It is to be regretted that these organisations, which I believe can exist without causing ill-feeling, should be sometimes represented by advocates, who, by using language needlessly offensive to the masters, frequently alienate their sympathies from the men in their legitimate grievances."

The following passage, which occurs in the annual report of the Eastern Counties Federation for 1892, cannot, I think, fail to produce irritation and nothing else, and is certainly directly contrary to the evidence given me privately, and at public meetings, by labourers :—

"The present distressed condition of many farmers is brought about by their own conduct towards their agricultural labourers, and the sooner they alter their course of action and treat their working men as human beings, and as Christians, instead of making slaves of them and treating them worse than cattle, as they have done in the past, the better it will be; we may then get on the highway to agricultural prosperity."

* * * * * *

"The farmers of Suffolk are just now forcing the labourers into rebellion. We have offered peaceful arbitration, and some of the farmers have returned our kindly offer with insulting language. Still they are members of Christian churches: no wonder at our churches being unpopular."

In the same report the following suggestion is made, which, if acted on, I believe would produce endless friction between employers and employed, would still further add to the grave difficulties the farmers have to face, and would demoralise the labourers :—

"In my opinion when a farmer reduces wages without accepting our offers of arbitration, the men are 'justified in doing a lesser amount of work for a lower amount of wages.' This is a strong weapon in the hands of the workers and much more powerful than strikes."

That this suggestion is not confined to the report, for a speaker who frequently delivers addresses on behalf of the Federation, at a meeting at the Norton branch, reported in the "Bury Free Press" on 11th March 1893, said as follows :—

"When it wasn't advisable to strike, if wages were reduced 1s. a week, it was the easiest thing in the world to do 2s. a week less work. Work according to pay was an effective weapon if properly handled, and there was a score and one little ways in which labourers could make themselves a nuisance to the powers that be."

I confess that the preaching of this doctrine by the Federation is difficult to reconcile with the estimable sentiments with which their annual report for 1892 concludes :—

"We know we cannot be perfect here below, but anyhow, let us aim at some grand idea — at a state of society in which each is working for another's good. If we do this, peace and happiness will reward us."

Chapman, A 148.

Mr. Chapman says on this subject :—

"Since the Agricultural Labourers' Union was founded in 1872, and gradually dwindled to insignificant proportions in 1888, there has been no systematic combination amongst agricultural labourers. In Thame there has been some experience of strikes promoted by the Dockers' Union in 1891. That experience was not a happy one, but it did some slight good in raising the wages in particular places."

Bear, A 14. Wilkinson, A 87.

Mr. Bear and Mr. Wilkinson report that no labourers' unions exist in any of the districts which they visited.

Reports of the Chief Registrar of Friendly Societies, 1893 Part C. App. (M.).

367. The Annual Reports of the Chief Registrar of Friendly Societies contain the names of registered trade unions, and the more recent reports give particulars of the funds, income, and expenditure, and the number of members of those unions which have made returns in pursuance of 34 & 35 Vict. c. 31. In the return for the year ending December 1892, the only registered trade unions which appear to be chiefly or largely composed of agricultural labourers are the following :—

Register Number.	Year of Establishment.	Name.	Number of Members.
24	1872	London and Counties Labour League *	10,000
28	1878	Amalgamated Labour League - - -	104
164	1872	National Agricultural Labourers' Union -	15,000
520	1890	Eastern Counties Labour Federation - -	16,281

I am informed by the Chief Registrar that since this return was published five new trade unions of agricultural labourers have been registered. The counties in which these unions have been formed are Berks, Beds, Hereford, Herts, Warwick, and Wilts. The Eastern Counties Federation, which claims to have a larger number of members than either the London and Counties Labour League or the National Agricultural Labourers' Union, is of very recent date. It has been referred to as active in its operations in Suffolk, but its means were certainly not large at the date of the return, which appeared in 1893, when it had an income of 1,530l. and an expenditure of 1,267l.

Annual Returns to Registrar.

368. By the courtesy of the Chief Registrar, (E. W. Brabrook, Esq.) I have had the opportunity of examining the annual returns made by the officials of two of the larger trade unions to the registry for several years past, and I have extracted from these returns some particulars as to income and expenditure which may be of interest as showing the past and present position of the two larger and old established unions.

London and Counties Union or League.

369. The London and Counties Land and Labour League, which was formerly styled the Kent and Sussex Labourers' Union, was formed in 1872. In a memorandum upon the Richmond Commission,† I have given an abstract of the evidence given before that Commission by Mr. A. Simmons, who was then (December 1881) secretary to the union. In that evidence the original objects of the organisation were stated to be to increase wages, to assist the labourers with legal protection, and to assist migration and emigration. In 1875 a provident section was added for the purpose of securing sick benefit, funeral, and confinement allowances. At that time the number of members was said to be 14,000 or 15,000, of whom 8,000 or 9,000 belonged to the provident section. The income was 11,540l. in the year before the evidence was given; the contributions of members were 2d. a week for trade purposes and 4d. a week for provident purposes.

An examination of such annual returns as were available show results which are tabulated below. It must be noted that these returns have been made very irregularly and that there are intervals of several years between them. Under these circumstances I have taken such accounts as were available, and where a series of consecutive years could be found I have summarised the account by stating the average expenditure and receipts under the main heads.

LONDON AND COUNTIES LABOUR LEAGUE.

SUMMARY ABSTRACT of ACCOUNTS for different PERIODS.

RECEIPTS.

Table 97.

—	One Year 1877.	Average for Four Years [illegible]	Average for Three Years [illegible]	One Year 1893.
	£	£	£	£
Contributions from members	11,189	11,341	9,431	4,893
Interest on investments	129	130	183	97
Other receipts	20	171	164	53
Total receipts	11,337	11,642	9,678	5,045
Balance brought forward (average)	5,631	9,305	6,134	4,874
Total	16,968	20,947	15,808	9,919

EXPENDITURE.

—	One Year 1877.	Average for Four Years [illegible]	Average for Three Years [illegible]	One Year 1893.
Printing and stationery	277	143	278	320
Salaries and other expenses of management	1,601	1,238	1,372	1,318
Allowances and payments, trade purposes	1,188	68	740	734
" " sick and benevolent purposes	5,631	10,679	8,017	3,118
Total expenditure	8,597	12,148	10,419	5,421
Balance carried forward (average)	8,371	8,469	5,383	4,498
Total	16,968	20,917	14,802	9,919

Number of members (average)	13,000	9,950	12,300	8,900

It will be seen that comparing 1877 with 1893, the receipts have decreased by more than 55 per cent., while the expenditure has decreased by only 37 per cent. The balance in hand has decreased from 8,371l. to 4,498l., or about 46 per cent. The ratio of this balance to the total contributions of members for the year was in 1893 as 92l. to 100l., whereas in 1877 it was only 75 per cent. In the following statement the per-centage of the total expenditure under each of these heads at different periods is given:—

LONDON AND COUNTIES LABOUR LEAGUE.

Per-centage of Expenditure under different Heads.

Table 98.

—	1877.	Average [illegible]	Average [illegible]	1893.
	Per cent.	Per cent.	Per cent.	Per cent.
Printing, stationery, salaries, and other expenses of management	22·7	14·5	16·0	29·8
Trade purposes	13·8	0·5	7·1	13·0
Sick benefits, funerals, &c.	63·5	85·0	76·9	57·3
Total	100·0	100·0	100·0	100·0

It is evident that insurance against loss by sickness and other kindred objects have been the main objects of this Association of late years, though the expenditure for trade purposes was in 1893 relatively higher than in the four preceding years. If the number of members was 8,900, and the total amount of contributions was only 4,895l., the average subscription was only 11s. a year or 2½d. per week.

370. The National Agricultural Labourers' Union has in the past been the most prominent organisation of agricultural labourers for promoting the increase of wages National Agricultural Labourers' Union.

and raising the *status* of the class to which its members belong. I have in my memorandum upon the Richmond Commission* given an abstract of Mr. Joseph Arch's evidence with respect to this union in 1881. The objects of the Society then included the improvement of the social condition of the agricultural labourers, the increase of their wages, the making provision for sickness and old age, and the movement by migration or emigration of surplus labour where the market was overstocked. It combined the functions of a trades union and a provident society. At that time the number of members was said to be about 25,000.† These members were said to be spread over 22 counties, in which counties Mr. Arch thought that two out of every five labourers were members of the Union. This estimate of the proportionate number of labourers must have been absurdly exaggerated.‡

The rate of contributions for trade purposes was 2½d. a week, while contributions for sick benefit were graduated according to age at the time of entry.

The following abstract of such of the annual accounts as I have been able to obtain shows the variation in the fortunes of the Association:—

NATIONAL AGRICULTURAL LABOURERS' UNION.

SUMMARY ABSTRACT of RECEIPTS and EXPENDITURE at different PERIODS.

RECEIPTS.

	Average for Four Years 1876–1879	Average for Two Years [illegible]	Average for Two Years [illegible]	Average for Three Years [illegible]	Average for Two Years [illegible]	[illegible]
	£	£	£	£	£	£
Member's contributions:—						
Trade purposes	9,868	4,203	3,141	1,641	1,580	1,319
Sick and benevolent fund		3,601	3,665	2,091	132	—
Interest on funds	141	175	311	57	4	—
Other receipts	55	30	190	66	10	7
Total receipts	10,177	8,004	7,311	3,861	3,485	1,539
Balance at beginning of each year (average)	4,964	6,839	6,843	3,961	784	1,451
Total	15,141	14,893	14,304	7,829	4,269	2,990

EXPENDITURE.

Stationery and printing	443	139	65	13	253	105
Salaries and expenses of management	5,769	2,215	1,959	1,404	1,424	1,116
Trade purposes	4,007	304	1,116	164	400	699
Sick and benevolent purposes		3,979	4,370	3,012	819	—
Total	10,212	6,879	7,510	5,651	2,900	2,921
Balance at end of year (average)	4,964	7,019	6,800	2,000	1,299	119
Total	15,188	13,891	13,900	7,803	4,219	3,040
Number of members	42,000	14,000	10,300	1,600	15,000	14,700

It seems that recently this Union has ceased to receive contributions for sick benefits, and the rules have been altered so that the objects of association are simply those of union for trade purposes. The number of members is less than one-half, and their contributions are less than one-sixth of what they were 20 years ago, and the reserve fund has pretty nearly vanished. The appropriation of the money subscribed by members of this union for the purpose of insuring against loss by sickness, &c., to trade purposes, and the consequent failure of the Association to fulfil the obligations which it had contracted, has been referred to in evidence given before the Commission.

The late Chief Registrar, Mr. J. Ludlow,§ describes the application of the provident funds to trade purposes as a common incident in the administration of Trade Unions; but it appeared that in every other case that had come officially under his notice the Union had kept faith with the subscribers, and though the capital was spent, the allowances were continued and provided for by levies. In the case of the National Agricultural

* See App. Vol. V., Part II., A. (B.)
† The annual returns to the Chief Registrar give the number of members in 1879 as [illegible] and in 1889 as about [illegible].
‡ There were at that time more than [illegible] adult male agricultural labourers in England. [illegible] in the 22 counties over which the union extended [illegible] would be [illegible] instead of [illegible].)
§ See Report of Chief Registrar of Friendly Societies, &c., 1[illegible], 188[illegible].

Labourers' Union, the Union has simply wiped its hands of all liability in respect of sick and provident benefits. In the following table the proportionate part of the whole expenditure which was spent in management and the part appropriated to members is shown.

NATIONAL AGRICULTURAL LABOURERS' UNION.

PER-CENTAGE and TOTAL EXPENDITURE under different Heads.

Table [illegible]

—	Average [illegible]	Average [illegible]	Average [illegible]	Average [illegible]	Average 1891 1892.	1893
Stationery and printing	5·2	4·9	1·0	0·5	18·0	29·7
Salaries and other expenses of management	57·6	61·4	34·3	24·3	40·7	49·3
Trade purposes	37·2	7·3	17·8	9·6	30·9	21·0
Sick and benevolent purposes		26·3	36·9	65·6	8·4	—
	100·0	100·0	100·0	100·0	100·0	100·0

In the case of the London and Counties Labour League the total cost of management, including stationery and printing, ranged from about 14 to 29 per cent., but in the case of the National Agricultural Labourers' Union the expenses have never been less than 25 per cent. of the whole. In 1891–92 they were 60 per cent., and in 1893 they were 79 per cent. of all expenditure. In ratio to contributions from members these expenses were in 1891–92 nearly 52 per cent., or 10s. 4d. out of every pound contributed by members. In 1893 the contributions of members amounted to 1,512l., while the expenses of management, printing, &c., were 1,821l. The items of expenditure were stated in the balance sheet for the year ending 31st December 1893 to have been as follows:—

	£	s.	d.	£	s.	d.
Strike pay to members } Relief, migration, &c. }	683	10	9			
Contribution to other Trade Unions	15	0	0			
				698	10	9
Salaries of paid officers	693	1	1½			
Rent	50	6	0			
Other expenses of management	572	2	7½			
				1,315	10	3
Stationery and printing, postage and newspaper account				506	8	9½
Total				2,520	9	9½

The number of members being 14,746, and the amount of their contributions 1,531l., their average contribution would be 2s. 1d. a year or about ½d. a week. It is evident that the membership of many of the members must be merely nominal.

871. The Eastern Counties Labour Federation, which is the only other organisation of the nature of a Trades Union claiming a large number of members, has been active in the county of Suffolk, and Mr. Wilson Fox notices the action of this Association in his report on Thingoe and also in his Final Report. This Union was registered in 1890. The general statement of accounts for the year ending December 31st, 1893, gives as the total contributions of members during the year the sum of 1,038l., and the number of members as 11,342, the average contribution being about 1s. 10d. a year. The total receipts for the year amounted to 1,120l. The expenditure for trade purposes was 239l. The expenses of management and legal expenses, exclusive of printing and stationery, were 909l. The total expenditure was 1,259l., and the balance in hand was reduced from 421l. to 255l. Eastern Counties Federation. Fox, A. xv. R. i. 349, App. A. 1

372. With regard to strikes there are only five districts in which any are reported to have occurred; and in every case but one the strike was of very insignificant proportions. In his report on the Thame district Mr. Chapman alludes to a strike which was promoted by the Dockers' Union who visited certain villages "in order to persuade "the men to join them and not come up to London to take work at the docks . . . "the Dockers promised to pay the men 10s. a week if they struck, and the men following "their advice went out on strike last summer, but when the small allowance ceased "the strike had to come to an end." Mr. Wilson Fox reports that there have been some strikes in the Swaffham Union in the last year or two, "and when they have Strikes. Chapman, B. i. 64. Fox, B. ii. iv.

"occurred farmers have sometimes gone and helped each other by working in the fields "themselves."

373. Mr. Wilson Fox also reports that the farmers have formed a union or federation, incorporated under the Companies Acts on July 23rd, 1891, for mutual protection and benefit. Each member pays a fee of 1d. per acre on all lands entered by him and is liable to calls of not more than 1s. per acre in a year.

In November 1892 a conference between representatives of this Association and members of the National Agricultural Labourers' Union was held at East Dereham at the suggestion of the Labourers' Union "for the purpose of discussing the question "of the wages of farm labourers in the eastern counties." At this meeting the formation of a board of arbitration which might settle a current rate of wages for a definite period of three or four months was suggested by Mr. Arch, M.P. The representatives of the Farmers' Federation urged that their Association was purely a defensive one, and that they had no power to bind their members to accept the award of a board of arbitration, while on the other hand the Labourers' Union could not speak for those who were not members. Beyond allowing an opportunity for an interchange of views, in which both parties seem to have adopted a conciliatory attitude, the conference seems to have been productive of no result.

The Annual Report of the Farmers' Federation refers to this conference in the following terms:—

"Considerable interest was evidenced in this conference, but the impossibility of binding either the employers or the employed proved an insuperable difficulty. If it even resulted in no other good the conference was of value for eliciting the admission from the labourers' representatives that the demand for increased wages last summer (1892) was unjustifiable, and was not sanctioned by the executive of the Union, and that their average weekly wages were considerably higher than the public had previously been led to suppose was the case."

The Association numbers more than 700 members in Norfolk and Suffolk. In the year 1892–93 there were strikes on no less than 22 farms in the occupation of members, and some of these lasted for three or four months. The Federation was successful in all but about four cases.

374. In the spring of 1893 a strike occurred at Gayton, near Lynn, and the labourers on five farms, containing altogether about 3,000 acres of land, went out. They gave notice on the Monday that they should leave work on the Saturday following unless 1s. a week more was paid. I put myself in communication with one of the farmers concerned, and after hearing his account of what took place I offered to meet the representative of the Labourers' Union in order that I might have a statement of the case from their point of view; but without directly refusing to give me any information the officials of the Union neglected the opportunity which I had given them, and I received no information from them. I was informed by the employer whom I met that he offered to give his men the advance of 1s. a week which was demanded if they would undertake to make no further demand of a similar character for a period of two months, but his offer was rejected. This gentleman gave me particulars of the wages which he was paying at the time of the strike. These ranged from 12s. to 14s. a week, the team men getting, in addition, cottages and gardens rent free, and harvest wages of 7*l*. 10s. to 8*l*. for an average period of four weeks. These additions to wages would amount to about 3s. 6*d*. per week, and the total earnings would be from 15s. 6d. to 17s. 6*d*. a week for men living on the farm.*

The stock on this farm at the time of the strike was 400 sheep folded on turnips, 30 head of feeding cattle in the yards, and 30 horses; 14 men and boys left work, one man and a boy remained with the farmer. During the first fortnight considerable inconvenience was experienced, but assistance was given by neighbours, and the Federation supplied labourers who were hooted and threatened at first, but no actual violence was done. In all about 40 men and boys went out on strike in this parish. Those who were members of the Union were allowed strike pay at the rate of 9s. a week; for others a collection was made. The wives of the strikers continued to work, and the exceptional character of the season (1893) very much reduced the amount of field work in hoeing and weeding. In the month of June the resources of the strikers failed, and they intimated to the farmers that they were "fit to come back." It required some little

* The farm contains 500 acres arable, 111 acres grass, total 611 acres. The total sum paid for labour [illegible] was [illegible], which is [illegible] an acre over the whole farm, or [illegible] an acre for the arable land and [illegible] an acre for the pasture. The money received by two of the strikers in the year ending Michaelmas 1892 was [illegible], or on average for the two men of [illegible] a week. One of them had however been absent through illness three weeks, the other earned on an average [illegible] a week. The [illegible] the Commissioners and proved that he had [illegible].

time to arrange for the departure of the strangers who had been imported into the district, and owing to the drought which prevailed the farmers found it impossible to take on the labourers at once, but they were reinstated as soon as this could be conveniently arranged. I could not ascertain that any of the strikers left the parish.

The gentleman to whom I am indebted for the statement of facts given above offered me every facility for verifying his statements; he gave the names of the labourers to whom he paid the sums stated, and I can only express my regret that my overtures to the representatives of the labourers met with no response.

375. It does not appear as a result of the whole inquiry that the several Trade Unions which exist among the agricultural labourers have enrolled a sufficient number of members to enable them to speak with authority, and to negotiate terms with any association representative of farmers. To estimate the number of agricultural labourers who are members of some Trade Union or other at the very highest they cannot be put at more than 50,000, which is less than one-tenth of the adult males in the class of wage-earners in agriculture.*

376. There can, I think, be little doubt that in the past a powerful incentive to labourers to join the National Agricultural Labourers' Union was the prospect which was held out to them of insuring against sickness and old age. Mr. Arch, M.P., in his evidence before the Richmond Commission put this prominently forward; he stated that many of the village clubs were rotten and were going to grief, that the "sick "benefit fund was entirely under the control of the sick members themselves." Whatever justification may be found for the employment of the sick benefit fund for trade purposes it cannot be denied that the thousands of labourers who, according to Mr. Arch's evidence, subscribed to the Union increased sums with the hope of providing against sickness and old age have suffered a cruel disappointment in finding that in this respect the Union has proved no better than one of the rotten village clubs.

8.—GENERAL RELATIONS BETWEEN EMPLOYERS AND EMPLOYED.

377. There is to be found in nearly all the Reports of the Assistant Commissioners evidence of some dissatisfaction being felt by both classes, employers and employed, with respect to their mutual relations. In some districts this is more felt than in others, but in none does it seem to have been at the time of the inquiry (1892-93) an actual feeling of hostility. "Pacific but not cordial" is an expression used by Mr. Richards, and it appears to sum up the situation very generally. On this point the opinions of the Assistant Commissioners may be quoted.

Mr. Bear says:—

"In all my districts the relations of employers and employed were generally friendly, although in all I heard many complaints from each class in relation to the other."

Mr. Chapman reports as follows:—

"The relations of employers and employed are marked everywhere by a want of cordiality, and in a great many places by mutual suspicion. The familiar and quasi patriarchal terms upon which farmers used to live with their men are fast giving way to more conventional relations. Things are at present in a transition stage; farmers resent the notion of men being independent of them, and dread being left in the lurch at busy seasons. They begin to see that nothing but money will keep a man upon a farm, and money is more than ever difficult to get. They could better afford to give a farm cottage, a good garden, and potato ground and fuel, but it often happens that the men will not have them. On the other hand, men are everywhere struggling for independence. They ride at loose anchor wherever they are employed, and no longer look upon themselves as fixtures upon a farm. They prefer to live in villages and depend upon allotments, but they are not satisfied with their independence. They regret many of the perquisites which they received when they were dependent, and complain that farmers have given up taking any interest in them. This state of things has resulted in a good deal of undeserved suspicion on both sides, and is most unsatisfactory, but there are signs of improvement. Masters everywhere treat their men with more consideration than they did, and men are beginning to realise in a great many places that farming is not such a profitable business as they believed it to be. When the transition stage is passed greater frankness on both sides may be expected."

Mr. Chapman proceeds to classify the several districts which he visited thus:—"An "example of the older condition of things may be found in the Builth Union of "Breconshire, but of the English districts Crediton, with its farm cottages, is the best

---

* In 1891 there were in England and Wales [illegible] wage-earners in agriculture of 20 years and upwards.

"type, and Atcham the next best. Of the new condition of things North Witchford "is the best example, Thame the next, then Truro. Wantage and Buntingford are "at the bottom of the list; they are affected by the spirit of independence without "the power." And he goes on to remark upon—

"The factors which combine to make this change of relationship are—

"(1) the giving up apprenticeship in farm-houses,
"(2) the tendency to live in village cottages,
"(3) the abolition of payment in kind;
"(4) the loss of perquisites;
"(5) the decay of local benefit clubs;
"(6) the absence of club feasts, harvest dinners, and other occasions for local conviviality;
"(7) the decrease in the number of allotments."

Mr. Wilson Fox says on the same subject:—

"The relations between employers and employed are of a more cordial character in the Northern counties than in the Eastern, though many farmers in the north say the men are more independent than they were 20 years ago. On the whole, the relations between the masters and men in the Eastern counties are not unsatisfactory, though the general opinion is that they are not so good as they were some years ago. Why this should be is difficult to say. Many farmers say it is due to doctrines preached by the unions. The men usually assert that the only cause of complaint they have is about the question of wages."

In another paragraph Mr. Wilson Fox attributes the more satisfactory relations of the Northern counties to the higher rate of wages, the custom of so many men living and boarding in the farm-houses, and the fact of there being in Cumberland and Lancashire but little social distinction between the classes.

Mr. Richards compares his several districts of inquiry thus:—

"At Stratford-on-Avon, where there is more solidarity of opinion among the agricultural labourers than is found elsewhere, there is an absence of cordiality in the relations amounting almost to an armed neutrality. There is a feeling of complete independence on both sides; there is so much work for so much pay, or so much pay for so much work, and nothing more, or as Canon Bury, of Harlestone, puts it 'merely a cash nexus.' . . . . . At Monmouth, where opinion is not so solid, and where almost all labour, except on large farms, is migratory, the relations are much about the same. In most of the other districts there is a queer compromise between the old order and the new. Labourers while striving for more freedom and more wages cling to the idea that their employers are under certain obligations to them, not comprised in the pay, while the employers (the larger ones) strive in some degree to meet these expectations.

"Nantwich and Belper represent the most cordial relations existing between the two sections of the community. In the former place these are probably traceable to the great improvement in cottage accommodation, and the steady development of cottage holdings; in the latter to the circumstance that the men have fairly good wages, and that the smaller farmers worked work as hard as their labourers."

Mr. Aubrey Spencer states his conclusions on the point in the following terms:—

"In all the districts visited labourers were said to be more 'independent' than they used to be, by which is meant, I think, that they regard their relation to the farmer more as a strictly commercial light than they used to, and that the quasi-family tie which used to exist between farmer and labourer has nearly ceased to exist. I do not, however, gather that there is much real hostility between the two classes in any district. In some cases I was told that relations were now more friendly than they were 12 or 15 years ago.

"At the same time it is right to point out that in every district I heard a good deal of discontent from the lips of labourers, especially from the younger men, rather more, I think, than would be usual in men following other occupations. At public meetings of labourers the spokesmen often showed a bitter feeling towards their employers, and blamed them for not employing more labour and not paying higher wages. I do not, however, think that too much weight should be attached to this demonstration of feeling, as the discontented men who exist in every class and occupation of life naturally come to the fore at a public meeting, while the more contented ones remain silent. . . . . . That there are a considerable number of men fairly well contented I can speak from my personal experience, gathered from men to whom I talked privately, in the field, in their cottages, or elsewhere than at public meetings. The discontent, such as it is, is greater, I think, amongst men who are ordinary labourers than amongst those who are more skilled, such as carters, stockmen, shepherds, thatchers, and the like. It is worthy of notice that such ill-feeling as was shown appeared to be, if anything, rather more marked in districts such as Kent, Surrey, and Essex, where the rate of pay is comparatively high, than in the lower paid districts of Wiltshire and Dorsetshire. In Somersetshire the presence of a newly formed trade union has rendered feeling in some, but not in all, cases rather strained. Taking all things into consideration I do not think that the relations of the better labourers toward their masters, when the latter are, as is frequently the case, kind and considerate, is even at the present day anything but very friendly, though men are probably not so easily satisfied as they were formerly."

Mr. Wilkinson reports that in some of the districts surveyed by him—

"There has been an interruption of the harmony existing between the farmers and their men, the reason that was said being, in Easingwold, 'Somehow there is slight friction, I can scarcely tell you how it is,' and, in Wetherby, 'There is a fair feeling, and it would be just as friendly as in the old days, if it were not for the professional agitators going about with apparently no other object than to make bad blood between us.' In Driffield, I heard several complaints of the trouble often given now by the young horsemen, and several instances of what I called (and I can still think of no better term) unfriendly conduct on the part of the men. But there was little general complaint on the part of the farmers, and there are few who have not had many men stay on with them year after year, men for whom they obviously feel a real regard which it is impossible that the men should fail to reciprocate. I say the same, too, of Holbeach, though that district is generally looked on as one where mischief-makers have carried all before them, and had exceptional success in instilling implacable hatred of the farmers in the minds of the men. It may be so, but, as others' feelings for one are apt to be intuitively felt and reciprocated, I am not inclined to believe implicitly in that version, for I did not hear a word on the part of the farmers indicating anything but kindly feeling towards their men, or anyhow for the men who worked regularly with them. They recognised that in many cases there was not the cordial friendliness which used to exist, but hoped for its restoration as time went on."

378. An examination of the District Reports will show that while there is hardly one district which does not exhibit some signs of estrangement, there are none where some evidence of kindly and friendly feelings are not forthcoming. If the several districts are classified in accordance with the general effect of the Reports on this point it must be understood that within many of these districts wide differences prevail, while the difference between one district and another is often slight, and the division into classes is merely that of a graduation and not that of a distinctive difference. In the following classification of districts I have attempted to show (1) those where the most friendly feelings and comparatively happy relations between the classes are reported as existing; (2) those where the relations are on the whole not unsatisfactory, but some qualification has to be introduced in describing the situation, and (3) those where the feeling between masters and men is described as "not good," or in some such terms.

379. Districts classed in respect of relations between employers and employed:—

1. Good or Satisfactory	2. Fairly Satisfactory, Generally Friendly, Fairly Good, &c., Amicable	3. Unsatisfactory, Strained, not Cordial
Belper (b).	Atcham.	Buntingford.
Cirencester.	Basingstoke.	Langport.
Crediton.	Brixworth.	Monmouth.
Garstang (a).	Bromyard.	St. Neots.
Glendale (a).	Dorchester.	Stratford-on-Avon.
Godstone.	Driffield.	Swaffham.
Hollingbourn.	Easingwold.	Thame.
Maldon.	Holbeach.	Truro.
Melton Mowbray.	Louth.	
Nantwich (b).	North Witchford.	
Southwell.	Pershore.	
Thingoe.	Pewsey.	
Wigton (a).	Thakeham.	
	Uttoxeter.	
	Wantage.	
	Wetherby.	
	Woburn.	
(13)	(17)	(8)

380. It is difficult to find in the conditions under which the labourers live a sufficient explanation of the above arrangement.

accommodation. Four of these districts,* where the relations are said to be good, have good cottages, and in four † they are fair.

As regards engagements in four of these districts, the engagement is for ordinary labourers generally a yearly one, in eight it is chiefly a weekly one, and in one it is a mixed system of yearly and weekly engagements.

Again, though the possession of land, either in small holdings or allotments, may distinguish some of these 13 districts, they are not singular in this respect.

But the most remarkable circumstance is perhaps this, that Mr Richards, who reports the relations of employers and employed as satisfactory in Cirencester, nevertheless classes that district as the lowest in the scale in respect of the average condition of the agricultural labourer of all the seven districts which he visited.

It is clear that the conditions under which the best relations are preserved are not uniform, and that these relations do not necessarily imply high wages, short hours, good cottages, particular engagements, or facilities for obtaining land, although in some cases, no doubt, the conditions are favourable in respect of one or more of these.

381. On the other hand, it will be found that the eight districts in which the evidence seems to show that the least friendly feelings exist between the two classes, are districts of comparatively low wages and of inferior cottages.

It need be no matter of surprise if what I had previously described as an economic revolution has disturbed and dislocated the old ties which formerly connected the employers and employed. The farmer has been losing ground; while the labourer has been advancing the resources of the employer have diminished. The labourer has been able to make better terms for himself, to reduce the hours of work, and, as is generally alleged to be the case, he works less diligently than formerly; his ideas have been expanded, and his demands have increased; he will not be contented with what his father accepted, and, if he consents to remain an agricultural labourer, he exacts conditions which his employer finds it difficult to comply with.

It is satisfactory to note that in the opinion of the Assistant Commissioners the mutual relations of the two classes have improved during the last few years, and both are accepting the inevitable change of circumstances.

D.—THE GENERAL CONDITION OF THE AGRICULTURAL LABOURER.

382. There is throughout the Reports of the Assistant Commissioners a general consensus of opinion that the condition of the agricultural labourer has greatly improved during the last 15 or 20 years, and if the review be extended to a more remote period, it will be found that this improvement has been continuous.

Pursuing the plan which I have throughout this Report adopted, I shall proceed first of all to quote from the Final Reports of the Assistant Commissioners the conclusions at which they arrived on this point.

He then proceeds to test the alleged improvement by reference to facts in a series of paragraphs in which he states that—

(i.) Wages have fallen off since the period 1872 to 1878, though they have risen above the level between 1888 and 1889, and he thinks that the upward tendency will be maintained.

(ii.) Cottages have improved in particular villages, but the majority are growing worse and worse, and landlords who can afford to improve are few and far between. "The general condition "of the cottages is not satisfactory, especially in the open villages, but there is a decided "and a natural tendency to an improved state of things."

(iii.) Allotments have increased, "but in a good many places the novelty has worn off, they are not "felt by the labourer to be of such advantage to him, and the supply is rather above than "below the demand."

(iv.) The hours of labour have been lessened in some districts, but "the improvement in this "respect is not very widespread."

Mr. Chapman then states on the authority of the Registrar General's Report that there is a tendency among the labourers to defer their marriage to a later period, inferring from this "greater prudence "and an increasing reluctance to be tied to the soil."

Employment is more continuous, free education has relieved the married labourer's pockets, and the spending power of his wages has increased. After discussing this point he continues thus:—

"It would be a great mistake to suppose that the condition of the average agricultural labourer is satisfactory. It is only necessary to compare the weekly budgets with the weekly earnings to realise that the large majority of labourers earn but a bare subsistence, and are unable to save anything for their old age or for times when they are out of work. An immense number of them live in a chronic state of debt and anxiety, and depend to a lamentable extent on charity. Their cottages are bad and often contain a minimum of furniture. It is very difficult for them to get milk for their children, and the supply of good water is in many districts deficient. For six days a week they live on vegetables, bacon, and bread, and on Sunday the change is more often to pork than to beef or mutton." (Chapman, A. [illegible]; Chapman, A. [illegible])

"In conclusion it may be stated that, although there have been material gains with increased number of allotments, the shortening of the hours of labour, the gradual improvement of cottages, the decreased price of necessaries, and free education, there still remains much to be done."

Mr. Wilson Fox sums up his conclusions in the following paragraph :—

"The condition of the agricultural labourer has improved in the last 20 years in the following particulars :— (Fox, A. [illegible])

(1.) Wages have gone up appreciably in the three Northern counties, and in the Eastern counties it is satisfactory for the labourers that the wages there are no lower now, in a time of severe agricultural depression, than they have been for the past ten years.

(2.) Work is less arduous, owing to the working hours being more defined to fixed limits, and to the introduction of machinery, and to the better class of implement now used.

(3.) Cottages built in recent years are generally far superior in all respects to those erected in former times, many of which, unfortunately, still remain.

(4.) Prices of food and clothing are considerably cheaper than they were, the result being that the labourer lives better than he did, spends more on trips by train to towns, thus getting his views and ideas enlarged.

(5.) There is less drunkenness everywhere.

(6.) Allotments have, generally speaking, been placed within the reach of those who require them in Norfolk and Suffolk.

(7.) The supply of water has much improved owing to the sinking of wells, and drainage is better attended to.

(8.) The opportunities of education given to the present generation have largely increased. The labourers all much appreciate the benefit of the *Free Education Act*."

Mr. Richards says :—

"On all hands the testimony is that the agricultural labourer is better off than he has been in the past." (Richards, A. [illegible])

He quotes a communication received by him from Canon Bury :—

"As to the material condition of the agricultural labourer it is vastly improved. He is better housed, fed, clothed, and educated, and his amusements are less gross. The moral improvement is that he is more sober, provident, and independent (*i.e.*, less dependent upon charity and the poor law). On the other hand he is less contented (although I am far from saying that discontent is a bad thing), less industrious, takes less interest in his work, and has less pride in doing it well."

"To the same effect is the evidence of a very intelligent labourer in Cirencester :—

"It (the general condition) is certainly better than that of his forefathers, but his improvement is far behind that of other workmen. In only too many cases his home and his work are so bound together that he has not that liberty which is so essential to the progress that he would otherwise endeavour to make."

Mr. Richards then compares the position of a labourer in the country with that of one in the town, and calculates that the former saves at least 5s. to 6s. a week in house rent and the value of his garden produce.

Mr. Aubrey Spencer's observations on this subject are as follows:—

"All the evidence I received points to the fact that the condition of the agricultural labourer has greatly improved, and that he has either not suffered at all from the agricultural depression or by no means to the same extent that the farmer and landowner have done.

"In most places there appeared to have been a short period, some 15 or 20 years ago, after Mr. Arch's first movement, when wages rose to an abnormal point. They then fell again, but latterly have been gradually rising, so that now they are as high as they have ever been, with the exception of the above-mentioned short period, though in some districts it was said that a fall was likely to take place in the winter which has just passed. In some counties (e.g., Essex, Worcestershire, Somerset) there has been a rise of wages within the last two or three years, owing to the diminution in the supply of labour.

"As compared with 30 or 40 years ago, the present rate of wages shows a remarkable increase in all cases.

"In estimating the comparative prosperity or the reverse of the agricultural labourer it is, however, as important to consider the purchasing power as the actual amount of money received, and I think there can be no question that this is much greater than it ever was before. Almost all the first necessaries of life, such as bread, tea, lights, clothes, groceries, are cheaper than they have been known before. This fact is not denied by labourers themselves, and obviously tends to make their condition one of greater comfort than it used to be. [*See* labourers' balance sheets in Dorchester, (19), Pewsey, (31), Hollingbourn, (54), Langport, (52).]

"As evidence of their improved condition, it was pointed out to me that the clothing of labourers and that of their children, and the furniture and belongings of their cottages, showed a great advance, and my observations confirmed this. I saw many cottages neat, well furnished, and bespeaking the general comfort of the inhabitants, and, though it is only fair to say that many were very much the reverse, I think that the former predominated considerably, and that where the cottage bore a poverty-stricken appearance it appeared to be more often due to the unthrifty character of the occupier or his wife than to the scantiness of their earnings.

"The hardest time in the life of the agricultural labourer is, I have no doubt, when he has a wife and several small children to support, none of whom bring any earnings into the family purse, and I think he often feels the pinch of poverty severely in such a case, though his burden has been somewhat lightened by the Free Education Act. When his boys are able to go to work in the field, and his girls to service, he reaches a time of comparative prosperity, and the income of a family where, as is often the case, there are two or three lads earning wages and living at home, comes to a respectable figure.

"The worst feature of the case, and one that affects a great number of agricultural labourers, is the defective house accommodation which often has to be put up with. This is, I think, gradually being improved, but the rate of improvement is slow. Another matter to be regretted is that the great majority of agricultural labourers who outlive their powers of work have no resource for the support of their old age except the poor law."

Finally Mr. Wilkinson reports thus:—

"I cannot doubt that the condition of the agricultural labourer in all these districts is comparatively better than it was a few years ago, and positively satisfactory in the majority of cases. As to the former, there is unanimous testimony, that of the men themselves being included, for, even if in some cases wages have dropped rather than risen, the fall has, in their opinion, been more than balanced by the greater cheapness of most necessities.

"Generally, however, the wages have risen rather than fallen. I am speaking, of course, of the time up to the autumn of 1891. Since then a general drop, in some cases, as in Holbeach, a severe one, has, I believe, taken place. This, unless very temporary, will, of course, alter the complexion of affairs considerably. One had evidence of a positively satisfactory state of things, in cottages nicely furnished, in greater variety of food, in good clothing, and general appearance of fairly comfortable circumstances.

"It is a common remark that men do not save more now than they used to do, though wages are double what they were 40 or 50 years ago, and everything then was much dearer. I should doubt that. I expect that there is a great deal more invested in savings banks, and much more provision made for sickness by membership of benefit societies. Even if many without actually squandering their income, do not put by much more than their fathers did, are they to be altogether blamed for that? Is there a class which does not at the present day live with more comfort, one might almost say, with greater luxury than it did a generation back, and, if others may and can do this, why not the labourers also.

"Of course, I do not mean to say that the shoe does not pinch very hard the labourer, even though making a fair steady income, who has a wife and a family of young children, of whom not one is able to add anything to the family income, and who has not a little money put by to provide for such a state of things.

"It must be admitted that in every district there are some in poverty whose poverty may fairly be attributed to their own fault. Several have no steady employment, but it is because they will not take it. No district, perhaps no considerable village is without its contingent of loafers, men who are quite content if they get some catch-work three or four days in the week. These men are sometimes first-rate workers when they will work at all, but more often are but indifferent hands in point both of skill and industry. They are the most fastidious as to the work they will accept, they ask the highest wages, and are the first who lay down their tools a quarter of an hour or more before the agreed time rather than risk giving a minute over it. I saw many who were unmistakeably of this class, and of whom the steady men expressed quite as poor an opinion as the farmers did. As whenever they are doing nothing they will say it is because no work is to be had, nothing would be easier than to get a chorus of testimony that things are in a bad way with the agricultural labourer. But whatever the future may bring forth, I am convinced that as regards the state of things in 1893 the opinion I have expressed is generally correct."

383. I have quoted the opinions of the Assistant Commissioners on this important point at some length, and it will be seen that all of them arrive at the conclusion that the material condition of the labourer has greatly improved. It is true that Mr. Chapman qualifies this statement by pointing out that the improvement is not the same in all districts, and that the present condition is not to be regarded as altogether satisfactory, and upon these points probably few would be found to disagree with him. It is, however, satisfactory to note that there has been from various causes a considerable amelioration of the position of the labourer, and that the progress which has been reported on the occasion of previous inquiries of a similar character has been fairly maintained, and this notwithstanding the fact that other classes connected with agriculture have been for a long period suffering from serious depression.

Present opinions of Assistant Commissioners.

384. If the present circumstances be compared with those existing 25 years ago it is indisputable that the earnings of all classes of labourers have increased, and that the purchasing power of money has also increased; the hours of work have been lessened; machinery has relieved the labourer of much of the severe work which he had then to perform. In many counties the wives of the labourers have been entirely emancipated from field work; for many years past the employment of young children has been prohibited; greater opportunities for free education have been given, and as regards the dwellings of the labourers, it cannot be doubted that, with all their defects, the average standard of accommodation has risen greatly. The labourer of the present day, who is better fed, better clothed, better housed than his father was, may not be fully conscious of the improvement which has taken place, because his ideas have expanded, and his wants, like those of persons in every other class, have grown. But none the less he lives in less discomfort, his toil is less severe, his children have a better prospect before them and opportunities which he himself never enjoyed.

Comparison with results of previous inquiries.

I have stated that each successive inquiry into the condition of the agricultural labourer records progress and improvement.

Mr. T. E. Kebbel, in his book on "The Agricultural Labourer," to which I have previously referred, after reviewing the Reports of "the Commission on the Employment "of Children, Young Persons, and Women in Agriculture," wrote thus in 1870:—

"On a general retrospect of the ground we have now travelled over, the conclusion seems to be that the condition of the agricultural labourer is slowly but surely on the rise." In 1887 a new edition of this work was published, and the author appended to the statement just quoted this note:—

Kebbel. The Agricultural Labourer, 1870, p. 191.

"This prophecy, it is needless to say, has been abundantly confirmed."

Sir James Caird, in his book on The Landed Interest, which was written in 1878, says:—

"The general condition of the agricultural labourer was probably never better than it is at present. Compared with that of 300 years ago, in the time of Queen Elizabeth, wages have risen sixfold, while the price of bread has only doubled. Two centuries later, in 1770, the farm labourer's wage was 1s. 2d. a day, when the price of wheat was 46s. a quarter. In 1846, immediately before the repeal of the Corn Laws, wages were 1s. 7d. when wheat was 53s. At the present time wages have risen 60 per cent., while wheat has diminished in price. In other words, the labourer's earning power in procuring the staff of life cost him five days' work to pay for a bushel of wheat in 1770, four days in 1846, and two and a half days in 1878. He is better lodged than he ever was before, though in many parts of the country there is still much room for improvement in that respect. Compared with the labourer in towns his position is one of greater comfort."

Caird. The Landed Interest, London, 1878, p. 65.

The Richmond Commission, a few years later, reported that:—

Richmond Commission.

"While the difficulties of the farmers have increased, higher wages and more general employment have proportionately improved the condition of the labourer. It is most satisfactory to be assured that the labouring class has been scarcely, if at all, affected by the distress which has fallen so heavily upon owners as well as occupiers. Provisions have been cheap and employment abundant, while wages, in a few districts only, have been slightly reduced."

Richmond Commission Final Report, 1882.

The Reports of the present Commission show that progress and improvement have been continued.

Wages and earnings.

385. I have in a previous part of this Report stated that the evidence obtained does not indicate a rise of wages since the inquiry under the Richmond Commission [1879–81] and that no large increase is shown in the average wages between 1870 and the present time, but I have stated the reasons which make the comparison of the available statistics somewhat difficult. Under the present inquiry the wages reported are those current in particular districts, which districts are, as there is reason to suppose, those where lower wages than the average wages of the county prevail; and further there are grounds for supposing that in the case of previous inquiries wages and earnings were frequently treated as synonymous terms, while the wages and earnings of the higher classes of labourers were frequently included with those of ordinary labourers, and thus raised the average rate. The same remarks will apply to the labour statistics which contain returns of wages of agricultural labourers in 1860–61 and 1869–70. It is evident that wages and earnings are not distinguished, and the rates given include those of all classes of labourers.

Vide ante, p. 63.

Returns of wages. C 5172, 1887.

It seems probable then that the advance in the wages and earnings in ordinary labourers has on the average been greater than is indicated by the comparative tables which I have given (Tables 59 and 65).

Earnings of labourers' families.

386. With regard to the wages of working members of the labourer's family, there has been undoubtedly a great increase. Where women work their wages are much higher than they were 25 or even 12 years ago. I have shown (page 80) that in Glendale women's wages rose by 17 per cent. between 1883 and 1890. In 1867–68 Mr. Henley reported to the Commission on the Employment of Children, &c., the ordinary wages of women in the district as 1s. a day. In 1880 they had advanced to 1s. 3d., and in 1890 they had risen to 1s. 6d., a rise of 50 per cent. in little more than 20 years. The wages of children who have been set free from school, and those of young persons have also increased much more than those of men (page 87). These earnings in many cases form a very important part of the family income (see Family Earnings, par. 219 *ante*).

But undoubtedly the labourer has benefited by the cheapness of the necessaries of life and the increased purchasing power of his money than by a direct increase in the amount of cash received.

Wages in ratio to wheat prices.

387. In a passage which I have quoted from Sir James Caird the ratio of wages to the value of wheat is taken as a test or standard of measurement. No authority is given for the statistics which form the basis of comparison, but the author's name is a guarantee for their substantial accuracy. If at the present time a similar comparison were made between wages and wheat prices, it would show that whereas in 1880 it took two-and-a-half days to earn a bushel of wheat, it now takes only one-and-a-quarter days or one-half what it took 14 years ago. But it would be manifestly unfair to base the comparison upon the price of wheat alone since that article exhibits the greatest decrease in value of anything which the labourer buys. But it may be pointed out that Professor Thorold Rogers was in the habit of applying this standard when he desired to prove that the agricultural labourer was far better paid in the middle ages than he has been in the nineteenth century. In his "Six Centuries of Work and Wages" he says that in the fourteenth century the wages of a day labourer were 2s. a week, while a quarter of wheat was worth 6s., so that it then took three weeks to earn a quarter. He contrasts this with Arthur Young's time when wheat was 40s. a quarter, and wages 7s. a week, at which rate it took about 34 days to earn a quarter. During the last four or five years an ordinary labourer has been able to earn the value of a quarter of wheat in 12 days. Measured solely by their ratio to the value of wheat then the agricultural labourer's wages would appear to be very much higher than they ever have been before. It is, however, necessary to take into account other items of expenditure to ascertain the spending power of wages.

Rogers' Six Centuries Work and Wages, [illegible], p. [illegible].

Wages in ratio to cost of subsistence. "Nineteenth Century Magazine," No. 196, June 1893.

388. In a recent number of the "Nineteenth Century Magazine" an article by Gustav F. Steffen, entitled "Six Hundred Years of English Poverty," compares money wages and food prices at different periods.

For the purpose of this comparison the writer estimates "the minimum diet required "to maintain an adult man of medium weight working with moderate intensity," and expresses this in wheat and beef and mutton. He takes the average family as comprising five persons, a man, his wife, and three children, and assumes that the average consumption of this family will be three times that of an adult male; and he finds that 6 lbs. 14 oz. of wheat and 1 lb. 6 oz. of meat supplies a daily ration, containing the nutritious elements required to sustain the family in question. Having ascertained the daily wages of two classes of labourers (a carpenter and an agricultural labourer) from

A.D. 1250 to the present time, the writer shows by tables and diagrams the per-centage of wages required to buy the wheat and meat necessary to maintain a family; the balance of wages left after providing these necessaries of life; and the quantity of wheat which could be bought by a day's wages at different periods. I do not propose to enter into the question of the remote past, I will simply point out that we must go back to about 1500 to find an agricultural labourer's wages in ratio to wheat prices as great as they were in 1890. Taking wheat and meat together, the portion of wages absorbed in buying the quantities previously named has steadily declined since about 1820, when it would have required about 10 per cent. more than the amount of the wages to provide the required quantity of food. According to these statistics there never has been a period since 1570 when the agricultural labourers' wages would buy so much wheat and meat in due proportions required to nourish and sustain a family as in the period of 1881–1890.

It would not be fair if I quoted these very interesting tables without pointing out that the author expressly states that these figures deal only with the proportion between "money wages for a day's work and the prices of the necessaries of life." He contends that since mediæval times the English workman has gradually lost other means of supporting himself and his family, and that he has been growing more and more exclusively dependent upon his money wages. He also asserts that house rent has absorbed a rapidly increasing per-centage of wages. As regards the average agricultural labourer, this I believe to be an entire mistake. He alludes to that curse of the wage earner, irregularity and uncertainty of employment, which is certainly not a characteristic of agriculture generally, and where it prevails it is mainly by the wish of the labourer; and finally the writer mentions as "a very serious draw-"back peculiar to modern economic life," such evils as extremely long hours, robbing the workman of his health and efficiency, and *child and female labour*, which make his housekeeping bad and wasteful. It does not appear from these arguments which are used to minimise the effect of the statistical facts that the writer has an intimate practical acquaintance with the agricultural conditions in England at the present time.

I take the liberty of extracting from one of the tables printed by Mr. Steffen in the article referred to some particulars as to wages and their purchasing power during the last 60 years.

Table 102.

Periods of 10 Years.	Daily Wages of an Agricultural Labourer.	Price (in Pence and Decimals) of			Percentage of an Agricultural Labourer's Wages required for buying		Pounds of Wheat that could be bought with Daily Wages of an Agricultural Labourer.
		6 lbs. 14 ozs. of Wheat and 1 lb. 8 ozs. Meat.	5 lbs. 5 ozs. of Wheat.	1 lb. 8 ozs. of Meat.	6 lbs. 14 ozs. of Wheat.	1 lb. 8 ozs. of Meat.	
	s. d.	d.	d.	d.	Per cent.	Per cent.	lbs.
1831–1840	1 6	[illegible]	[illegible]	[illegible]	[illegible]	[illegible]	[illegible]
1841–1850	1 9	[illegible]	[illegible]	[illegible]	[illegible]	[illegible]	[illegible]
1851–1860	1 11	17·19	[illegible]	[illegible]	[illegible]	[illegible]	17
1861–1870	2 1	[illegible]	11·71	[illegible]	[illegible]	[illegible]	[illegible]
1871–1880	2 4	[illegible]	[illegible]	[illegible]	[illegible]	[illegible]	[illegible]
1881–1890	2 2½	15·45	6·15	[illegible]	[illegible]	[illegible]	[illegible]

In the first of these six periods 93 per cent. of the wages were required to buy the same quantity of food as could be bought in the last decade for 58 per cent. of those wages. In the earlier period the margin for other expenses was 7 per cent., in the latest period it was 42 per cent. If the last three years were dealt with in a similar manner the purchasing power of money would be shown to have gone on increasing, since wheat has gone down in value by at least 12½ per cent.

389. It may be true that in taking into account the values of certain articles of food, a correct idea of the actual power of money is given, but we may carry the investigation one step further and ascertain the comparative cost at different periods of such commodities as the agricultural labourers buy, and by multiplying the quantities consumed by the ascertained prices arrive at an approximate standard of value. The wholesale contract prices given for a series of years at a well-managed union workhouse will afford an approximate record of prices. In Mr. Chapman's Report on the Atcham district a full account of prices of different articles is given. These prices are, of course, wholesale, and it is not assumed that a labourer can buy at the same price, but we may fairly suppose that the per-centage to be added to bring these prices to the level of retail prices would be about the same at different periods, Estimated purchasing power of wages on commodities usually consumed. Chapman, B.

and at least it would not have increased in recent years when competition has been much keener than formerly. If we divide the whole series of 32 years for which prices are given into four periods of eight years we shall minimise if not eliminate those fluctuations which are accidental and temporary. For the purpose of calculating comparative expenditure I shall take the case of a single young man living in lodgings and what I have ascertained to be the average consumption of such a man on my own farm. I have been obliged to substitute mutton for pork as the prices for the latter meat are not quoted, but it is the meat which is almost always consumed, not because beef and mutton are unprocurable, but because pork is considered more serviceable and it is preferred. In addition to the food which they purchase these young men pay to the foreman's wife about 2s. a week for lodging, cooking, plain or fruit puddings, pepper, salt, &c. Potatoes are provided by the farmer without charge.

Prices of commodities.

390. The average prices paid at Atcham for several articles of general consumption during four periods of eight years each between 1860 and 1891 were as follows:—

Table 108.

	Average Prices (in Pence and Decimals).			
	1860–1867.	1868–1875.	1876–1883.	1884–1891.
	d.	d.	d.	d.
Flour, per stone	25·31	24·50	16·42	15·87
Mutton, per lb.	6·75	7·34	7·34	6·12
Butter „	13·60	14·87	14·00	11·00
Cheese „	4·13	4·87	4·12	3·80
Tea „	31·63	23·00	18·25	18·06
Sugar „	4·00	3·20	2·20	1·71

Cost of one week's provisions for single man.

391. The comparative value of these articles consumed by one adult male per week at different periods was as follows:—

Table 109.

Week's Consumption.	1860–1867.	1868–1875.	1876–1883.	1884–1891.
	d.	d.	d.	d.
Flour, 1¼ stone	31·64	30·62	20·52	19·81
Mutton, 6 lbs.	40·50	44·04	44·04	36·72
Butter, ½ lb.	6·80	7·43	7·00	5·50
Cheese, 1 lb.	4·13	4·87	4·12	3·80
Tea, ¼ lb.	3·95	2·95	2·28	2·00
Sugar, 1 lb.	1·00	3·20	2·20	1·71
	87·91	92·44	80·25	68·34
Ratio to first period of eight years	100·	102·83	89·37	77·17
If 2s. be added for lodging the totals will be	24·	24·	24·	24·
	111·91	116·44	104·25	92·34
Ratio to first eight years	100	104·33	93·73	82·55

From this table it appears that the value of the articles purchased was in the last period of eight years nearly 25 per cent. below that of the same articles during the earlier period, and more than 25 per cent. below the cost in the period between 1868 and 1875.

The total expenditure (exclusive of the cost of clothing and such indulgences as beer, tobacco, &c.) was nearly 20 per cent. less in recent years than between 1860 and 1867, and 16s. was equal in purchasing power during that period to 1l. in the former period.

I have not attempted to carry out the comparison with respect to a labourer with a wife and family. It is clear that he could not frame his budget on such a liberal scale, but in so far as he substituted bread, tea, and sugar for meat he would benefit to a greater extent by the reduced prices of these commodities which have decreased in value much more in proportion than meat.

Some changes advantageous to labourers.

391a. Of the smaller changes which have taken place in recent years which have tended to the comfort and convenience of the working classes in rural districts there is one which is frequently lost sight of; not only have the village shops improved in the character of the goods which they supply, but the removal of turnpike tolls, the abolition of the assessed taxes on horses, and the improved roads have encouraged the shopkeepers in great numbers to send round carts which regularly call at the cottages and deliver meat, groceries, flour or bread, paraffin oil, and indeed almost everything that the labourer's wife wants to buy. This regular service has conduced to punctual payments, as the accounts are generally settled weekly, and the running accounts of indebtedness to the village shopkeeper, which was once so common, is now much less frequent than it was. I have myself inspected several account books extending over a long period, and I have been surprised to find how punctually these accounts are in many cases discharged. Those who are within reach of a good weekly market take advantage of these opportunities, no doubt, but many of those who live in districts remote from towns are saved the trouble and inconvenience of fetching and carrying their weekly supplies of goods.

Wants and wishes of labourers.

392. I have in my *Review of the Evidence*, which has been laid before the Commission, stated what appear to be the principal wants and wishes of the labourers. These vary widely in the different parts of the country. In some districts a desire for land in large allotments or small holdings prevails; in others, and these the districts of highest wages, there is not any demand for land in any form; in others, grass holdings are desired; higher wages and shorter hours of work are naturally wished for. In those districts where weekly or daily engagements are customary there is dissatisfaction with the practice of those who do not pay or employ their labourers in wet weather; and somewhat inconsistently, those who urge this grievance, demand for the labourer the option of working for himself in his allotment whenever he wishes, and for the farmer at other times.

There is reported to be in several districts a great objection on the part of the labourers to the holding of farm cottages at the will of the farmer and conditionally upon the occupant continuing to work for the particular farmer who sublets the cottage, but this objection is apparently not felt at all in the north of England, and in many other parts the dislike to the system is overcome by allowing the labourers to hold the cottages rent free, although in such cases the wages of the holder are decreased, or he gives extra hours of work in return. When all the grievances and all the aspirations of the agricultural labourers are recapitulated and considered it will be found that few of them require legislation for their redress or fulfilment. The independence of the labourer, his power to defend himself, and to secure that which he desires have greatly increased. He receives a much larger share of the gross produce of the land than was ever allotted or enjoyed by the labourer in recent times. Nothing but the utter failure of British agriculture will arrest the course of progress and improvement which have been so marked a feature in the history of the last 50 years.

CONCLUSION.

393. I had intended to summarise the results of the inquiry in Wales, Scotland, and Ireland, and to draw attention to the more interesting subjects of my colleagues' Reports on those divisions of the kingdom, but I am warned that my Report must now be brought to an end. I have, in the Review which has been laid before the Commission, noticed the principal topics of interest, and I must refer to those Reports for full information on the different subjects of inquiry. At the conclusion of the Review which I have presented to the Commission I ventured to sum up what appeared to me to be the principal conclusions to be deduced from the evidence which has been received in the following paragraph.

In conclusion I would venture to state very briefly what seem to me to be the principal conclusions to be deduced from the evidence which has been received.

1. The number of those competing for employment in agriculture has everywhere decreased.
2. The decrease in the number of wage earners in agriculture has been most marked in Ireland; but the effect of a decrease has been most felt in Scotland, where only there is a general complaint of a scarcity of labourers.
3. In England a general contraction of employment in agriculture has proceeded concurrently with the decrease of wage earners and to some extent balanced the supply and demand.
4. The decrease in the number of labourers has improved the chance of obtaining regular work by those who desire it.
5. The universal withdrawal of women from field work is an evidence of an improvement in the circumstances of the labourers.

6. The material condition of the labourer has everywhere improved, though there are still very wide and striking differences as to the amount of remuneration received by them in different localities and parts of the United Kingdom.
7. This improvement, though in some measure due to an increase of earnings, is, however, very largely the result of the cheapening of commodities which are the necessaries of life.
8. The least satisfactory circumstance affecting the life of the labourers is the condition of the dwellings which a considerable number of them are compelled to live in.

Before concluding this Report I ask leave to express my high opinion of the ability, zeal, and tact with which my colleagues have discharged the duties entrusted to them, and to acknowledge the very willing and cordial manner in which they have uniformly accepted such suggestions as I ventured to make to them from time to time during the progress of the inquiry.

I desire again to acknowledge the great assistance which you have personally given me, and I should like to add that I am much indebted to Mr. F. V. Hornby, the assistant secretary, for his good offices and ready helpfulness. I would also wish to say that several members of your staff have laid me under great obligations by the careful revision of proofs which they have conducted.

I annex to this Report a copy of the Heads of Inquiry which formed the instructions to the Assistant Commissioners and also an Index to the Reports of the Assistant Commissioners. I have arranged the Index under the following heads: A.—Districts surveyed; B.—Counties with reference to Districts of Inquiry and Assistant Commissioners reporting thereon; and C.—Districts of Inquiry with Name of Assistant Commissioner reporting thereon and Reference to Report.

I have, &c.,
WILLIAM C. LITTLE.

Stag's Holt, March,
20th June 1894.

For General Circulation.

ROYAL COMMISSION ON LABOUR.

THE AGRICULTURAL LABOURER.

Notes for the Inquiry to be conducted by Assistant Commissioners.

Facts are desired bearing upon the following points :—

1. The present supply of labour.
2. The conditions of engagement of the labourers.
3. Wages and earnings.
4. Cottage accommodation.
5. Gardens and allotments.
6. Benefit societies.
7. Trade unions.
8. General relations between employers and employed.
9. The general condition of the agricultural labourer.

1. The Supply of Labour.

(a.) Sufficiency for present requirements.
(b.) Increase or decrease during the past 10 or 15 years.
(c.) Immigration of workers at particular seasons.
(d.) Comparative efficiency of labourers :—
 (i.) As compared with former times.
 (ii.) As compared with other districts.

2. Conditions of Engagement.

(a.) Employment regular and continuous, or casual and intermittent.
(b.) Engagement by year, month, week, or otherwise.
(c.) Hours of work :—
 (i.) Limits of time.

Class.	Summer		Winter	
	From	To	From	To
Carters, horsekeepers, stockmen, or others in charge of animals.				
Ordinary labourers				
Women				
Children				

 (ii.) Meal hours allowed.
 (iii.) Hours of labour, excluding meal times, but including time occupied in going to work and returning.
 (iv.) Proportionate number employed in Sunday work and hours of employment.

3. Wages and Earnings.

(a.) Current rate of weekly wages during preceding twelve months
(b.) (i.) Opportunities of adding to wages by piece-work.
 (ii.) Nature of piece-work put out to contract.
 (iii.) Prices of piece-work.
 (iv.) Mode of payment adopted in—
  (i.) Haytime.
  (ii.) Harvest.

(c.) Additions to wages by—
  (i.) Perquisites.
  (ii.) Allowances.
  (iii.) Payments in kind.

(d.) Wages earned by employment during a part of the year in occupations other than agriculture, e.g. wood-cutting, seaweed gathering, quarrying, &c.

(e.) Estimated annual earnings, including all allowances, piece-work, &c. of—
  (i.) Ordinary labourers.
  (ii.) Labourers skilled in special departments.
  (iii.) Shepherds.
  (iv.) Men in charge of horses, cattle, &c.

4. Cottage Accommodation.

(a.) Supply (i.) in respect of number, and (ii.) as compared with the past.

(b.) Situation:—
  (i.) As regards distance from work.
  (ii.) Whether concentrated in villages or hamlets or dispersed on farms.

(c.) Condition and construction:—
  (i.) State of repair.
  (ii.) Materials of which composed.
  (iii.) Accommodation.
    Number of rooms.
    Size of rooms.
    Ventilation.
    Drainage.
    Water supply.
    Out-houses.

(d.) Ownership and tenure:—
  (i.) Held directly by labourer of an estate owner.
  (ii.) Held by tenant farmer, who hires of the landowner and sub-lets to the labourer.
  (iii.) Hired from independent owners.
  (iv.) Owned by labourers.
  (v.) Conditions of tenure (a) held on condition of working on a particular estate, (b) for a particular employer.
  (vi.) Period of tenure and notice required for termination of the tenancy.
  (vii.) Rent—amount.
  (viii.) Accommodation for which rent is paid, e.g. garden included.
  (ix.) Amount of rates charged.
  (x.) By whom such rates are paid.

5. Gardens, Allotments, &c.

(a.) Gardens adjoining or attached to cottages:—
  (i.) Size.
  (ii.) Cultivation.

(b.) Allotments (as defined by Allotments Act, 1891):—
  (i.) Supply adequate to demand or insufficient.
  (ii.) Proportionate number of labourers in possession of allotments.
  (iii.) Size.
  (iv.) Rent.
  (v.) Cultivation prescribed.
  (vi.) Crops chiefly grown.

(c.) Potato grounds provided by farmers:—
  (i.) Size.
  (ii.) Conditions upon which they are held.

(d.) Cow runs, cow gates, or cow pastures.

(e.) Live stock kept by labourers (including bees).

6. Benefit Societies.

(a.) Extent to which agricultural labourers avail themselves of them.

(b.) Class of societies:—

(1.) General.
(2.) County.
(3.) District or parochial.

(c.) Whether such societies are registered or not.

7. Trade Unions of Agricultural Labourers.

Strikes and lock-outs of past ten years.
Effect of such trade unions.

8. General Relations between Employers and Employed.

9. The General Condition of the Agricultural Labourer.

Index to the Reports of the Assistant Commissioners.

A.—Districts Surveyed.

ENGLAND.

No. on Map	District	County	Reference to Reports
	Bear, W. E.	Vol. I., Part I.	B.
7	Basingstoke	Hampshire	IV
20	Melton Mowbray	Leicestershire	VI
26	St. Neots	Hunts and Beds	II
27	Southwell	Nottinghamshire	V
30	Thakeham	Sussex	III
38	Woburn	Bedford	I
	Chapman, C. M.	Vol. I., Part II.	B.
1	Atcham	Shropshire	VI
8	[illegible]	Herefordshire	VII
9	Crediton	Devon	IV
23	North Witchford	Cambridgeshire	III
31	Thame	Oxon and Bucks	I.
33	Truro	Cornwall	V
35	Wantage	Berkshire	II

England—continued.

No. on Map	District.	County.	Reference to Reports.
	Spencer, Aubrey. Vol. I., Part V.		B.
9	Dorchester	Dorset	I.
14	Godstone	Surrey	VII.
16	Hollingbourn	Kent	III.
17	Langport	Somerset	IV.
19	Maldon	Essex	V.
24	Pershore	Worcester	VI.
25	Pewsey	Wiltshire	II.
	Wilkinson, R. Vol. I., Part VI.		B.
10	Driffield	Yorks, E. Riding	II.
11	Easingwold	„ N. Riding	III.
15	Holbeach	Lincolnshire	VI.
18	Louth	„	I.
31	Uttoxeter	Stafford and Derby	V.
35	Wetherby	Yorks, W. Riding	IV.

WALES.

No. on Map	District.	County.	Reference to Reports.
	Thomas, D. Lleufer. Vol. II.		B.
39	Anglesey	Anglesey	VI.
40	Bridgend	Glamorgan	I.
42	Dolgelly	Merioneth	IV.
43	Llanfyllin	Montgomery and Denbigh	III.
44	Narberth	Pembroke and Carmarthen	II.
45	Pwllheli	Carnarvon	VII.
46	Ruthin	Denbigh	V.
	Chapman, C. M. Vol. II.		B.
41	Builth	Brecon and Radnor	VIII.

SCOTLAND.

Counties.	Reference to Reports.
Rutherfurd, H. Vol. III., Part I.	B.
Caithness, Orkney, Sutherland, and Ross	I.
Stirling and Dumbarton	III.
North Lanark and Linlithgow	IV.
Dumfries, Wigtown, Kirkcudbright	V.
Ayr, Renfrew, Bute, and S. Argyle	II.
Gillespie, G. R., the late. Vol. III., Part II.	B.
Moray, Banff, and Nairn	VI.
Aberdeen and Kincardine	VII.
Forfar and East Perth	VIII.
Pringle, R. Hunter. Vol. III., Part II.	B.
Fife, Kinross, Clackmannan	I.
Edinburgh and Haddington	II.
Perthshire and N. Argyle	III.
Inverness and Ross	IV.
Wilkinson, R.	B.
Berwick and Roxburgh	V.
Peebles, Selkirk, &c.	VI.

No. on Map.	District.	County.	Reference of Reports.
	McCarthy, R. Vol. IV., Part I.		B.
1	Ardee	Louth and Meath	III.
3	Ballymahon	Longford and Westmeath	XI.
4	Ballymena	Antrim	VIII.
5	Ballyshannon	Donegal, Fermanagh, and Leitrim	II.
9	Castleblayney	Monaghan and Armagh	IX.
11	Clones	Monaghan and Fermanagh	V.
12	Cookstown	Tyrone	I.
14	Downpatrick	Down	IV.
15	Dromore West	Sligo	X.
20	Letterkenny	Donegal	VI.
21	Limavady	Londonderry	VII.
	O'Brien, W. P., C.B. Vol. IV., Part II.		B.
7	Carlow	Carlow and Queen's Co.	XI.
8	Cashel	Tipperary	V.
16	Ennistimon	Clare	IV.
17	Kanturk	Cork	II.
18	Kenmare	Kerry	I.
19	Kilmallock	Limerick and Cork	IX.
23	Lismore	Waterford	VII.
24	Mountmellick	Queen's and King's Cos.	X.
25	Naas	Kildare and Wicklow	III.
28	Thomastown	Kilkenny	VIII.
30	Wexford	Wexford	VI.
	Richards, R. C. Vol. IV., Part III.		B.
2	Baillieborough	Cavan	IV.
6	Balrothery	Dublin	VI.
22	Loughrea	Galway	I.
26	Roscrea	Tipperary, King's Co., and Queen's Co.	II.
	Fox, A. Wilson. Vol. IV., Part IV.		B.
10	Castlerea	Roscommon and Mayo	II.
13	Delvin	Westmeath	IV.
27	Skibbereen	Cork	III.
29	Westport	Mayo	I.

B.—Counties with reference to Districts of Inquiry and Assistant Commissioners reporting thereon.

ENGLAND.

County.	District.	Assistant Commissioner.	Reference to Vol. I. Part.	Reference to Vol. I. Index No. of Report.
Bedfordshire	Woburn	Bear, W. E.	I.	I.
"	St. Neots	Bear, W. E.	I.	II.
Berks	Wantage	Chapman, C. M.	II.	II.
Bucks	Thame	Chapman, C. M.	II.	I.
Cambs	N. Witchford	Chapman, C. M.	II.	III.
Cheshire	Nantwich	Richards, R. C.	IV.	VI.
Cornwall	Truro	Chapman, C. M.	II.	V.
Cumberland	Wigton	Fox, A. Wilson	III.	IV.
Derby	Belper	Richards, R. C.	IV.	VII.
"	Uttoxeter	Wilkinson, E.	VI.	V.
Devon	Crediton	Chapman, C. M.	II.	IV.
Dorset	Dorchester	Spencer, A.	V.	I.
Durham	—	—	—	—

ENGLAND—*continued.*

County.	District.	Assistant Commissioner.	Reference to Vol. I. Part.	Index No. of Report.
Essex	Maldon	Spencer, A.	V	V.
Gloucester	Cirencester	Richards, R. C.	IV.	III.
"	Monmouth	Richards, R. C.	IV	IV
Hampshire	Basingstoke	Bear, W. E.	I.	IV.
Hereford	Bromyard	Richards, R. C.	IV.	V.
Hertfordshire	Buntingford	Chapman, C. M.	II.	VII
Huntingdon	St. Neots	Bear, W. E.	I	II.
Kent	Hollingbourne	Spencer, A.	V.	III
Lancashire	Garstang	Fox, A. Wilson	III	V
Leicestershire	Melton Mowbray	Bear, W. E.	I.	VI
Lincolnshire	Holbeach	Wilkinson, E.	VI.	VI.
"	Louth	Wilkinson, E.	VI	I.
Middlesex	—	—	—	—
Monmouth	Monmouth	Richards, R. C.	IV	IV.
Norfolk	Swaffham	Fox, A. Wilson	III	II.
Northampton	Brixworth	Richards, R. C.	IV.	II
Northumberland	Glendale	Fox, A. Wilson	III	III
Notts	Southwell	Bear, W. E.	I.	V.
Oxon	Thame	Chapman, C. M.	—	I.
Rutland	—	—	—	—
Salop	Atcham	Chapman, C. M.	—	VI.
Somerset	Langport	Spencer, A.	V	IV.
Stafford	Uttoxeter	Wilkinson, E.	VI.	V.
Suffolk	Thingoe	Fox, A. Wilson	III.	I
Surrey	Godstone	Spencer, A.	V	VII.
Sussex	Thakeham	Bear, W. E.	I.	III.
Warwick	Stratford	Richards, R. C.	IV.	I
Westmorland	—	—	—	—
Wiltshire	Pewsey	Spencer, A.	V.	II
"	Cricklade	Richards, R. C.	IV	III
Worcester	Pershore	Spencer, A.	V.	VI
Yorks, East Riding	Driffield	Wilkinson, E.	VI	II.
" North Riding	Easingwold	Wilkinson, E.	VI	III
" West Riding	Wetherby	Wilkinson, E.	VI.	IV.

WALES.

County.	District.	Assistant Commissioner.	Reference to Vol. II. Index No. of Report.
			B.
Anglesey	Anglesey	Thomas, D. L.	VI.
Brecon	Builth	Chapman, C. M.	VIII.
Cardigan	—	—	—
Carmarthen	Narberth	Thomas	II
Carnarvon	Pwllheli	Thomas	VII.
Denbigh	Ruthin	Thomas	V.
"	Llanfyllin	Thomas	III
Flint	—	—	—
Glamorgan	Bridgend	Thomas	I.
Merioneth	Dolgelly	Thomas	IV
Montgomery	Llanfyllin	Thomas	III.
Pembroke	Narberth	Thomas	II
Radnor	Builth	Chapman, C. M.	VIII.

SCOTLAND.

County	Assistant Commissioner reporting	Reference to Report, Vol. III. Part	County	Assistant Commissioner reporting	Reference to Report, Vol. III. Part
Aberdeen	Gillespie, G. B.	I. – VIII.	Kinross	Pringle, R. H.	II. – I.
Argyle, South	Rutherfurd, H.	I. – II.	Kirkcudbright	Rutherfurd, H.	I. – V.
" North	Pringle, R. H.	II. – III.	Lanark	Rutherfurd, H.	I. – IV.
Ayr	Rutherfurd, H.	I. – II.	Linlithgow	Rutherfurd, H.	I. – IV.
Banff	Gillespie, G. B.	I. – VI.	Nairn	Gillespie, G. B.	I. – VI.
Berwick	Wilkinson, E.	II. – VI.	Orkney	Rutherfurd, H.	I. – I.
Bute	Rutherfurd, H.	I. – III.	Peebles	Wilkinson, E.	II. – V.
Caithness	Rutherfurd, H.	I. – I.	Perth, East	Gillespie, G. B.	I. – VIII.
Clackmannan	Pringle, R. H.	II. – I.	" Mid	Pringle, R. H.	II. – III.
Dumbarton	Rutherfurd, H.	I. – III.	Renfrew	Rutherfurd, H.	I. – II.
Dumfries	Rutherfurd, H.	I. – V.	Ross and Cromarty	Rutherfurd, H.	I. – I.
Edinburgh	Pringle, R. H.	II. – I.	—	Pringle, R. H.	II. – IV.
Elgin or Moray	Gillespie, G. B.	I. – VI.	Roxburgh	Wilkinson, E.	II. – VI.
Fife	Pringle, R. H.	II. – II.	Selkirk	Wilkinson, E.	II. – V.
Forfar	Gillespie, G. B.	I. – VIII.	Shetland	—	—
Haddington	Pringle, R. H.	II. – I.	Stirling	Rutherfurd, H.	I. – III.
Inverness	Pringle, R. H.	II. – IV.	Sutherland	Rutherfurd, H.	I. – I.
Kincardine	Gillespie, G. B.	II. – VII.	Wigtown	Rutherfurd, H.	I. – V.

IRELAND.

Province	County	District	Assistant Commissioner reporting	Reference to Vol. IV. Part	Reference to Vol. IV. Index No. of Report
Connaught	Galway	Loughrea	Richards, R. C.	III.	I.
	Leitrim	Ballyshannon	McCrea, R.	I.	II.
	Mayo	Claremorris	Fox, A. Wilson	IV.	II.
	"	Westport	Fox, A. Wilson	IV.	I.
	Roscommon	Castlerea	Fox, A. Wilson	IV.	II.
	Sligo	Dromore West	McCrea, R.	I.	X.
Leinster	Carlow	Carlow	O'Brien, W. P.	II.	XI.
	Dublin	Balrothery	Richards, R. C.	III.	III.
	Kildare	Naas	O'Brien, W. P.	II.	III.
	Kilkenny	Thomastown	O'Brien, W. P.	II.	VIII.
	King's Co.	Mountmellick	O'Brien, W. P.	II.	X.
	"	Roscrea	Richards, R. C.	III.	II.
	Longford	Ballymahon	McCrea, R.	I.	XI.
	Louth	Ardee	McCrea, R.	I.	III.
	Meath	Athboy	McCrea, R.	I.	III.
	Queen's Co.	Carlow	O'Brien, W. P.	II.	XI.
	"	Mountmellick	O'Brien, W. P.	II.	X.
	"	Roscrea	Richards, R. C.	III.	II.
	Westmeath	Ballymahon	McCrea, R.	I.	XI.
	"	Delvin	Fox, A. Wilson	IV.	IV.
	Wexford	Wexford	O'Brien, W. P.	II.	VI.
	Wicklow	Naas	O'Brien, W. P.	II.	III.
Munster	Clare	Ennistimon	O'Brien, W. P.	II.	IV.
	Cork	Kanturk	O'Brien, W. P.	II.	II.
	"	Kilmallock	O'Brien, W. P.	II.	IX.
	"	Skibbereen	Fox, A. Wilson	IV.	III.
	Kerry	Kenmare	O'Brien, W. P.	II.	I.
	Limerick	Kilmallock	O'Brien, W. P.	II.	IX.
	Tipperary	Cashel	O'Brien, W. P.	II.	V.
	"	Roscrea	Richards, R. C.	III.	II.
	Waterford	Lismore	O'Brien, W. P.	II.	VII.
Ulster	Antrim	Ballymena	McCrea, R.	I.	VIII.
	Armagh	Castleblayney	McCrea, R.	I.	IX.
	Cavan	Bailieborough	Richards, R. C.	III.	IV.
	Donegal	Ballyshannon	McCrea, R.	I.	II.
	"	Letterkenny	McCrea, R.	I.	VI.
	Down	Downpatrick	McCrea, R.	I.	IV.
	Fermanagh	Ballyshannon	McCrea, R.	I.	VI.
	"	Clones	McCrea, R.	I.	V.
	Londonderry	Limavady	McCrea, R.	I.	VII.
	Monaghan	Castleblayney	McCrea, R.	I.	IX.
	"	Clones	McCrea, R.	I.	V.
	Tyrone	Cookstown	McCrea, R.	I.	I.

C.—Districts of Inquiry with Name of Assistant Commissioner reporting thereon with Reference to Reports.

ENGLAND. Vol. I.

No. on Map.	District.	Assistant Commissioner reporting.	Reference. Part
1	Atcham	Chapman, C. M.	II. B. VI.
2	Basingstoke	Bear, W. E.	I. ,, IV.
3	Belper	Richards, R. C.	IV. ,, VII.
4	Bosworth	Richards, R. C.	IV. ,, II.
5	Bromyard	Richards, R. C.	IV. ,, V.
6	Buntingford	Chapman, C. M.	II. ,, VII.
7	Cirencester	Richards, R. C.	IV. ,, III.
8	Crediton	Chapman, C. M.	II. ,, IV.
9	Dorchester	Spencer, A.	V. ,, I.
10	Driffield	Wilkinson, E.	VI. ,, II.
11	Easingwold	Wilkinson, E.	VI. ,, III.
12	Garstang	Fox, A. Wilson	III. ,, V.
13	Glendale	Fox, A. Wilson	III. ,, III.
14	Godstone	Spencer, A.	V. ,, VII.
15	Holbeach	Wilkinson, E.	VI. ,, VI.
16	Hollingbourne	Spencer, A.	V. ,, III.
17	Langport	Spencer, A.	V. ,, IV.
18	Louth	Wilkinson, E.	VI. ,, I.
19	Maldon	Spencer, A.	V. ,, V.
20	Melton Mowbray	Bear, W. E.	I. ,, VI.
21	Monmouth	Richards, R. C.	IV. ,, IV.
22	Nantwich	Richards, R. C.	IV. ,, VI.
23	North Witchford	Chapman, C. M.	II. ,, III.
24	Pershore	Spencer, A.	V. ,, VI.
25	Pewsey	Spencer, A.	V. ,, II.
26	St. Neots	Bear, W. E.	I. ,, II.
27	Southwell	Bear, W. E.	I. ,, V.
28	Stratford-on-Avon	Richards, R. C.	IV. ,, I.
29	Swaffham	Fox, A. Wilson	III. ,, II.
30	Thakeham	Bear, W. E.	I. ,, III.
31	Thame	Chapman, C. M.	II. ,, I.
32	Thingoe	Fox, A. Wilson	III. ,, I.
33	Truro	Chapman, C. M.	II. ,, V.
34	Uttoxeter	Wilkinson, E.	VI. ,, V.
35	Wantage	Chapman, C. M.	II. ,, II.
36	Wetherby	Wilkinson, E.	VI. ,, IV.
37	Wigton	Fox, A. Wilson	III. ,, IV.
38	Woburn	Bear, W. E.	I. ,, I.

WALES. Vol. II.

No. on Map.	District.	Assistant Commissioner reporting.	Reference. Part
39	Anglesey	Thomas, D. L.	B. VI.
40	Bridgend	Thomas, D. L.	I.
41	Builth	Chapman, C. M.	VIII.
42	Dolgelly	Thomas, D. L.	IV.
43	Llanfyllin	Thomas, D. L.	III.
44	Narberth	Thomas, D. L.	II.
45	Pwllheli	Thomas, D. L.	VII.
46	Ruthin	Thomas, D. L.	V.

IRELAND. Vol. IV.

IRELAND. VOL. IV.—*continued.*

No. on Map	District	Assistant Commissioner reporting
8	Cashel	O'Brien, W. P.
9	Castleblayney	McCrea, R.
10	Castlerea	Fox, A. Wilson
11	Clones	McCrea, R.
12	Cookstown	McCrea, R.
13	Delvin	Fox, A. Wilson
14	Downpatrick	McCrea, R.
15	Dromore	McCrea, R.
16	Ennistimon	O'Brien, W. P.
17	Kanturk	O'Brien, W. P.
18	Kenmare	O'Brien, W. P.
19	Kilmallock	O'Brien, W. P.
20	Letterkenny	McCrea, R.
21	Limavady	McCrea, R.
22	Lismore	O'Brien, W. P.
23	Loughrea	Richards, R. C.
24	Mountmellick	O'Brien, W. P.
25	Naas	O'Brien, W. P.
26	Roscrea	Richards, R. C.
27	Skibbereen	Fox, A. Wilson
28	Thomastown	O'Brien, W. P.
29	Westport	Fox, A. Wilson
30	Wexford	O'Brien, W. P.

www.ingramcontent.com/pod-product-compliance
Lightning Source LLC
Chambersburg PA
CBHW030845270326
41928CB00007B/1222
* 9 7 8 3 7 4 1 1 9 9 6 0 8 *